AFTER THE REBELLION

After the Rebellion

Black Youth, Social Movement Activism,
and the Post–Civil Rights Generation

Sekou M. Franklin

NEW YORK UNIVERSITY PRESS
New York and London

NEW YORK UNIVERSITY PRESS
New York and London
www.nyupress.org

References to Internet websites (URLs) were accurate at the time of writing. Neither the author nor New York University Press is responsible for URLs that may have expired or changed since the manuscript was prepared.

Library of Congress Cataloging-in-Publication Data
Franklin, Sekou M.
After the rebellion : black youth, social movement activism, and the post-civil rights generation / Sekou M. Franklin.
pages cm   Includes bibliographical references and index.
ISBN 978-0-8147-8938-4 (hbk.) — ISBN 978-0-8147-6481-7 (pbk.)
1. African Americans—Social conditons—20th century.
2. Civil rights movement—United States—History—20th century.
3. Youth, Black—United States—History—20th century. I. Title.
E185.615.F723   2014
305.2'3509730904—dc23   2014004206

New York University Press books are printed on acid-free paper, and their binding materials are chosen for strength and durability. We strive to use environmentally responsible suppliers and materials to the greatest extent possible in publishing our books.

Manufactured in the United States of America

10 9 8 7 6 5 4 3 2 1

Also available as an ebook

CONTENTS

Acknowledgments   vii

Abbreviations of Organizations and Initiatives   ix

Introduction   1

PART I

1 Movement Activism and the Post–Civil Rights Generation   15

2 The World beyond the Campus   47

3 From Civil Rights to Anti-Apartheid   71

4 The New Haven Youth Movement   95

PART II

5 The Origins of the Black Student Leadership Network   115

6 Organizing for Change   142

7 The Collapse of the Black Student Leadership Network   183

PART III

8 Reclaiming Our Youth: Policing and Protesting
   Juvenile Injustice   209

9 We Are Labor Too   235

Conclusion   253

Appendix A: Study Design and Methodology   263

*Appendix B: Interview Methodology and Biographies
of Interviewees*   265

Appendix C: Profiles of Principal Organizations and Networks   271

Notes   273

Bibliography   319

Index   343

About the Author   366

ACKNOWLEDGMENTS

The completion of this book would not have been possible without the help of family, friends, colleagues, and mentors. This research project began while I was at Howard University. Robert Brown, Martell Teasley, and Robert Vinson from Howard deserve special mention for guiding me throughout the writing process. Michael Frazier gave further assistance and Lorenzo Morris provided insightful comments on earlier drafts of this work. Clarence Lusane and Elizabeth Clark-Lewis, two notable scholars, also helped with my transition through Howard University.

A large part of my scholarly development is due to Robert C. Smith. He has been a mentor and friend, who first taught me African American politics as a graduate student at San Francisco State University. Professor Smith (and his wife Scottie) handed me to Howard University, where Richard Seltzer gave me additional mentorship during my doctoral years. Donn Davis is another advisor and comrade who still serves as my "social movement" advisor years after I departed Howard University. Joseph P. McCormick has been a valuable resource and mentor who always demands the best of his students, while celebrating their innovation and career benchmarks. For this, I am eternally grateful to him and his wife, Janet.

Portions of this book were read by numerous scholars at conferences hosted by the National Conference of Black Political Scientists, the Southwest Labor Studies Association, the Southern Political Science Association, and the Popular Culture Association. I am also grateful to the anonymous reviewers for the book as well as numerous colleagues and friends, many of whom read or reviewed parts of this book. Over the years, I learned a great deal from Melanie Njeri Jackson, Hanes Walton, Frank Pryor, Alex Willingham, Wendy Smooth, Diane Pinderhughes, Sundiata Cha-Jua, Cedric Johnson, Artemesia Stanberry, Baruti Jahi, Janet Flammang, Jesus Martínez-Saldaña, Dennis Gordon, Dorian Warren, Byron D'Andra Orey, Boris Ricks, Adonijah Bakari,

Andra Gillespie, Tyson King-Meadows, Dionne Knox, John Williams, Pearl Ford Dowe, Angela Lewis, Evelyn Simien, Joy Banks, Nell Levin, Calvin Hill, Stephen Morris, John Davis, David Montague, Todd Shaw, Lynn Hampton, Adolphus Belk, Monét and Marilyn Brown, Jermaine Hardy, Jackie Sims, Louis Woods, Peter Brannon, Lorna Gonsalves, Gwen Sumlin, Alvin Thornton, John Vile, Jacques Bolivar, Sylvanna Falcon, Evonne Tisdale, Melina Abdulla, Denise Carlson, Keith Caldwell, Pam Davis, Rose Harris, Melanye and Melynda Price, Christie Williams, Thomas Bynum, Ida Jones, Kenneth Caine, Rev. James Lawson's Nonviolent Resistance Group, and Rev. Henry Blaze's Ad Hoc Committee for Equity. I also thank my editors at NYU Press, Ilene Kalish and Caelyn Cobb.

I owe special thanks to Lisa Y. Sullivan, Kia Chatmon, Claudine "Candy" Taffe, Nicole Johnson, Steven White, Helene Fisher, and Felicia Verdin. These individuals gave me access to their personal archives detailing the activities of the Black Student Leadership Network and connected me to former members of the organization. Lynda DeLoach also made a special effort to help me navigate the archives of the AFL-CIO's Union Summer Program at the George Meany Memorial Archives.

In addition, I thank the University of Illinois's Afro-American Studies Program as well as the Faculty Research and Creative Projects Committee and Department of Political Science at Middle Tennessee State University for financially supporting this book project. The Office of Institutional Equity at Middle Tennessee State University, led by Forrestine White Williams and Barbara Patton, also provided financial assistance toward the completion of the project. And, I was fortunate to receive a grant from the W. T. Grant Foundation to research juvenile justice activism in Louisiana, Maryland, and New York in 2004 and 2005.

My family has been especially supportive throughout this book project. This includes my aunts and uncles (Boose, Clyde, Harold, Helen, Curtis, Ron, Evelyn, Jonell, Pete, John, Neil, Shirley, and Grant); my brothers (Malik and Tyrone); my father, mother, stepfather, and grandmother (Thomas Franklin, Georgia Pierson, Rev. Robert Pierson, grandmother "Penny"); and my in-laws (Rudy, Dollie, and Rasheed). Finally, this book is dedicated to my lifelong partner, Tené, and our two daughters (Sojourner and Langston) for traveling with me during this long journey.

ABBREVIATIONS OF ORGANIZATIONS AND INITIATIVES

AAPRP	All African People's Revolutionary Party
AAYC	African-American Youth Congress (New Haven)
AFL	American Federation of Labor
AFL-CIO	American Federation of Labor–Congress of Industrial Organizations
ALSC	African Liberation Support Committee
ANLC	American Negro Labor Congress
APRI	A. Philip Randolph Institute
BCCC	Black Community Crusade for Children
BL	Black Liberators
BPP	Black Panther Party
BSLN	Black Student Leadership Network
CBP	Central Brooklyn Partnership
CBTU	Coalition of Black Trade Unionists
CDF	Children's Defense Fund
CDGM	Child Development Group of Mississippi
CIO	Council of Industrial Organizations
CNAC	Cambridge Nonviolent Action Committee
COFI	Community Organizing and Family Issues
CORE	Congress of Racial Equality
CP	Communist Party (American Communist Party)
CWYPF	City-Wide Young People's Forum
DMZ	Democracy Multiplied Zone
EBCPTI	Ella Baker Child Policy Training Institute
FFLIC	Families and Friends of Louisiana's Incarcerated Children
FSAM	Free South Africa Movement
GAPP	Greensboro Association of Poor People
GPSA	Georgia Progressive Black Student Alliance
JJPL	Juvenile Justice Project of Louisiana
JJRM	juvenile justice reform movement

MFDP	Mississippi Freedom Democratic Party
MJJC	Maryland Juvenile Justice Coalition
NAACP	National Association for the Advancement of Colored People
NBPA	National Black Political Assembly
NNC	National Negro Congress
OI	Organizing Institute
PBSA	Progressive Black Student Alliance
PMP	Prison Moratorium Project
SCAR	Student Coalition against Apartheid and Racism
SCLC	Southern Christian Leadership Conference
SEIU	Service Employment International Union
SLAC	Student Labor Action Coalition
SNCC	Student Nonviolent Coordinating Committee
SNYC	Southern Negro Youth Congress
SOBU	Student Organization for Black Unity
SP	Socialist Party
USSA	United States Student Association
YEP	Youth Empowerment Project
YOBU	Youth Organization for Black Unity

Introduction

Our Country opens wide the door of opportunity to the youth of the world but slams it shut in the faces of its Negro citizenry. The great masses of Negro youth are offered only one-fifteenth the educational opportunity of the average American child. The great masses of Negro workers are depressed and unprotected in the lowest levels of agriculture and domestic service while the black workers in industry are generally barred from the unions and grossly discriminated against. Their housing and living conditions are sordid and unhealthy; they live in constant terror of the lynch mob, shorn of their constitutionally guaranteed right of suffrage, and humiliated by the denial of civil liberties.
—Mary McLeod Bethune, letter to President Franklin Delano Roosevelt, 1937

Youth-based activism has been central to black political historiography in the past century. The Southern Negro Youth Congress (SNYC), though vastly understudied, emerged as a preeminent social movement organization in the 1930s and 1940s. In addition to mobilizing young blacks in support of civil rights and racial desegregation campaigns, the SNYC implemented economic justice initiatives for black workers in the South. The Student Nonviolent Coordinating Committee (SNCC) was formed two decades after the SNYC's formation. SNCC quickened the pace of the civil rights movement, advanced a participatory democratic framework of community organizing, and challenged racial terrorism in southern jurisdictions. The rebellious impulse of black youth after World War II was further exemplified in the Student Organization for Black Unity (SOBU). Situated in Greensboro, North Carolina, SOBU developed racial and economic justice programs as well as Pan-African, solidarity initiatives.

By the mid-1970s the militant phase of the civil rights, black power, and New Left movements was virtually over and transformational movements—high-risk, geographically diffuse movements—declined toward the end of the twentieth century. The demobilization of these movements was due to political repression, movement fatigue, party realignment, and the triumph of the conservative agenda in the last three decades of the century. Institutional leveraging also contributed to the weakening of transformational movements. Institutional leveraging occurs when the energy and resources of movement infrastructures— the organizational processes and networks of activists that cultivate movement-building activities and supply activist groups with resources and legitimacy—are channeled into established bureaucratic and political institutions.[1] It represents both a strategic and cultural shift in the evolution of movement politics that privileges elite mobilization strategies and tactics such as electioneering, negotiation, interest group lobbying, and specialized advocacy.

This book examines social movement activism among activists of the post–civil rights generation or the generation of activists (students, youth, and young adults) who came of age after the civil rights, black power, and New Left movements. The title of the book, *After the Rebellion: Black Youth, Social Movement Activism, and the Post–Civil Rights Generation*, underscores the argument that the political terrains and constraints on popular mobilization in the post–civil rights era made it particularly difficult for young activists to jump-start and sustain transformational movements. While this book is highly critical of the political and social contexts that circumscribe movement activism among the post–civil rights generation, I recognize that young activists maintain the desire to effect social change. As George Crane points out, "A movement is not necessarily a slave to context."[2] With assistance from the leaders of youth-based organizations or what I call movement bridge-builders, youth-based movements can transcend the constraints of institutional leveraging.

Movement bridge-builders frequently use an ensemble of creative organizing strategies to elevate the social and political status of black youth such that they become vehicles for contentious politics. Creative organizing strategies such as framing, the appropriation of indigenous resources, and positionality are used by movement bridge-builders to propel youth-based movements. These strategies discussed at great length in this book can have a multivaried impact on policy implementation, political institutions, intergenerational collaboration initiatives, and other movement-building initiatives.

The organizations and infrastructures examined in this book offer unique insight into youth-based activism in the post–civil rights era. The Free South Africa Movement and the New Haven youth movement of the 1980s, the Black Student Leadership Network (BSLN) in the 1990s, the juvenile justice reform movement (JJRM) initiatives, and the labor-backed Union Summer campaign of the 1990s and 2000s help to explain the challenges associated with institutional leveraging and creative organizing. I also situate these youth-based movements within a historical context and give attention to black student and youth activism dating back to the 1930s.

My interests in youth activism are both personal and political. For four summers, as an undergraduate and graduate student, I participated in the BSLN's Summer Freedom School program in Oakland, California. Our cadre of several dozen activists set up three freedom schools that were affiliated with the Children's Defense Fund and coordinated by the Oakland-based Urban Strategies Council. Although we were formally called "summer interns," we were required to participate in an intensive, two-week training, much of which was rooted in community organizing and direct action theories. After 1993, the approximately two hundred interns or organizers working annually in freedom schools across the country were sent to the Alex Haley Farm in eastern Tennessee for the training session. For activists working in the San Francisco Bay Area, especially in the summers of 1993 and 1994, our political education was bolstered by workshops facilitated by local grassroots activists as well as former members of SNCC and the Black Panther Party. The origins, national and local organizing activities, and strengths and weaknesses of the BSLN are documented later in this book.

The political status of youth of color, particularly African Americans, is another area of interest. As exhibited in Mary McLeod Bethune's letter to President Roosevelt at the outset of this chapter, the political status of black youth is not isolated from political discourse. Bethune was perhaps the most respected champion of black youth and women in the first half of the twentieth century.[3] She created the National Council of Negro Women in 1935 and a year later began working in Roosevelt's National Youth Administration, where she became the director of the Division of Negro Affairs.

Bethune sent the letter a year after covening the "National Conference on the Problems of the Negro and Negro Youth" from January 6 to January 8, 1936. The letter summarized the problems affecting black youth such as racial segregation, severe patterns of economic deprivation and exclusion, and civil rights abuses. She insisted that these problems reflected the systemic marginalization of the black working class. Finally, the letter outlined a series of recommendations adopted by the more than one hundred delegates attending the national conference, and urged the federal government to take the lead in abolishing racial segregation.

Although this conference convened decades ago, young blacks are as pivotal to contemporary social movements and political discourse as they were in the 1930s. In some respects, the post–civil rights generation has been cannon fodder for political and economic elites seeking to retrench antipoverty and civil rights programs. Cathy Cohen, Jennifer Tilton, and Lester Spence all describe how representations of youth of color are central to neoliberal debates about the role of government. Public figures advancing neoliberal agendas—bootstrap individualism, market-oriented policies, self-help programs, and the retrenchment of social welfare programs as alternatives to government interventionism—often point to (or exploit) the so-called moral failings of black youth to make their case.[4] They frequently argue that social expenditures privilege the black poor, lazy youth, and others who fall under the umbrella of the so-called undeserving.

These neoliberal agendas were partially advanced by political observers who claimed that Barack Obama's presidential victory in 2008 ushered in a new era of postracialism. Postracialism rested on the belief that racial and class hierarchies had all but disappeared or were inconsequential to the life circumstances of young blacks.[5] Yet Apollon's study of eighteen- to twenty-five-year-olds found that young blacks have mostly rejected this notion of postracialism. Many believe that racial hierarchy and other inequities continue to have a dynamic influence on their lives despite the election of the nation's first black president.[6]

Even the Occupy Wall Street movement, one of the most authoritative resistance movements to the power of large financial institutions and deregulation in the past decade, was criticized for advancing a left-oriented version of postracialism. Rinku Sen of the Applied Research Center, a leading racial justice think tank, points out that blacks and Latinos challenged this predisposition by organizing to "make space for people of color to join the [Occupy] movement."[7] Groups such as Occupy the Hood and Occupy Harlem emerged as a counterweight to the Occupy movement. These groups and other activists advanced an intersectional approach to movement building that addressed the twin evils of racial and economic injustices.

The main point is that political debates and movement-building initiatives are often affixed to competing representations of black youth. These representations may create openings or allow for acute criticisms of systemic inequalities as demonstrated with Bethune's letter to Roosevelt. They can be used to expand the boundaries of inclusion within social movements as exemplified with the struggles inside the Occupy movement. Or black youth (and representations of black youth) can be exploited by political and economic elites to advance political agendas.

Case Study Selection and Methodology

This book weaves together several case studies of youth-based social movement activism. I offer a historical account of movement activism during the protest cycles of the 1930s to 1940s and the 1950s to 1970s, and examine youth-based movements in the post–civil rights era. Included in this book are case studies of SNYC, SNCC, SOBU, the student divestment movement of the 1980s, the New Haven youth movement, BSLN, the AFL-CIO's Union Summer program, and youth-based activism in JJRMs.

I used five strategies for selecting the case studies for this book. First, I assessed youth-based activism through the prism of social movement organizations and advocacy groups. Youth-based activism has been typically coordinated or facilitated by three types of groups: youth-led organizations, multigenerational (or intergenerational) organizations, and network-affiliated groups or advocacy coalitions that support youth activities.[8] All the activists in this book (youth, college-age students, young adults, adult allies, and movement bridge-builders) articulated their grievances through social movement organizations and advocacy groups delineated by this three-part typology. These groups were embedded in a larger network or movement infrastructure of activists. I therefore analyze youth-based activism and intergenerational politics by focusing on social movement organizations, advocacy groups, and movement infrastructures as the units of analyses.

The politics of race and racial inequities is central to this investigation of youth-based movements. The movement formations in this book attempted to remedy structural inequities that harm marginalized blacks and poor people or immersed black students, youth, and young adults in popular mobilization campaigns. While blacks compose much of the cast of movement actors in this book, in a few cases, such as the movements to reform juvenile justice systems and the Union Summer campaign, the initiatives were coordinated by multiracial, network-affiliated groups or coalitions.

Whether the movement activities were facilitated by black or multiracial networks, the distinguishing characteristic in the case study selection process is that black youth form the principal variable in this book. The movements relied on young blacks as foot soldiers and bridge-builders, or, as exemplified in the juvenile justice initiatives, network-affiliated organizations mobilized opposition to public policies that were disproportionately injurious to young blacks. This means that nonblacks (whites and other people of color) are also critical to this examination as long as they participated in movement formations that were directly connected to the politics of young blacks. For example, the voting rights struggle in the 1960s is intrinsically linked to racial justice; was propelled by civil rights and black indigenous groups; engaged young people in movement activism through SNCC, the NAACP, the Southern Christian Leadership Conference, and the Congress of Racial Equality (CORE); and received active support from white allies and students. An assessment of youth-based participation in this movement may thus warrant a discussion of blacks as well as nonblacks.

The third criterion for case study selection is the "diverse method" that allows for inferences to be made from the cross-case analyses between movements.[9] This approach offers a better appreciation of the leadership styles and creative organizing strategies of movement bridge-builders, as well as the political contexts that affect movement infrastructures. Cross-case analyses further allow for temporal-based comparisons between youth-based movements. Comparing youth-based groups, for example the SNYC in the 1930s and the Union Summer campaign in the 1990s, gives us some understanding of the varying political contexts that shaped youth activism in their respective periods.

In addition, the diverse method permits comparisons between activists within a given movement, but based on *when* they join movements. There is some indication that activists emerging in the early stages of insurgent campaigns are more likely to benefit from the movement's successes than those whose maturation comes later in the protest cycle.[10] Early risers can expose the vulnerability of those in power, create leverage positions, and garner valuable resources for themselves.[11] Because of shifting contexts and diminishing resources, late risers (those joining a movement later in a protect cycle) may be forced to innovate with new strategies or tactics. This strategy of "elaboration" can help sustain an organization or movement in a changing political context.[12] Later in this study I examine how this dynamic influenced SNCC's development in the late 1960s.

In addition, I focus on extra-campus activism, or youth-based activism that transcends the walls of college campuses. This is somewhat challenging given that collective action tends to be structured based on where individuals work, live, and go to school.[13] Yet, youth-based activism outside the campus environs offers greater insight into intergenerational collaborative initiatives and coalition work with indigenous activists. Even the student divestment movement, though targeting college campuses, was part of a nationwide campaign comprising civil rights activists, internationalists, college students, and trade unionists.

Last, federated student and youth groups or youth-based movements that had a geographically diffuse scope are included in the case selection. For example, the SNYC, SNCC, SOBU, BSLN, and Union Summer attempted to set up regional or national entities that immersed young people in local organizing campaigns. Although the New Haven youth movement discussed in chapter 4 was limited to a small locality, the movement was intrinsically linked to black students and youth who participated in Jesse Jackson's presidential campaign in 1988 and assisted with the BSLN's formation.

At first glance, the juvenile justice initiatives examined in the last chapter were local campaigns. Yet they were part of national movement to reform state or local juvenile justice systems. This movement was wedded by national conferences, philanthropic institutions, and advocacy groups such as the DataCenter, Human Rights Watch, the Justice Policy Institute, and the American Youth Policy Forum. An abundance of resources actually poured into juvenile justice initiatives in the late 1990s and early 2000s in order to blunt the explosion of zero-tolerance policies approved by state and local governments. I selected three movement campaigns in Louisiana, Maryland, and New York. These initiatives account for the regional diversity that shaped youth-based activism in juvenile justice initiatives.

Altogether, the cases selected in this book share the following characteristics:

a. They were propelled by youth-led, multigenerational, or network-affiliated organizations embedded in a movement infrastructure

b. African American youth, either as activists themselves or through policy issues that disproportionately impacted them, were fundamental to the movement campaigns

c. The movements allow for cross-case analyses, temporally or across time, as well as intermovement comparisons of strategies, leadership patterns, and the infrastructures

d. The movements immersed young people in extra-campus initiatives and policy issues

e. The movement groups were geographically diffuse and, in a few circumstances, attempted to develop national-level or federated organizations

Based on this methodological approach, the case studies constitute a representative sample of youth-based activism, thus reducing selection bias. Excluded from this book are case studies of environmental activism and environmental justice, the United States Student Association's campaigns, and locally based youth development initiatives. Although useful for understanding youth activism, these activities do not allow for the in-depth, cross-case analyses as the case studies selected in this book.

Plan for the Book

This book offers a historical and empirical account of social movement activism among the post–civil rights generation. The book further addresses the limitations and opportunities for popular mobilization among black youth and young adult activists since the passage of the major civil rights legislation of the 1960s. I rely on qualitative data to assess youth-based movements: archival sources, including rarely used and noncatalogued archives; interviews with eighty-one activists and advocates involved in youth-based movements; and participant observation. An extensive discussion of these data is in appendices A to C.

The first chapter offers a conceptual overview of youth-based activism. I focus on four theoretical concerns: the political status of black youth in the post–civil rights era, the significance of movement infrastructures that buttress youth-based activism, the impact of institutional leveraging on transformational movements, and how movement bridge-builders use creative organizing strategies (framing, indigenous resources, and positionality) to stimulate youth-based movements and expand the opportunity structure of youth activism. The remaining chapters help to illuminate these theoretical concerns.

Although most of the book follows a chronological time frame spanning from 1965 to 2006, included in part I is an examination of black youth radicalism in the 1930s and 1940s. Chapter 2 focuses mainly on the origins, development, and collapse of the SNYC, and its interaction with a diverse movement infrastructure composed of black progressive and white leftist groups. The SNYC was the most important black youth formation of the pre–Cold War era. It implemented grassroots initiatives that pushed for voting rights, desegregation, and economic justice for black workers. Its collapse was largely attributed to the anticommunist hysteria after World War II that moderated the political orientations of veteran activists within the progressive-left community.

The evolution of African Americans and youth-based movement activism from the 1960s to the 1980s is examined in the third chapter. This period covers SNCC's organizing initiatives, SOBU activities from 1969 to 1975, and student activists who participated in the Free South Africa Movement in the 1980s. In this chapter, I examine how these groups experimented with creative organizing strategies as a response to the shift by prominent black groups toward institutional leveraging.

The last chapter of part I investigates the New Haven youth movement in the late 1980s. The youth movement, or Kiddie Korner as it was called, underscored the significance of black youth participation in urban organizing campaigns. Fostered by a coalition of black college students and working-class youth, the New Haven youth movement coordinated an antiviolence/anticrime initiative designed to combat the burgeoning gun violence between rival street gangs, participated in a protest campaign for equitable public school funding, and mobilized black youth in support of two grassroots electoral organizing campaigns.

Part II (chapters 5–7) investigates the BSLN's activities from 1991 to 1996. Chapter 5 describes the BSLN's parent organizations, the Black Community Crusade for Children (BCCC) and the Children's Defense Fund (CDF). It also looks at the BSLN's leadership development and popular education programs. Through its Ella Baker Child Policy Training Institute and Advanced Service and Advocacy Workshops, the BSLN trained over six hundred black students and youth in direct action organizing, social movement building, voter education, child advocacy, and teaching methodology and developed freedom schools in dozens of urban and rural jurisdictions. Chapter 6 extends these discussions by assessing the BSLN's organizing initiatives from 1993 to 1996: the Summer Freedom School program; its antiviolence campaign coordinated with the CDF and BCCC; and local organizing initiatives in New York City, North and South Carolina, and California.

Chapter 7 discusses the BSLN's attempt to implement two large-scale projects: Citizenship 2000, a comprehensive civic and electoral organizing campaign, and the One Thousand by Two Thousand project that targeted an additional one thousand members for recruitment into the organization. These initiatives were initiated, in part, to counteract the institutional leveraging pressures of the BSLN's parent organizations. Included in this chapter is a discussion of the intergroup tensions between the BSLN and its parent organizations, which contributed to underlying disputes within BSLN's leadership nucleus. Both sources (intergroup and intragroup) of disagreement weakened the BSLN and contributed to its collapse in the summer of 1996. The BSLN's collapse was further attributed to its inability to reconcile its relationship with the CDF and BCCC, the principal groups of its movement infrastructure. The tensions between the BSLN and its parent groups increased after the CDF jump-started the Stand for Children campaign in 1995. The campaign attempted to mobilize opposition to the Personal Responsibility and Work Opportunity Reconciliation Act (also known as the Welfare Reform Bill) that was passed by Congress in 1996. Despite the good intentions of Stand for Children, the BSLN's leadership nucleus feared that the campaign would neutralize its agenda and channel the group's energies into supporting a political agenda that was predetermined by its parent organizations.

Part III of the book assesses post–civil rights activists in JJRM and the labor movement from the mid-1990s to the mid-2000s. As discussed in chapter 8, the JJRM campaigns in New York, Maryland, and Louisiana attempted to deinstitutionalize the juvenile justice system and combat disproportionate minority confinement. I also examine how the makeup of the JJRM's movement infrastructures, combined with the regional and local political cultures that shaped the orientations of their key activists, influenced the trajectory of the campaigns.

Chapter 9 looks at whether the reform measures instituted by President John Sweeney of the AFL-CIO in the mid- to late 1990s created opportunities for young blacks to participate in the labor movement. Black youth participation in labor-backed initiatives was limited due to an outmoded set of organizing approaches used to mobilize black working-class communities. These approaches failed to address the concerns of black youth and young adults whose social and political orientations were radically shaped by a postindustrial economy.

The concluding chapter discusses the tribulations and triumphs of social movement activism among the post–civil rights generation. I argue that the constraints placed on movement activism, especially among young black activists, will likely remain as long as progressives and blacks have access to institutional channels to exercise political influence. While this may curtail transformational movement initiatives that use extra-systemic pressures, youth-based groups must routinely adjust and reconfigure ways to create opportunities for black youth to participate in social justice campaigns.

PART I

1

Movement Activism and the Post–Civil Rights Generation

The other thing that's quite important is that all of us [sixties activists] are talking from a context that is utterly and radically and permanently different than today's context. You cannot underestimate how important it was that no black person in the South could vote, and no college student in America could vote. The two active constituencies did not have the option of working in the system open to them. . . . Civil disobedience and speaking out were the options open. Today, I suppose to most people civil disobedience seems strange if you haven't first voted and tried to work within the system. So it's a hopelessly different context.
—Tom Hayden, SNCC Conference at Trinity College, April 1988

The Peoples' Community Feeding Program was created in 1994 by a contingent of black students from Hunter College in New York City. Similar to the feeding programs created by the Student Nonviolent Coordinating Committee (SNCC) and the Black Panther Party in the 1960s and 1970s, the initiative tackled malnutrition and hunger, feeding close to two hundred people each month in its Central Brooklyn neighborhood. Supported through in-kind contributions from churches and activists, the program was eventually taken over by activists affiliated with the Black Student Leadership Network (BSLN), a national organization allied with the Children's Defense Fund (CDF), a prominent child advocacy group. The BSLN affiliate, officially called the New York Metro chapter, also was cultivated by the Central Brooklyn Partnership, an economic justice organization that served as an informal gathering place for young activists from the Bedford-Stuyvesant, Crown Heights, and Fort Greene sections of Brooklyn.

In the early 2000s, the Youth Media Council in the San Francisco Bay Area and the Youth Force in the South Bronx, two activist groups composed of youth of color, initiated a campaign highlighting the misrepresentation of urban youth in the mainstream media. Conducted in collaboration with a national media strategy organization called We Interrupt This Message, the campaign analyzed the news coverage of black and Latino youth by the *New York Times* and San Francisco Bay Area's KTVU Channel 2 News. The youth groups found that most of coverage of youth of color unfairly portrayed them as pathological, dysfunctional, and inclined toward criminal behavior.[1] The findings were then disseminated to community organizers and political activists who were mobilizing against racial profiling and zero-tolerance youth policies in their respective jurisdictions.

Another promising campaign, occurring in 2000, involved the mobilization of hundreds of youth of color against Proposition 21 in California. The statewide ballot initiative permitted prosecutors to charge fourteen-year-olds as adults if they were involved in violent crimes. The measure, backed by conservative interest groups, intended to charge young offenders "as adults without a judicial review and made it easier to incarcerate youths with adult inmates."[2] It was the latest of several voter initiatives within the previous decade that adversely affected the state's black and Latino youth, the others being an anti–affirmative action measure and a ballot proposition penalizing illegal immigrants. The measure was opposed by many youth groups and activists in the San Francisco Bay Area, and the campaign experienced some of the largest protests of young people since the 1970s. Though the ballot initiative was approved in March 2000, it was widely rejected in the Bay Area and received its greatest opposition in San Francisco and Alameda Counties, the two areas that experienced the stiffest amount of youth resistance.

This book charts the development of social movement activism and popular mobilization among young activists of the post–civil rights generation. The post–civil rights generation describes young people who came of age after the collapse of the civil rights, New Left, and black power movements that occurred from the 1950s to the early 1970s. Andrea Simpson refers to the post–civil rights generation as the "integration generation" because they were the first cohort of young people whose political orientations were shaped by the realities of post–de jure segregation.[3]

By documenting social movement activism among the post–civil rights generation, this book examines the limitations and opportunities for youth and young adult participation in movement-building initiatives. I am also concerned with explaining the status and participation of black youth and young adults in popular mobilization campaigns and social movement infrastructures, or the diverse organizational processes and networks of activists, advocates, and allies that reinforce movements and social activism.[4] I focus on mobilization campaigns that targeted regressive measures and public health dilemmas that had particularly damaging consequences on poor and working-poor black communities in the late twentieth and early twenty-first centuries.

Social movements offer an entry point for engaging students and youth in what Holloway Sparks refers to as a "dissident citizenship," or a type of civic engagement that encourages marginal groups to challenge the social and political order.[5] They serve as socializing agents that link disaffected communities with public policy agendas, especially when elected officials and authoritative decision makers neglect their grievances. In a general sense, progressive social movements entail a mix of contentious social justice activism, popular mobilization campaigns, popular education and consciousness-raising activities, grassroots organizing, and legal and institutional pressures. As demonstrated in the youth initiatives discussed at the beginning of the chapter, movement campaigns use a broad array of strategies and tactics, and are led by an assortment of activists, networks, and organizations.

I rely on a loose interpretation of social movements and interchange this concept with popular mobilization campaigns, extra-systemic pressures, resistance movements, movement-building initiatives, and contentious politics.[6] However, I distinguish between transformational forms of movement-building exercises and contained protest movements. *Transformational* movements (or mobilization campaigns that have a transformational character) are diffuse and involve high-risk strategies and tactics that have a sustained impact on political culture; their goals are adopted by a diverse group of movement networks; occasionally, they influence the emergence of new mobilizing structures; and at times they disrupt or effect the implementation of public policies. *Contained* movements or mobilization campaigns, on the other hand, are episodic and discontinuous; they are short-lived, are restricted, and have difficulty shaping public policy and political attitudes, usually because of limited mobilization opportunities or unfavorable conditions external or internal to the movements.[7] Despite these differences, both forms of movement activism are anchored in social justice frames and attempt to foster leadership among rank-and-file members from aggrieved communities.

A major argument of this book is that there has been an overall shift in the post–civil rights era toward institutional leveraging among progressive movements and mobilizing structures (or what I call movement infrastructures) that typically fuel mobilization campaigns. Institutional leveraging occurs when movement infrastructures channel their energies and resources into established bureaucratic and political institutions in order to safeguard their interests in a hostile political climate or because they seek institutional power.[8] This leveraging process usually takes place at the expense of buttressing transformational campaigns.

As a result of institutional leveraging and the ascent of the conservative movement, popular mobilization campaigns have been contained in the post–civil rights era, at least compared to the movements of the 1930s and 1960s. Notwithstanding these constraints, the second argument guiding this study is that the post–civil rights generation activists did not completely eschew movement activism. As demonstrated in the movement initiatives discussed at the outset of the chapter, young activists and veteran activists allied with their causes challenged the limitations and boundaries of these constraints, and created opportunities for new groups of young people to participate in mobilization campaigns. They contested the push and pull toward institutional leveraging, and in the process attempted to elevate the social and political status of poor and working-class black youth as an important variable in popular mobilization campaigns. Documenting these movement struggles, their impact on intergenerational relations within progressive movements and advocacy campaigns, and their intersection with black politics and left-oriented multiracial campaigns in the post–civil rights era is the objective of this study.

The principal actor in the book is black youth and young adults, most of whom were under twenty-five years of age during the height of their activist years. Also included in this study are veteran or adult activists and advocates from mobilization campaigns that focused on issues that

impacted or depended upon the participation of black youth or students. These campaigns were coordinated by movement infrastructures
composed of youth-led organizations, multigenerational organizations,
and network-affiliated groups that supported youth organizing. Most of
the campaigns took place in community struggles outside the university environs including urban-based organizing initiatives, labor/union
and economic justice activities, antihunger campaigns, popular education activities, criminal and juvenile justice reform campaigns, and
racial justice initiatives.

With the exception of the historical overview of black youth activism in the 1930s and 1940s examined in the second chapter, I focus specifically on the period spanning from the mid-1960s to the mid-2000s.
This period saw the demobilization of the civil rights, black power, and
New Left movements; the conservative movement's growing influence
as exhibited with the presidential administrations of Richard Nixon,
Ronald Reagan, George H. W. Bush, and George W. Bush and the
Republican Party's takeover of Congress subsequent to the 1994 mid-
term elections; the capture of the Democratic Party by its moderate/
conservative wing as demonstrated with the Democratic Leadership
Council's growing power in the late 1980s; the retrenchment of New
Deal social welfare programs; the shift from an industrial to a service
economy; and the emergence of the youth vote as a result of the passage
of the Twenty-Sixth Amendment in 1971.

The Problem of Generations: Youth as a Social and Political Variable

Youth-based activism was an important part of progressive social movements throughout much of the twentieth century. Historian Charles
Payne refers to activists from the SNCC, one of the most influential youth
formations in the twentieth century, as the "shock troops" of the civil
rights movement. This was because of their unique brand of courage,
strategic and tactical innovation, and willingness to organize in racially
hostile communities that frightened many veteran activists.[9] SNCC
activists contributed a tremendous amount of time, energy, and personal commitment, or what Jo Freeman refers to as "people resources,"
to the civil rights movement.[10] Their efforts debunked the argument by

some political observers such as Mancur Olson that individuals join collective action initiatives to maximize selective or monetary incentives.[11] Dennis Chong further argues that rather than selective incentives, participation in civil rights initiatives was propelled by social pressures, friendship, reputational enhancement, the viability of movement success, and social acceptance.[12] Indigenous resources such as communication infrastructures and long-standing civic groups also prepared young activists for high-risk activism in the civil rights movement.[13] Youth participation in the civil rights, black power, and New Left movements of the 1960s, as well as the labor-left movements of the 1930s, truly involved great personal risk that far outweighed any selective rewards that might be obtained from participating in these initiatives.

Despite the contributions of young activists to social movements, it is important to discuss the conceptual and empirical shortcomings of situating youth, or what Karl Mannheim and others called "political generations,"[14] at the forefront of social and political analyses. I am cautious about concluding that post–civil rights "youth" by virtue of their age and because of adultism, or the subordination of youth, should be positioned at the forefront of popular mobilization campaigns. Still, some activists and intellectuals insist that youth are best prepared to lead movement campaigns or participate in high-risk initiatives because of their age and social location, and because they have fewer family and personal commitments.[15]

While recognizing the significance of generational resistance and consciousness, situating youth as the vanguard of social change initiatives can actually detach them from comprehensive community struggles.[16] It advances what O'Donoghue, Kirshner, and McLaughlin call an "overly romantic notion of youth involvement" in mobilization campaigns,[17] because it assumes that a younger cohort of activists is destined to be more progressive or supportive of social justice claims than older ones. Karl Mannheim warned political observers against associating age with political radicalism. He said, "Nothing is more false than the usual assumption uncritically shared by students of generations, that the young generation is 'progressive' and the older generational *eo ipso* conservative."[18] His commentary is particularly relevant for analyses of the post–civil rights generation. The idea that youth should be the vanguard of modern resistance movements has been discussed at virtually every political and activist conference and in electoral organizing initiatives that claim to advance progressive causes. This narrative has been reinforced by popular culture, especially hip-hop culture, which claims to represent the sentiments of disillusioned ghetto youth. Yet there is little evidence that post–civil rights youth are more progressive in their political orientations compared to adult activists of the sixties generation. Survey data and research reveal that younger blacks have actually been more conservative than older ones on some policy issues.[19]

In addition, the narrative fails to appreciate that regardless of how altruistic youth activists may be in asserting a generational consciousness, it is difficult and perhaps impossible for them to win significant political victories without marrying their concerns to public agendas and movement infrastructures that emerge out of broader mobilization campaigns. Because racial and class inequities are exacerbated by policies that cannot be resolved solely by young people themselves, student and youth activists must interact, form coalitions, and organize with veteran activists who make up complex movement infrastructures. Moreover, movement campaigns that recruited significant numbers of young blacks have traditionally been shaped by veteran activists and organizers who have helped to politicize young people and recruit new activists, offered them direction, and educated them about organizing and politics.

Generational analyses that contend youth should be at the vanguard of social movements further assume that activists who belong to the same age category share a uniform or fixed identity, or represent a unified political actor.[20] The argument, however, discounts the multiple identities among young activists and varied interpretations of what exactly is a *youth* activist. Plotke reminds us of the problems with assuming that activists share "a single, totalizing identity."[21] Young activists, including those in the same organization and from the same racial background, may be equally influenced by competing identities such as gender, region, and class. Within mobilization campaigns, these identity-based distinctions among young activists can have differential influences on their social and political outlooks.[22] For example, Apollon's investigation of millennial activists (those born after 1980) found divergent views among activists who participated in the Occupy Wall Street movement that targeted the financial industry in the fall of 2011.

Non-Occupy protestors were more likely to point to racial justice as their primary concern compared to young progressives involved in the Occupy movement.[23]

Furthermore, "youth" is a transitory or "relational" concept that, according to Wyn and White, "has meaning only in relation to the specific circumstances of social, political and economic conditions."[24] For example, a nineteen-year-old black male student activist in the 1930s had a different set of experiences than an eighteen-year-old black woman who worked in a factory, was married, and had two children. Whereas the former can be said to still be in his youth, the latter, despite being younger, but due to life circumstances, has experienced a social condition that might accurately be categorized as adulthood. Likewise, a twenty-year-old Howard University student activist has a different set of experiences than a twenty-year-old unemployed, inner-city young adult who has two children, even if the two individuals grew up in the same neighborhood. These differential locations in the opportunity structure, more than age or generation, have a varied impact on their involvement in social justice campaigns and in defining what "youth" means to them.

Bedolla's study of Latino youth involved in protests against Proposition 187, the anti–illegal immigration initiative that was approved by Californians in 1994, provides an interesting look at the social and political attitudes of native-born and immigrant high school students. She found that despite being influenced by the same protest movement and attending the same high schools, the youth had multiple identities that shaped their enthusiasm for politics, their views about racial stigma, and their political efficacy. Class, gender, their location in social networks, and when and from where their families immigrated to the United States all had as much of an impact on their political orientations as did age.[25]

Another example of how multiple identities had as much of an impact as age or generational consciousness on youth-based activism can be found in the mobilization campaigns to reform the juvenile justice system in the first decade of the twenty-first century. The trajectory of the campaigns and avenues for youth participation were shaped by federalism as well as local and regional political cultures. As demonstrated later in the book, the movement to reform the juvenile justice movement in Louisiana initially relied on legal advocates who were better prepared to tackle a rigid, Jim Crow political culture that was embedded in the juvenile justice system. Yet seasoned activists from New York City, where there was a thriving youth organizing culture, encouraged youth-led groups to take the lead in the juvenile justice reform initiatives.

Another point worth noting is the distinct political orientations among youth who join the same movement organization or mobilization campaign at different periods of time. Whittier refers to these groups of activists as "micro-cohorts" or "clusters of participants." Despite joining a movement two or three years apart, they may be "shaped by distinct transformative experiences that differ because of subtle shifts in the political context."[26] This can produce dissimilar political orientations among young activists in the same organization or movement campaign. Young activists who joined SNCC in the early 1960s were influenced by a different political context than those who participated in the group's initiatives after the passage of the Voting Rights Act of 1965. The mood of the country, the varying political events, and the rise of the black power movement had differential impacts on the two micro-cohorts, even though they belonged to the same political generation and organization.

Another reason why it is problematic to think of youth as a vanguard group with a shared identity relates to how social and political actors of all types—social movement organizations, the media, social workers, politicians, and law enforcement agents—all play competing roles in constructing and reconstructing their interpretations of what it means to be youthful. Peter Edelman notes that political elites did not give attention to "youth" as a separate and distinct social phenomenon until the early twentieth century. This was due to changes in the economy, industrialization, the advent of compulsory, elementary education in the United States, and child labor regulations.[27] After these changes Congress, the president, public interest groups, and social movement organizations gave additional attention to the problems of youth. President Franklin Roosevelt created the National Youth Administration in the mid-1930s. During the same period, the American Council on Education sponsored several studies analyzing the problems of black youth.[28] Many radical left organizations also made concerted efforts to recruit and mobilize young people, including the Young Communist League, the Southern Negro Youth Congress (SNYC), and militant labor unions. Inevitably, students of political generations must account for how the concept of youth is constructed, both socially and politically, and how this process involves a political struggle between competing actors that affects movement-building initiatives. Because multiple actors play a dynamic role in shaping, defining, and reproducing competing notions of youth culture and participation, it is difficult to organize youth around a common political agenda or identity, or to assume that they should be vanguards of movement struggles by virtue of their age.

Considering the major challenges to conceptualizing generational consciousness and youth participation in social movements, why do the aforementioned viewpoints continue to shape generational interpretations of movement campaigns? The main reason is because young activists, especially those who share militant or social justice orientations, fear that the energy and resources will be co-opted by adult activists who are presumably (and often mistakenly assumed to be) more conservative, antidemocratic, and vulnerable to elite forms of mobilization. A common argument is that young activists should be cautious of participating in adult-led movement organizations or infrastructures due to the belief that they will be manipulated or used to augment political agendas that are predetermined by veteran activists who eschew extra-systemic pressures.[29] The belief is that a patron-client relationship will emerge, where youth are considered clients and as subordinate to the political preferences of antidemocratic, adult-led movement infrastructures.[30]

These concerns are not necessarily new to progressive-left movements. As Christine Kelly argues, they existed during the student phase of the anti-apartheid movement and impeded the student activists from formalizing their initiatives into a long-term social movement.[31] The roots of this debate, she argues, date as far back as the identity-based movements and countercultural politics of the 1960s. During this period, many student activists established social movement organizations that were independent from adult-led groups that were perceived to be elitist or hierarchical.

These concerns are further rooted in a misinterpretation of the generational debates that took place inside the civil rights movement, primarily between SNCC and adult-led organizations. Ella Baker was one of the principal architects of SNCC. She argued that SNCC had to be autonomous from the civil rights leadership strata and white-led progressive groups in order to engage in effective grassroots organizing.[32] As the primary staff member for the Southern Christian Leadership Conference (SCLC), she organized the Southwide Leadership Conference in April 1960. The gathering brought together black students who were involved in the southern sit-in movement earlier that year, as well as student leaders and youth advocates from a number of student organizations. The SCLC, the Congress of Racial Equality (CORE), and the Fellowship of Reconciliation all were in attendance at the conference, along with white progressive formations such as the National Student Association, the Students for a Democratic Society, and the National Student Christian Federation.

At the conference, there was a debate over whether black students should form an independent formation or formally incorporate their efforts into the established civil rights organizations. Some groups at the conference attempted to recruit the students into their fold. Although the SCLC had the inside track, partially due to Baker's insistence, the conference leaders decided to form a separate organization that eventually became SNCC.[33]

Youth activists point to this debate as the main reason why young activists should be at the forefront of community-based struggles. Because Baker and others feared co-optation by established civil rights groups, SNCC's formation was viewed as a validation for autonomous youth formations that articulate a distinct identity from adult-led groups. Yet historian Barbara Ransby claims that the divide at SNCC's founding conference "was not generational," and Baker herself believed "youth was no guarantee of political radicalism, and age did not always mean moderation." Instead, Baker wanted to preserve the autonomy of radical youth and "did not want them shackled by the bureaucracy of existing organizations."[34] She would have made the same argument, as she did on numerous occasions, had the debate involved middle-age radical activists or sharecroppers instead of youth. Accordingly, the debate was not necessarily about generational divisions or the attempt as some might believe to separate youth from adults, as it was about the optimum strategies for cultivating radical democratic approaches to movement building.

There is some indication that the SCLC and Dr. Martin Luther King, Jr. were less enthusiastic about co-opting the student activists at SNCC's founding meeting than is generally portrayed in the literature. King was part of a bridge generation of activists, who because of their age and political orientations were in the camp of neither an old and moderate civil rights guard or the young people who affiliated with SNCC.[35] Furthermore, a closer examination of SNCC underscores the fact that it relied extensively on the philosophical thrust and mentorship of veteran activists including Baker, James Forman, Gloria Richardson, Amzie Moore, Fannie Lou Hamer, Herbert Lee, Septima Clark, and Miles Horton. Hence, a misinterpretation of divisions in the civil rights movement may be one of the reasons why some contemporary activists attempt to separate young people from adult activists.

The notion that black youth share a uniform identity and should be at the vanguard of resistance movements has been further advanced by hip-hop culture. Since its emergence in the 1970s hip-hop's far-reaching influence, both domestically and globally, has offered a discursive treatment of the drudgeries of postindustrial ghetto life.[36] Progressive hip-hop artists such as New York's Rosa Clemente in the mid-2000s formed the National Hip-Hop Political Convention, which sponsored workshops on electoral organizing, voter education, and gang mediation.[37] Boots Riley of the radical hip-hop group The Coup is another progressive activist-artist whose music offers biting criticisms of racism and class exploitation.[38] Some service agencies even carry out "'Hood Work" that uses hip-hop to empower urban youth to support education reform, restorative justice, and economic justice initiatives.[39] Some scholars further contend that hip-hop has produced a fourth wave of feminism that criticizes neoliberal and global restructuring programs.[40]

However, the stature of progressive artists and 'Hood Work has been eclipsed by artists who promote materialist consumption, consumerism, and chauvinism. The commodification of some elements of hip-hop has made them impotent when it comes to advancing a radical politics that can remedy the material conditions of disaffected communities. As stated by activist Yvonne Bynoe, "Unfortunately, many activists and their supporters have not fully considered the prospect that Hip Hop culture's co-option by 'Corporate America' and 'Madison Avenue' may have stripped it of its radicalism. Realistically, how revolutionary can a 'Hip Hop' movement be if its primary motivator is a market-driven entity?"[41] Despite the progressive components of hip-hop, the culture's influence is further overshadowed by the corporatization of the genre. This includes corporate influence on the types of rap music played on mainstream radio stations, and the ascent of market-oriented hip-hop moguls such as Russell Simmons, Sean "Puffy" Combs, and rapper 50 Cent. This, in turn, allows the most financially astute (and usually most wealthy) hip-hop entrepreneurs to position themselves as the authentic representatives of ghetto youth, such that their prestige and voices are exalted within corporate and mainstream artistic and political circles.

Spence's assessment of hip-hop and rap music is instructive in this regard. He contends that neoliberal ideology—bootstrap individualism, the promotion of market-based initiatives over government programs and human rights, and the attribution of cultural dysfunction as a leading cause of black poverty—is rampant in rap music.[42] Even some hip-hop organizations such as the Hip Hop Summit Action Network reproduced neoliberal orientations, which then allowed its lead organizer, Russell Simmons, to assume the role of broker between white politicians and black and Latinos activists.[43]

Equally problematic is that hip-hop reproduces the same conceptual missteps that confront generational analyses. It relies on the inaccurate assumption that young people—or what is referred to as the "hip-hop generation," a concept that has become synonymous with the "post–civil rights generation"—have a distinct or shared identity. Many hip-hop artists and intellectuals claim to articulate a unique generational consciousness that transcends the political diversity within hip hop and the multiple and competing identities among young blacks and Latinos. This interpretation downplays the fact that hip-hop's influence cuts across generational lines and involves micro-cohorts. Young people who came of age during the incipient stages of hip-hop in the 1970s and the latter stages of the black power movement have a different set of experiences than hip-hop activists whose political socialization was shaped by the devolution policies of the Reagan and Bush years, or those who came of age in the first decade of the twenty-first century.

The major point of this discussion is that young activists belonging to the same age-specific categories have multiple identities. Despite the utility of generational analyses, one has to be cautious about essentializing the experiences of young people, especially activists, of the post–civil rights generation. The activist movements discussed throughout this book involve a small contingent of young people. Although all embrace social justice narratives and were socialized by movement infrastructures and social networks, they are politically diverse. They have multiple identities that transcended age-specific categories and influenced the trajectory of their activism.

Conceptualizing Contemporary Youth-Based Activism

In assessing movement activism among the post–civil rights generation, I have two theoretical concerns: first, to explain the broader constraints on social movement activism among the post–civil rights generation; second, to describe how young activists have circumvented these constraints and expanded the boundaries of movement activism. A major challenge with the study of social movements is explaining how activists from aggrieved communities are able to advance ameliorative demands despite shifting political contexts. Kurt Schock insists that "not only do social movements respond to political opportunities, but they also strategically overcome political constraints, thereby reshaping the political context."[44] Addressing these two realities—the constraints on movement activism and how young activists have overcome these constraints—is the objective of this discussion.

Next, I describe several factors that have influenced the constraints, obstacles, and opportunities for youth-based mobilization: (1) the evolution of movement infrastructures since the mid-1960s and their impact on youth-based activism, (2) the impact of institutional leveraging on social movement activism, and (3) the use by movement bridge-builders, or the leading activists of movements, of innovative strategies and tactics,[45] or what I call *creative organizing*, as a vehicle to jump-start youth-based mobilization.

Movement Infrastructures and Youth-Based Movements

This book examines youth-based activism, or movement activities and popular mobilization campaigns involving and coordinated by youth, students, and young adults. These activities are affiliated with youth-oriented groups that are best described in Sherwood and Dressner's discussion of the "landscape" of youth work and HoSang's portrait of youth organizing: youth or student-led organizations, some of which are affiliated with national or federated youth organizations; multigenerational (or intergenerational) organizations; and network-affiliated groups or coalitions that bolster youth-centered organizing projects.[46]

I extend this three-part typology by insisting that young activists, youth groups, and their adult allies in a given movement operate within what Curtis and Zurcher called a "multi-organizational field" or multilayered network of activists and organizations.[47] Although social movement scholars use several concepts to explain this multiorganizational field—mobilizing structure, social movement community, social movement industry, youth development infrastructure, and social movement sector[48]—I prefer the term "movement infrastructure." This concept describes an organizational process composed of a complex leadership structure, multiple organizations that have centralized governing structures and decentralized affiliate groups, formal and informal activists, and a resource base (i.e., funders, patrons, contributors, etc.) that coalesce around the same causes.[49] The leaders of movement infrastructures, through the maintenance of norms and standards and the adoption of strategies and tactics, shape their constituents' political orientations and movement-building initiatives. Their interactions with nonyouth groups and even nonmovement actors, as indicated in Rucht's study of social movements, also dictates their strategies for social change and movement outcomes.[50]

To be certain, youth-based movements are not the only ones influenced by movement infrastructures. Health care justice activists operate within a movement infrastructure, as do homeless rights activists, children's rights activists, peace organizations, and labor unions. And at times, the policy objectives of a movement infrastructure intersect or are shifted to support allied movements.[51] This was exemplified during the Memphis sanitation workers' strike in 1968 when the civil rights movement's activities intersected with the labor movement.

Yet my understanding of movement infrastructures has particular relevance for youth activists and organizations. Despite romantic notions that youth activists should be autonomous from adult-led formations, it is impossible to divorce young activists from movement infrastructures. Youth-based mobilization activities require resources, linkages with indigenous organizations, and political education, much of which involves intergenerational and interactive work with adult allies. The three youth-based groups (youth-led, multigenerational, network-affiliated groups) operate within a movement infrastructure composed of a constellation of organizations and activist networks. These groups are influenced by nonyouth groups, networks, and indigenous activists. Tilton's investigation of the anti–Proposition 21 campaign in the Bay Area found that it "was nurtured by a densely networked infrastructure of nonprofit youth services" including youth organizing groups, adult-led advocacy organizations, and even radical black and Latino activists who came of age in the 1960s and 1970s.[52] For youth or student-led movement organizations, it may be impossible to separate them from a complex, organizational process. These groups interact with and are influenced by nonyouth groups and routinely rely on adult allies to assist with resource support, fund-raising, and capacity-building activities.[53] Equally important is that youth-led groups help to shape the political orientations of adult allies and often push more established leaders and groups to adjust their policy objectives.

An additional concern about movement infrastructures is that shifting and declining political opportunities can destabilize cooperative relations between various groups inside a given movement infrastructure, including adult and youth groups, as well as movement and nonmovement actors. Some groups inside of a movement infrastructure will actually adjust their policy objectives depending on changing political contexts, as exhibited in the examination of the SNYC's initiatives discussed in the next chapter.

SNCC's prominent role in the Mississippi civil rights movement of the 1960s is an example of a complex movement infrastructure. To prevent intramovement conflict and competition for resources, SNCC, SCLC, CORE, and the NAACP established a formal coalition called the Council of Federated Organizations (COFO). Also sprouting out of this infrastructure was the Mississippi Freedom Democratic Party (MFDP), a parallel political party that attempted to replace the segregationist (white) state Democratic Party. Founded in 1964 with the support of SNCC, the MFDP was probably best characterized as an intergenerational formation. In the late 1950s and early 1960s, some activists from

COFO-affiliated organizations and networks attended organizing training sessions at the Highlander Folk School, a movement center in Tennessee that provided organizers' training, capacity building, and popular education to labor and civil rights activists in the South.[54] SNCC's organizing activities were undoubtedly shaped by its interactions with the COFO groups, the MFDP, Highlander, and a cadre of local activists, some of whom were active in civil rights initiatives long before SNCC's arrival and COFO's formation. And, nonmovement actors and the shifting political context significantly impacted SNCC's organizing work in Mississippi.

Although a movement infrastructure brings together like-minded activists, they may have ideological and philosophical disagreements about the optimum strategies that can best advance their causes.[55] SNCC activist Stokely Carmichael coexisted in the same movement infrastructure as the national NAACP president Roy Wilkins. Both belonged to organizations that adamantly opposed Jim Crow segregation and black disenfranchisement. Yet they had distinct approaches to combating racial hierarchy that were shaped by ideology, age, and their connections to different social and political networks. Because movement infrastructures consist of activists with different political orientations and positions within the social and political structure, it is often the case that competing claims will emerge among activists who share the same political grievances.

Furthermore, it is common for hierarchies to emerge within movement infrastructures based on how groups prioritize issues. Advocacy groups may choose to fight harder for issues that affect marginalized subgroups that have more resources and greater status than other subgroups. In her study of more than two hundred advocacy groups, Strolovitch found that "issues affecting advantaged subgroups are given disproportionately higher levels of attention, whereas issues affecting disadvantaged subgroups are given disproportionately low levels."[56] This creates a double standard in which "the quality of representation [for disadvantaged subgroups] is inferior to that received by advantaged subgroups."[57] This double standard was indicative of the response to the HIV/AIDS crisis by black political, advocacy, and civil rights groups. These groups were slow to respond to the HIV/AIDS crisis because of the marginalization and stigmatization of lesbian, gay, bisexual, and transgendered communities. When they did respond to the HIV/AIDS epidemic, the framing of their early mobilization activities deemphasized the crisis among black homosexuals—presumably because of stigma and homophobia—and instead focused on heterosexual blacks who contracted the virus through intravenous drug use.[58]

Movement infrastructures may also be burdened by class hierarchies that privilege well-educated activists, and racial justice movements may subordinate women, youth, or low-income activists. These hierarchies or what some feminist scholars refer to as divisions of labor within movement infrastructures may circumscribe some cohort groups within movements.[59] Aaronette White's examination of revolutionary movements underscores how nationalist movements and armed insurrections, including those that fought against colonial regimes, reinforced masculine identities and relegated revolutionary women to subordinate positions.[60] These movements were widely supported and romanticized by the left, but nonetheless reproduced hierarchies that many social justice activists in the United States and the West struggled against in their own countries.

Hierarchies may be exacerbated by external factors such as changes in the political environment and the flow of resources from allies to a select group of activists in the movement infrastructures. Haines and McAdam, in separate studies of the civil rights movement, found that elite patrons distributed and shifted monetary contributions and resources to the "Big Five" civil rights organizations (the NAACP, the National Urban League, SNCC, SCLC, and CORE) according to which organizations were viewed as less confrontational.[61] This occurred when the civil rights movement was perceived to have become more militant in the late 1960s.

Understanding that movement infrastructures influence the trajectory of protest and claims making is critical to this discussion. To summarize, movements are facilitated by infrastructures or organizational processes that promote certain strategies and tactics, minimize conflict or dissent among competing groups that are allied around the same cause, encourage groups to follow a set of norms and standards that shape movement activism, are shaped by broader political changes external to movements, and may be rife within internal divisions and hierarchies. These factors can limit or create opportunities for young people to participate in mobilization campaigns.

Institutional Leveraging and Movement Infrastructures

Contemporary social movements, especially those involving young people, have been inhibited by movement infrastructures that privilege institutional modes of political change. The institutionalization of progressive movements and the expansion of single-issue advocacy groups that practice insider negotiation strategies have moderated movement infrastructures and subsequently constrained transformational movements and mobilization opportunities for young activists.[62] Debra Minkoff's research of contemporary civil rights and women's rights groups argues that the growing power of progressive movements in the 1960s encouraged many groups—groups that one might conclude would be at the forefront of movement activities—to downplay social justice activism in exchange for leveraging their influence inside of political institutions. The conservative movement's growing influence, the need to safeguard the legislative measures that were won in the 1960s and early 1970s, and the struggle to survive in a hostile political environment encouraged many social justice groups to channel their energies and resources into safe and conventional modes of political activism.

Minkoff insists that political elites offered these groups and movement infrastructures a tangle of incentives or "institutional niche" inside and in relation to political institutions.[63] This niche, though limiting transformational movement initiatives, gave the most influential and resource-abundant organizations inside these infrastructures resources, access to political elites, legitimacy, protection, and stability in an evolving political environment.[64] In exchange, these groups were encouraged to moderate their strategies and tactics and minimize the use of confrontational protests. By doing this, these groups were able to present themselves as viable alternatives to other movement organizations that appeared to be confrontational or threatening.[65]

Accordingly, movement infrastructures that should support transformational movement activity among young people have moderated their activities as a result of the leveraging or channeling process expanded at length by Minkoff. When leveraging is not overtly promoted, some groups inside of movement infrastructures still simulate the norms and standards of political elites, philanthropic allies, and bureaucratic institutions.[66] This activity privileges established groups, some of which embedded their influence at the end of the civil rights, black power, and New Left movements. It further elevates groups that are staffed by highly trained professionals who understand the dictates of elite mobilization such as interest group lobbying, fund-raising, and strategic planning and are readily prepared to navigate the Byzantine nature of political institutions.

Institutional leveraging has become salient in the post–civil rights era due to the expansion of the nonprofit sector and single-issue advocacy groups. Domhoff claims that a "parallel government of nonprofit organizations" has emerged in recent years, partially composed of advocacy, social welfare, and civil rights groups working in marginalized communities.[67] These groups generally receive funding from philanthropic institutions and must comply with a complex set of rules and regulations, such that they are typically led by a well-educated and professionalized staff.[68] One activist in Apollon's study of young organizers referred to this phenomenon as a "non-profit industrial complex" that exercises too much control over civil rights advocacy, youth development, and movement activities.[69] In reality, leading activists have become sophisticated in mobilizing resources, recruiting foundation resources, and placing allies in grant-making institutions. Nonetheless, the expansion of nonprofits potentially creates a "self-limiting radicalism" that moderates transformative initiatives and encourages institutional leveraging strategies.[70] Since young activists or youth-based formations operate inside of movement infrastructures that are shaped by the culture of nonprofits—or because they depend on the support of nonprofits, their professional staff and expertise, and leaders inside of movement infrastructures—their initiatives and demands have also become shaped by these organizational processes.[71]

In some cases, activists inside movement infrastructures who gain an institutional niche assist incipient movement formations, including black student and youth activist groups. Yet leveraging can make it difficult for young activists inside of these movement infrastructures to promote transformational initiatives, especially if they conflict with veteran activists and advocates who have access to the routine decision-making apparatuses and resources, and have strong commitments to institutional elites.

Institutional leveraging may further reinforce hierarchies and clientelism within movement infrastructures. For example, low-income and working-class activists may be subordinated inside of movement infrastructures that are controlled by middle-class advocacy groups. Movement infrastructures may be ripe with sexism, thus exacerbating unequal relations between women and men. Similarly, youth may be relegated to an unequal partner or client in these movement infrastructures. This is particularly the case when pairing movement formations or groups that garner a niche in the political universe, and thus are able to acquire resources and legitimacy, with youth who develop creative strategies to mobilize aggrieved communities but lack the resources and communication infrastructures to fully implement them. The consequence of this dynamic is that groups that garner an institutional niche and benefit from institutional channeling may then assume the status of patrons inside movement infrastructures. They may support resource-poor organizations or youth-led groups, but regulate or control their activists if they are considered too disruptive.

In reality, institutional leveraging was used by groups during the civil rights movement and even during the left movements of the 1930s. Yet, it is now part of the larger family of institutionalized strategies (electioneering, interest group lobbying, insider politics, and bargaining) that are widely used by post–civil rights activists and politicians. Some movement groups willingly choose to use leveraging processes even if it means offsetting transformational mobilization strategies. Hasan Jeffries documents the experiences of movement activists who were at the forefront of the Lowndes County Freedom Party (LCFP) in the 1960s. For half a decade, the LCFP provided a national model for "freedom politics" that challenged the segregationist Democratic Party in Alabama. However, by the early 1970s, some LCFP activists used their influence in the organization and the broader Lowndes County movement to negotiate private agreements with political elites for public office.[72] They essentially leveraged the LCFP's reputation and resources to garner public offices for themselves, even though this strategy undermined the organization's mobilization activities.

Complicating matters has been the dramatic reduction in youth militancy since the 1970s. This was partially due to the disillusionment resulting from the Vietnam War and the Watergate scandal.[73] The passage of the Twenty-Sixth Amendment in 1971, which gave eighteen-year-olds the right to vote, also moderated political insurgency among young people. As indicated by Tom Hayden's commentary at the beginning of this chapter, the Twenty-Sixth Amendment gave youth an alternative and institutionalized mechanism for exercising political influence other than the use of protest.[74]

Among young blacks, militancy took a spiral downward as a result of political repression, organizational fatigue, and intramovement conflict, all of which diminished the influence of and eliminated many civil rights and black power organizations.[75] The decline in militant-style protest coincided with deteriorating economic conditions in poor and working-class black communities, deindustrialization and suburbanization, and the shift from a manufacturing to a service-based economy. These crises ended almost thirty years of economic growth that helped to develop a bourgeoning black middle class.[76] They also left working-poor blacks in urban areas isolated away from major employment opportunities.

The rise of the conservative movement had a particularly sobering effect on black youth militancy. President Reagan eliminated important social, educational, and economic programs and funds that served as a social safety net for poor black youth, and by the mid-1980s federal cutbacks to education contributed to a drop in black college attendance rates.[77] This confluence of factors had a moderating effect on black political insurgency and progressive youth activism.[78] These factors also made the utilization of institutional leveraging more attractive to progressive movements and advocacy groups. Many of these entities no longer used militant political action or direct action to mobilize youth or to challenge racial and class hierarchies due to fear of neglect or repression.

Certainly, youth-based movements are not the only movements influenced by institutional leveraging and the broader shift toward institutionalization. The political culture undergirding contemporary civil rights and liberal advocacy groups has also been impacted by these phenomena. Many of these organizations no longer used militant political action to mobilize constituents, and as Adolph Reed explains, they now "earn their insider status by providing a convincing alternative to popular political mobilization."[79] In order to survive and garner political stature, these groups modified their goals or methods of mobilization such that they conformed to the norms and standards of dominant political institutions.[80]

This is not to suggest that institutional leveraging was completely absent from the movement strategies of the earlier generations of activists. Civil rights activists and even black power radicals used an assortment of institutionalized strategies. These strategies, however, were part of a repertoire of tactics deployed by activists and usually complemented militant forms of political action.[81]

The challenges emerging from institutional leveraging are examined in chapter 3's assessment of SNCC and the MFDP and the attempts by conservative Democrats to subvert their organizing activities. I also examine institutional leveraging in chapters 5 through 7. The chapters look extensively at the organizing activities of the BSLN, the Black Community Crusade for Children (BCCC), and the CDF in the 1990s. I suggest that the BSLN's movement bridge-builders or leadership core—national staff, field organizers, and National Coordinating Committee—were frequently in a tug-of-war with its parent organizations, especially the BCCC's Steering Committee, over the optimum strategies for effecting change in low-income black communities. While the leadership core did not eschew electioneering—and instead created a comprehensive program for engaging young people in voter education and outreach—the group was wary about shifting too much of its energy and resources into established bureaucratic and political institutions. This produced tensions between the BSLN and its parent organizations and, at times, between the BSLN's local affiliates and national staff.

Creative Organizing: Expanding the Youth Opportunity Structure

The discussion of movement infrastructures and institutional leveraging offers valuable insight into the complicated set of factors that inhibit social activism among the post–civil rights generation. Yet despite the limitations of leveraging, it would be incorrect to conclude that there has been an absence of social justice claims by young blacks. Institutional leveraging, though rendering transformational campaigns episodic, has not been completely deterministic or insurmountable. Through creative organizing strategies, young and veteran activists have been able to expand the opportunity structure of activism and contested the boundaries of movement infrastructures.[82]

Several scholars insist that movement activists can circumvent political contexts that appear to contain transformational activism. Todd Shaw, in his examination of black grassroots activism in Detroit, argues that the protest variation of grassroots activism can force political institutions and public officials to positively respond to grievances by neglected constituents such as fair housing and homeless rights advocates. Yet, grassroots activists and disruptive coalitions must appropriately time their actions, use flexible and adaptive tactics, and recognize when political regimes are vulnerable and can be coerced to support redistributive and judicious policies.[83]

Another compelling study, by Marshall Ganz, looks at organizational tensions within the movement infrastructure that shaped the California farm workers movement of the 1960s.[84] He compares the mobilization strategies of the United Farm Workers (UFW) organization and the AFL-CIO's Agricultural Workers Organizing Committee (AWOC). Through "strategic capacity," or the creation of a flexible leadership team that implemented innovative strategies, the UFW had better success mobilizing immigrant agricultural workers than the well-resourced AWOC. McAdam also states that civil rights activists used "tactical innovation," which entailed the use of dynamic strategies and tactics, in order to enhance their perceived powerlessness when the political opportunity structure appeared to be shifting against them.[85] Tera Hunter further notes that in the late nineteenth and early twentieth centuries, black washerwomen fought against discrimination and class exploitation despite the retrenchment of civil rights policies. In addition to forming a labor union, the women organized strikes and fought for the right to set their own wages.[86] Other scholars claim that under repressive conditions, marginal and resource-poor groups found ways to resist, sometimes through the use of survival strategies or covert forms of political activism.[87]

I modify these earlier assessments by arguing that movement bridge-builders can generate opportunities for young people to participate in movements by utilizing creative strategies that seek to elevate the social and political status of youth. These strategies must situate youth as an important variable in movement infrastructures and as vital to addressing the material realities of working-poor communities. I distinguish bridge-builders from Belinda Robnett's use of the concept "bridge leaders."[88] Both sets of activists organize diverse constituency groups in support of a movement's objectives and help to bridge generational divisions among activists. Yet Robnett claims bridge leaders are marginalized or excluded from formal leadership positions due to generational or gender biases. On the other hand, I argue that bridge-builders are not marginal in movements, but are the most important resource for sustaining movement campaigns beyond their incipient stages.

One component of creative organizing is the use of strategic *framing* devices. Framing is an "interpretive schema" that allows movement leaders to package a belief system or set of explanations about material conditions or policies that appeal to aggrieved communities and encourage youth to be socially active.[89] The importance of framing should not be underestimated; it is used by political elites and social movement actors across the ideological spectrum. Yet in contrast to political elites who frame issues through sophisticated and expensive media and advertisement campaigns, community activists and organizers must link the framing process with on-the-ground organizing initiatives and solutions.[90] They must identify a problem, assign blame or cause to it, and then offer solutions to resolving the problem.[91] Bob Moses and Charlie Cobb, both former SNCC activists, point to the central tenets of the framing process—they refer to it as "consensus" building—at the height of the civil rights movement. They write,

> Effective organizing in 1960s Mississippi meant an organizer had to utilize the everyday issues of the community and frame them for the maximum benefit of the community. Staking out some area of consensus was necessary, but an organizer could not create consensus, an organizer had to find it. And it took time and patience to search out where it was lodged beneath layer after layer of other concerns. Then, if the organizer found it, the question of how to tap into the consensus, how to energize it and use it for mobilization and organization remained.[92]

Hence, the framing process is evolutionary and dynamic. Movement bridge-builders must adjust and readjust their interpretations of material conditions that affect marginalized youth as a vehicle for mobilizing them to support a cause. Furthermore, movement activists can use framing as an agenda-setting strategy in order to advance causes that resonate among young people or promote issues that are neglected by political elites. The media reform campaign coordinated by the Youth Force and Youth Media Council used framing to highlight the mistreatment of black and Latino youth by the mainstream media. The groups claimed that it was difficult to address racial profiling and high incarceration rates among ghetto youth without understanding the mainstream media's stereotypes of black and Latino youth.

Another component of creative organizing involves the use of indigenous resources or preexisting organizations, networks, and institutions that are used for stimulating movement participation. Aldon Morris's analysis of the civil rights movement found that black indigenous institutions such as activist churches, civic groups, and colleges played a critical role in buttressing civil rights protests and creating communication infrastructures for diffusing collective action.[93] They helped to recruit students and young people into the civil rights movement, and provided the necessary training and resources to the students involved in civil rights protests.

Despite the utility of the indigenous resource perspective, it deserves some revisions when applied to contemporary youth activists. This is because preexisting groups can hinder youth activists from adopting innovative strategies, or they may reinforce hierarchies within movement infrastructures.[94] Some preexisting groups may resist creative strategies because of their concrete commitments and linkages to political and economic elites. Subsequently, they may place barriers in front of alternative forms of leadership, including youth leaders, especially those who are deemed as threats to their interests. The 1963 civil rights campaign in Birmingham, Alabama, experienced some resistance from indigenous groups in the black community that had linkages with political elites and business leaders. Some activists, business leaders, and ministers feared that Martin Luther King, Jr. would invite more repression and urged him to halt the protests in the city.[95]

To overcome this problem, movement activists must make creative use of indigenous resources, especially those organizations and networks that have access to marginalized youth. McAdam, Tarrow, and Tilly assert that it's not the existence of indigenous resources that is useful to protests, but it is how these resources are *appropriated* or transformed into vehicles of contention.[96] Appropriation occurs through organizing and cultural work that synthesizes the interests and collective identities of indigenous groups with the goals of young people and broader movements. This creates a context for interest convergence, or what the authors call an "attribution of similarity."[97] Movement bridge-builders, through appropriation, can establish an attribution of similarity or interest convergence between youth activists and preexisting actors in order to convince the latter group to assist youth-based movements. In other words, the purpose is to activate indigenous groups and activists in order to create more flexible and deliberative movement infrastructures, and turn them into vehicles that can nurture young activists and support transformational movement demands.

Furthermore, this strategy can bridge two movement infrastructures or single-issue campaigns, thus developing cross-movement linkages between different sectors of activists. For example, SCLC and SNCC activists synthesized the interests of the civil rights and antiwar movements, in part by insisting that both were essential to advancing the philosophy of nonviolence. This created a window or opening for the formation of new coalitions and new avenues for young people to support the demands of the civil rights movement in the late 1960s.

Positionality is another strategy that movement bridge-builders have used to create opportunities for young people to participate in mobilization campaigns. It occurs when movement bridge-builders intentionally alert youth, allies, donors to movement campaigns, and veteran activists within their movement infrastructures about the harmful effects of regressive policies on disaffected black youth. The intent is to heighten the sense of urgency or dramatize the impact of these policies on young people. Consequently, the status of marginalized youth—or the impact of regressive policies on their life circumstances—serves as a "canary in the mine" or an alarm that warns potential youth activists, veteran organizers and advocates, and allies about the urgent problems affecting marginal communities,[98] and the need to accelerate extra-systemic pressures and recruit new activists in support of mobilization campaigns. Positional tactics can thus shape policies by encouraging their implementation, or they can be used to interfere or disrupt policies—what I call policy interference—that are deemed harmful to youth.

The movement against Proposition 21 discussed at the beginning of this chapter used a positional strategy to mobilize young people who were previously disengaged from social activism to join the mobilization campaign against the measure. Movement bridge-builders argued that the ballot initiative was emblematic of a systematic attempt to use voter initiatives to advance policies that harmed communities of color. Similarly, labor activists may heighten the problem of black youth unemployment in order to recruit new activists or young blacks to the labor movement, or mobilize their support for job training programs. And, education advocates may raise the public's awareness about high school drop-out rates or the disproportionate placement of blacks in special education programs as a means for mobilizing young activists around expenditures for public schools.

Thus, positionality is useful for awakening a dormant or latent contingent of young people and dramatizing issues that impact their life circumstances. It is equally useful for convincing veteran activists and advocates to dedicate resources that create opportunities for young people to participate in movement campaigns that target urgent problems. Positional tactics can also cultivate intergenerational collaborative initiatives; and they can convince veteran activists that the problems affecting black youth reflect more systemic problems that adversely affect different cohorts in underdeveloped communities. Positionality actually expands the meaning of youth-based activism. It allows the status of youth to be used as an instrument for stimulating intergenerational struggles even if young people are subordinated in these campaigns.

Measuring the Consequences and Outcomes
of Creative Organizing Strategies

The previous section outlined three creative organizing strategies deployed in youth-based movements: framing, the appropriation of indigenous resources, and positionality. Movement bridge-builders will use creative organizing strategies to expand opportunities for young people to participate in movement campaigns. In addition to shaping institutional outcomes, either through policy implementation and elections, movements can produce new actors and assist other movements, lead to the political recognition of previously ignored groups, and cause broad cultural shifts in the body politic.[99] They may also yield unintended outcomes and "spin off new challenges or factions

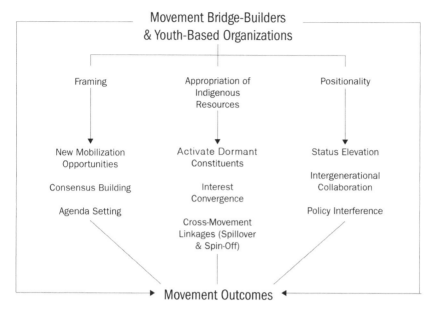

Figure 1.1. Creative Organizing Strategies and Measuring Their Impact

even after a cycle of protest declines."[100] These new forms of claims-making activities may be entirely different from the progenitor movements that created them.

The aforementioned consequences or outcomes of creative organizing strategies are outlined in figure 1.1. Movement bridge-builders use *framing* to develop narratives that explain a particular problem that has relevance to marginalized groups. For grassroots movements, the best framing strategies are not imposed or dropped on marginalized communities, but emerge from interactions between movement bridge-builders and aggrieved communities. The urgency assigned to a problem can thus build a consensus between different groups, including advantaged and disadvantaged subgroups, in marginalized communities. And, it can thrust an issue in dispute to the forefront of a political agenda. Depending on the urgency assigned to a problem, this strategy can also create new opportunities for young people and disadvantaged subgroups to participate in movement politics.

The SNYC and SOBU discussed in the succeeding chapters used framing to create new opportunities for youth-based activism. The

SNYC and its adult allies framed the Great Depression as uniquely injurious to working-class and poor black youth. In addition to mobilizing
young blacks in extra-campus activities, this strategy focused attention
on economic exploitation and a range of economic justice initiatives
that could ameliorate black despair. SOBU also used framing to situate black youth resistance within black working-class politics and Pan-
African movements.

In addition, movement bridge-builders can transform indigenous
groups (e.g., preexisting networks, local activists and organizations,
and even nonpolitical/apolitical civic and volunteer groups) into
vehicles of movement contention. This strategy of *appropriation* can
activate or encourage these groups to support incipient mobilization
campaigns. This was demonstrated with the New Haven youth movement (see chapter 4) and the AFL-CIO's Union Summer campaign (see
chapter 9). Or it can be used to develop cross-movement linkages—it
allows movements to spill over into other movements as well as spin
off into new movements—because it pulls different groups under the
same movement infrastructure. In the third chapter, I describe SNCC's
attempt to build cross-movement linkages with the Black Panther Party
and the Black Liberators. Though these efforts failed, they represented
the types of cross-movement-building opportunities that emerge
from the appropriation strategy. The BSLN's formation and ideological development, examined in chapters 5 through 7, were also directly
attributed to indigenous activists who came out of the anti-apartheid
movement, the Jesse Jackson presidential campaigns, and local organizing activities.

The strategy of *positionality* occurs when bridge-builders intentionally position the status of youth as critical to a specific policy debate.
This can elevate youth and youth-based groups as important voices
within a hypercompetitive political environment. It encourages adult
allies or reputable advocacy groups to pay attention to marginalized
youth such that policies disproportionately affecting them are thrust to
the forefront of the political landscape. This strategy further legitimates
youth-based activities that are potentially disruptive or that interfere
with policies that are on the fast track to implementation. Both the
BSLN and JJRM coalitions (see chapter 8) used positional strategies to
address zero-tolerance policies and child poverty. Decades earlier, black

and white radicals employed a positional strategy to call attention to the suffering of black working-class communities in the Great Depression. This allowed them to mobilize the resources as well as raise the consciousness of young people and adults, thus creating opportunities for young blacks to participate in movement campaigns.

These creative organizing strategies explain how youth-based movements have attempted to effect change, notwithstanding shifting political contexts and the push and pull of institutional leveraging. They point to the vitality of youth-based movements, the innovation and leadership styles of movement bridge-builders, and the role of youth within social movement infrastructures.

Conclusion

Overall, the theoretical framework attempts to account for the challenges confronting movement activists of the post–civil rights generation. The existence of movement infrastructures suggests that young activists operate within a broader and complex network of activists. Mobilization campaigns led by movement infrastructures rooted in social and racial justice claims nonetheless are still likely to have divisions, hierarchies, and an unequal distribution of resources that are allocated to the most influential activists or movement organizations.

Another argument in this study, which is explained in this theoretical overview, is that the political context of the post–civil rights era has made movement infrastructures more susceptible to institutional leveraging. The institutional leveraging process is another facet of political incorporation that pertains uniquely to contemporary social movement organizations and advocacy groups, especially those that are well resourced and have strong connections to political elites. Leveraging provides these groups with some resources and protection in hostile political environments. Yet, at times, it can discourage groups that have an institutional niche from expending the energy and resources on nurturing militant youth.

Finally, the existence of movement infrastructures and the constraints of institutional leveraging have not deterred activists of the post–civil rights generation from joining mobilization campaigns. Although these campaigns were episodic and in some cases lacked the transformational character of the 1930s and 1960s movements, they were still important. Through creative organizing, young activists and veteran organizers can contest the institutional constraints on youth-based activism and generate opportunities for young activists to become involved in diverse movement initiatives. This further underscores the importance of leadership—the skills of movement bridge-builders, their ability to deploy resources and use frames to mobilize constituents, and varied leadership styles[101]—which is an undervalued component of social movement activities.

2

The World beyond the Campus

Some serious-minded adults gravely pronounced in innu-
merable articles, books and speeches, that ours was a "lost
generation." Such was the dismal future for the mass of the
youth; but the outlook of Negro youth, what with all the multiple patterns of discrimination and oppression, was more
hopeless yet. However, Negro youth, as the whole of American people, refused to accept such a fate for themselves.
—Esther Cooper Jackson, *This Is My Husband*, 1953

When James Jackson died in September 2007 at the age of ninety-two,
few contemporary activists acknowledged or understood his valuable
contribution to progressive social movements, black radicalism, and the
development of a black student and youth activist tradition in the twentieth century. Jackson was part of a small cadre of young black radicals
who cofounded the little known, but no less important, Southern Negro
Youth Congress (SNYC) in the late 1930s. The SNYC was a social movement organization that provided a blueprint for black student and youth
organizing two decades before the student protests of the 1960s. It was
instrumental in linking the economic justice claims of the black working class with the civil rights demands of middle-class leaders, many of
whom were drawn from the ranks of black colleges and advocacy groups.

In a 1931 speech to his Virginia Union freshman class titled "The
World beyond the Campus," Jackson offered an important commentary on the prospects of movement activism among black students

and youth. Although he was only sixteen years old at the time, Jackson urged his peers to reject the trappings of a middle-class lifestyle and dedicate themselves to improving the lives of poor and working-class blacks who were not afforded the opportunity to attend college. He insisted that black youth participation in social movements and popular mobilization campaigns was critical to combating the dogmatism of the Jim Crow code that brutalized rank-and-file blacks, shut them out of labor unions, and denied them labor protections.[1]

Six years after his speech, Jackson and a cadre of black students and young adults—this included his future wife and intellectual soul mate, Esther Cooper (also referred to by her married name, Esther Cooper Jackson or Esther Jackson), Ed Strong, C. Columbus Alston, and Louis Burnham—formed the nucleus of the SNYC. Operating from 1937 to 1949, the SNYC preceded the more well-known Student Nonviolent Coordinating Committee (SNCC) by a generation. The SNYC launched its first organizing campaign in 1937 against the British American Tobacco Company that was just a "stone's throw away" from Jackson's childhood home. Organizing in concert with black tobacco workers and labor organizers, the group attacked the mega-factory elite who doled out pittances to black workers, which Jackson later described as just a "cut above starvation wages."[2]

This chapter examines the participation of black students, youth, and young adults in high-risk social justice campaigns in the 1930s and 1940s, with a close look at the SNYC's origins, development, and collapse. Movement bridge-builders allied with the youth group and other young progressives used the creative organizing strategies of framing and positionality to create intergenerational collaborations and new opportunities for young people to participate in movement activism. Movement bridge-builders argued that militant action was needed to remedy the deprivation of black youth and working-class black communities in the Great Depression era. This viewpoint was embraced even by some black activists and professionals who in another time period would have been lukewarm to anticapitalist criticisms.

This chapter gives additional attention to the movement infrastructure that nurtured young black radicals. This infrastructure consisted of black progressives and left organizations and even white leftists groups, including the National Negro Congress (NNC), the NAACP, the

Communist Party (CP), and the Congress of Industrial Organizations (CIO). This movement infrastructure was dynamic, routinely changing, and shaped by the shifting political, economic, and international contexts of the Great Depression and World War II periods, which further influenced the political orientations of black radical youth. More important, movement organizations in the 1930s and 1940s initiated community organizing initiatives and popular mobilization campaigns that pushed for civil rights, labor protections for black workers, and economic recovery programs.

The first part of the chapter offers a detailed account of the emergence of black youth, movement formations in the 1930s, and why the social status of black youth was a central concern of black progressives during this period. I then examine movement activism among black youth, before and during World War II, with a particular focus on the activities of the SNYC. Afterward, I discuss the SNYC's positions on the U.S. intervention in World War II and black conscription and explain how their views were influenced by the political and economic climates of the period. Finally, I examine the collapse of the SNYC organization, which was partially due to the anticommunist hysteria and the increasing shift among black leaders away from militant political action in the late 1940s.

The Origins of Twentieth-Century Black Student Youth-Based Movements

It is difficult to determine when black youth first became involved in transformational movements. Historian John Lovell insists that youth and young adults between the ages of ten and thirty made up a large segment of the black slave population in the mid-nineteenth century and were heavily involved in the slave revolts.[3] Decades later, in the 1920s, students revolted against the conservative administrations, policies, officials, and philosophies at historically black colleges and universities.[4] The 1930s also experienced an unprecedented rise of political activity and community organizing among black youth. At the beginning of the decade, the infamous Scottsboro case in 1931 helped to raise the political consciousness of many young blacks about the horrors of racial segregation. Similar to the Emmit Till incident two decades later, it hastened young people's involvement in social and political activism.

In Baltimore, Maryland, Juanita Jackson helped to establish the City-Wide Young People's Forum (CWYPF), a multiclass youth formation that combated unemployment and racial segregation. Assisted by NAACP lobbyist Clarence Mitchell, the CWYPF successfully lobbied retail stores, the local library, and the Family Welfare Association in an effort to combat racial segregation and black youth unemployment.[5] It also lobbied Congress to eliminate segregation, worked with the national NAACP office on local issues, and mobilized Baltimore's black youth around a "Buy Where You Can Work" campaign at local department stores.[6] In New York, Ella Baker, who would later assist in the formation and development of SNCC, along with then progressive George Schuyler (later a conservative), formed a youth economic cooperative called the Young Negro Cooperative League in response to the economic crises of the Great Depression.[7] Also in New York, black and white youth organizations, assisted by the NAACP's Youth Council, formed the United Youth Committee, which rallied support for the National Labor Relations (Wagner) Act and an antilynching bill in Congress. Toward the end of the 1930s, a number of national level youth formations surfaced, including the NNC Youth Council and the NAACP Youth Council in 1936, and the SNYC in 1937.

These formations focused attention on the economic plight of blacks during the Great Depression, as well as the exclusion of blacks in the nation's leading trade unions and some of President Franklin Roosevelt's New Deal programs.[8] Racial exclusion inside of labor was especially disconcerting to the civil rights community decades before the New Deal. Between World War I and the late 1920s, some black trade unionists and white progressives aggressively challenged racial hierarchies inside of labor unions. They even deliberated several resolutions at the American Federation of Labor (AFL) Annual Conventions such as that introduced by Jordan Chambers, a delegate from St. Louis representing the Railway Coach Cleaners. Chambers introduced a resolution at the Forty-First Annual AFL Convention recommending that unions operating at work sites with black workers "strike" the word "white" out of their constitutions and make every effort to be racially inclusive.[9]

Even still, it was fairly common for black trade union leaders to defend the AFL's position on race, especially when criticisms came from groups with radical and socialist leanings. In the mid-1920s, twenty-seven black trade unionists from Chicago wrote several black state legislators explaining that "an examination of the records of the American Federation of Labor will show that it has always stood for justice to the Negro workers."[10] The trade unionists attempted to dissuade the legislators from voting against prounion laws after the latter group expressed concerns about the rampant discrimination in trade unions. Despite black protestations and vocal support from white progressives inside the AFL leadership infrastructure, racial exclusion was a way of life for most unions, partly because their autonomous structures allowed them to ignore directives from the AFL Executive Council.

Further evidence of racial exclusion inside of trade unions was provided by civil rights and black radical groups in the 1920s. A survey of ninety-four unions administered by the Chicago Commission of Race Relations documented entrenched racism in the labor movement.[11] A second survey of hundreds of trade unions, administered by the American Negro Labor Congress (ANLC) from 1925 to 1926, uncovered severe patterns of racial exclusion.[12] The ANLC was founded in 1925 with the purpose of advocating for racial and social equality inside of labor. Some black trade unionists downplayed the ANLC's concerns because of its ties with leftist groups, but its investigations reflected a prevailing concern among black leaders about racial hierarchy inside of labor.

By the mid-1930s, there was growing concern among black leaders about the dim prospects for black economic recovery from the Depression. The Joint Committee on National Recovery (JCNR) and Howard University's Social Science Division sponsored a conference in 1935 to look at the economic status of blacks in the New Deal era. Afterward, some conference participants, including labor and civil rights activist A. Philip Randolph, John P. Davis of the JCNR, and Ralph Bunche, the chair of Howard University's Department of Political Science, met to discuss the prospects of developing a united front, umbrella organization that would mobilize blacks to support economic recovery programs and civil rights policies.[13] A year later, in 1936, they organized another gathering in Chicago that gave birth to the NNC and its Youth Council.

The first conference of the NNC drew thousands of participants who covered a vast ideological spectrum, 817 of whom represented 585 organizations.[14] Randolph was elected the organization's president and Davis its executive secretary. The election of Randolph and Davis to the

NNC's two key leadership offices represented a symbolic, temporary union between members aligned with two competing leftist organizations, the Socialist Party (SP) and the CP.[15] While Randolph was a former member of the SP, Davis was a young upstart in the CP.

The consolidation between these two leaders on the left may have reflected, at least from the perspective of the CP, a willingness to forge stronger alliances and united front organizations with other leftist organizations. The CP initially scolded members of the SP, trade unions, and other leftist organizations because of their perceived opposition to radical socialist revolution, and their purported reliance on trade union activism and "bourgeois" democratic, parliamentarian procedures in order to achieve economic equality and socialist objectives.[16] Yet in 1934 and 1935, the CP began to embrace other leftist organizations under a popular united front banner, especially after Hitler's fascism encapsulated Europe. Under this banner, it endorsed a policy of "collective security" and "social patriotism" against European fascism and the mobilization of the working class in collaboration with other left-wing groups in both Europe and the United States.[17] Hence the unification of Randolph, Davis, and other black leaders on the left and inside of the NNC may have been a local manifestation of this larger international, united front policy involving radical and other left-wing groups that were historically at odds with each other.

The NNC was instrumental in advocating for racial and economic justice when it organized fifty-six local councils between 1936 and 1940. In Chicago, the local council helped to secure jobs for black motormen and organized rent strikes and protests against slum landlords. In Washington, D.C., the NNC chapter combated police brutality and inadequate recreational activities that serviced the needs of the city's black residents. In other cities, such as Oakland, Boston, Newark, New York, and Baltimore, the NNC gained a foothold in local political affairs.[18]

Approximately two hundred youth activists representing 125 youth organizations attended the first NNC conference. Thirty-three of these delegates formed the Youth Continuations Committee of the NNC (also referred to as the Youth Section of the NNC and the NNC Youth Council).[19] The Youth Continuations Committee chose prominent New Deal youth organizer Ed Strong as its chairperson. After the conference, the NNC Youth Council organized youth councils in different cities intended "to carry out the program of the National Negro Congress."[20] Many of these youth councils were organized as mini-congresses and united front organizations that consisted of representatives from local youth groups drawn together under one umbrella organization in a particular city or jurisdiction.

Despite the early success of the NNC and the cordial relationship between its adult and youth leadership, there was some dissatisfaction among the Youth Council members that they were given a second-ary role inside the organization. In addition, Youth Council members were disappointed that many of its participants were drawn from the North and not from the South.[21] Although the Youth Council had con-tacts in the South, many of its energies were directed toward mobiliz-ing the black urban working class that emerged as a result of northern migration and industrialization. These factors led some members of the NNC's Youth Council to initiate the formation of the SNYC.

For those CP members inside the NNC's Youth Council, the consider-ation of assisting in the development of a youth formation like the SNYC was logical and fell in line with the party's efforts to win over southern blacks. As early as 1928, the CP began considering a policy called the Black Belt Thesis (also called the Black Republic Thesis). Under this pol-icy, the CP advocated for the creation of an independent black nation in the South and the right to secession and self-determination by southern blacks because of their dominant presence extending from the eastern part of Virginia to the border of Texas.[22] Yet as the CP moved toward "collective security" and "social patriotism" in the mid-1930s, it concen-trated less of its energies in organizing southern blacks.[23] Accordingly, the prospects of assisting in the development of a youth formation such as the SNYC, by CP members inside and outside the NNC, may have reflected their renewed efforts to organize blacks in the South.

Less than a year after the NNC's founding conference, Ed Strong, chair of the NNC Youth Council, along with Louis Burnham of the American Student Union, sent out a call to a number of southern youth activists to attend the First Annual All-Southern Negro Youth Confer-ence in Richmond, Virginia, in February 1937. The conference brought together over five hundred delegates. At the gathering, the delegates decided to "establish an independent Southern Negro Youth Con-gress with Richmond, Virginia, serving as its headquarters and that it be fraternally associated with the Youth Section of the National Negro Congress."[24] Throughout its history, the SNYC shared an especially close relationship with the NNC (and the NNC Youth Council).[25]

Initially, the SNYC's organizational structure was divided into several layers. At the first level, there was an Executive Committee, which consisted of nationally elected officials who were required to be from the South. Included on the Executive Committee were local officers drawn from the area or jurisdiction where the SNYC hosted its annual conferences. The Executive Committee members were then included on the SNYC's Regional Council, which consisted of fifty additional youth activists, five of whom were each drawn from ten southern states. During its organizational history, the SNYC's adult advisory board members and mentors included prominent black intellectuals and activists such as Mary McLeod Bethune, Frederick Patterson, the president of Tuskegee Institute, W. E. B. Dubois, Alaine Locke, Charles S. Johnson, Horace Mann Bond, E. D. Nixon, and Charlotte Hawkins Brown of the Palmer Institute, who at one time served as the SNYC's principal advisor.[26]

The emergence of the NNC Youth Council and the SNYC occurred concurrently with the upsurge in progressive sociopolitical activity by black youth in the 1930s, and their linkages with diverse movement infrastructures. A few of the SNYC's enthusiastic leaders were involved in progressive, white national organizations such as the American Youth Congress (AYC), the American Student Union (ASU), and the National Student League (NSL). Louis Burnham of the ASU, who was also a leader of the militant Frederick Douglass Society at City College of New York, as well as James Jackson and Edward Strong of the AYC, all became important figures inside the SNYC.[27] Strong had also been involved in an earlier, short-lived effort in Chicago to establish the International Negro Youth Movement.

Moreover, throughout the 1930s, several conferences were held on the plight of black youth. In 1933, the NSL organized the Student Conference on Negro Student Problems and held its annual convention at Howard University in the same year. In addition, Mary McLeod Bethune, director of the Negro Division of the National Youth Administration (NYA), organized the National Conference on Problems of the Negro and Negro Youth in 1937 and the National Conference of Negro

Youth in 1939. Bethune was an esteemed figure in black America, particularly among youth advocates and the SNYC activists. As a member of President Roosevelt's "black cabinet," she lobbied the administration to allocate New Deal jobs and services to southern black youth.[28] While this provided a renewed sense of hope for black youth activists, the impact that these lobby efforts had on improving the daily life conditions of poor black youth in the Deep South was questionable.

Despite the significance of Bethune's Negro Division, the NYA may have been reluctant to aggressively challenge racial segregation and institutional racism within its own organization's state and local administrative offices. In many localities, the NYA had dual state and local advisory committees—one black and one white—that determined black participation in their programs. The white advisory committees exercised more control over resources and policymaking than those controlled by blacks. On the other hand, the state and local NYA policymaking bodies that were black controlled were usually limited to middle-class or well-connected blacks.[29] Many of these prestigious blacks accepted racial segregation inside the NYA as a customary practice and did little to challenge southern mores.

Notwithstanding the NYA's racist machinery, Bethune was able to leverage the agency to offer job training and employment opportunities to perhaps as many as three hundred thousand black youth in the 1930s and 1940s.[30] Even more important, the establishment of the Negro Division symbolized the overall push by various segments of the black leadership ranks (both young and old) to critically examine the problems of black youth.

Adding urgency to the situation was a series of studies sponsored by the American Council on Education's American Youth Commission that examined black youth sociopolitical culture in the late 1930s and early 1940s. These studies looked at how the economic conditions of the Depression Era shaped black youth attitudes about political efficacy, ideology, social mobility, strategies for improving the black predicament, and intraracial socioeconomic divisions.[31] The studies revealed the depths to which black youth suffered from severe forms of economic deprivation, institutional racism, and political alienation. These conditions spurred debates in the black community about how to create a more equitable society.

Meanwhile, some NAACP youth and young adults became radical-
ized in the 1930s and encouraged their adult counterparts to incorporate young people into influential leadership positions. Early in the
decade, a collective of young intellectuals inside the association known
as the "Young Turks" pressured the NAACP to embrace more progressive economic initiatives and to aggressively advocate for antilynching
legislation.[32] The restlessness of some of its young members forced Joel
Spingarn, the association's president, to organize a meeting involving
young NAACP members in Amenia, New York, in 1933. Initially, this
meeting faced some resistance by notable NAACP figures, including
Walter White. This delayed the conference for one year (it was originally set to take place in 1932) and forced Spingarn to appoint White's
archrival, W. E. B. Dubois, to take over as head of the conference's planning arrangements.[33]

The Amenia Conference brought together young intellectuals
between twenty and thirty-five years of age,[34] who attempted to bridge
the concerns of younger blacks with those of the older cadre of activists
inside the association. Influenced by a Marxist orientation, which had
become popular among some social and political activists and advocates of the 1930s, many conference attendees were anticapitalist and
favored working-class unity between black and white workers.[35]

The progressive push by youth and young intellectuals inside the
NAACP early in the 1930s eventually led it to establish a youth council
in 1936, just one month after the founding of the NNC Youth Council.
Afterward, NAACP youth directed their energies toward the passage of
a congressional antilynching bill. Arguably one reason why the NAACP
decided to establish a youth section in 1936, and not in 1932–1933, was
because it was losing young people to other organizations. Many young
people who were disenchanted with the NAACP's middle-class stature
and detachment from southern civil rights struggles began to drift into
more radical organizations.[36]

In Harlem, a hotbed of black political activity, the NAACP feared
growing competition from the NNC, which had "helped to spur the
NAACP to implement a youth movement of its own with an activist
orientation."[37] The SNYC's maturation as a southern-based entity in
1937 was actually indicative of the NAACP's failure "in developing a
youth program and in organizing in the South."[38] The NAACP did not

hold a major conference meeting in the South for most of the 1920s and the first half of the 1930s. By the time that it did wage a more broad-base campaign in the Deep South, the SNYC and more radical associations were already invested in southern jurisdictions.

Interestingly, the NAACP's annual convention in 1937 attracted over three hundred youth delegates. In the same year and just a few months after the establishment of the SNYC, the association's Board of Directors granted twenty-three charters to youth councils and college chapters, eleven of which opened up in the Deep and Upper South.[39] Walter White, the organization's president, then welcomed youth participation despite his objections a few years earlier, perhaps because he saw the youth as bolstering the organization's membership rolls at a time when it was competing with other newly formed organizations.

However, White specified the conditions for incorporating a youth wing into the NAACP. First, he discouraged the independent organizational thrust of the Youth Council and insisted that it remain tightly confined as a subordinate to the association. Second, he urged the association's youth activists to accept a gradual approach to leadership and "wait their turn" in ascending to leadership positions. In this regard, he stated,

> The Youth Council offers an opportunity for young people between the ages of 16 and 25 to work together on the problem of racial advancement to which the N.A.A.C.P. is dedicated. It offers the N.A.A.C.P. to get into its membership large numbers of young people who might not otherwise join. It is important to recognize that the Youth Council is a part of the N.A.A.C.P. not separate from it. . . . Having the Youth Council and the adult groups part of the same organization offers the strength of numbers and makes possible all sorts of cooperative activities, combining experience with new enthusiasm. Also, since they are all a part of the same organization, it will seem natural for the young people to take their places in the adult groups when the time comes.[40]

White's position on the NAACP Youth Council is understandable since one of the objectives of a national organization is to add new members. Such an objective legitimizes an organization to external allies and financial contributors who, in turn, want to support a successful entity. The addition of new members can legitimize an organization in the eyes of individuals in influential political positions who may be more willing to consider the demands of an organization that has strength in numbers. Still, despite the incorporation of the Youth Council and even its extension into the South after the mid-1930s, the NAACP's passive and lackluster approach disappointed much of its younger cadre.

Movement Activism and the Southern Negro Youth Congress

Many activities of the SNYC focused on economic recovery initiatives. At its inaugural conference in 1937, the SNYC committed itself to organizing sharecroppers and domestic and agricultural workers. It approved several resolutions including labor protections for black workers, a child labor amendment, and the desegregation of labor unions and industries.[41] In addition, it used the National Labor Relations Act (also called the Wagner Act), passed in 1935, to advocate for black unionization. Civil rights activists were disappointed that the Wagner Act failed to eliminate racially disparate pay scales between blacks and whites and racially segregated work sites.[42] However, the Wagner Act's collective bargaining provision created a more favorable context for social movement organizations such as the SNYC to enlist rank-and-file black workers in grassroots labor campaigns.

Following the SNYC's founding conference, the youth group began laying the ground work for what would be its most important economic justice campaign, taking place in Richmond, Virginia. The SNYC activists joined with black tobacco workers to form the Tobacco Stemmers and Laborers Industrial Union. In the same year, the union carried out major strikes involving a total of five thousand black workers. This coalition of SNYC activists and tobacco workers was able to secure higher wages for black tobacco laborers and helped to improve working conditions in the tobacco industries. It forced the major industries to reclassify some black workers from laborers and helpers to skilled machine operators and tenders.[43]

In many respects, the Richmond tobacco strike stands out in the social history of southern-based radical social movements because it occurred in one of the epicenters of the Confederacy. Accordingly, James Jackson believed it was the "first blow against [racial] tyranny [in the South] since the civil war."[44] The victory of the tobacco workers was significant also for women who dominated the tobacco industry workforce and made up the bulk of the strikers. Although the strike sparked an internal debate among the black clergy, the activists eventually won over the support of some progressive ministers who allowed them to use their church basements as meeting places. Also, high school students played an active role by handing out flyers and watching over the children during the planning of the meetings. This was particularly important because many women were forced to bring their children to meetings.[45]

The Richmond strike increased the SNYC's positional influence inside of civil rights, labor, and radical circles in the 1930s. In addition to the Richmond campaign, the SNYC worked with the CIO to organize black workers in the Miami Shipbuilding Company and pressured the city government and Miami's Civil Service Commission to desegregate the municipal postal service.[46] It also spent considerable energy on developing the leadership capacity of black youth and indigenous, local workers. It set up labor schools in Nashville, Tennessee, New Orleans, Louisiana, Birmingham and Fairfield, Alabama, and other localities. The schools were used to educate black workers and local union leaders "on the present problems of the labor movement, as well as of techniques for improving the effectiveness of their particular union meetings and procedures."[47] The SNYC's Labor Youth Clubs were further established to "acquaint more people with ideals of trade unions," and "provided educational and cultural programs in union halls for their members, taught classes in history, current events, parliamentary procedure and even in reading and writing."[48] Finally, the SNYC sponsored leadership development seminars and citizenship schools.

Voting rights and protection against mob rule and lynching were additional concerns of the SNYC. The SNYC investigated lynchings and police brutality, and issued reports that publicized racial violence.[49] It struggled to protect prospective black voters and initiated voter education campaigns in southern localities. In 1939, its youth councils and affiliate groups set up committees to pay the poll taxes levied against southern blacks. In 1940, the SNYC sponsored the Right to Vote Campaign and held demonstrations protesting the poll tax.[50] A year later, it organized the Abolish the Poll Tax Week. These efforts, according to Robert Cohen, "aired the demand for the franchise more boldly than it had ever been in the South during the Depression decade."[51]

Another SNYC initiative was the development of youth legislatures in Alabama and South Carolina. The legislatures passed bills outlining the positions of black and progressive white youth on labor policy, foreign policy, and voting rights.[52] Although these bills failed to win support in the regular state legislatures, the youth legislatures provided a model of organizing that closely resembled Chana Kai Lee's description of "parallel" institutionalism in the 1960s, as exhibited with the SNCC-initiated freedom schools, the "Freedom Vote" campaign, and the Mississippi Freedom Democratic Party.[53] The organizing campaigns in South Carolina were shaped by indigenous activists such as Modjeska Simkins and Osceola McKaine, the cofounder of the Progressive Democratic Party, an independent black political party in South Carolina. Both activists were widely respected inside of black progressive and radical circles, and served as SNYC advisors.

Most of the SNYC's activities were carried out by its youth centers and local councils. Youth centers were established in Birmingham, Alabama, the SNYC's central headquarters beginning in 1939, and in Fairfield, Alabama, as well as other southern localities. The youth centers sponsored black history courses, discussions about World War II, and trade union meetings.[54] Similar to the NNC's youth councils, the SNYC's councils were organized as localized federated organizations that consisted of youth leaders and representatives of different youth organizations in a particular area. Although cooperation between the local councils and the national executive committee was encouraged, for the most part the councils were given the autonomy to develop separate projects.[55]

Women played a prominent role in the activities of the SNYC. During World War II, when some of its key male activists joined the wartime efforts, women held prominent positions in the organization and kept it afloat. Undeniably, sexism was pervasive inside the SNYC and arguments took place between men and women over domestic responsibilities. However, on the issue of gender equality, the SNYC was more progressive than most black organizations. According to the former executive secretary of the SNYC, Esther Cooper Jackson, there was a "conscious effort that this [the SNYC] was part of a revolutionary movement where women and men are equal," especially in the organization's hierarchy.[56] She added,

I would say that people like Louis Burnham, Ed Strong, Christopher Alston, James Jackson [male leaders in the organization] were all feminists: [They] were dedicated revolutionaries and as a part of being dedicated revolutionaries, believed in the equality of women, believed in promoting women. In fact, when I came to Birmingham [the headquarters of the SNYC during most of its life cycle], I wanted to work on drafting leaflets and doing things behind the scenes and Ed Strong and James Jackson and other people pushed me into taking a leadership role, which I was reluctant to do.[57]

The Marxist beliefs among some of the SNYC's leading activists actually made them more receptive to feminist positions. Many of them believed that sexist practices were in direct contradiction to radical social movements and reinforced class hierarchies. However, despite the attempts among the SNYC's leadership apparatus to equalize gender relations at the top ranks of the organization, some local activists were not used to seeing women such as Esther Cooper Jackson in leadership positions. She said that it took some time for local activists to accept the "strange young women" who were organizing in their communities.[58]

Despite the class orientation of the SNYC and its connection to diverse movement infrastructures, its leading activists strongly believed that it was appropriate for young blacks, instead of whites, to take the lead in organizing the black community. This emphasis on race-based organizational building did not preclude the SNYC members from embracing the notion that cross-racial coalitions were essential to the overall objective of combating capitalist exploitation. In fact, the SNYC activists embraced the notion that black and white working-class unity was a prerequisite to socioeconomic equality, but this had to be achieved through working with race-based organizations.

This strategic position persisted not necessarily as a result of high levels of racial consciousness among the SNYC's leadership, but because it was simply the most realistic method of organizing. After all, white progressives had penetrated the South during this time period, but had difficulty organizing black workers due to Jim Crow segregation and white supremacy. As Robert Cohen notes, "the problem of southern segregation was so massive it could only be battled effectively by a black-led southern organization, devoted exclusively to helping black people fight for equality."[59] In addition, the SNYC's white allies faced the problem of organizing blacks in the Deep South because of their "peculiar hold of traditional religious beliefs," which often conflicted with the white left's beliefs that religion was the opium of the masses.[60] Thus it was important for white radicals to rely upon groups like the SNYC to weather the political and religious terrains of the Deep South.

The Shifting Political Context of the 1940s

A major theme of this chapter is that movement activism among black youth radicals during 1930s and 1940s was influenced by the shifting political contexts of this period. The shifts in the political and international environments altered the relationship between these youth and allies situated inside of their movement infrastructures, including black adult activists, white radicals, and organizations such as the NNC.

By 1940, internal conflicts and dissension within the NNC had an effect on the SNYC's maturation given their close alliance with each other. One source of these conflicts centered on the influx into the NNC of members from the CP and the CIO, which A. Philip Randolph believed undermined the group's autonomy. Besides John P. Davis, NNC's executive secretary, Max Yergan of the Black YMCA was associated with the CP. The CP's influence also extended into the ranks of the SNYC's leadership. James Jackson and Ed Strong, the two most influential SNYC leaders, were CP activists.

As indicated earlier, the CP had always had some influence inside the NNC and the SNYC since their foundings in 1936 and 1937, respectively. Some political observers believed the CP's participation inside the NNC was initially welcomed by Randolph and others, during the CP's popular front years, until the early 1940s.[61] Yet, at the beginning of the 1940s, Davis and other NNC members lobbied the CP and the CIO for greater financial and delegate support. Because Davis was responsible for the NNC's day-to-day operations, he exercised the most influence inside the group and was able to encourage greater participation in the organization from the CP.[62]

In exchange for greater financial resources and delegate support from the CP and CIO, their supporters campaigned to ensure that the NNC's agenda items and resolutions strongly reflected the positions of the CP and the CIO.[63] The extensive outreach to these groups brought more white radicals into the NNC. By 1940, almost one-third of the delegates at its annual convention were white, prompting Randolph to resign and state, "I quit the Congress because it is not truly a Negro Congress."[64] This set of events was the turning point in the NNC because it gave the impression that the white left was undermining the NNC's autonomy.

Another source of tension inside the NNC was its policy shift toward U.S. involvement in the impending war in Europe. Since its founding, the NNC had expressed support for "collective security" against fascism and U.S. intervention in Europe. But a series of events in 1940 caused the NNC to reconsider its policy on collective security. Hitler's advance across Europe caused so much consternation among Soviet Union leaders that it resulted in the signing of the historic Nazi-Soviet Pact (nonaggression treaty). With the signing of the treaty, the CP reversed its position and opposed U.S. involvement in Europe and collective security. The CP now believed that a U.S. interventionist strategy in Europe would sully relations between Germany and Russia, and interpreted this type of intervention as imperialism.[65]

The Nazi-Soviet Pact had ramifications inside the NNC and the SNYC. CP activists inside the NNC pushed for it to adopt the CP's policy shift toward the war in Europe. This debate took center stage at the NNC's third annual convention in 1940 (the NNC had only three conventions between 1936 and 1940). With the CP and CIO's increased involvement in the NNC, members of both organizations were able to influence the NNC's resolutions and agenda. As a result, these organizations influenced the NNC to pass resolutions indicating its support for the CP's "reversal" on the collective security issue.

These transactions sparked a debate inside the NNC and within black activist and intellectual circles about whether the NNC really exercised organizational autonomy that was independent of external (white left) patrons. It exposed growing fears among some elements of the black leadership ranks that the white left was trying to co-opt much of the NNC's enthusiasm. It also reinvigorated a discussion inside the NNC over whether it should endorse black enlistment in the wartime efforts. This debate engulfed the SNYC activists due to their close ties with the NNC and white radicals. It also occurred around the same time that John

P. Davis called for the NNC's extension into the South, and advocated for a closer relationship between the SNYC and the NNC's leadership.[66]

In some respects, the expanding European conflict and the SNYC's position on collective security provide an in-depth look into how its policies closely paralleled those of the CP and the NNC. For example, in 1940 the SNYC took a middle-range approach in its position on black conscription into the U.S. Army. It concluded that because racism was a systematic and unresolved feature inside the U.S. armed forces, it should concentrate its energies on the more pressing issues of securing better education and housing for blacks, as well as the right to vote and protection against lynching.[67] In addition to the SNYC's commitment to racial and economic justice policies, this was probably a strategic decision by the SNYC. Perhaps it did not want to take an overt position against the war out of concern that it would sully relations with some of its adult advisory board members and other black activists who supported U.S. engagement. On the other hand, the SNYC may have wanted to reflect the NNC and CP's initial antiwar position.

However, in 1941, the SNYC reversed its policy on collective security and black participation in the war. This occurred after Germany invaded the Soviet Union in the same year and after the CP reverted to its pre-1940 position of supporting collective security and U.S. involvement in Europe. Thus, following the lead of the CP, both the NNC and the SNYC embraced their earlier pre-1940 support of U.S. intervention, social patriotism, and collective security and stepped up their attacks against Hitler and Germany.

Did the close relationship between CP and SNYC activists, as reflected in their parallel support of the war, have a profound, adverse impact on the efforts by both groups to combat racial hierarchy and economic inequality in the South? This may have been the case. In 1941, the SNYC insisted that some of its energies should be redirected toward supporting its eclectic foreign policy positions. After the CP's reversal in 1941 and its subsequent retreat from attacking racial segregation, the youth group did not expend a lot of energy assisting A. Philip Randolph's planned March on Washington, which attempted to combat racial segregation in wartime industries. Many CP members also believed that the 1941 March on Washington would thwart anticipated U.S. intervention in Europe.[68]

By the end of 1941, the SNYC exerted much of its energies toward supporting the war, and in some southern communities, its campaign against Hitler was the only one of its kind.[69] The anti-Hitler campaign was the central focus of its annual conference in Tuskegee. In a letter to adult sponsors of the SNYC's Fifth Annual Conference in Tuskegee, Alabama, SNYC organizer Louis Burnham stated, "The war against Hitlerism is our war. The future of Negro youth depends upon a decisive victory for the United Nations. In order to play our part in guaranteeing that victory, this conference will be devoted to the discussion of ways and means of increasing the opportunities of Negro youth to serve the nation in this hour of peril."[70] Although some evidence suggests the Youth Congress's shifting frames toward the war—a shift that paralleled the CP and the NNC—may have reduced its interest in combating racial and economic justice, Esther Cooper Jackson strongly disagreed. She insisted that the SNYC's wartime efforts did not reduce its domestic fight and that it still helped to organize black people for Randolph's March on Washington. She commented, "We continued much of the same work that we were always doing. . . . Some of the men went into the army, this is true, and fought Jim Crow within the Army. But at the same time the Southern Negro Youth Congress continued all of the activities, the militant activities that we had always been doing all along, and the women in particular came into leadership at that time."[71] Furthermore, the SNYC argued that its support for World War II had less to do with the CP's maneuverings, and more to do with its endorsement of the "Double V" (Double Victory) campaign—victory against fascism abroad and racism at home—waged by the larger black leadership strata. The SNYC received some encouragement on this point. During the war, President Roosevelt sent a correspondence to the SNYC activists, insisting that he would pay serious attention to the problems of black youth after the end of World War II.[72] The SNYC's prointerventionist policy also curried the favor of mainstream black leaders and young intellectuals who were supportive of greater black involvement in the wartime efforts. This occurred until the SNYC reversed its position toward U.S. intervention in Europe and black conscription in the military, shortly after World War II, at the inception of the Cold War.

Another criticism directed toward the Youth Congress was that the shifting political conditions and the group's close relationship with the CP undermined the SNYC's autonomy and ability to build a progressive, independent movement in the South. In terms of the CP, certainly it played a significant role in organizing blacks to fight racial segregation. However, there was a quid pro quo. The CP and other external organizations such as the CIO benefited from the involvement of black youth inside and in alliance with their organizations. Black activists provided strength in numbers to these organizations and gave them increased standing and legitimacy inside the black community.[73] Also, the CP had a tremendous amount of resources, intellectual capacity, and a critique of the southern racial caste system and was very well organized. More important, it had the fortitude to organize in the South, vis-à-vis groups like the SNYC and labor organizations, during a period where racial terror dominated southern politics. James Jackson, one the SNYC's chief organizers, stated "that without the Communist Party there would never have been a Southern Negro Youth Congress."[74] Thus, it was logical and pragmatic that progressive and radical black youth would become the CP's ally.

To some extent the CP's influence inside the SNYC may be the reason why the organization's impact has been underappreciated. Ralph Bunche, who was a one-time supporter of the SNYC and drafted several members to help him collect data that eventually were included in Gunnar Myrdal's seminal work, *An American Dilemma*, stated,

> The Southern Negro Youth Congress is a flame that flickers only feebly in a few Southern cities today. It started with promise but, lacking competent leadership, it failed to catch the imagination of the young Negro in the South. Its program has been diffuse and recently, at least, seems to take its cue in the major essentials from the "line" laid down by the American Communist Party. . . . Moreover, no serious effort has been made to reach the lower class Negro youth of the South who are in dire need of guidance and encouragement. In its present form the Negro Youth Congress is run by and for a select group of Negro school boys and girls who are themselves terribly confused and frustrated. It can contribute but little toward progressive development of the Negro.[75]

It is true that the CP influenced much of the activities of the SNYC. As stated earlier, the SNYC's key leaders had been actively involved in the CP and the Young Communist League. The SNYC also developed close alliances with CP-influenced organizations such as the CIO, the League of Young Southerners, and the Sharecropper's Union. Yet, as historian Robin Kelley points out, many of these organizations did admirable work in black communities throughout the North and South.[76] They also organized in the southern region during a period in which many of the traditional civil rights organizations and black labor activists were reluctant to take on such activity.

Despite these concerns with the NNC and the CP, the SNYC was the leading black national-level or federated student/youth formation of its era, and laid much of the groundwork for SNCC activists who came along two decades later.[77] Earlier in its organizational history, it organized over twenty councils/chapters in a number of states and jurisdictions, including Florida, Mississippi, Alabama, Louisiana, West Virginia, South Carolina, and North Carolina. By the 1940s, the SNYC had an estimated 115 councils throughout the South and even received a request from a group in La Boca, Panama to charter a youth affiliate.[78]

Moreover, contrary to Bunche's conclusions, the SNYC did reach out to low-income blacks. In April 1938, over five thousand black youth and young adults attended a rally as part of the SNYC's Second Annual All-Southern Negro Youth Conference in Chattanooga, Tennessee, which was "one of the largest mass meetings held by Negro youth."[79] The conference attendees included miners, factory and mill workers, sharecroppers, and trade unionists.[80] Augusta Strong, a prominent SNYC activist, further stated that the hundreds of delegates at the conference represented the "various strata" of African Americans, including fifty whites.[81]

The Demobilization of the Southern Negro Youth Congress

The SNYC collapsed because of organizational fatigue and because it was targeted for political repression and surveillance during the early years of the Cold War. At least since 1940, the SNYC had been under surveillance by the FBI. By the end of World War II, the FBI initiated a secret surveillance campaign of SNYC affiliates in at least a dozen cities.[82] After the war, the SNYC even faced repression from Birmingham, Alabama, police commissioner "Bull" Connor. He pressured local churches to distance themselves from the SNYC's activities, which partially disrupted its plans to hold an annual conference in Birmingham in 1949.[83]

In addition, the SNYC had to answer repeated claims by the House Committee on Un-American Activities of being a communist-front organization, and U.S. attorney general Tom Clark considered it a subversive organization.[84] The FBI infiltrated the SNYC during World War II in order to monitor its connections with communist and other radical groups. The irony in this, which is symbolic of the pathology of the "red" hysteria, was that government repression of the youth formation occurred despite the fact that the SNYC and the CP were in strong support of U.S. engagement during the height of World War II and committed much of their resources to encouraging numerous blacks to join the U.S. armed forces.

The red baiting and intensified antagonism toward the SNYC drove previous members of the black left to embrace a more moderate position in achieving racial, social, and economic equality. Some black leaders, adult advisors, and labor allies to the SNYC distanced themselves from the organization after the end of World War II. Other activists who remained committed to the organization's ideological orientation diverted their energies to assisting Henry Wallace's 1948 presidential campaign. These events were too much for the SNYC, and it collapsed in 1949.

The changes in the political and international environments after World War II contributed to the SNYC's declining influence and collapse. As the United States advanced under its Cold War policy, groups such as the SNYC came under attack by government officials for their political postures. This made organizing under the umbrella of radical organizations extremely difficult and dangerous. In addition, the shifting political contexts changed the internal political dynamics of the black community. Few indigenous organizations and networks of activists inside of the black community would assist the SNYC's organizing efforts after World War II.

Conclusion

This chapter highlighted the vital role that black students and youth activists played as social change agents in the first half of the twentieth century, especially in community organizing and social movement initiatives in impoverished and disenfranchised communities. The participation of students and youth in organizations such as the NNC Youth

Council, the SNYC, and the NAACP Youth Council blossomed out of broader efforts by national leaders and indigenous activists to combat systemic patterns of racial segregation and economic inequality. Through creative organizing, black student and youth activists helped ameliorate oppressive conditions confronting economically distressed black communities.

This chapter further illustrated that shifting political conditions facilitated, accelerated, and marginalized black youth and young adult participation in social movement campaigns in the 1930s and 1940s. Some of these changes, such as the Great Depression and industrialization, extended beyond the control of the youth formations. Yet the deprivation brought on by these environmental conditions made the SNYC and other radical and progressive formations attractive to young people. The SNYC's reliance on labor organizing and its anticapitalist orientation made the organization attractive to young blacks, who themselves had suffered socioeconomic deprivation during the 1930s. Many of the SNYC activists were part of a small, emergent black middle class, but were alienated from employment opportunities as a result of racism and economic stagnation. Others were poor and working class and segregated outside of labor unions and major industries.

The dialectical exchange between political contexts and movement activism among young blacks is important for understanding why some organizations and movement infrastructures eventually collapse, despite the fact that they once had a large following. This is most evident when looking at the example of the SNYC. Although the SNYC attracted many young people who were alienated due to the political economy of the 1930s, its organizational trajectory was impacted by World War II and the anticommunist hysteria. Thus while the SNYC leaders were embraced by prominent blacks in the late 1930s, and while it maintained good relations with the Roosevelt administration in the midst of World War II, shortly after the war, its allegiance to Marxism and proximity to CP members brought on governmental repression and abandonment by many black leaders who feared government retribution. This points to difficulties that student and youth activists have in sustaining organizations in diverse movement infrastructures, particularly when they take positions that are at odds with the prevailing ideological sentiments of the dominant political/economic order.

The next chapter examines the evolution of movement activism among black students and youth from the 1960s to the 1980s. This includes a discussion of the Student Nonviolent Coordinating Committee and the Student Organization for Black Unity, two influential youth formations during this period. The chapter concludes with a look at the student wing of the South African divestment movement of the 1980s, which, despite emerging in the post–civil rights era, displayed a contentious variant of politics that was heavily influenced by the militant activism of the 1950s and 1960s.

3

From Civil Rights to Anti-Apartheid

I think the nearest thing to an answer that's short of changing the system is a greater degree of real concentration on
organizing people. I keep bringing this up. I'm sorry, but it's
a part of me. I just don't see anything to be substituted for
having people understand their position and understand
their potential power and how to use it. This can only be
done, as I see it, through the long route, almost, of actually
organizing people in small groups and parlaying those into
larger groups.
—Ella Baker, 1969

The Southern Negro Youth Congress (SNYC) was the most influential
youth formation to emerge out of the black protest movement in the
1930s and 1940s. Its radical orientation and militant opposition to Jim
Crow segregation was part of a larger wave of youth activism among
black and white young people. The black protest movement would not
have to wait long before the emergence of another transformational
wave of student and youth activism. In the late 1950s and continuing
into the mid-1970s, young African Americans participated in the most
militant period of youth-based activism in the twentieth century.

Similar to participants in the SNYC's activities in the 1930s and 1940s,
young blacks in the post–World War II period were nurtured by indigenous networks, adult activists, and prominent civil rights and social
justice organizations. The murder of Emmett Till in 1955, similar to the
Scottsboro case in 1931, affected the sensibilities of many youth who
came of age after the 1940s. The positional influence of black youth

inside the movement infrastructure that shaped black protest activity was also influenced by the *Brown v. Board of Education* decision in 1954; the NAACP Youth Council sit-ins in Kansas in 1958; the school desegregation campaign in Little Rock, Arkansas (also known as the "Little Rock Nine"); the 1958 and 1959 Youth Marches for Integrated Schools organized by A. Philip Randolph and Bayard Rustin; the Nashville sit-in movement in 1959 and 1960; the 1960 sit-in movement, which saw thousands of students challenging racially segregated public facilities; and the formation of the Student Nonviolent Coordinating Committee (SNCC), a pioneering youth formation that gained prominence in the 1960s.

As the 1960s came to an end, the Student Organization for Black Unity (SOBU) continued to mobilize southern blacks around racial and economic justice claims. Founded in May 1969, SOBU was one of the most important national youth formations of this period. The upsurge of activism in the late 1960s extended the opportunity structure of movement activism and produced a culture of grassroots organizing for young people to model after the demobilization of the civil rights and black power movements. In the 1980s, young blacks and whites, drawing their enthusiasm partially from the 1960s, were active participants in the South African anti-apartheid movement that encapsulated college campuses around the country.

This chapter examines the evolution of black student and youth activism from the 1960s to the 1980s. First, I focus specifically on SNCC's organizing efforts after the passage of the Voting Rights Act of 1965 and efforts to implement new strategies that intended to help the organization adjust to a different political context in the second half of the 1960s. My objective is to examine how institutional leveraging and the urban rebellions outside of the South impacted SNCC's organizing work. In addition, I look at how SNCC used the strategy of appropriation (also called the appropriation of indigenous resources) to counter institutional leveraging, expand its reach outside of the South, and develop cross-movement linkages with non-SNCC groups.

The second part of this chapter examines SOBU's organizing activities from 1969 to 1975. SOBU used framing and appropriation to marry African American students to black working-class politics and Pan-African movements. SOBU's experiences illustrate how black youth formations attempted to shift their strategies and tactics to respond to, if not offset, the changing political environment and the trend toward institutionalized leveraging among prominent black groups.

The last section of the chapter gives attention to black student activism in the Free South Africa Movement (FSAM) of the 1980s, the last nationwide or broad-based transformational campaign of the twentieth century. I discuss how the anti-apartheid campaign heightened the political consciousness of hundreds of students and youth about racial justice and transnational politics. This section explains why the student wing of the divestment movement failed to develop a national youth formation that could transfer its energies into grassroots racial justice campaigns after the demobilization of the divestment movement. The racial and ideological tensions inside the student wing of the movement and the fear of co-optation by adult or veteran activists of the FSAM made it difficult for the student activists to implement innovative or creative strategies that could sustain the enthusiasm of black and white students. Thus, despite producing some of the most dynamic student protests since the early 1970s—protests that led to the passage of the Anti-Apartheid Act of 1986—the student wing of the FSAM collapsed in the late 1980s.

SNCC and the Civil Rights Movement Infrastructure

Generally viewed as the most influential black student and youth formation of the twentieth century, SNCC emerged in the aftermath of the 1960 student sit-in movement that encapsulated the South. In April of that year, Ella Baker of the Southern Christian Leadership Conference (SCLC) organized the Southwide Leadership Conference, which brought together sit-in participants, youth advocates, and student leaders. Out of this conference, student leaders organized a temporary organization that was later renamed SNCC.

During its first five years, SNCC concentrated much of its activities on fighting racial segregation and political disenfranchisement, as well as developing economic and educational initiatives throughout the South. In addition to its participation in the freedom rides and various protests throughout the South sponsored by the Congress of Racial Equality (CORE), the youth group initiated community organizing campaigns in rural areas throughout the South beset by racial terrorism.[1] In fact, it was common for SNCC to embed itself in a community for a couple of years and organize, while simultaneously urging local constituents to shape the agenda and programs that were relevant to that particular community. According to Gloria Richardson, the head of the Cambridge Nonviolent Action Committee in Cambridge, Maryland, SNCC's philosophy was "to teach them [local people] organizing tactics and let the local people run their own show."[2] This allowed SNCC to expand its constituency beyond the ranks of traditional student and youth members. It also created a pathway for incorporating older and poorer constituents into the SNCC fold, particularly those who had been shut out of the local political process.

In addition, SNCC provided avenues for young people to hold important leadership positions that would have been difficult to obtain had it been an extension of the more established groups. Its political orientations and approach to community organizing were dramatically shaped by Baker, who encouraged the young activists to develop the leadership capacity of indigenous activists, some of whom were isolated from mainline civil rights organizations. As indicated in Baker's comments at the beginning of the chapter, this was an incremental process that had the potential to yield long-term results.

SNCC resembled the SNYC in that it initially put forth a recommendation that all members of its central committee should be from southern states.[3] Despite SNCC's much popularized autonomy, similar to the SNYC, it welcomed advice from "adult organizations which [were] supportive of the movement."[4] Yet, in order to maintain its autonomous structure, it excluded the adult organizations from participating as voting members of its central committee and relegated them to the role of participant observers.[5] Similar to the SNYC, SNCC used parallel institutionalism to address racial antagonisms in the South. It set up mock elections, such as the Freedom Vote, in places where blacks could not vote.[6] It assisted with the formation of a satellite political party, the Mississippi Freedom Democratic Party (MFDP), to challenge the segregationist Democratic Party and eventually helped to get blacks into public offices in the South.

By the mid-1960s, the changing political landscape was beginning to adversely affect SNCC's internal operations and relations with other black activist groups. The urban rebellions, black power radicalism, and growing white resentment in the North presented several challenges to SNCC concerning the role of whites in the movement, the withdrawal of financial support by external patrons as a result of SNCC's growing militancy and its opposition to the Vietnam War, and SNCC's concerns about political co-optation and institutionalized leveraging as a moderating influence.

By the mid-1960s, a contentious debate engulfed SNCC regarding interracial organizing and the role of whites. A small contingent of white activists were SNCC members dating back to at least 1961, but most were from the South or had an acute understanding of southern black culture. For a short while, during the 1964 Freedom Summer campaign, SNCC also assisted with the creation of the short-lived White Folks Project, a community organizing project that intended to use white students to organize working-class white communities in the Biloxi, Mississippi, area.[7]

Yet, white students from nonsouthern universities were recruited for the 1964 Freedom Summer campaign, and some remained with the organization afterward. In discussing the plans for Freedom Summer, some SNCC members and longtime white staffers opposed the recruitment of whites into the Summer Project. They believed nonsouthern whites were unaccustomed to the mores of indigenous blacks in Mississippi. Many SNCC staffers were further disappointed because much of the media attention focused on these newly arriving volunteers.[8]

The emergence of black power politics also sparked an internal debate about the role of whites in SNCC-related activities. For example, SNCC's Atlanta Project staff adopted a black nationalist posture that insisted upon a diminished role for white organizational members. Whites were not necessarily expelled from SNCC, however in 1966 they lost their ability to vote on policy issues adjudicated by SNCC's Central Committee. A year later whites left the organization after a failed attempt to regain their voting status inside the Central Committee.[9]

By 1967, some SNCC members pushed the organization to embrace an international outlook. These members attempted to develop philosophical and political alliances with revolutionary movements and leaders throughout the world. SNCC also was the first major civil rights organization to openly oppose the war in Vietnam and criticize the Arab-Israeli War. These positions, in concert with its black power posture, brought on continued political repression and surveillance by the government, as well as ostracism from traditional white allies, liberals, and black moderates. Subsequently, many financial patrons who backed SNCC's efforts in the early 1960s withdrew their support and viewed the organization as too militant, unpatriotic, and moving toward racial separatism.[10]

Another challenge facing SNCC centered on the institutional leveraging strategies by some black leaders inside of its movement infrastructure. An early indication of this problem occurred at the Democratic Party's presidential nominating convention in 1964. In the months leading up to the convention, SNCC worked closely with the MFDP, a political party that served as a racially inclusive alternative to the racist Democratic Party in Mississippi. The MFDP mobilized voters and recruited candidates for local offices in order to challenge the regular Mississippi Democratic Party's process of selecting delegates to the national convention.[11]

Since the end of Reconstruction, the Mississippi state Democratic Party had a history of disenfranchising black voters and excluding blacks from participating as delegates to the national convention. After a failed challenge by the MFDP for delegate representation at the Democratic Party's statewide Mississippi convention, the MFDP took its demand to the national convention in Atlantic City. Despite growing public support for equal representation at the convention and a rousing speech condemning the practice of Jim Crow segregation by SNCC-MFDP activist Fannie Lou Hamer, the MFDP was offered two seats for nonvoting "delegates-at-large."[12] Furthermore, the group was unable to garner the full support of several high-profile black leaders who were at the convention, including labor activist Bayard Rustin, Dr. Martin Luther King, Jr., James Farmer of CORE, and Roy Wilkins of the NAACP. In the end, the MFDP delegates rejected the symbolic gesture of nonvoting representation.

The Atlantic City challenge underscored the frustrations that SNCC-MFDP had with institutional leveraging and its allies inside the civil rights movement infrastructure, whom SNCC believed were increasingly unenthusiastic about protest politics. Bayard Rustin, the one-time radical and advisor to Dr. King during the Montgomery Bus Boycott, told SNCC and MFDP members, "You must be willing to compromise. If you don't, then you are still protesting."[13] NAACP President Roy Wilkins also told Hamer that "she and the other people from Mississippi had made their point—they should go back home and leave politicking to those who knew how to do it."[14] The fact that the MFDP's insurgent challenge came from poor Mississippians was even more problematic for the high-profile group of black leaders who served as clients to the Democratic Party and organized labor.[15]

In reality, SNCC feared co-optation by government officials. Ella Baker, SNCC's most respected advisor, warned the young activists about this. Her past experiences revealed that political elites have a way of "burying off of potential leaders by rewarding them with positions within the structure."[16] This allowed the moderates to reap the benefits produced by the movement, or as historian Charles Payne points out, "when it became clear that the movement was going to bear some fruit, those who worked hardest to make it happen were systemically pushed aside."[17] By 1965, after MFDP gained some standing in Mississippi, tensions surfaced between grassroots organizers affiliated with the SNCC-MFDP coalition and moderate black leaders who had close ties to the state's political establishment. After the 1964 Atlantic City challenge, the Loyal Democrats of Mississippi, a moderate political party supported by the national Democratic Party, won the support of blacks unaffiliated with the MFDP. In turn, the Loyal Democrats undermined SNCC and the confrontational elements of the Mississippi civil rights struggles.

While this concern intensified after 1965, especially after the passage of the Voting Rights Act, it had always existed within SNCC. As early as 1962, it almost split the organization when SNCC members debated their involvement in the Voter Education Project (VEP), a program sponsored by the U.S. Justice Department. SNCC believed the Kennedy Administration created the VEP to co-opt and defuse the student movement.[18] Some SNCC members believed the voting project would complement their ongoing efforts to register voters, and that the federal government would protect civil rights activists who registered people to vote.[19] To the contrary, SNCC received little protection from the federal government. Yet, it was able to integrate the VEP into its overall direct action and social change efforts. Later through its MFDP challenge, Stokely Carmichael's efforts in Lowndes County, and Julian Bond's challenge for a Georgia state legislature seat, SNCC members made electoral organizing a part of their direct action campaigns.

Another challenge facing SNCC after 1965 was the increasing pressure by the federal government to reduce financial support of successful programs that were largely SNCC-influenced. For example, President Lyndon Johnson's Office of Economic Opportunity, along with Mississippi's political establishment, made a concerted attempt to undermine the SNCC-influenced Child Development Group of Mississippi (CDGM). As part of Johnson's War on Poverty program, the CDGM provided free meals to school-aged children, preschool training, and medical care and employed hundreds of Mississippians.[20] Initially, SNCC was apprehensive about the CDGM and other War on Poverty programs due to concerns that they would derail the militant orientation of the movement.[21] But instead, SNCC and social activists absorbed CDGM programs. By the mid-1960s, the CDGM had served thirteen thousand children in over one hundred seventy centers in thirty-seven counties throughout Mississippi; they had forty-nine other centers that operated on a voluntary basis in association with the CDGM that assisted four thousand additional children; and it became a major source of employment for many poor Mississippians, employing almost one thousand people statewide.[22]

The CDGM's success brought about a systematic response by Mississippi's political establishment. R. Sargent Shriver, the head of Johnson's Office of Economic Opportunity (OEO), also believed that the CDGM was too independent and publicly associated with black power advocates. In response, the OEO diverted funds to the Mississippi Action Plan, a more moderate community action program.[23] CDGM workers also had to fend off attacks from the federal government that they had misappropriated funds.

Recounting SNCC's conundrum with moderate black leaders is important for understanding the challenges facing progressive student activists. It is also important for understanding the internal complexity of the movement infrastructure that encapsulated SNCC. Certainly, there has always been a moderate black leadership class. Yet in the mid-1960s, one began to see traditional protest leaders discourage protest politics in favor of institutionalized leveraging practices. This occurred, in part, because these leaders began to receive more rewards from the political system and gained greater access. Also, political elites intentionally backed a moderate black clientele who presented themselves as alternatives to SNCC-influenced activists.

This combination of factors adversely affected grassroots mobilization and youth organizing. As black politics shifted toward institutionalized leveraging practices, political elites persisted in developing an obedient leadership class as an alternative to the militant wing of the civil rights movement. While this leadership class gained access to resources, it eschewed more radical or progressive forms of political agitation.

However, institutional leveraging is not the only factor that contributed to SNCC's collapse. Another argument is that SNCC collapsed because it focused too much attention on a "northern strategy" after 1965 that addressed urban poverty and racism outside of the South.[24] This strategy may have altered the "social base" of the civil rights movement that was rural, southern, and augmented by the black church.

Yet, the northern strategy's contribution to SNCC's demise is largely misinterpreted. Urban poverty, ghetto rebellions, and campus protests also encapsulated the South. These phenomena had an equally dynamic impact on the political orientations of black youth who were targeted by black grassroots organizations in the South. Furthermore, by 1960, SNCC had already suffered from institutional leveraging, organizational fatigue, internal conflicts and the departures of key staff due to philosophical disagreements, and the aging out of SNCC members who joined the organization in the early 1960s.

The northern strategy exemplified what Judith Taylor calls "organizational elaboration." This "involves annexing and creating new organizational forms over time to preserve or increase resources, autonomy, and legitimacy."[25] Movement leaders or bridge-builders will utilize this strategy to improve the morale of their members and constituents, and to expand the spheres of influence of their organizations during periods of crises.

Organizational elaboration helps to explain SNCC's attempts to develop cross-movement linkages with movement organizations outside of the South.[26] This was illustrated in SNCC's short-term alliances with the Black Panther Party (BPP) and the Black Liberators of St. Louis, Missouri, in 1967 and 1968, two radical formations that had influence in urban centers outside the South. SNCC believed the BPP's constituency of young adults, college students, poor and working-class youth would help reenergize the organization in urban

centers outside the South. Unfortunately, the alliance never materialized into a full-fledged coalition due to personality conflicts between
SNCC and BPP leaders.

SNCC's alliance with the Liberators seemed more promising. SNCC's
Phil Hutchings and Charles Koen, a leading figure in the Liberators
and the former chairperson of the Cairo (Illinois) Nonviolent Freedom
Committee, were critical to solidifying this alliance.[27] SNCC offered two
positions on its Central Committee to the Liberators. In return, and
for "reasons of publicity," H. Rap Brown and James Forman of SNCC
accepted the titular positions of general of human justice and general
of foreign affairs, respectively, for the Midwest organization. The Liberators then accepted SNCC's political codes of conduct and pledged to
organize young blacks from the Midwest into SNCC chapters.

The SNCC-Liberators alliance was short-lived. Historian Clayborne
Carson speculates that the alliance may have been used by SNCC's staff
to counter the BPP's influence on the organization. He adds that the
SNCC-Liberators alliance may have been undermined by factional
disputes inside of SNCC over its coalition with the Panthers.[28] Yet in
reality, the alliance was on shaky ground from its inception. Political
repression decimated the Liberators, along with factional conflicts with
local black groups. Koen, the group's most influential leader, left St.
Louis by 1968, a year after its formation.[29] These events destabilized the
coalition work between these two formations.

The Student Organization for Black Unity

The late 1960s was the height of black power and attendant Pan-African
consciousness among young blacks. This was exemplified with the black
student rebellions during this period, which Biondi claims was more
prevalent than the anti–Vietnam War protests on college campus.[30]
Along with the growth of black elected officials, black power radicals
gained popularity as traditional civil rights leaders and organizations
such as SNCC, the SCLC, CORE, and the NAACP lost influence. The
popularity of black power radicalism grew as black students, youth, and
progressives were influenced by notable national and international figures, such as Malcolm X, Che Guevara, and Franz Fanon. Radical and
nationalist organizations attracted militant youth who were influenced

by the Vietnam War and liberation movements in Africa and Latin America. One of the last attempts by youth activists of the 1960s and the early 1970s to create a national youth formation was SOBU.[31]

Greensboro, North Carolina, was a training ground for social change activities in the 1960s. Students at North Carolina A&T University in Greensboro developed relations with indigenous organizations such as the Greensboro Association of Poor People (GAPP), Malcolm X Liberation University, and the Foundation for Community Development. SOBU emerged out of this political context on the campus of North Carolina A&T, with a commitment to engaging college students in social change activities outside of the university environs. The transition from campus to community was an easy one for many members of SOBU who had been active in community organizing activities even before its founding.

SOBU's signature initiative occurred in 1969 when it assisted the protest efforts of local students from Dudley High School. The students protested what they considered to be an inappropriate use of authority by local school administrators, who attempted to overturn the results of the school's student election. The election of Claude Barnes as the student council president was opposed by school administrators because of his affiliation with GAPP, the Youth for the Unity of a Black Society, and the Black Students United for Liberation.[32] In response to the attempts by school administrators to nullify the elections, students at Dudley High School, assisted by SOBU and other local activists, protested this and other "dictatorial practices of school officials."[33] Before it was all over, the protests became violent as school administrators requested intervention by the police, who then used force to repress the high school protestors. As SOBU and other activists from A&T aided the young activists, local law enforcement authorities responded with even more repression.[34]

The response by SOBU to the Dudley High School protests positioned this organization as one that was serious about engaging its members and A&T students in community organizing beyond the walls of the university. The necessity for students to organize in poor communities and to transcend their own class predilections became a constant theme inside SOBU. The national chairperson, Nelson Johnson, constantly challenged students that they must seek more than

just a middle-class lifestyle.[35] In addition, SOBU challenged the plu-
ralist notions of democratic participation and provided a fundamental critique of U.S. democracy at a time when the first wave of blacks
was elected to major public offices. In 1970, SOBU stated, "In the past
months elections have been big business for black people and a great
deal of our time and energy has gone into voter registration, education,
and participation. Yet, the real results of all those efforts [elections of
blacks] are not the political offices which have been captured, for they
are only temporary and external. And the elected officials themselves
are limited because in all cases, they are subordinate to a larger external
structure or internal majority."[36] SOBU doubted that mainstream electioneering could produce transformational gains for blacks. Instead, it
backed the formation of a black political party and the "development
and support of institutions–educational, political, economic, medical
and otherwise."[37] In the early 1970s, SOBU assisted in the formation
of the Black Peoples' Union Party of North Carolina, which organized
poor and working-class families around the acquisition of jobs, housing, and welfare reform.[38]

SOBU's support of a black political party logically led to its involvement in the National Black Political Convention (NBPC) in 1972. Its
participation in this endeavor intensified between July and September
1972 when it participated in the 110-member North Carolina delegation of the NBPC. This then led to the formation of the North Carolina Black Assembly (NCBA), the state affiliate of the National Black
Political Assembly (NBPA).[39] Yet, the national infrastructure of the
black political convention movement was plagued by ideological tur-
moil. Nationalists and radicals routinely clashed throughout the convention and assembly meetings during the 1970s, and both sets of activists sparred with elected officials and civil rights groups.[40] The FBI also
infiltrated the convention movement in order to bolster moderate leaders to counteract nationalists and radicals.[41]

Still, SOBU's fellowship with the NBPA and NCBA is not all that
surprising. As SOBU's national chair, Johnson was skilled in building
constructive partnerships with diverse organizations, which included
building bridges between militant organizations and activists that used
institutional leveraging as their method of organizing. Even before his
involvement in SOBU, he had an innate ability to establish relationships

with groups, local activists, and students who were not in ideological agreement with him. For example, although SOBU criticized NAACP President Roy Wilkins for his antagonisms toward militant and radical organizations, Johnson still participated in NAACP voter registration drives. He also worked for the election of blacks to city offices.[42] At the same time, he was able to maintain authentic relationships with militant activists in Greensboro. After the founding of SOBU, he continued to work with the GAPP, which gained prominence in North Carolina for its work on behalf of poor people, high school and college students.[43] His involvement in GAPP, which actually occurred before SOBU's formation, allowed him to build coalitions between college campuses and the community.

A considerable amount of SOBU's energies were dedicated to organizing high school and college students; building alliances with prisoners; working on the creation of black political parties; implementing survival programs in impoverished communities; setting up a speaker's bureau and a community development press; and establishing clothing centers, food-buying clubs, and community service centers. These activities were amplified by SOBU's bimonthly newspaper, the *African World*, which at its height had a circulation of ten thousand people.[44]

SOBU's ideological underpinnings reflected a black nationalist orientation that later evolved into a Pan-African socialism.[45] As such, it developed cross-movement linkages with other Pan-African and black nationalist student and youth formations in Africa and the black Diaspora. Some of these groups were the Pan African Students' Organization in the Americas, the Student Movement for African Unity in Ghana, the Student Movement for Liberation of Southern Africa, the Pan African Students Association, and the African Students Association. These linkages underscored the importance of black transnationalism in SOBU's development and how much its international outlook was shaped by African and Caribbean independence movements. One of SOBU's chief advisors, Owusu Sadauki (also known as Howard Fuller), was in fact the architect of the African Liberation Day activities in the 1970s and a lead organizer in the development of the African Liberation Support Committee (ALSC).[46] These initiatives injected a radical internationalism into the fabric of SOBU's local activities.

Toward Organizational Clarity: From SOBU to YOBU

The most important years for SOBU occurred between 1971 and 1972 when it sponsored several regional conferences with the purpose of building a national Pan-African student and youth movement. It started local affiliates in a dozen cities, including New Haven, Connecticut; Houston, Texas; Kansas City, Kansas; Omaha, Nebraska; and Denver, Colorado. Through the *African World*, it had a communications vehicle that kept its members and allies informed about local SOBU initiatives such as combating police brutality and prison-based organizing. By the early 1970s, SOBU shifted its focus to organizing young adults and youth who were situated in nontraditional college settings.

Another important development that took place in North Carolina was the formation of the Youth Organization for Black Unity (YOBU) in 1971. YOBU was a "state-wide coalition of black student groups" that affiliated itself with SOBU.[47] Immediately after its founding, YOBU, led by such figures as Ron Ivey and Sandra Neely, organized a five-thou-sand-person rally of black youth to protest the reorganization of histor-ically black colleges and universities. YOBU's programs were situated around four initiatives: an antidrug and antialcohol initiative for black youth; a campaign to save black colleges and universities; electoral orga-nizing and voter education, including discussions about developing an independent, alternative political structure outside the two major par-ties; and intergenerational organizing.[48]

In 1972, SOBU underwent several transformations. It hosted its first National Assembly with one hundred young people in attendance. The editor of SOBU's newspaper, Milton Coleman, resigned apparently because his request that the *African World* be independent of SOBU was denied. In the same year, SOBU merged with YOBU and assumed its name. The merger and name change reflected the group's growing class consciousness.

SOBU's name change has its origins in the group's encounter with Stokely Carmichael as early as 1970.[49] In that year, Carmichael traveled to attend a SOBU-sponsored rally commemorating the Sharpeville (South Africa) massacre. Despite Carmichael's participation, SOBU's leading activists were angered by his lackadaisical response to their invitation to speak at the rally. After the rally, Carmichael and SOBU met to resolve their differences. It was at this meeting that he urged the group to "gain a deeper understanding of the class dimensions of the Pan African movement."[50] Subsequent to this meeting, several SOBU members revised the organization's "statement of purpose and place a greater emphasis on class and the international role of imperialism."[51] This underscored an ideological shift in SOBU that was further enhanced by the organization's dialogues with African youth formations and with Guinea-Bissau and Cape Verde Island revolutionary leader Amilcar Cabral. By 1972, SOBU changed its name to YOBU. The intent of using the word "youth" rather than "student" demonstrated SOBU's move to the left and attempt to use a framing strategy to identify with low-income youth.

Some SOBU members believed this ideological shift reinforced their work, much of which was already concentrated in working-class communities. Others believed it may have alienated black nationalists in the organization.[52] Historian Che Wilkins suggests that it exposed the programmatic challenge of synthesizing Pan-African socialism with on-the-ground struggles in these communities. He writes that "the difficulty of translating these broadly defined political objectives into everyday practice forced some YOBU members to rethink the relationship of their local community work to broader political objectives concerned with Africa."[53] Notwithstanding this concern, YOBU was still dedicated to grassroots organizing after the name change and ideological shift.

In 1973, YOBU launched a campaign to save black colleges and universities from being "reorganized" and eliminated. In Washington, D.C., the YOBU chapter, led by Kimoko Ferut Bey, coordinated initiatives focusing on welfare, housing, and prisoners' rights and assisted government workers in collaboration with the Government Employees United Against Racial Discrimination.[54] By the end of 1973, Washington, D.C., became the home base for the newly named YOBU as it moved out of Greensboro. By early 1975, SOBU/YOBU turned its attention to the February 1st Movement. Named after the first date of the 1960 sit-in movement, which was initiated by students from North Carolina A&T University, the February 1st Movement group comprised students and youth from SOBU/YOBU, the Black Student Collective from Harvard University, the National Save and Change Black Schools Project, the Peoples College of Tennessee, the Harambe Organization from New Jersey, and other progressive student groups.

Despite these efforts, SOBU/YOBU collapsed in 1975. One factor that contributed to its declining influence was that the overall mood of the black community began to change by the mid-1970s. Black power radicalism began to wane and the overall tone of the country had become increasingly conservative. Another difficulty that presented problems for SOBU was the changing nature of black leadership. The post-1965 era of black political participation ushered in a new black leadership class, and the locus of black politics shifted the energies of young blacks away from grassroots organizing to institutional leveraging.

Political scientist Ronald Walters argued that this new black leadership class was accorded legitimacy by "the arrival of a formidable support base in the black middle class, which had taken advantage of the occupational and educational opportunities of the 1960s and 1970s and had achieved a degree of socioeconomic mobility."[55] The arrival of this new black leadership class, along with the growth of the black middle class, made it difficult for black power advocates to recruit students into progressive and radical organizations such as SOBU. Nelson Johnson referred to this phenomenon as a cultural shift—an "inertia, a kind of cultural pull to conformism"[56]—in which transformational movement activism began to lose its saliency among black students. Students, who several years earlier would have been attracted to groups such as SOBU, were encouraged to eschew militant activism in exchange for mainstream professionalized, career opportunities, and occupations. The overall impact of mainstream culture and professionalization had a deradicalizing effect on SOBU and its potential recruits.

One of the arguments emphasized throughout this book is that after the collapse of transformational movements such as the civil rights movement and black power radicalism, it became far more difficult for young blacks to reproduce national-level or federated student and youth formations in the same molds as SOBU, the SNYC, and SNCC. The energy and focus of black leadership had shifted from protest and movement-style activism to institutional leveraging. This shift had an effect on SOBU, particularly because it "changed the entire leadership equation" in the black community.[57] Organizations such as SOBU, which Johnson said were "born out of the black power and community control" movement, were forced to organize or compete with this new leadership class.[58]

Furthermore, SOBU may have more effectively served its purposes had its home base stayed in Greensboro, rather than moving to Washington, D.C. Greensboro was a breeding ground of progressive, indigenous activity and had been the driving force behind the founding of SOBU. The District of Columbia was also well known for such activism, but it was still a city dominated by long-established political figures. In terms of its radical elements, prominent organizations such as Stokely Carmichael's All African People's Revolutionary Party (AAPRP) and the African Liberation Support Committee (ALSC) had already established their headquarters in Washington.

On the other hand, SOBU's former national chair, Nelson Johnson, disagreed with the premise that the organization's exit from Greensboro may have contributed to its collapse. He insisted that the move to Washington, D.C., may have been in its best interests since many of its influential members were involved in coordinated activities with the AAPRP and ALSC, both of which helped to broaden SOBU's base. Yet, one-time editor of SOBU's *African World* Milton Coleman hinted that the move from Greensboro to Washington, D.C., may have hurt SOBU's ability to recruit students at black colleges and universities in the Deep South.

Despite its short life (1969–1975), SOBU was a leading Pan-African/ nationalist organization in the 1960s and early 1970s. It gave equal treatment to challenging racism and capitalist exploitation and its various manifestations (institutional racism, white supremacy, colonialism/ neocolonialism). Its activities, in coordination with several black grassroots organizations in Greensboro and the surrounding communities, made the city the "center of Black Power in the South" during this period.[59] Similar to the student and youth formations that came before it, SOBU was influenced by the mood of the political environment that influenced its initial formation. Whereas the youth of the SNYC were influenced by Marxist political orientations and believed in interracial working-class unity, which was common for political activists of the 1930s, SOBU embodied the spirit of militant black nationalism and Pan-African socialism, an adherence to direct action and protest tactics, and self-determination.

The Free South Africa Movement

Though white students were involved in many of the student protests around divestment in the mid-1980s and assumed some of the key leadership roles in the movement, black students and young activists had been involved in the struggle to end South African apartheid since the 1960s and 1970s. In many ways, the emergence of organizations such as the SOBU, the AAPRP, and the ALSC in the early 1970s signaled a tactical shift by young black activists toward organizing around foreign policy and international solidarity issues.[60] Much of this was filtered through a Pan-African lens shaped by African and Latin American independence movements.[61] Student activists also took center stage in the anti-apartheid efforts in South Africa in the late 1960s and early 1970s. Some of these organizations were the South African Students' Organization, the National Youth Organization, and the Soweto Student Representative Council.[62]

The struggle to end apartheid during the 1960s and 1970s was sharply focused on linking U.S.-born blacks with revolutionary movements in Africa. Two decades later, in the mid-1980s, students of color and progressive whites ignited protests on college campuses against the South African regime. The protests pressured elite universities to relinquish their business activities with corporations that had financial investments in South Africa. Students set up campus-based shantytowns or makeshift "shacks" that symbolically represented the "living conditions of many black South Africans."[63] Most of the student activists focused their energies on college campuses, while others limited their efforts to specific regions of the country. Some youth formations involved in the anti-apartheid movement were multiracial, while others were predominantly black. For example, the Progressive Black Student Alliance (PBSA) blossomed in the early 1980s and organized against apartheid in South Africa and other foreign policy issues such as U.S. involvement in Grenada and Nicaragua. As explained by Keith Jennings, one of the PBSA's principal leaders, the organization participated in the planning of the student section of the twentieth anniversary of the March on Washington in 1983, and lobbied March organizers to ensure "that apartheid was a major plank in what we talked about and discussed."[64]

Despite this success of the divestment movement, the student wing of the movement was beset with racial and ideological tensions. Some black student leaders were quick to challenge their white counterparts for their resolute opposition to racism abroad, but disregard for confronting similar racist behavior in the United States.[65] Jennings said there was a constant effort by black anti-apartheid activists "to remind them [progressive white student leaders] that we didn't just need to be against apartheid in South Africa, we also needed to oppose racism at home."[66] This was a recurring struggle inside the anti-apartheid movement, which in part propelled the creation of the Student Coalition against Apartheid and Racism (SCAR) in Washington, D.C., in the mid-1980s. SCAR started out as a multiracial coalition of progressive students that attacked racism in South Africa and in the United States. Yet at the forefront of SCAR's leadership infrastructure were black students and young adults such as Marty Ellington, Marguerite Fletcher, and Ray Davis.

Tensions over leadership and the role of whites inside the divestment movement almost thwarted the efforts of the student activists who formed SCAR. At its founding meeting, some Pan-African students opposed the cross-racial linkages between black and white students. The students even rejected the name of "South Africa" and endorsed the designation "Azania," in solidarity with the radical South African Pan-African Congress, which used this moniker to refer to their country. As a result of these tensions, the collective decided to form its own organizational entity instead of joining forces with the newly formed SCAR.[67]

These tensions highlighted ideological differences in the South Africa divestment student movement and underscored the larger debate over who (blacks or whites) was going to be at the forefront of the movement's leadership. Matthew Countryman, a divestment movement leader from Yale University, believed this issue created tensions between black and white students. As he explained, it came down to a question of leadership in the movement, and "do black student organizations have the right, a kind of moral imperative to claim a leadership role, or should leadership be completely democratic or consensual."[68] Countryman's viewpoint about black involvement in the South African divestment campaign was similar to sentiments among SNCC's leadership staff regarding the involvement of blacks in anti-apartheid struggles. In the 1960s, Dona Richards, a SNCC staff member, stated that "the Movement has been almost completely silent [regarding South African divestment], and the very insignificant, mostly ineffective protests which have occurred has been organized by a handful of whites in the North."[69] In order to mobilize support among blacks for anti-apartheid efforts, SNCC developed the African Project, which backed African independence and liberation movements.

One of the factors that made it difficult to insert black students into leadership positions, at least in the 1980s, was actually "jump-starting" activities on black campuses. Jennings recalled,

> The debate was going on [regarding] who should be in the leadership of the movement [and] many people thought that it should be black students and stuff like that and I was one of them. But at the same time we were rather challenged because when I went down South I realized that nothing was happening on college campuses, so we decided to start working there. We created the Georgia [Progressive] Black Student Alliance (GPBSA). One of the projects of the Georgia [Progressive] Black Student Alliance was Atlanta SCAR. There were SCARs popping up everywhere. In Atlanta we made sure we went to Spelman College because that was the college we thought [would be] most receptive and the women were very active.[70]

The GPBSA took a lead role in organizing students from black colleges and universities. Along with the Atlanta SCAR, the GPBSA was successful in coordinating a nationwide boycott of Coca-Cola for its investment policies in South Africa during the mid-1980s. Outside of the South, the divestment movement was influenced by black leaders from the Washington, D.C., chapter of SCAR and Greg Moore of the United States Student Association (USSA). After working with the GPBSA, Jennings worked with the USSA's Third World Coalition, which helped to coordinate national events to build opposition against apartheid among students.

Other groups that mobilized student dissenters against the apartheid regime were the Progressive Student Network, the National African Youth Student Alliance, and the Democratic Socialists of America's Youth Section, which included Matthew Countryman, a leader in the student takeover at Yale University in 1986. The student wing of the divestment campaigns, along with the wide-scale protests and lobbying activities of protest leaders and public officials, all contributed to the passage of the Comprehensive Anti-Apartheid Act of 1986, the first major congressional measure condemning the South African regime.

One disappointment espoused by some student divestment leaders was their inability to coordinate the diverse organizing initiatives occurring across the country. Some divestment leaders believed these initiatives should have been merged into a national network or federated organization. Others insisted that local and campus autonomy was vital to the overall independence of their own initiatives. According to Countryman, these activists "guarded their autonomy and saw any effort to set up regional or national units as an attempt to dictate how they must organize locally."[71] Although autonomy was significant, student leaders had difficulty sustaining their activities beyond the initial protests in the mid-1980s. Countryman argued that the downfall of the student divestment movement was the students' failure to develop a unified, national organization to continue the student movement and coordinate its efforts after the passage of the anti-apartheid legislation.

Countryman had been a leading activist in the divestment campaigns at Yale University during the height of student protests (1984–1986). Despite the passage of the Anti-Apartheid Act, he suggested that the legislation may have had a deradicalizing effect upon the student movement because it gave many student activists the illusion that they had won the good fight.[72] He was disappointed that students did not capitalize on the momentum they had built leading up to the passage of the bill. He said, "What we did not succeed [in doing] is turning that single-issue movement against racism in South Africa into a broader movement against racism and all the various forms."[73] Furthermore, he and other student activists were somewhat disappointed with the legislation because they believed it was too watered down and did little to combat apartheid and entrenched racial divisions in South Africa.

Consequently, when the legislation was passed, student protests began to wane after 1986 due to perceptions among the young activists that they were victorious. With no national organization in place to coordinate their dispersed activities, student divestment leaders had difficulty maintaining social justice initiatives after the initial burst of dissension. There was a possibility for student leaders to reach out to "adult" lobby groups such as TransAfrica Forum and the American Committee on Africa to assist in this coordination, but some students distrusted the groups because of their concerns about autonomy. Moreover, the student organizations that embraced intergenerational collaboration received little support from adult allies and lobby groups.[74]

The racial tensions that were present during the outset of the student movement in the 1980s eventually proved to be the movement's most difficult challenge. By the latter part of the decade, these tensions invited doubts among black student activists about the prospect of developing long-term progressive, multiracial coalitions between students of color. According to Countryman, "The divestment movement spawned more attempts to build campus multiracial coalitions in eighteen months than had occurred in the previous decade, yet few would argue that it had much success. As black and Third World students we found ourselves in fundamental disagreement with white students over tactics, agendas and decision-making structures."[75] He added that even if there had been a push to develop a national infrastructure to coordinate the dispersed activities, "it is debatable whether such a process could have overcome internal racial tensions."[76] By the mid-1980s, many students had turned their attention away from the divestment campaigns and more toward "building black groups to work against racism on their campuses or at the regional and national level."[77] This turn toward building black groups increased with the rise of black nationalist sentiments among young blacks in the latter part of the 1980s.

The rise of black nationalist sentiments was somewhat expected in the late 1980s and continuing to the early 1990s. The conservative upswing during this period made racial attacks more acceptable in everyday practices and rhetoric. The attacks were fueled by the rhetoric and policies of the Reagan-Bush administrations and their successful efforts to use subtle appeals to exacerbate racial animus among whites.[78] This, in effect, filtered down to college campuses, neighborhoods, and political institutions. Young people were the targets of these attacks inside and outside of the university. The Howard Beach (Queens, NY) killing of a black teenager named Michael Griffith in December 1986, the racial attacks of black students at predominantly white universities, the rejection by the Democratic Party of Jesse Jackson's platform in

1988, the retrenchment of affirmative action programs by the Supreme Court,[79] the Virginia Beach confrontation that resulted in police attacking young blacks on a spring break celebration in 1989, and the attempt by Howard University to appoint conservative Lee Atwater to its Board of Trustees,[80] all created a mood of militancy and heightened racial consciousness among younger blacks.

The racial consciousness during this period mirrored that of the late 1960s and early 1970s, which also experienced heightened levels of black nationalist sentiments. These sentiments emerged partially in response to the white backlash to the civil rights movement and the growing power of the conservative movement as exhibited with Richard Nixon's presidency. Black power advocates were also influenced by the urban rebellions and the African independence and anticolonial movements during this period.

Conclusion

A major objective of this chapter was to highlight the integral role that national/regional student and youth activists played as agents of social change in the second half of the twentieth century, especially from the 1960s to the 1980s. The participation of students and youth in organizations such as SNCC, SOBU, and the FSAM underscored their willingness to combat systemic patterns of racial injustice, disenfranchisement, and economic marginalization. This chapter further illustrated that the formation of activist-oriented student and youth formations in the black community is part of the long tradition of transformational black activism and community organizing celebrated by Ella Baker at the beginning of the chapter. In fact, the contributions of black student/youth activist organizations were a central ingredient of black politics in the twentieth century.

This chapter also underscored the difficulty youth organizations and activist networks have sustaining their work over long periods. The emergence, development, and demobilization of student and youth formations and networks are influenced by forces internal and external to their movement infrastructures. The transient nature of student and youth formations almost guarantees that these organizations will be short-lived, unless they recruit new members, develop new leaders, or regenerate resources. Nelson Johnson of SOBU concluded that many influential activists who were at the vanguard of these organizations grew into adulthood and were forced to take upon a different set of responsibilities. As their core constituencies advanced into full-fledged adults, the leaders of these organizations did not spend enough time replenishing the organization with new younger members.

In addition, the changes in the political and economic environments or shifting political contexts have a dynamic impact on the livelihood of youth-influenced movements and movement infrastructures that rely on the vitality of young activists. For example, SNCC's organizing efforts, combined with the activities of other civil rights groups, helped to usher in civil rights measures such as the 1964 Civil Rights Act and the Voting Rights Act of 1965. Ironically, this opposition helped to transform the political and economic environments such that it made more militant modes of organizing less attractive to activists.

The next chapter examines locally based youth activities in New Haven, Connecticut, during the late 1990s and early 1990s. The young people involved in the New Haven youth movement were influenced by the legacies of resistance movements of the 1960s, as well as the anti-apartheid movement and the Jesse Jackson presidential campaigns of the 1980s. Yet, they also operated in a political environment shaped by black political elites and a powerful political machine that inhibited their movement from becoming the transformational force that could spread to other cities. Nonetheless, the youth movement experimented with innovative organizing strategies and cultivated a host of young activists who remained committed to social justice after the initial phase of the movement.

4

The New Haven Youth Movement

[The New Haven activists represented] a new breed of young people who were not invested or interested in that machine [but who were interested in] creating empowerment for communities that weren't receiving any power in our view.
—Steven White, campaign manager for John Daniels's mayoral election campaign

In recent years, political observers have speculated about a potential resurgence of black youth activism in American politics. Indeed, during each presidential cycle, the prospect of a reinvigorated youth movement that attracts large numbers of young blacks and other youth of color is the subject of much debate among activists and the media. In the 2004 and 2008 presidential elections, youth groups and youth-based voter mobilization organizations registered thousands of voters, including Black Youth Vote, Rock the Vote, the NAACP Youth Council, Americans Coming Together, the League of Young Voters, US Action, and a collection of hip-hop activist networks. Yet these groups and the recent discussions about youth movements are not novel to the post–civil rights era. As discussed at the end of chapter 3, young activists protested on college campuses against South African apartheid during the 1980s. Others were actively involved in Jesse Jackson's 1984 and 1988 presidential campaigns, locally based community organizing initiatives, racial justice protests on college campuses, and campus-based living wage campaigns.

One set of campaigns, fostered by a cadre of black student and youth activists in the late 1980s, was the New Haven youth movement. Activists involved in the New Haven youth movement, or Kiddie Korner as it was euphemistically called, organized a youth-led antiviolence/anticrime initiative, protested and lobbied for equitable school funding, and participated in two electoral organizing campaigns that helped to elect New Haven's first black mayor and reform the police department. Symbolizing a "new breed" of activists, the youth movement's success caught the attention of prominent civil rights activists and social justice advocates around the country. When Rev. Jesse Jackson of the Rainbow/Push Coalition and NAACP President Benjamin Hooks visited New Haven in 1989, they were impressed by the outpouring of young blacks involved in voter mobilization and social change activities.[1]

The New Haven youth movement underscored three characteristics of post–civil rights activism. First, it showed how young people can be catalysts for social change in urban municipalities plagued by decaying political machines and social stratification. Second, it demonstrated how young people, through their participation in progressive urban movements, can be valuable resources to community workers, activists, and public officials who seek to challenge racial hierarchies and economic injustices in municipalities. Third, the youth movement pointed to the difficulties youth activists have in sustaining resistance campaigns that challenge power structures, especially when allied with public officials and black leaders inclined toward institutional leveraging.

Youth mobilization initiatives during this period existed in other cities, such as New York and Boston, but they lacked the cohesion and internal diversity that were seen in New Haven. New Haven's fairly small population of 130,000 allowed youth organizing to spread in different neighborhoods in a relatively short amount of time. In addition, the youth movement developed a unique cross-class coalition that brought together students from Yale University and Southern Connecticut State University, as well as high school students and youth from the city's poor and working-class black neighborhoods.

Many young people involved in social activism were recruited by movement bridge-builders into several community-based organizations: the African-American Youth Congress (initially called the Black Youth Political Coalition), cofounded by Michael Jefferson and Gary Highsmith; a reinvigorated Greater New Haven NAACP Youth Council led by advisors Lisa Y. Sullivan and Kevin D. Houston; and the Alliance of African Men, coordinated by Roger Vann, a young activist and counselor at the Dixwell Community House. The African-American Youth Congress and the NAACP Youth Council, in particular, made concerted efforts to recruit youth from several of New Haven's public housing developments. The youth movement received additional support from another young activist and local store owner Scot X Esdaile, who worked with both organizations and had a unique ability to mobilize black youth from the city's poorest neighborhoods.[2] This cross-class coalition integrated the concerns of politically active youth with latent youth networks that had been neglected by political elites.

In examining the New Haven youth movement, this chapter addresses how young people can shape community and institutional politics. The focus of this chapter is on three interrelated grassroots campaigns, the first of which was an antiviolence initiative that attempted to broker a truce among the rival street crews to reduce the rise of gun violence and crime. Second, the young activists mobilized high school and college students in support of a black superintendent, John Dow, and his contentious battle with City Hall to increase public expenditures for the city's public school system. The third initiative involved youth participation in two electoral organizing campaigns. In 1988, young people from the African-American Youth Congress and the NAACP Youth Council served as foot soldiers for Althea Tyson's campaign for the Registrar of Voters. Although Tyson suffered a controversial defeat, her electoral bid added momentum to John Daniels's mayoral campaign in 1989 and his attempt to become the city's first black mayor. Young activists, drawn from the various youth formations, were given "insider" positions in this campaign, while they simultaneously functioned as rank-and-file foot soldiers, registering hundreds of eligible voters on college campuses and in poor and working-class neighborhoods. These three initiatives, occurring between 1987 and 1989, underscore the utility of creative organizing strategies (framing, the appropriation of indigenous resources, positionality) that were used to foment movement activism.

Antiviolence, Education, and Electoral Politics in New Haven

As discussed at the outset of the book, creative organizing is best understood as the course of action taken by movement bridge-builders to compel young people to participate in movement campaigns, and generate opportunities for them to influence community and political struggles. Movement bridge-builders may encourage young people and potential recruits to engage in activism by creating opportunities for them to elevate their political status and exercise leverage through social movement participation. Or they may emphasize intergenerational collaborative activities in order to garner resources and expertise from seasoned activists and public officials. These collaborations can aid mobilization campaigns as long as there is continuity between the goals and objectives of both cohort groups. In addition, the New Haven activists used framing to organize youth and to heighten the awareness of city officials about the urgent problems facing ghetto youth, particularly around anticrime measures and education concerns.

Antiviolence/Community Intervention

The New Haven youth movement occurred at a time when political opportunities were somewhat unfavorable due to the adverse impact of deindustrialization and the reduction in federal aid to cities experiencing high poverty rates. The reduction of federal aid beginning with President Nixon's New Federalism and worsening under President Reagan's devolutionary policies exemplified how urban fiscal and economic problems were aggravated by political decisions external to cities. By the 1970s and continuing into the 1980s, virtually every urban city in the industrial North and Midwest experienced budget deficits, economic recessions, and soaring unemployment rates.[3] These problems were exacerbated by middle-class and white flight, suburbanization, and public sector downsizing measures in many urban cities.[4] These difficulties fueled public health epidemics in many poor and working-class black neighborhoods, including rising homelessness, AIDS, soaring crime rates, and escalating gun violence and incarceration rates, largely resulting from the involvement of underemployed and unemployed youth and young adults in the drug culture.[5] These conditions presented a unique set of challenges that had the potential to handicap youth activism.

In New Haven, from 1947 to 1997, the number of factories declined from 444 to 106 and the factory wage-earner population diminished from 28,000 to 2,800.[6] By the 1980s, according to all social indicators, entrenched poverty characterized parts of the city. It had one of the highest infant mortality rates for a U.S. city with more than 100,000 people,[7] its public school system was in shambles, and there was a significant increase in violent crime in many neighborhoods where the city's 40,000 black residents lived. Unemployment and underemployment, along with the infusion of crack cocaine, produced deadly gun violence among the city's impoverished youth and young adult population. To make matters worse, New Haven had a severe budget deficit in the late 1980s and early 1990s,[8] and Yale University did little to improve the city's bleak economy.[9]

The aforementioned problems made the 1980s a difficult period for residents of New Haven as young blacks from chronically distressed neighborhoods fell victim to the drug culture. In just a short time, poor neighborhoods turned into seedbeds of gun violence between rival street crews that fought over the drug trade. By 1989, New Haven's homicide rate ranked ninth in the country when controlling for population size.[10] Community leaders, elected officials, and the police offered no substantive solutions to the escalating crime rates. In 1988, a group of clergy appealed to Connecticut governor William O'Neil to send the National Guard into New Haven's crime-ridden neighborhoods.[11] Although the police chief and mayor disagreed with this action, they both lobbied state and federal officials for more prisons, prosecutors, and police officers. As crime worsened, so did police-community relations. Similar to those of other urban cities, the New Haven police department had a reputation for brutality against poor black youth.

Despite the negative responses by these leaders and the neglect by others, the Youth Council and Youth Congress worked overtime to curb the violence. In 1989, they organized a memorial service attended by four hundred youth to discourage them from resorting to gun violence.[12] In August of the same year, Scot X approached the youth groups for assistance with a proposal to negotiate a truce between the rival factions in the city.[13] He owned a restaurant in the Newhallville section of the city, which also functioned as an unofficial safe space for local street youth.[14]

The other activists involved in the truce were well known throughout the city. Vann, a New Haven native, ran a "rites-of-passage" program at the Dixwell Community Center. Highsmith, also from New Haven, and Jefferson formed the nucleus of the Youth Congress's leadership. Jefferson, a student at Southern Connecticut State University, was the more outspoken of the two leaders. He worked at the local juvenile detention center, which gave him access to marginal youth, many of whom were from the same communities victimized by gun violence.

Sullivan and Houston advised the NAACP Youth Council. Although they were not native residents of New Haven and were Yale University graduate students, their entries into the city's political and community organizing circles differed from those of the typical Yale student. Houston, almost immediately upon his arrival from Atlanta in the mid-1980s, immersed himself in community organizing activities and became the youth director of the Elks Club. As he was a divinity student, his philosophy reflected a mix of black nationalism and black liberation theology.[15]

Coincidentally, Houston and Sullivan knew each other when both labored together with the Progressive Black Student Alliance (PBSA) as undergraduate students in Atlanta, Georgia.[16] Sullivan moved to New Haven after graduating from Clark University, where she also worked with the Atlanta NAACP Youth Council. Upon her arrival to New Haven, she decided to live in a public housing development close to Yale University. Thereafter, she spent most of her time absorbed in community-based and grassroots initiatives, learning from seasoned activists in the city. While in graduate school, she worked as a legislative liaison for John Daniels, the state Senate's first black pro tempore and New Haven's future mayor, who recommended that she advise the NAACP Youth Council.[17] Both Houston and Sullivan purposely distanced themselves from campus-based political activities due to their belief that black college students needed to transcend their class biases and submerge themselves in community struggles.[18]

Houston and Sullivan's efforts exemplified how movements are able to develop cross-class coalitions. As advisors to the NAACP Youth Council, they helped to alter the youth wing's traditional middle-class composition. Similar to most youth councils around the country, the Greater New Haven chapter was made up of middle-class youth and the sons and daughters of longtime organizational members. Yet, Houston and Sullivan recruited youth from poor neighborhoods.[19] Hence, by the end of the decade, the two activists helped to transform the organization into one of the more innovative and progressive youth councils in the country. It became one of the few youth councils that actually engaged in aggressive on-the-ground outreach activities involving young people who were traditionally not members of the NAACP.

Before the antiviolence campaign gained momentum, the Youth Congress and Youth Council agreed to form a coalition and develop a recruitment strategy for each group. The Youth Congress enlisted high school students, youth in the detention center, and students at Southern Connecticut State University. On the other hand, the Youth Council directed its energies on youth from public housing and students from Yale University.

Combating gun violence was an urgent issue that affected the Youth Congress and the Youth Council's constituent groups.[20] The antiviolence campaign highlighted structural and socioeconomic inequalities that rendered impoverished blacks without the resources to combat public health ills. Jefferson of the Youth Congress scolded community leaders for blaming young people for the gun violence without getting to "the root of the problem"[21]—that is, the combination of poverty and the neglect by City Hall and Yale University of New Haven's deteriorating neighborhoods. The soaring crime rates further underscored the growing class fragmentation and generational divide in the city. Poor residents and young people, especially ghetto youth, were ignored by many older and middle-class blacks who offered few judicious solutions to the problems.[22]

Unfortunately, the antiviolence campaign did not lead to immediate results. Homicides continued after the truce, before declining in the early 1990s. However, the antiviolence campaign made two important contributions. First, it augmented the young activists' stature in poor neighborhoods and among established black politicians, and it demonstrated that they were a nascent resource for mobilizing aggrieved communities in forthcoming political campaigns. Second, it preempted conservative and punitive responses to crime by offering a model for how community-based organizations could engage in crime-solving measures. For example, a couple of years after the youth movement's collapse, Scot X founded the Elm City Nation. This grassroots organization comprised black youth, young adults, and former gang members who attempted to combat gun violence, poverty-related public health dilemmas, and risk behavior among ghetto youth.[23]

The Fight for Equitable Funding for Public Schools

School reform was another issue that consumed the energies of the youth activists. Similar to many urban school districts, by the mid-1980s New Haven's public school system was mostly composed of black and Latino children and suffered from a depleted tax base, bureaucratic inertia, and scarce resources.[24] Yet Superintendent John Dow's arrival in 1984 ushered in significant changes in the school district. Dow instituted innovative measures, including college outreach programs and partnerships between the school district and child development specialists from Yale University, staff and teacher recruitment and development, and programs designed to encourage parental involvement. His efforts won the support of students, parents, and the youth-based movement organizations.

At the time, the youth activists considered Dow to be what Santoro and McGuire call an "institutional activist." Institutional activists are public officials who advance the same goals and objectives of movement activists, yet "hold formal positions within the polity and use their offices' resources to affect policy change."[25] Youth leaders believed that, at least during his initial tenure as superintendent, he displayed a certain degree of independence and distanced himself from the political machine's power brokers.[26]

Dow repeatedly clashed with City Hall over school funding, such as the case in 1988, when the Board of Finance rejected his $106 million budget request and instead proposed the reduced amount of $95 million. Afterward, the Youth Congress and the NAACP mobilized support for Dow's budget request. In May of that year the two groups organized a walkout of four hundred high school students, who then marched to City Hall in support of Dow's proposal. In his public statements to the press, Dow discouraged the student/youth protest and insisted that *adults* needed to get involved in the fight for educational funding.[27] He did this, however, to juxtapose their activism to that of some black leaders who were unwilling to challenge City Hall.

Months after the walkout, the youth organizations published an editorial advertisement in the *New Haven Independent* titled "An Open Letter to Mayor Biagio DiLieto, 'Don't Sacrifice the Education of Black and Hispanic Youth for the Sake of Political Power.'" The young activists condemned City Hall for rebuffing Dow's demand and for "shirking responsibility to educate its youth."[28] They wrote, "Instead of protecting public education in New Haven, Mayor DiLieto chose during the same period to offer tax abatements for large out-of-town developers. That was his prerogative and he showed us then just how much he really cared about our future."[29] The letter was signed by fifty black and Latino high school and college-age young people.

Although downtown officials did not concede to the demands of the youth protestors, the education campaign heightened the political consciousness of New Haven's youth and exhibited how youth groups can use the framing process to mobilize support for ameliorative policies. Similar to the antiviolence initiatives described above, the education reform campaign gave young people the opportunity to draw attention to the adverse treatment of low-income blacks by those who controlled the city's political and economic resources. It provided them with a political opportunity to highlight the "racial duality" in the city's education system, one in which black and Latino children received unequal educational resources in comparison to children in the suburbs.[30] It further demonstrated the potential power and resourcefulness of a new breed of young political and community activists. This campaign also exemplified the willingness of youth activists to interact and work in intergenerational collaborations with local officials.

Black Students/Youth and Electoral Organizing

The initiative that gained the most attention was the participation of youth in the 1988 and 1989 municipal elections. New Haven was governed by an antiquated political machine best symbolized by Mayor Richard Lee, who ran the city from 1953 to 1969. Under Lee's direction, New Haven became a model city for urban renewal development.[31] He used a provision in the Federal Housing Act of 1949 to leverage $500 million in urban renewal funds during his mayoralty, and used the revenue to distribute patronage and harvest support among his constituents.[32] His use of urban renewal dollars thus made him one of the most influential post–World War II mayors and probably the most powerful small city mayor of this period. Yet, similar to the situation in many Snowbelt cities, Lee's industrial population base dramatically changed in the 1950s and 1960s. Deindustrialization and white flight, along with upsurge of black militancy,[33] pushed him to co-opt moderate black leaders in order to maintain his hold on the city. Although the city did little to alleviate black poverty, it handed out patronage to some black leaders and their constituents, who simultaneously discouraged progressive political activity and social change initiatives.

Some youth organizers were initially skeptical of conventional politics because their issues were often ignored by City Hall. Yet three factors convinced them to embrace electoral politics. First, the young activists were encouraged by Jesse Jackson's 1984 and 1988 presidential campaigns. Notwithstanding their idealism, the possibility that Jackson's campaigns could push the Democratic Party to the left created a sense of optimism among these young people. In New Haven the Youth Congress, the Youth Council, and Scot X recruited youth to register voters for Jackson in 1988.[34] Deirdre Bailey, the most prominent student activist in the city, was a member of the NAACP Youth Council when she participated in the electioneering activities. She said, "I was instrumental in getting over 200 students to register [to vote], with the help of the school administration, my [NAACP] youth council advisors and my sister."[35] New Haven, to some extent, was also a microcosm of Jackson's struggles within the Democratic Party. It was a one-party town, at least since World War II, and the winner of the Democratic Party primary was the de facto winner of the mayoral election. Thus, contentious electoral battles were between moderates and liberals within the Democratic Party, or between machine insiders and outsiders. Similar to the Jackson campaigns, the New Haven youth movement was interested in moving the local party to the left and outside of the controls of the machine.

A second reason why the youth were attracted to electoral organizing was because they saw it as vehicle to challenge the local party machinery, and to challenge the docile group of black elected officials who were unwilling to oppose it. Hence, the youth cadre framed electoral organizing as a challenge to the downtown establishment that neglected the black community's concerns.

Third, related to the electoral organizing campaigns was the possibility that the youth organizers could persuade a new mayor, subsequent to the 1989 election, to reform the police department. Shortly before the 1989 election, there were several high-profile incidences of police abuse against black youth.[36] Since New Haven had an executive-centered political system that vested a great deal of power in the mayor's office,[37] the youth were convinced that a new mayor could use unilateral authority to replace the police chief. Accordingly, the youth organizers were able to frame the 1989 election as an opportunity to elect the city's first black mayor and as a referendum on the police department. This appealed to many youth, poor people, and progressive activists, particularly those who were skeptical of electoral politics.

Furthermore, the earlier campaigns (the antiviolence and educational reform initiatives) amplified the youth groups' stature. When they turned their attention to electoral politics, they were already positioned as fixtures in New Haven's political circles. As early as 1987 and 1988, the youth groups began to coordinate their activities with a few black officials who believed that a new mobilized constituency—and in this case, youth organizations—could assist them in their own political struggles with the machine.

In 1987 Bill Jones, a longtime political operative, ran for mayor. Though he lost badly, collecting only 24 percent of the primary vote and winning only three out of thirty wards,[38] his campaign helped to lay the foundation for a successful mayoral challenge by John Daniels two years later. More important than the Jones's campaign was Althea Tyson's 1988 bid to become the first black woman elected as the city's Registrar of Voters, an office that supervised voting registration and election precinct activities. As the city's first black assistant registrar of voters, she was the presumptive favorite for the higher office. Also the seat had been vacated before the election, and usually the assistant to the registrar had received the party endorsement for an open-seat race. However, in her case, she was rejected by the party based on what many believed to be racism.[39] This angered the Youth Congress and the Youth

Council, and young people who actively campaigned for Tyson. Bailey, the NAACP Youth Council member, "got involved with a voter registration drive with some community leaders," and convinced about twenty to thirty NAACP Youth Council members to volunteer for her campaign.[40] Also influential in her campaign were black women organizations and state senator John Daniels, one of the few black politicians who strayed outside of the machine to lend his support.[41]

Though Tyson ran a strong campaign, she lost by eight hundred votes. Nevertheless, her campaign shed light on a deeper reality that faced black progressives if they were going to mount a serious challenge to the local machine. This was the continued patron-client relationship between City Hall and some black elected officials, many of whom did not support Tyson. Thus a successful challenge, either for the registrar or the mayor's office, necessitated that the candidate build a strong coalition of progressives who were not obedient to the machine.

The Jones and Tyson campaigns, along with the youth organizing initiatives, were springboards for John Daniels's 1989 candidacy for the open mayoral seat that was vacated by the retiring incumbent, Biagio DiLieto. The activists had mixed feelings about Daniels's candidacy. Some thought he was too moderate and not fully committed to promoting the causes of marginalized blacks. Steven White, Daniels's "youthful" campaign manager, recalled, "Privately I knew that people wanted Bill [Jones] to run [for reelection] because they didn't trust John, frankly, to deliver to them as he was delivered into political power. They were worried that we might get John Daniels in, [and] John would forget about us. . . . At the same time, we all recognized, he had the greatest opportunity, he was the most fundable, he was the most liked. He had the greatest momentum. He had been reelected to the [Connecticut] Senate."[42] Notwithstanding his centrism, Daniels passed two litmus tests for the young activists: he endorsed Tyson for registrar of voters and backed Dow's school funding initiative. His alliance with Dow was particularly significant because quality public education was the centerpiece of his campaign and his mayoral exploratory committee paid for youths' editorial advertisement in the *New Haven Independent*.[43] Therefore, when Daniels opened his mayoral campaign, he was armed with a politicized young cadre of community activists. His campaign, similar to Tyson's electoral challenge, fused the interests of older, institutionalized activists and public officials with those of younger activists.

Young activists played additional roles in the inner circle of his campaign. Bailey, the Youth Council activist, was a member of Daniels's exploratory committee as a high school student, making her the youngest person on his campaign staff. Steven White, despite being in his mid-twenties, was hired as his campaign manager. This decision upset older black politicians, who took this to mean that Daniels was not serious about winning the mayoral race.[44] Yet in many respects, the hiring of White was a politically astute move, especially when it became clear to Daniels's supporters that the machine would not back him. It was feared that some black officials, who were prime candidates for the campaign manager position, were or would be compromised by the machine and could not be trusted.

White, on the other hand, was independent of the party machinery and was young, only twenty-five years old at the time. In fact, he was one of the youngest campaign managers leading a successful mayor bid in an urban city during this period. Despite his youth, he was no stranger to political activism, having been introduced to campaign politics as a young teenager. Later, in 1987, he campaigned for Bill Jones and operated as his de facto deputy campaign manager. During this campaign, White ran for a council seat in the predominantly white Twenty-Sixth Ward. Although the district had no inclinations of electing a black candidate, he used the race to promote Jones's campaign and build alliances across racial lines.

White's service to Jones's campaign gave him valuable insight into local politics and allowed him to learn from seasoned politicians. At the same time, his youthfulness put him in good standing with the leadership of the Youth Congress and the Youth Council, which he had known before the campaign.

Lisa Y. Sullivan, the NAACP Youth Council advisor, was another activist who had an influential role in the mayoral campaign and was one of the few women on Daniels's exploratory committee. As a bridge-builder, she had connections with women groups such as the African-American Women's Agenda that supplied the energy and resources to Daniels's campaign and gave her access to certain constituencies not afforded to the other youth leaders.[45]

In addition to her position as an NAACP Youth Council advisor, Sullivan was a legislative liaison for Daniels. Yet, she resigned from this position once Daniels decided to run for mayor and became the field organizer for his campaign. She was also the project director of Operation Big Vote, which registered hundreds of new voters for the election.[46] Due to New Haven's history of corruption and reports of fraud that adversely affected Tyson's campaign a year earlier, she urged Daniels to pay for fifteen young people to serve as notary publics, or commissioners hired by the state who could verify voter registration cards. This would allow Daniels's supporters to bypass local registrars, whom they believed would eliminate black voters from the registration lists. With the assistance of the notary publics, voters were allowed to use universal mail-in registration cards that went directly to the secretary of state, who then verified the legality of the registrations without the approval of New Haven's Registrar of Voters.[47]

In addition, the youth organizations were intent on creating a new voting constituency that was carved out of the city's poor communities and public housing developments. Scot X was instrumental to this effort. When the youth groups planned to set up voter registration sites in several housing projects, Scot X used his contacts to persuade street youth to temporarily vacate their usual hang-out spots in these areas. This allowed the groups to register voters in relatively secure environments for extended periods of time. The registrars then entertained these neighborhoods with music and food, while registering voters. Generally, many adults were wary about venturing out of their apartments for long periods of time due to high incidences of gun violence. However, the youth activists told the children that if they wanted more food, they had to go to their apartments and return with as many adults as possible so they could register to vote.

The voter registration drive was an example of the framing process discussed in the first chapter. Framing is more than message packaging. It is a coherent rationale, reinforced by movement bridge-builders, that helps explain the multifaceted predicament of a community, and then attempts to link this analysis with on-the-ground solutions to the identifiable problems. Chana Kai Lee, in her biography of civil rights activist Fannie Lou Hamer, refers to a similar strategy used by civil rights activists called the moral pragmatic approach to organizing. She writes,

The approach of moral pragmatism involved tending to whatever needed to be done wherever because this was only right. If there was a need in a community for food, clothing, or housing, the moral pragmatist in the civil rights movement directly addressed those needs alongside the task of tearing down the walls of Jim Crow. For moral pragmatists like Hamer [as well as Ella Baker, Bob Moses, Myles Horton, and Septima Clark], the most pressing community needs determined one's political agenda . . . With need as their guide, moral pragmatists kept their attention focused on conditions in their own communities; they were localistic in orientation.[48]

This approach is rooted in the southern black freedom movement and the labor movement's community unionism tradition. Whether it's more aptly called framing or moral pragmatism, it underscores the utility of linking interpretative schema to service provision and political participation. The Youth Congress and Youth Council believed that the best way to register poor voters was not only to emphasize voting, but to interpret crime and hunger as impediments to black political participation and a decent quality of life. By feeding children, as well as creating a safe haven for the public housing residents, they provided them with much-needed services. They then used these services as a vehicle to introduce the residents to the political process.

The Youth Council and Youth Congress recruited dozens of high school youth and college students to assist with the voter registration activities. In addition, they coordinated electioneering activities with black women activist networks and even reached out to Latino groups to garner support for the Daniels's campaign. Due to these efforts, over fifteen hundred new voters turned out to cast ballots and voter turnout doubled in the black precincts—the highest increase in the state.[49] Overall, voter turnout in 1989 increased by over 5 percent compared to the previous mayoral election. Bailey said that "the youth pulled him [Daniels] over the hurdle,"[50] as he received 59 percent of the primary vote and 68 percent of the general election vote.[51]

After Daniels's election victory, due to the pressures from community activists and the youth groups, he replaced the police chief with Nicholas Pastore. Pastore used unconventional methods to reform New Haven's police department. He created a Child Development-Community

Policing Program in cooperation with Yale Medical School's Child Study Center. He dismantled the police department's militaristic-style training academy. The new academy emphasized "the importance of academics, original research, communication skills, critical thinking, community involvement and offer[ed] discretion and dialogue." As part of the training, police cadets were required to take culturally competent classes ranging from "Non-Violent Alternative Dispute Resolution" to a "New Haven Needle Exchange Program." The department also organized national and regional conferences that concentrated on the "Police and the Black Family" and "Domestic Violence."[52]

Pastore enlisted NAACP activists to advise the department on police-community relations. He brought in experts from the departments/schools of law, medicine, divinity, psychiatry, public health, and social policy at Harvard and Yale Universities, as well as from the New Haven AIDS Project, to work as consultants to the department's training academy.[53] The most important innovation was the establishment of a Board of Young Adult Police Commissioners. Composed of youth from local high schools, the Young Adult Board was given direct access to the police chief and advised him regularly on police-community relations.

Daniels won two (two-year) mayoral terms, serving from 1989 to 1993 as New Haven's first and only black mayor. For progressives who made up the nucleus of the New Haven youth movement, his mayoralty produced mixed results. He inherited the mayor's office during a fiscal crisis or "economic tsunami" that led to municipal layoffs during his first term.[54] The decade-long devolution policies of the Reagan and Bush administrations also dampened aspirations that Daniels could rely upon federal grants to address entrenched poverty. When he had access to federal funds such as the Urban Development Action Grants, he followed the progrowth policies of his predecessors by distributing them to developers.[55] These realities underscored the inherit weakness of the New Haven youth movement and the institutional leveraging approach that it used to assist the Daniels campaign. Beyond grassroots networks in black communities, the young activists had little influence in elite and economic decision-making circles in the city.

In addition, the Daniels administration was plagued by tensions with unions and "well-capitalized nonprofits" such as Yale University.

Representatives of these groups were entrenched in the city bureaucracy or, in the case of nonprofit representatives, had decades of experience working with municipal officials. Yet both sets of groups had few blacks in their leadership hierarchies and Daniels had little control over the city patronage system outside two dozen positions.[56] Consequently, the decision-making apparatus that was anchored in the private sector was mostly exclusive of blacks and the young activists.

Where blacks and the youth movement had influence were in the areas of public safety and public health. The hiring of Pastore as police chief was directly related to the elevated concerns that young activists had about deteriorating police relations. Daniels was also one of the first mayors and perhaps the most widely publicized elected official to openly advocate for a needle exchange program in poor neighborhoods to combat the spread of HIV and AIDS.

Overall, the electioneering activities of young black activists displayed the strengths and limits of institutional leveraging. Young blacks proved to be a vital constituency in New Haven's elections from 1988 to 1991 such that they were able to position concerns about police harassment within the inner circle of Daniels's campaign team. Yet, they had little influence leveraging the political and economic superstructure—elite policymakers, business and private sector leaders, high-ranking union members, and powerful nonprofits—to implement redistributive measures on behalf of the city's distressed communities.

Conclusion

This chapter looked closely at the New Haven youth movement in the late 1980s. Movement scholars generally conclude that a movement's successes or limitations are determined by the contextual realities shaping their activism, or the structure of political opportunities afforded to them. In reality, the structure of opportunities during the late 1980s in New Haven was not necessarily conducive to a youth-based grassroots movement. The city was governed by an antiquated political machine, and many black leaders were married to it. Gun violence, the drug culture, and poverty intensified alienation among ghetto youth. Moreover, deindustrialization and a bad political economy created a host of fiscal problems for New Haven.

Notwithstanding these trends, the New Haven youth movement was demonstrative of an effective local, grassroots effort. The collection of young activists who led or participated in the three local campaigns (antiviolence, public school reform, electoral organizing) demonstrated that young people can impact community and institutional politics. They offered solutions to gun violence, challenged the city's public school funding policy, and immersed themselves in two electoral organizing campaigns. The youth movement performed these tasks by building cross-class coalitions, framing issues that were pertinent to youth and institutional allies, collaborating across generational lines, and providing services that satisfied the immediate needs of their constituent groups. Paying closer attention to these strategies and tactics offers insight into how aggrieved populations can draw upon their own resources to facilitate social change.

In addition, the New Haven youth movement had a spin-off effect—that is, it provided a resource base of activists that gave birth to a new youth formation. This organization, the Black Student Leadership Network (BSLN), was propelled by several New Haven activists, including Lisa Y. Sullivan, Steven White, and Deidre Bailey. The BSLN also held its first regional meeting in New Haven in 1992. Another ally of the New Haven youth movement, anti-apartheid activist Matthew Countryman, was equally influential in the BSLN's formation. After leaving Yale University, he became an organizer for a national student group called Youth Action. The BSLN's formation, evolution, and collapse are examined in the next three chapters.

PART II

5

The Origins of the Black Student Leadership Network

How do we revive the sense of militancy, activism, and independence within African-American politics as we enter the twenty-first century? Organizationally, we need several new kinds of institutions. First, and perhaps foremost, we need a new "SNCC" (Student Nonviolent Coordinating Committee), a youth-oriented formation which taps the energies and abilities of the Hip-Hop generation. A militant black youth movement, directed and led by young people themselves, could target issues of black-on-black violence in a more effective manner. It could help develop the leadership skills among young people, acquainting them with the whole range of political intervention and tactics, such as economic boycotts and civil disobedience.
—Manning Marable, 1992[1]

A major challenge that activists and leaders of an aggrieved population encounter is the shortage or low supply of monetary resources and selective incentives to help facilitate social movement activities. The shortage of resources available to progressive organizations can limit their ability to spread collective action and sustain long-term, movement-building initiatives targeting regressive policies.[2] Consequently, Aldon Morris argues that aggrieved populations have come to rely upon internal resources (indigenous activists, preexisting organizations, and networks of activists) and the "mobilization capacity" of movement infrastructures in their communities to help spread collective action.[3] Under such conditions, young people serve as a potential resource base for encouraging popular mobilization campaigns that attempt to ameliorate various inequities.

Arguably, it is difficult for established groups and older activists to engage in social movement building without the mobilization capacity and assistance of young people. Not only do young people bring an extraordinary amount of energy to social change work, they also tend to have less family and financial commitments and have more flexibility than older activists.[4] Thus, there is an expectation that adults and youth operating within the same movement infrastructure will rely on each other, not only because of ideological congruity between the two entities, but out of necessity. Although young activists are a potential resource base and have the capacity to mobilize aggrieved populations and other young people, this alone is not enough to build a movement. The development of social movement organizations or social change organizations (e.g., Southern Negro Youth Congress, Student Nonviolent Coordinating Committee, and Student Organization for Black Unity), as indicated by historian Manning Marable, is essential to engaging young people in social movement activities.

This and the next two chapters examine the development of the Black Student Leadership Network (BSLN), a national youth formation that was created in the early 1990s as the student/youth wing of the Children's Defense Fund's Black Community Crusade for Children (BCCC) initiative. The BSLN represented an extensive effort on the part of post–civil rights student and youth activists to develop a federated youth formation that could address poverty, racism, and public health crises in low-income black communities. This chapter gives specific attention to the origins of the BSLN and its linkages to the Children's Defense Fund (CDF). I also look closely at the BSLN's leadership development and popular education programs with a particular focus on its Ella Baker Child Policy Training Institute (EBCPTI) and freedom school initiatives. The EBCPTI (also referred to as the Training Institute) was an activist training center for hundreds of young people who participated in the BSLN's freedom school programs. It allowed the BSLN and its parent organizations to form linkages with local-level, indigenous groups. More important, through the Training Institute, the BSLN used framing strategies to explain why youth-based movements were essential to the survival of working-class black communities. The EBCPTI allowed the BSLN to develop a distinct political identity rooted in an ethos of collective leadership and grassroots organizing. The BSLN's origins, the Training Institute, and a summary of the BSLN's initiatives in 1992 and 1993 are discussed in the remainder of the chapter.

The Black Community Crusade for Children

It is impossible to separate the BSLN's formation from the political tenor of the post–civil rights era, especially the late 1980s and early 1990s. During this period, young blacks were cautiously optimistic about the prospects of igniting popular mobilization campaigns on campuses and in communities. Evidence of this was seen in the South African divestment protests, black student participation in Jesse Jackson's presidential campaigns, student opposition to the 1991 Persian Gulf War, and community-based initiatives such as those that occurred in New Haven. Moreover, in the 1980s, there was a heightened sense of black consciousness among young people due to the rightward shift in the nation. Groups such as the Black Nia Force from Howard University, which also had a chapter in the New York/New Jersey area, and the Black Consciousness Movement in New York emerged with a particular appeal to black youth.[5] These initiatives preceded the BSLN's formation. Though most were short-lived and plagued by disorganization and a lack of resources, they created an indigenous resource base of activists that assisted in the BSLN's formation and youth organizing initiatives in the 1990s.

The New Haven youth movement was the most important initiative that influenced the BSLN's formation, mainly because it caught the attention of Marian Wright Edelman, the founder and president of CDF. In addition to being the most vocal advocate of the modern movement against child poverty, she was an alumnus of Yale University and was a member of its Board of Directors during the peak of the New Haven youth movement. These responsibilities allowed her to frequent New Haven and become somewhat familiar with the youth-oriented activities of the young people in the city. In late 1990 Edelman requested a meeting with Lisa Y. Sullivan, one of the activists at the forefront of the youth movement in the city.

Prior to the meeting, Edelman had begun to organize prominent black public and social policy advocates, activists, and intellectuals in support of a national campaign against child poverty. She encouraged these officials to support an agenda that would address the growing concerns facing children and families, especially those situated in impoverished black communities. Edelman had many reasons for such concern. As president of the CDF, part of her constituency (black children and families) was adversely impacted by the rise in poverty, child hunger, and related public health crises. Furthermore, Edelman was well aware that the body politic had shifted to the right, that spending for social welfare programs had lost support among some Americans, and that poverty and the public health epidemics in black America were rooted in structural inequalities.

The explosion of gun violence and disintegration of black social and political institutions during the 1980s also surprised Edelman and other longtime civil rights organizers. When Edelman began to have meetings with other black leaders, she did so under the notion that it was "SOS time for Black folk." She believed that as a result of these public health epidemics, African Americans faced their "greatest crisis since slavery."[6] She may have overstated the intensity of this crisis, but nonetheless the statement highlighted her own anxieties about the intersection of poverty, crime, institutional racism, and social welfare conservatism, and their collective impact on the most marginalized black communities at the end of the twentieth century.

Edelman's efforts at organizing a cadre of longtime social and political activists also brought a certain amount of legitimacy to the issue of black child poverty, given her own long history of activism. She was one of the initial participants in SNCC's founding conference while a student at Spelman College. After graduating from Yale Law School in 1963, she served as an advisor to Senator Robert Kennedy's antipoverty investigations. She also was the first black woman in Mississippi history to pass the state bar examination, and urged Dr. Martin Luther King, Jr. to organize the Poor People's Campaign in 1968.[7]

Edelman founded the CDF in 1973. Under her tutelage, she brought in prominent political figures to serve as the organization's chairperson, including Hillary Rodham Clinton and Donna Shalala, who later served as the head of the U.S. Department of Health and Human Services under President Bill Clinton. Since the 1970s, CDF has issued numerous reports highlighting child poverty in attempt to influence public policies at both the national and state levels. Throughout the 1980s, Edelman and the CDF won important victories despite the conservatism and opposition from the Reagan-Bush era. These legislative victories included safeguarding Head Start and the Women, Infants, and Children (WIC) nutrition program and pushing for the expansion of

Medicaid coverage and the passage of a child care bill in 1990.[8] The CDF also conducted extensive outreach efforts outside the Beltway. It opened regional, state, and local offices in Edelman's hometown of Marlboro County–Bennettsville, South Carolina; Minneapolis, Minnesota; Cleveland-Cuyahoga County, Ohio; Oakland and Los Angeles, California; New York City; Detroit, Michigan; and Hartford, Connecticut.[9]

In order to advocate on behalf of poor black families and children, Edelman pulled together prominent black activists and intellectuals under a campaign referred to as "A Crusade for Black Children." The initial efforts of this crusade came as early as March 1990, when Edelman secured funds from the Van Ameringen Foundation, Inc., as part of an effort to "train a core group of leaders in the black community who [it insisted] will advocate for black children and ensure that the needs of at-risk children are met."[10] Two months later, on May 12, Edelman gave the commencement address at Howard University. In her speech, she admonished the black community—perhaps directed more at the black middle class—for the "abandonment of responsibility for ourselves, for each other, and for our children."[11] She further urged the audience to "help jumpstart the black community and the nation to action to save black children—and all children—and to replace the current climate of despair with one of hope and struggle." She made strong connections in her speech among racism, poverty, and the disintegration of black community institutions. Even though she did not mention the names of Ronald Reagan and George H. W. Bush, much of her speech was clearly an attack on their administrations and the conservative right. She made reference to "misguided national investment priorities" and "national and community inattention" as contributing to black poverty. She pointed to a host of data demonstrating that during the Reagan years there was a worsening of infant mortality, black college graduation rates, and declining black family income.

Six months after the speech, in early November, Edelman brought together a group of prominent blacks for a meeting in Leesburg, Virginia. The purpose of the meeting was to have "an overview and discussion of the crisis facing America's black youth, steps for mobilization and an action plan within America's black communities."[12] Included on the list of attendees to the November meeting was a talented group of black educators, social policy experts, civil rights activists, and intellectuals.

The meeting "was designed to set the stage" for a retreat organized a month later in Bellagio, Italy, by Edelman at the Rockefeller Center.[13]

Despite her initial attempts to bring together prominent activists, initially this initiative almost began without the inclusion of young activists, especially those working with grassroots organizations in the same type of communities that the crusade wanted to mobilize. Accordingly, the meeting between Edelman and Sullivan in late 1990, in New Haven, was an important step to bring a "younger" voice to the table.

This meeting was somewhat of a litmus test for Sullivan. Edelman was well known around Yale University circles, and her prior experiences in the civil rights movement had won her the admiration of many young activists, even among those who were further to the left. Yet, in her first informal discussion with Edelman, Sullivan conveyed a political astuteness and knowledge of social history and the civil rights movement.[14] Sullivan "told Edelman she believed young African Americans genuinely want to complete the unfinished business of the civil rights movement, but they have no one to bridge the generation gap between old and young, the way Ella Baker had done during the creation of the Student Nonviolent Coordinating Committee in the 1960s."[15] Edelman was impressed by this interaction, and she invited Sullivan to the Bellagio retreat scheduled for December 10 to 15, 1990.

The Rockefeller Center in Bellagio appeared to be an odd place for the second retreat, especially for a meeting involving those individuals who attempted to help "jump-start" a movement on behalf of poor black children and families in the United States. However, the Bellagio site had been conceived in 1959 solely for the purposes of bringing individuals together to discuss issues related to international understanding, human rights, and tolerance. Also, Edelman probably offered Bellagio as a place to convene prominent activists, leaders, and intellectuals in order to convince them to actually attend the meeting. Under normal circumstances, intense work schedules may have prevented the invited participants from being able to attend a five-day meeting if it were held in the United States. Moreover, Bellagio was more than an ideal place given that one of the participants was Hugh Price, vice-president of the Rockefeller Foundation, where he worked on educational and outreach initiatives for underrepresented groups. (Price was appointed president of the National Urban League in 1994.) Price had strong connections to New Haven, where he attended Yale Law School and served as the administrator of human resources for the city.[16]

Twenty-three participants attended the Bellagio retreat, including historian John Hope Franklin and civil rights leader Dorothy Height, both of whom agreed to serve as this meeting's official co-conveners. Additional invitees included Hugh Price; Harvey Gantt, the two-term mayor of Charlotte, North Carolina, who twice ran a competitive race for the North Carolina Senate seat against racially conservative senator Jesse Helms; noted scholars Cornel West, Roger Wilkins, John B. Turner, and James Comer; Barbara Sabol, the first black woman to be named administrator/commissioner of the New York City Human Resources Administration; and William Lynch, Jr., New York City's deputy mayor for intergovernmental affairs and campaign manager for David Dinkins's 1989 mayoral victory.

At the meeting, Edelman asked the collective to draw up plans for expanding their network to recruit seasoned activists and policymakers who would be willing to develop concrete solutions to address poverty and public health crises in low-income black communities.[17] Edelman viewed this initiative as complementing her overall push to create a broader vision for the CDF, which included, among many things, helping black children and families.[18] The Bellagio retreat's participants agreed to recruit leaders from twelve constituency groups representing the broad spectrum of the black community: religious/church; college students/youth; corporate/business/foundation; media; sports/entertainment/celebrities; national politics; state and local politics; higher education, elementary and secondary education; health; family and income supports; social workers and direct service providers; and grassroots.[19] They also agreed on their name, the Black Community Crusade for Children (BCCC), and to have the CDF coordinate their efforts out of its national office.

Developing a national movement on behalf of black children and families, despite rising poverty rates and the retrenchment of social welfare programs, was a monumental task. Dr. Reed Tuckson, a prominent medical professional and the former president of Charles R. Drew University of Medicine and Science in Los Angeles, remembered the Bellagio participants deliberating the viability of national campaign or organization that could bring together disparate black networks and organizations. He explained, we "first had to determine if it was possible to mobilize and energize a multidisciplinary effort that could bring the challenges and plight of black children to the forefront."[20] Sabol, of New York City's Human Resources Administration, was an enthusiastic proponent of the BCCC and is credited by some for coining the popular CDF moniker "Leave No Child Behind." After the BCCC's formation, she chaired the group's Human Services Committee. Reflecting Tuckson's concerns, she said "it was often difficult to get a straight consensus" on different issues because each of the human services commissioners was "operating in very different political environments."[21] Enola Aird, who worked with the CDF and BCCC from 1993 to 1995, also said that it was extremely hard "to build a critical mass of African Americans around the country who [were] committed to one agenda, a very similar agenda."[22] Although she didn't attend the Bellagio meeting and later inherited the role of acting director for the organization, she understood that philosophical and ideological divisions among black groups would be an obstacle to the BCCC's development.

Notwithstanding these concerns, most of the attendees believed a nationwide campaign was critical to reshaping the political discourse about black families and the working poor. Steve Minter, the executive director of the Cleveland Foundation, joined the BCCC shortly after the Bellagio retreat. He supported the BCCC's attempts to build intergenerational linkages, believing it could bring together researchers and grassroots activists.[23] The BCCC provided another purpose, from his vantage point, which was to create a dialogue about internal divisions among black leaders, such as allowing for a broader conversation on why some faith-based leaders held socially conservative views.

At the outset, the BCCC outlined several objectives highlighting its grassroots mobilization strategy: (1) to coordinate a movement to reverse public policies that adversely impacted low-income families and children, (2) to tackle a host of issues around poverty and crime, and (3) to internally mobilize the black community's resources, particularly grassroots activists, social policy analysts and advocates, and the clergy to combat public health crises.[24] This was later formalized into the campaign titled "A Healthy Start, a Safe Start, a Fair Start, and a Head Start," which focused on four issues: health care, curbing gun violence and crime, advocating for antipoverty and employment initiatives, and mobilizing the black community's support for educational equity, access to good schools, child care, and preschool expansion.[25]

After the December 1990 meeting in Bellagio, the BCCC coordinated three dozen follow-up meetings with national, civic, religious, civil rights, professional, and community leaders, "in an effort to develop a strategy to improve the condition of black families and children."[26] On March 29, 1992, the BCCC convened a follow-up meeting in Washington, D.C., to offer an update of its mobilizing initiatives. A few months later, in July 1992, the group held another five-day meeting in Bellagio. A year later, on March 9, 1993, the BCCC officially announced itself to the public when it sponsored a two-day meeting that attracted 250 leading black activists, intellectuals, and policymakers.

The BCCC's initiatives were carried out by a Working Committee comprising three dozen academicians, policymakers, social advocates, religious leaders, and civil rights activists. The Working Committee members were divided into task forces: the Religious Advisory Board, a Media Advisory Committee, a Human Services Advisory Committee, an Anti-Violence Task Force, a Juvenile and Family Court Judges Working Committee, an Education Advisory Committee, African American Males Project, and the Beat the Odds Committee. Two additional task forces were established that focused on the BSLN and the freedom school program. Some of the activists who attended the first and second Bellagio retreats volunteered to be a part of the BCCC's Working Committee, and from this group, twelve members sat on a Steering Committee.[27] By the mid-1990s, the BCCC established an Advisory Committee of approximately three hundred leaders, policymakers, and civil rights activists from around the country who provided consultation on important issues.

By 1994, the BCCC had several regional offices. Angela Glover Blackwell, executive director of the Urban Strategies Council in Oakland, California, and Carolyn Reid-Green of the Charles Drew Development Corporation in South Central Los Angeles coordinated the western regional offices. Geoffrey Canada, president of the Rheedlen Centers for Children and Families in Harlem, New York, headed the eastern regional office. Lolita McDavid of the CDF's Cleveland office spearheaded the Midwestern regional activities.[28] By 1996, the BCCC opened up other offices, including another Midwestern office in Cincinnati,

Ohio, a southern regional office in Jackson, Mississippi, and another office in St. Paul, Minnesota. The regional directors assisted with the Summer Freedom Schools, developed coalitions with state and local agencies, and worked on anti–child hunger initiatives.[29]

The BCCC had additional linkages to the CDF's office in Marlboro County, South Carolina, which was coordinated by Edelman's sister, Olive Covington. Edelman also urged the BCCC to work with the CDF's office in Austin, Texas, which focused largely on health care issues and was the "laboratory for developing and sustaining multiethnic coalitions to promote community building primarily among black and Latino communities."[30] The BCCC also discussed plans to develop local and regional support networks in Detroit, Atlanta, and Chicago.

Sullivan was the only representative of young people who attended the Bellagio retreat. Realizing that there was an opportunity to pressure leading black "movers" and "shakers" to support a national student and youth formation, before attending the retreat, she discussed the initiative with several young activists in New Haven as well as some divestment movement activists. She held additional conversations with young activists outside of New Haven to gauge their interest about Edelman's efforts and a potential marriage between young people and older, more established black leaders who would be attending the Bellagio retreat.

Some of Sullivan's peers warned that such a marriage would limit a national youth formation from carrying out a full-scale popular mobilization campaign. As young activists organized their communities, they often faced opposition from older activists and were told to wait their turn when it came to leadership. Despite the impressive record of the social activists involved in the Bellagio retreat, many of the younger activists who participated in discussions before and after the meeting questioned its potential efficacy and viewed this national campaign by black leaders with a great deal of caution. Although the CDF worked hard at lobbying on behalf of poor children, this national coalition of black leaders was viewed as anything but radical. Some of the younger cohort of activists familiar with the CDF perceived it as overly middle-class and as staffed with too many whites who were unfamiliar with black political culture. They also perceived the CDF as far more comfortable with leveraging its influence inside of Beltway political institutions instead of engaging in grassroots organizing.

Despite the skepticism, Sullivan believed such a marriage was the only way to gain the type of support that young people had been looking for to assist large-scale movement-building activities. She admitted, "I understood why [my peers] were skeptical and with good reason, but I didn't really see any other options at the time that would provide us with an opportunity to build an infrastructure."[31] Still, out of these discussions, there was some interest in an adult/youth alliance as long as Bellagio participants were willing to leverage their resources to develop the leadership capacity of a new cadre of young leaders.[32]

Others recognized that the older leaders had a serious concern for black children and youth and the crises that faced them. During the early years of the campaign, Edelman repeatedly expressed a strong desire to recruit and train one thousand new young black leaders/advocates under the age of thirty. Thus the young activists viewed their marriage with older activists as a unique opportunity, especially given that Edelman's move toward developing a black-led mobilization campaign had attracted black leaders who were strategically situated in important public policy positions. Furthermore, the young activists were already mobilized and had been involved in their own local and campus-based initiatives leading up to the Bellagio retreat. They had their own constituencies and autonomy.

Another reason why some of the initial members of the BSLN chose to participate in this kinship with the BCCC and CDF was because of the resources that flowed from these organizations. The BCCC and CDF offered the infrastructure support that many student/youth activists and advocates believed was necessary to spearhead a social movement organization. Matthew Countryman, who had known Sullivan since his days as a leading activist in the divestment movement at Yale University, was especially important in these early discussions. Shaped by his experiences in the anti-apartheid movement, he was attracted to the idea that a national organization like the BCCC could provide the resources and infrastructure support to young activists. This was something that did not happen in the anti-apartheid movement. Countryman articulated these concerns shortly after the BSLN's founding conference in 1991. In a letter to Edelman, he wrote, "The inability of student activists to effect change in national politics in recent years is testament more to the failure of progressive organizations to put essential resources and organizing skills into student mobilization than it is to student apathy and/or self-centeredness."[33] Furthermore, forming a black student organization that worked on behalf of black children had the potential of bringing together a broad section of "black student activists—liberals, leftists, entrepreneurs, and nationalists."[34] In other words, such a political formation could bridge ideological differences among black students.

The BSLN Comes Together

The BSLN was founded six months after the Bellagio conference in June 1991 with funding provided by the CDF.[35] The CDF loaned two of its staff members, Marty Rodgers and Amy Wilkins, to assist with the founding meeting. As appropriate, the meeting was held at Howard University, where Edelman had just given the graduation commencement address the year before, and where two years prior student activists led a widely publicized protest against the appointment of Republican Party stalwart Lee Atwater to the university's Board of Trustees.[36]

Forty participants attended the founding meeting. The gathering focused on generational divisions, how to develop community service programs, how to develop a budget and strategy for raising funds, and how to work with media outlets in order to shape public discourse on important public policy issues.[37] Before the close of the meeting, the participants agreed to establish a Working Committee that would coordinate follow-up activities, develop a mission statement, assist with hiring a full-time staff person who would coordinate future activities of the national organization, develop a quarterly newsletter and training manual for black college-age activists, and plan a follow-up conference within the next ten months.[38]

The Working Committee developed a proposal formalizing these ideas and provided a detailed budget for the initiative that was then submitted to Edelman. Kasey Jones, a Howard University student, was one of the key volunteers on the Working Committee. Previously, she had been active in the Washington chapter of the SCAR and the Concerned Black Awareness Council. Also on the Working Committee were Errol James, a student at John Jay College of Criminal Justice and a senior member of the Harlem Writing Crew; Jeff Robinson, a recent graduate of Michigan State University, where he served as the president of the campus NAACP; and Leslie Watson, a Southern University student and volunteer with the National Student Mobilization group that opposed the Persian Gulf War in 1991.[39] Sullivan also joined the Working Committee, as did Countryman shortly after the founding conference. Richard Gray was another key member on the Working Committee. As an activist at Brown University in the mid-1980s, Gray was involved in the antiracism mobilization efforts at the university. After moving to Boston, he served as the young adult advisor to the Free My People Youth Organization, a social justice group composed of high-school-aged youth in the Roxbury, Mattapan, and Dorchester sections of the city that challenged the police department's stop-and-frisk tactics, which disproportionately targeted black and Latino youth.[40] At the time, Gray was the co–executive director of the National Coalition of Advocates for Students, a group that provided educational opportunities for at-risk youth. Assisting the Working Committee were Marty Rodgers, a CDF staff employee, and Leah Williamson, a University of Maryland student who previously served as the co-chair of the Malcolm X Leadership Summit and was member of the National Collegiate Black Caucus.

Finally, the Working Committee and Edelman, upon the recommendation of Sullivan, drafted Steven White, the former campaign manager for John Daniels in New Haven. White had been a member of Daniels's cabinet and assisted Daniels's in his second mayoral victory in 1991. He also set up a political action committee, the 21st Century Leadership, which assisted the New Haven NAACP Youth Council in its voter registration efforts. White accepted the offer and subsequently became the BSLN's first director by December 1991.

As the BSLN's full-time director, White was responsible for administering its day-to-day activities and coordinating the recruitment efforts. Although he had recently finished working on New Haven's mayoral campaign, the challenges he faced as the first BSLN director proved to be just as difficult and painstaking. He had few monetary resources to lead a full-fledged movement campaign. Other than the Working Committee selected at the founding conference, there was no governing body or functional organizational structure to conduct the organization's day-to-day activities. The CDF allocated some resources to the BSLN as well as office space at its central headquarters in Washington,

D.C. Yet White's challenges in administering the day-to-day operations of the BSLN were complicated by the fact that its parent organization, the BCCC, was also an embryonic entity and had yet to hire a permanent national coordinator or director. Hence, White generally consulted with Edelman and a few other BCCC members to help run the daily operations of the BSLN.

After being hired, White attempted to capitalize upon the enthusiasm generated at the 1991 founding conference. He met with conference attendees, the Working Committee, and others who were interested but unable to attend the founding meeting. The significance of these discussions, according to Richard Gray, a young adult advisor to the BSLN, was for White to understand "where they [BSLN activists] were coming from, what they saw as the issues, and the role of BSLN,"[41] especially since he was not involved in the initial planning phase of the organization. Out of these conversations, BSLN members decided to develop a mobilization strategy to recruit new members and allies to the organization. As part of this strategy, the BSLN's leading activists identified grassroots and campus-based organizations to help coordinate regional meetings.

BSLN members organized regional meetings in 1992 and 1993, mainly along the East Coast and the Mid-Atlantic corridor, in order to expand its constituency. Drawing upon the BSLN's New Haven connections and network of activists, YaSin Shabazz, a founding member, and Wendy Battles, a graduate student at the University of New Haven, organized a regional meeting at Yale University in February 1992. The meeting offered workshops on community organizing, media advocacy, and fund-raising to about one hundred students from twenty-five colleges and universities as well as community activists from the Northeast.[42]

Six months later Kasey Jones and Kim Freeman organized a regional meeting, "Youth Reclaiming Youth: Community Service, Leadership Development, and Political Advocacy in the 1990's," at Howard University. The meeting attracted fifty students from neighboring universities and an additional twenty community activists from local organizations.[43] Both Jones and Freeman had been instrumental in facilitating the BSLN's development at a time when it had no administrative infrastructure. In fact, Jones became the organization's first national field organizer in 1993,[44] and Freeman was selected as the first editor of its quarterly newspaper, *We Speak! A Voice for African American Youth.*

In total, BSLN activists organized four regional meetings in 1992 in New Haven, in Washington, D.C., at Vassar College in Poughkeepsie, New York, and at Duke University in Raleigh, North Carolina. The BSLN continued to organize regional meetings the following year. Similar to rallies and protest marches, the meetings or what some activists called "gatherings" served as rallying points for mass action.[45]

Despite the enthusiasm at regional meetings, they were usually one-shot events that allowed for little follow-up and postmeeting organizing. Another weakness was that they mostly attracted college students rather than noncollege youth or young people situated outside of mainstream political and educational institutions. The BSLN's leadership cadre attempted to create a space for young college students to move beyond the insular world of campus politics. However, this tendency to recruit mostly college students represented a weakness in the network's ability to articulate an agenda that was inclusive of all youth, particularly noncollege young people. Later, as the BSLN matured, it developed an orientation toward youth participation that went beyond the boundaries of students on college campuses.

To develop a more operational mobilization structure, in 1992 the BSLN field team instituted small-scale meetings at the local level called "house parties." These "were informal gatherings of young black adults where participants interacted socially but discussed community problems, developed winnable solutions, and delegated responsibilities for follow-up."[46] They were patterned after the coffee/tea house parties generally organized by political strategists in order to recruit voters and campaign donors.[47] The house party model was a vehicle for engaging young people in organizing around important public policy issues, letter-writing campaigns, and public forums.[48]

In September 1993, the BSLN field team in collaboration with the BCCC expanded beyond the regional conferences and house parties and began implementing leadership development seminars called Advanced Service and Advocacy Workshops (ASAWs). The ASAWs provided intensive training to the BSLN's members, its key organizers, and non-BSLN youth advocates and activists who supported the organization. BCCC members assisted with training sessions for the first couple of ASAW seminars, which offered interactive discussions between adult activists and young people.

Mobilizing a base of constituents was not the only concern of the BSLN in 1992. During the organization's first year, it was still faced with the problem of having no coherent organizational structure, no issue agenda, and no distinct political identity. The process of developing a structure began at its March 1992 annual conference in Atlanta, Georgia, where the participants were given the responsibilities of setting "organizational priorities."[49] A Steering Committee was tasked with drafting a proposal for an organizational structure and constitutional bylaws for selecting a national governing body. At the Steering Committee's first follow-up meeting in August of that year, founding member Sullivan presented the draft proposal of the organizational structure, which was then amended and adopted. In November, the Steering Committee convened once again and prepared constitutional bylaws for presentation, amendment, and ratification at the annual conference in Washington, D.C., in March 1993.[50]

An important addition to the bylaws was the inclusion of a young adult advisory board to the BSLN that consisted of activists, social policy analysts, and intellectuals, who were five to ten years older than were the college-aged BSLN members. In addition to the formal young adult advisory group, the BSLN had an informal network of young adult advisors, intellectuals, and policymakers who offered their expertise to the organization. Together, they provided technical support and leadership development and sustained the overall vision of progressive activity for the young activists.

The remaining debate over the constitutional bylaws centered on two proposed amendments. The conference participants wanted to make sure that the BSLN's constitution had an inclusive definition of "student," mainly because they did not want to exclude noncollege young people from joining the organization.[51] The delegates defined a "student" as "any individual committed to the concept of education as (1) a fundamental component of social action, (2) a life-long endeavor, and (3) a process that occurs in both traditional and nontraditional institutions of learning."[52] This discussion and the constitutional provision reflected the apprehension among the delegates and outside observers that the organization was concentrating too much attention on recruiting college students rather than young people who were not in college.

The debate over the constitutional bylaws was filled with discussion about how the delegates could create a democratic, nationally elected governing body and an operational field team with full-time organizers. The delegates agreed that the national governing body, the National Coordinating Committee (NCC), would consist of eight members ages eighteen to twenty-nine. A provision was also included in the constitution, which indicated that the NCC had to be composed of an equal number of men and women. Within the constitutional bylaws, an additional guideline designated the NCC's leadership to two co-chairs, one man and one woman.

These concerns over student classification and gender equity were among the most important during the BSLN's first three years. Many of the delegates to the March 1993 conference, especially its core leadership staff, had a sophisticated understanding of the history of social activism and the internal contradictions that encompassed progressive social movements and student/youth organizations. The inclusion of a broad definition of "students" was an attempt to confront the class tensions within the black community and within various student and youth activist constituencies. It underscored the BSLN's internal struggles to preempt itself from becoming a "talented tenth" type organization. Clearly, many of the activists within the group had strong relations with grassroots organizations and understood that noncollege young people were disconnected from activist organizations and excluded from critical political discourses on public policy initiatives. With this in mind, BSLN members struggled to reach young people who were not in college. Writing a constitution that included a different understanding of "students" was an important step toward meeting this objective.

Gender equity was another concern that was critical to the constitutional debates of the BSLN in its early years. At the conference, some attendees were wary that women would be excluded from the high-profile leadership positions or as spokespersons for the organization, and assigned administrative and organizing roles. The division of labor and leadership responsibilities between male and female leaders within the national governing body was an attempt by core members to avoid replicating practices that marginalized women in other black activist and civil rights groups organizations. As Belinda Robnett argues, black women "have been excluded from formal leadership [within activist groups] on the basis of their sex" despite their significant role as rank-and-file organizers.[53] The delegates to the March 1993 conference were, therefore, intent on giving men and women equal representation on the NCC.

These discussions reveal that the BSLN wanted to combat various forms of oppression, such as institutional racism and poverty, as well as sexism and class tensions within the internal functions of black politics and leadership. The divisions also underscore how important it is for an organization to develop its own identity and distinguish it from other groups, especially during an organization's early development.[54] This exercise helps an organization's leading activists answer the essential question, "Who are we?," for potential recruits.[55] Answering this question helps to shape an organization's character, frames its mobilization goals and organizing initiatives, and heightens the political consciousness of its constituents and potential recruits.

Ella Baker Child Policy Training Institute and the Summer of 1992

The most promising initiative implemented by the BSLN during its first full year in operation was its direct action advocacy and community organizing school, the EBCPTI. Developing the institute was an important step for the BSLN in establishing an organizing strategy rooted in collective leadership and grassroots organizing. The institute was a two-week training session on a variety of topics, including direct action advocacy and community organizing, political education and social movement history, and media relations. After the session, the summer interns recruited for the Training Institute were then deployed to work with local organizations throughout numerous communities. Although the EBCPTI was carried out throughout the BSLN's tenure, its most significant period of operation occurred during the summer of 1992.

The BSLN's leadership cadre chose to name the institute after SNCC advisor and civil rights activist Ella Baker because they were attracted to her philosophy of community organizing, "group-centered" leadership, and participatory democracy.[56] Though Baker believed direct action was essential to altering institutional inequities and challenging racial segregation, she believed it was equally important to challenge the internal functions of the black community, particularly the antidemocratic style of many black leaders.[57] Her philosophy admonished some black leaders and civil rights organizations that were seen as too hierarchical and bureaucratic, and generally led by middle-class and mostly male spokespersons. She believed these groups often discouraged activists from low-income communities from enthusiastically participating in transformational movements because of their general bias toward incorporating spokespersons who were socially distinguished, middle-class, and less confrontational. As a result young people, poor people, and women had difficulty ascending to top leadership positions inside of these organizations. Countryman and Lisa Y. Sullivan, the institute's chief architects and longtime followers of Baker's philosophy, had operationalized it in their own experiences in political and community organizing. Accordingly, they attempted to institutionalize Baker's philosophy inside of the BSLN and in the Training Institute.

The planning for the Training Institute began in the spring of 1992 after Countryman secured a grant from the Fund for Southern Communities, a foundation that provided monetary resources for grassroots social change organizations in Georgia, South Carolina, and North Carolina. Because the grant was limited to organizations located in the Carolinas and Georgia, the BSLN members chose to have the first institute at Shaw University in Raleigh, North Carolina.

In June, the Training Institute welcomed its first group of workers. In preparation for the summer training, Countryman developed a direct action advocacy/community organizing training module adapted from the Midwest Academy/United States Student Association Grassroots Organizing Weekends training curriculum. The module was designed to assist indigenous people, particularly the least organized, to become aware of their own power.[58] Sullivan then incorporated the civil rights film series *Eyes on the Prize* into the training "to point out how movements and people get organized," and demystify how social change takes place.[59] The film series complemented the literature on civil rights movement history that the Training Institute's twenty-five participants were required to read. Martin Rodgers, a CDF employee, proposed that summer organizers be paid a small stipend and then paired to work with local BCCC members or black leaders.[60]

After the training, the summer organizers were sent in teams of four or five to work with local organizations in North Carolina. These organizations included the Hobgood Citizen's Group, North Carolinians Against Racial and Religious Violence, the APPLES program and the Communiversity program in Chapel Hill, and the Concerned Citizens of Tillery. The projects were very much steeped in the idea of collective leadership, identifying indigenous leaders, and assisting them with their own projects.[61]

In Durham, Paulette Quick and Kim Janey encouraged young mothers in the Scotland Neck housing development to lobby the town council for reductions in their enormously high utility bills, which in many cases took an entire week's paycheck to pay off.[62] Most residents had never before visited the town council and were hesitant about demonstrating against local political authorities. Quick and Janey were reluctant to lobby the town council themselves and worked hard to energize the residents to lead this effort. Quick addressed the residents and encouraged them that it was "crucial for someone from your community to go address your town council," because "we don't live here and we can't address your problems."[63] After some prodding, they drafted one of the residents, a young mother of two, to represent the community and pressure the town council for the utility reductions. The council responded by offering to help the residents find a solution to lowering their utility rates, and the manager of the housing development "told the women he would help them apply for a utility fund."[64]

This activity may seem insignificant compared to the civil rights movement's challenge to the southern racial caste system. However, in the isolated world of the Deep South, Quick and Janey's outreach efforts helped the housing development residents combat their own sense of isolation, fear, and alienation. Furthermore, this activity reaffirmed the importance of Baker's philosophy inside the BSLN as a useful approach to developing and empowering local-level leadership.

BSLN activists labored intensively in other North Carolina communities. BSLN summer organizers, Marcia Thompson and Jawana Johnson, spent their summer with the North Carolinians Against Racial and Religious Violence. They organized a council of teenagers to help find solutions on how to exercise their own political power to combat racism. According to Thompson, the initiative tried to "encourage young people to organize programs of their own and take leadership roles."[65] In the town of Hobgood, Nicole Burrowes assisted Easter Hillard of the

Hobgood Citizen's Group (HCG) in organizing residents in support of a community center that would eventually be turned into a school. This initiative came about after the town's only elementary school was closed down by the school board, which wanted to sell it to a private school.[66] Burrowes, a Brooklyn native and New York University student, began the summer by helping Hillard recruit the town's black residents into the HCG. Initially, some residents were cautious about joining the group and questioned the usefulness of the proposed community center, even though it intended to provide services to the community's children. To demonstrate to doubtful community residents the utility of having a community center, the HCG opened up a temporary school/child day care center out of Hillard's own house. Yet, even as Burrowes recruited parents to send their kids to the program, she recalled seeing resistance among some of them, particularly after the HCG announced that it would offer black history lessons to the children in the day care center. As Burrowes recalled, some of the residents "were like, why are you trying to start trouble," and feared the center would anger influential city officials.[67]

Eventually, Hillard and Burrowes convinced some of the residents to send their children to the child care program. They also encouraged broader community participation in the struggle to get a community center, and raised funds through a talent show and community donations. They also held community-wide hearings to gain support for their efforts and Burrowes wrote a grant to raise money for the center. After Burrowes's departure in August, the HCG was able to open up a community center. More important, its campaign became a model for surrounding communities that wanted to implement similar initiatives.[68]

About forty-five miles outside of Hobgood, North Carolina, Sean Greene, a college student from New Haven, was sent to work with the Concerned Citizens of Tillery (CCT). Led by Gary Grant, a prominent activist in the Halifax County region, the CCT was a community-based operation that organized residents around environmental justice issues, economic development, and rural health care and conducted outreach efforts directed toward at-risk youth. Although Greene directed a summer youth camp, his main responsibilities resulted in training local high school and college young people to take it over after he left and run the program for themselves.[69]

The Training Institute and organizing initiatives nurtured a collective of young people, many of whom went on to serve in important leadership positions inside the BSLN. The organizing initiatives, explained activist Darriel Hoy, offered them "the opportunity to put things into practice instead of just talking about them."[70] Perhaps the most important characteristic of those who attended the Training Institute was the diversity of the group that made up the first summer organizing campaign. Most of the young people were students from state colleges and universities, Ivy League schools and private institutions, and community colleges. A few were not in college or had fluctuated in and out of university environs. The summer organizers were also politically diverse, and although some had come to the BSLN with prior experiences in political and community organizing, others had virtually no previous involvement in these types of activities.[71] Rather than hindering the group, the BSLN's diversity was an attribute. Countryman stated,

[It was important to] build an all-black organization based not on unanimity or uniformity, but rather on diversity; that we come from different places, from different regions, from different [social] classes, and from different ideologies, but we can work together on common stuff. And, that we have to recognize that there isn't one way to be black, or one black experience, there are multiple experiences . . . [and] that we struggled through this question over how do you, what does it mean to be a black organization to work together when we we're so different from each other.[72]

The belief in collective leadership, developing the capacity of people to lead for themselves, and organizational diversity and uniformity clearly reflected Baker's philosophical influence on BSLN. In addition to mobilizing young people into its organization and implementing an organized campaign, the BSLN leadership worked hard to make this philosophy more than just a utopian idea of how young people could participate in social change. To a large extent, the network was successful in 1992 because of its strategic emphasis on "developing organizing skills and tactics to respond to the conditions that people face in their lives."[73] By taking this type of approach, BSLN's leadership gave less attention to emphasizing a hard "ideological line" as a primary motive in guiding this organization. This was a purposeful approach and reflected an attempt to avoid the pitfalls that forced many student and youth groups in the late 1980s to disintegrate.

Shortcomings and New Developments of the BSLN's Mobilizing Efforts

Despite the successes that the BSLN experienced in 1992, it still lacked a political program. Countryman attributed this weakness to the organization's decentralized structure and the belief that BSLN summer organizers would go back to their own communities and initiate their own programs. Yet this never happened in the formal way that the BSLN leadership expected because the organization was too weak organizationally and lacked the resources to extend its efforts beyond the summer months. In 1992, the BSLN did not have a field organizing team to coordinate follow-up activities, nor did it have an action plan to assist the summer organizers throughout the academic school year.

While the BSLN was busy mobilizing students during its first two years, BCCC members struggled with putting their organization together. Contributing to the struggles of the Crusade was that it did not have a permanent national coordinator for its first couple of years in operation. Despite the outreach activities of the BCCC Steering Committee, Edelman essentially coordinated the organization for the first three years. Angela Glover Blackwell, a well-respected activist and the founder of the Urban Strategies Council in Oakland, California, volunteered to coordinate the BCCC in 1993, but only on an interim basis. Yet she was removed from the BCCC's central office located at the CDF's headquarters in Washington, D.C., and was not privy to the organizational demands that BSLN director Steven White had to face on a day-to-day basis.

An additional problem with the BCCC during its first three years was that it lacked a strong administrative staff infrastructure and field organizers who could support its working and steering committees. Most staff members were on the CDF payroll or divided their time between their regular work demands at non-CDF agencies. To help increase the staff, Blackwell and BSLN members "lobbied for the incorporation of Ella Baker [Child Policy Training Institute] graduates into field staff positions."[74] In 1994 BCCC local initiatives coordinator Otis Johnson of the Savannah-Chatham (Georgia) Youth-Futures organization urged BCCC's faithful supporters to formalize its structure in more concrete terms, so that it could effectively carry out its programs. Johnson insisted that the BCCC needed to build a strong support base among local leaders who were willing to merge the BCCC's agenda with their own. He urged the Working Committee to meet at least twice a year, in January and July, and for the Steering Committee to conduct quarterly meetings.[75] These concerns were deliberated the previous year at the annual BCCC meeting in Santa Fe, New Mexico, but they went largely unresolved.[76] Johnson went a step further in an organizational position paper and added that a "comprehensive evaluation plan" of the BCCC was necessary for it to "track the process of implementation and the outcomes that result from BCCC activities."[77] He believed that even though the BCCC collaborated with other civil rights groups, it needed its own identity and should distinguish itself from other civil rights groups.

A couple of months after the 1992 summer initiative came to a close, the BSLN, its young adult advisory board, and other key allies met to develop a broader vision and program for the organization.[78] Organized by Keith Jennings, an informal advisor to the BSLN and the former divestment movement leader, the African American Young Adult Leadership (AAYAL) meeting took place between November 20 and 22, 1992 at the Martin Luther King, Jr. Center for Nonviolent Social Change and at Pascal's Hotel in Atlanta, Georgia. The meeting had the potential to provide the BSLN with a concrete agenda for improving the black predicament.

The meeting participants divided into five working groups that issued position papers on education, health care, the criminal justice system and violence, progressive economic development, and social, economic, and political empowerment.[79] For example, the Health Care Working Group maintained that successful national health care legislation needed the input from grassroots leaders and health care activists who were drawn from community-based health programs.[80] The Progressive Economic Development Working Group supported the establishment of economic institutions in impoverished black communities such as financial literacy programs and community-based credit unions.

The meeting participants identified strongly with the group-centered leadership philosophy that emerged from the EBCPTI and "reject[ed] the autocratic, command-control leadership model," which they believed disabled black organizations.[81] They believed that a progressive black agenda needed to challenge the black leadership establishment regarding its views on gender relations, black family formation, and homophobia.[82] Finally, reflecting their disappointments in the inability and unwillingness of black electoral leadership to advance programs that could ameliorate poverty and other forms of oppression, the group insisted that movement politics was essential to a progressive black agenda.

The AAYAL meeting provided BSLN's leadership with an opportunity to develop a constituency that was independent of the BCCC and that extended beyond its traditional student base. In many respects, the meeting resembled the NAACP's Amenia Conference held in 1933. Similar to the Amenia Conference attendees, the AAYAL consisted mostly of young adult organizers and intellectuals between the ages of twenty-five and thirty-five, who, despite their middle-class orientations, had firm commitments to progressive social and political agency.[83]

While the 1933 Amenia Conference helped to propel the NAACP to establish a youth council, the AAYAL meeting produced few results. Although the group planned to host regional meetings to expand its base, poor follow-up and the lack of resources prevented the group from turning its initial efforts into a viable organizational entity. Moreover, if they chose to spend their time and resources developing a new group, then the AAYAL attendees said they wanted to remain independent and autonomous from the CDF/BCCC/BSLN organizational structure. Jennings stated that the participants were wary about being absorbed into the BSLN and BCCC: "Some of our people were a little hesitant because we thought we were being organized into Marian Edelman's thing. And, we weren't going for that because that wasn't the purpose of the meeting. . . . We were not seeking to become part of the BSLN or Marian Wright Edelman's activities. We were here [at the AAYAL meeting] because we wanted to give some direction to the nation."[84] As such, the group never reconciled how it was going to engage in follow-up activities given the fact that it wanted to remain independent from the BSLN and BCCC. Jennings explained, "Part of the complications of follow-up had to do with the fact that we didn't arrive at a consensus at the end about where we were going to go. . . . I think it was a lost opportunity looking back at it."[85] This was an unfortunate circumstance not only for the BSLN but also because the group had the potential to become an innovative organizational mechanism.

Notwithstanding the failure by the AAYAL to establish a permanent organization, the meeting demonstrated the utility of indigenous activists in shaping the trajectory of an existing organization. At the outset of this book, it was suggested that networks and organizations composed of experienced activists are able to assist organizations like the BSLN in developing a program, agenda, and strategies for mobilizing young people. By linking these new strategies and programs with the current political context, indigenous activists can raise the political consciousness of the young people in their movement infrastructure. The AAYAL meeting was an example of this because it assisted the BSLN's leadership cadre in developing a larger vision for its organization, and gave it greater credibility among a slightly older cadre of seasoned activists who were not part of the organization.

Conclusion

Exercising its mobilization capacity and providing leadership development to a cadre of young college-aged activists in the areas of political and community organizing were central concerns of the BSLN's leadership core. This was exhibited with its national and regional meetings, house parties, ASAWs, and leadership development institute and summer organizing initiative. These programs allowed the BSLN to serve as a vehicle for mobilizing and training black students in social and political activism. The BSLN's leadership placed as much concern on the process of how young people are mobilized as it did with the implementation of on-the-ground initiatives. For this reason, the BSLN's emphasis on collective leadership as a community and political organizing tool and philosophy, as exemplified with the EBCPTI and the North Carolina organizing initiative in 1992, stands out in the network's history. More important, the BSLN's focus on collective leadership, grassroots activism, and antibureaucratic organizational structures was an attempt to create a distinct political identity for the organization.

In 1992, there was little tension between the BSLN and its parent organizations.[86] This was because White and other BSLN influential leaders were able to effectively balance the organization's agenda within the confines of the BCCC and CDF. Also, because the BCCC's own development took longer than expected, it did not necessarily have the leverage to pressure the BSLN to dramatically alter its course. On the other hand, the BSLN's mobilization capacity gave it tremendous leverage and brought its parent organizations some legitimacy among young people.

Despite promoting an innovative approach to community organizing, the BSLN lacked a coherent political program, thus making it difficult for the organization to sustain long-term mobilization efforts. The AAYAL meeting in Atlanta, Georgia, was an attempt to develop a larger vision for organizing the black community. It also underscored the potential capacity of the BSLN, which was more clearly articulated in its grassroots initiatives from 1993 to 1996. These initiatives, such as the freedom school program, the antiviolence campaign, and locally based organizing campaigns, are discussed in the next chapter.

6

Organizing for Change

The day-in-and-day-out work of organizing is developing
leadership and helping institutional leaders build the power
that's needed to make some changes. That work looks more
like teaching, training, mentoring, and weaving together
relationships so that there is mutual accountability, trust,
and strong operational unity among the different institutions and organizations that are part of the effort.
—Tony Massengale, Watts Wellness Promotion Violence
Prevention Program, 1995[1]

When the Black Student Leadership Network (BSLN) was formed in
1991, its lead organizers wanted to develop the leadership capacity of
young social and political activists, albeit within the narrow confines of
the Black Community Crusade for Children (BCCC), and connect them
to locally based, grassroots initiatives. They also wanted to shape the
BSLN into a political force that could weigh in on national policy debates
concerning the black predicament and marginalized communities.

Yet during the BSLN's early years, as it attempted to make connections with indigenous activists, it struggled to establish a formal organizing structure that was semiautonomous of the BCCC and Children's
Defense Fund (CDF). Many of the BSLN's local organizing initiatives
were carried out by loose coalitions and networks, rather than official chapters. As a result, some of its initiatives were led by activists
loosely connected to the BSLN, but also wedded to locally based and
autonomous activist networks. Because BSLN members developed

relationships with indigenous activists, some of the affiliates struggled to make their projects appealing to local people and groups.

Another challenge involved linking BSLN's goals, objectives, and program with its local constituents, members, and affiliates. For national-level or federated organizations, this is not always an easy task since local affiliates may wish to safeguard their autonomy against the encroachment of national leadership. Groups like the BSLN need the support of local activists who are often the driving force behind national programs. These local support bases also allow a national organization such as the BSLN to recruit new members or constituents and develop alliances with existing groups and networks. However, synthesizing the goals of BSLN's national infrastructure with local affiliates was difficult because some of its initiatives fell directly under the jurisdiction of the BCCC and CDF.[2] As a result, BSLN members at the local levels were often forced to divert their attention away from community-driven projects and instead toward implementing the programs of its parent organizations.

The BSLN's experiences underscore the broader set of concerns confronting movement formations that have a national staff or governing structure, but attempt to develop decentralized, semiautonomous affiliates. These formations allow for the rapid diffusion of policy objectives, as their local affiliates can quickly mobilize constituents in various jurisdictions. Federated organizations that have decentralized structures also create what Polletta calls "free spaces," or pockets of organizing for constituents lacking status-oriented credentials. These free spaces give "unqualified" activists the opportunity to articulate grievances that may be overlooked or shunned by the national body.[3] In addition, activists can institutionalize identities and ideological preferences in local affiliates, as well as experiment with tactics that best complement the political cultures that circumscribe their organizing work.[4] For example, activists belonging to national organizations may reside in communities with rich histories of environmental justice or feminist organizing, and thus are able to embed these identity-based grievances within local affiliates.

Despite the advantages with these formations, it is common for divisions to emerge between national governing bodies and their local affiliates. As Reger suggests, affiliates may promote ideologies and identities that are distinct from their national groups.[5] Managing national organizations, deciding which local grievances deserve attention, and raising money to sustain mobilization activities also complicate movement-building activities. For groups such as the BSLN that belong to complex and hierarchically based movement infrastructures—for example, the BSLN's attachment to the BCCC/CDF umbrella—developing national or federated movement formations is even more challenging.

This chapter examines three initiatives that were instrumental to the BSLN and BCCC's outreach efforts from 1993 to 1996. First, I look at the BSLN's Summer Freedom School program, the organization's most important initiative during its six-year history. An examination of how institutional leveraging within the CDF/BCCC/BSLN infrastructure influenced the freedom school program is included in this section. This is followed with a discussion of the antiviolence and juvenile justice campaigns coordinated by the BCCC and BSLN. I then assess the BSLN's organizing activities in three regions: the New York Metro chapter, the southern regional initiatives in North and South Carolina, and the western regional activities in the San Francisco Bay Area and Los Angeles, California.[6]

The Summer Freedom School Program

The Summer Freedom School program was the BCCC and BSLN's most important initiative during its six-year history. Freedom schools, or alternative educational institutions for poor children, were popularized in the 1960s by the Student Nonviolent Coordinating Committee (SNCC) and other civil rights activists who implemented a freedom school program as part of the 1964 Freedom Summer project. Yet the notion of using alternative educational institutions as pedagogical tools of protest is probably as old as slavery and was exhibited with the labor and citizenship schools of the Southern Negro Youth Congress, the Southern Christian Leadership Conference, and Highlander Folk School.[7] The SNCC freedom schools, however, had special significance because they were instituted at the height of civil rights movement activity.

The Mississippi freedom school program was a radical popular education project. Besides politicizing the young activists who served as teachers for the program, the freedom schools encouraged the children and teenage participants to challenge the separate, unequal, and oppressive school system in Mississippi. This was articulated best by

SNCC activist Charlie Cobb, who was mainly responsible for initiating the program,[8] when he stated that the freedom schools were used to draw "the link between a rotting shack and a rotting America."[9] By the middle of the summer in 1964, the Summer Project had established forty-one freedom schools in twenty communities throughout Mississippi that enrolled over 2,100 students, with almost two hundred college students recruited to teach in the program.[10]

The prospects of utilizing the BSLN's capacity to mobilize young people to coordinate a Summer Freedom School program was actually considered by Edelman just a few months after the BSLN's founding conference. A similar initiative had already been in operation in the CDF–Marlboro County office, in her hometown of Bennettsville, South Carolina, which had a great deal of success in combating child malnutrition and teenage pregnancy. As early as September 1991, Edelman made inquiries to her staff about implementing a freedom school program. Yet Martin Rodgers, a CDF employee who participated in the BSLN's founding meeting, advised her that logistical complications made it too difficult to implement a program at the time.[11] Hence, Edelman and other crusade members delayed the creation of freedom schools until after the BSLN's first full year of operation.

Arguably, the freedom school proposal may have become more attractive to some BCCC members in 1992 and 1993 with Bill Clinton's presidential election and the growth of the Congressional Black Caucus, which doubled in size as a result of majority-minority redistricting. Because of Edelman's close ties to the Clinton administration, the BCCC was in a good position to influence national policy targeting child poverty reduction. Edelman had known the Clintons for some time due to First Lady Hillary Clinton's association with the CDF. Clinton was a CDF staff attorney and, up until the 1992 presidential campaign season, the chair of the organization's board. After Clinton's presidential victory, Edelman was on a short list of candidates for a cabinet or senior staff position in the White House.[12] The Clinton administration opted to appoint Donna Shalala, who also had been the chair of the CDF, to the cabinet post. Other BCCC stalwarts were close to the Clinton administration, including Dorothy Height and John Hope Franklin, who served as the honorary co-chairs of the organization. Height, viewed by many as the mother of the civil rights movement, was routinely recognized by figures in the Clinton administration for her commitment to civil rights. Franklin was eventually appointed to lead President Clinton's national dialogue on race. These ties to the Clinton administration allowed the CDF to secure the White House as the convening venue for the BCCC's March 1993 national gathering.

The Clinton administration outlined several legislative packages that appealed to many BCCC members and allies, as well as complemented the CDF's own initiatives. Outlined in Clinton's campaign treatise, *Putting People First: How We Can All Change America*, these policies included a national health care plan, support for child care services (e.g., Head Start, Women, Infants and Children, etc.), and a national youth service corps.[13]

Ironically, some black progressives were disturbed by Clinton's election, given his alliance with the centrist Democratic Leadership Council (DLC). In the late 1980s and continuing to the 1990s, the DLC made a concerted effort to distance the party from its traditional social welfare agenda—a strategy that further weakened the New Deal coalition.[14] Nonetheless, a presidency from the DLC wing of the Democratic Party as opposed to another four years of a Bush presidency was a winnable trade-off for many black leaders despite their concerns about the Democratic Party's shift to the right.

With the political developments resulting from the 1992 election, a few BCCC members believed that they could leverage their access to the Clinton administration and liberal Democrats. Former BCCC national director/coordinator Angela Blackwell insisted that with the Democrats' increased political power, they "were more sensitive to our issues, so we had more access."[15] With this access, BCCC members believed they could leverage resources to agitate for social change and exercise their political muscle to influence governmental officials in support of favorable social policies.

Yet after Clinton's inauguration ceremonies, there was some disagreement with the assertion that institutional leveraging was an appropriate vehicle to remedy child poverty. During an informal conversation among BCCC and BSLN members at the CDF's headquarters, Roger Wilkins criticized several BCCC members for their disinclination to pressure the Clinton administration to champion ameliorative racial and public policies. Countryman recalled this conversation vividly:

The day of the inauguration, we all sat in a meeting in CDF on E Street, in which all the big heavy hitters were there: Hugh Price and Dorothy Height, Leon Higginbotham [as well as Edelman and others]. And it was all about how we had access . . . we were going to see Hillary [Clinton]. And Roger Wilkins who had been in this stuff from the beginning and gave this incredibly prophetic speech about Clinton, in which he said, the civil rights movement made [John F.] Kennedy a great president. And if you don't get too close to these people, if you fight them, if you push them, you would make Clinton the best president we ever had. But if you're too close to them, they'll suck you up. It was incredibly prophetic. . . . Nobody wanted to talk about that, they were all mad about that.[16]

Still, with Clinton's electoral victory, Edelman proposed an innovative way to link the BSLN's mobilization efforts and the freedom school program with the U.S. Department of Agriculture's Summer Food Service Program (SFSP), an entitlement program that offers free and reduced-price lunches to children in poor communities. Despite the utility of the SFSP, in the early 1990s the program reached only about two million out of the thirteen million eligible children. Many children receiving free or reduced-price lunches from their schools during the academic year were left to go hungry during the summer months. Many families were unaware of the summer program or did not know the location of the feeding sites.[17] Social advocates were convinced that the SFSP failed to reach eligible children and families because its feeding sites were poorly administered and inoperative. In some cases, families were discouraged from sending their children to these sites because they were rumored to serve unhealthy food.

To encourage participation in SFSP, Edelman insisted that the BSLN restructure its summer organizing initiative and implement freedom schools that would also be used as feeding sites for the USDA's program. The freedom schools could then be used to "increase the public awareness of the SFSP and increase the number of children served by the program."[18] They also could be used to influence public support for the feeding program since it was up for congressional reauthorization in 1994.

In addition, the freedom schools would give the BCCC greater legitimacy at a time when it still labored to expand its reach in local communities. Blackwell said the freedom school program "brought incredible credibility to the BCCC because it was a concrete thing on the ground . . . and that communities could look to it as they began to mobilize."[19] The program essentially became the centerpiece of the BCCC and BSLN's initiatives after 1992.

The BSLN's leadership cadre was receptive to the freedom school proposal, although it forced them to abandon plans for establishing an organizing initiative in the summer of 1993 that would have replicated the previous summer's activities in North Carolina. They also believed freedom schools could enhance the group's community organizing efforts, even as far as the West Coast, especially after Edelman insisted that she wanted the Ella Baker Child Policy Training Institute (EBCPTI) to train over one hundred college-aged young people who would staff the freedom schools. The idea of linking the USDA's SFSP with BSLN-run freedom schools created an opportunity to utilize the program as a vehicle for organizing low-income families.

Yet unlike SNCC's freedom schools, which were attractive to BSLN's leadership cadre because of their strong emphasis on community organizing, the BCCC's proposal gave less attention to community organizing and focused more attention on academic and cultural enrichment. Some BCCC members believed the program should emphasize more service (academic and cultural enrichment) initiatives, and that its linkages to USDA feeding sites could serve as a model for other programs across the nation. These concerns were shared at the BCCC's summer meeting in Santa Fe, New Mexico, in July 1993. BCCC members hoped that freedom schools would be looked upon with favor by political elites and philanthropic foundations so the program could be adequately financed, and then modeled by local communities and organizations around the country. Hugh Price believed the duplication of the program would be difficult to accomplish if the freedom schools appeared to be separate and lacked definitive funding.[20]

The Santa Fe meeting participants discussed the efficacy of the freedom school curriculum and how they were going to raise funds for the program. Some BCCC members urged the group to rely upon their connections to the White House and amiable congressional leaders to find ways for funding the program. Kent Amos of the Washington, D.C.-based Urban Family Institute and a member of the Steering Committee, suggested that the BCCC should leverage public monies from the Clinton administration in innovative ways that would not threaten the CDF's nonprofit status. He proposed that BCCC members solicit cabinet secretaries "who have discretionary money available to them—as this kind of request could easily become bogged down or lost if it were routed through traditional bureaucratic channels in the federal agencies."[21] Edelman thought this strategy was worth considering as long as there was an intermediary fiscal source that could best handle the distribution of funds, while at the same time it was "accountable to a group of steering committee members."[22] As early as the summer of 1993 and thereafter, the BSLN/BCCC used the Commission on National and Community Service as an intermediary source to allocate funds to local agencies and organizations that were hosting freedom school sites. This was a fairly common strategy as grassroots organizations lobbied to get resources from the commission in order to support different programs and projects.

Another viewpoint at the Santa Fe meeting was expressed by Yale University's Ed Gordon and James Comer, both members of the BCCC's Education Committee. Comer stated that the freedom schools had the "potential to serve as focal point for mobilizing the black community," particularly around educational and economic development initiatives.[23] Gordon saw the program as a "perfect vehicle for pulling youths back into the mainstream," and for bridging the growing class divide in the black community, or, as he stated, for connecting the "functioning" elements of the black community (college students) with "nonfunctioning" segments (economically disadvantaged children and families).[24]

In addition to these deliberations, the BSLN's leadership cadre envisioned a freedom school that strongly emphasized a SNCC-style community organizing project. They wanted the schools to serve as a launching pad for a comprehensive organizing initiative. BSLN's national director, Steven White, believed that such a program would attract progressive students who might have otherwise been "turned off by just solely working on children's issues."[25] Countryman and Sullivan put together a proposal for a freedom school curriculum directed toward community organizing and advocacy, which was to be implemented by the summer organizers at each of the freedom schools sites around the country. It was designed to have the summer administrators, as well as children who benefited from the program, organize local communities to evaluate the USDA summer feeding sites around the country. It included surveys and parental evaluations of the SFSP, door-to-door outreach efforts, and meetings with newspaper editorial boards and elected officials. The proposal intended to bring attention to the problems of the feeding sites.[26]

The curriculum was ambitious and would have been difficult to execute given the demands of running a temporary school-based program. Yet, it would have accommodated the BCCC's push to develop a model program that could simultaneously support the USDA's reauthorization efforts. At the same time, the curriculum would have engaged the summer workers and freedom school attendees in what Countryman called "the politics of the community" or grassroots projects that collaborated with indigenous organizations.[27] Unfortunately, this proposal was rejected for what some believed to be CDF's angst that it would have embarrassed the USDA by exposing its poorly administered and inoperative feeding sites. The proposal was then amended without the comprehensive organizing plan. As a substitute, the BSLN's leaders focused most of the training for the summer institute on civil rights movement history, community organizing, and direct action advocacy, all of which were still based on the philosophy of collective leadership. They brought in an additional group of educators and conflict resolution specialists who assisted the summer organizers with their teaching methodology, and prepared them to adjust to the demands of working with at-risk children in the freedom schools.

Toward the end of 1993, Countryman resigned as director of the EBCPTI to continue his graduate studies, but he remained as an advisor to the BSLN. He was replaced by Helene Fisher, who was initially recruited into the BSLN by Kasey Jones, a founding member of the organization. The Howard University graduate had been involved in the 1989 protests spearheaded by Ras Baraka's Black Nia Force organization, which opposed Republican strategist Lee Atwater's appointment to Howard University's Board of Trustees. In September 1992, she helped to organize the BSLN's regional meeting in Washington, D.C. A year later, she spent most of the summer as the area coordinator for Washington's freedom schools.

As the new director of the Training Institute, Fisher believed the freedom school program could be a "tool for community change" and as "the tool for young people to be involved in building their own communities."[28] She too pushed to have community organizing and direct action as a centerpiece of the freedom school program. In December 1993 she met with Countryman, Richard Lyn-Cook, the special assistant to the institute, Dr. Edmund Gordon of the BCCC's Education Committee, and BSLN activist Wendy Killian to develop an efficacy curriculum for the freedom schools. Several models were considered for the curriculum, all of which attempted to pair academic and cultural enrichment activities with community organizing and advocacy initiatives.[29] One model considered developing two tracks for the freedom school staff and interns: one track would have young people working on community organizing initiatives, and the other working exclusively with children in the freedom schools. Another proposal insisted that freedom school organizers be incorporated "into the community mapping and advocacy work that Field Organizers have been working on year-round."[30] Although the models were never implemented, they represented the BSLN's continued commitment to expand the boundaries of the freedom school program beyond academic and cultural enrichment activities.

The debate over the freedom school program and curriculum underscored larger philosophical differences between some of the BSLN and BCCC's key leaders. These differences were hinted at in an essay by White, Sullivan, and Countryman, the most influential members of the BSLN's leadership circle. Written before the summer 1993 campaign in the BSLN's newspaper organ, *We Speak!*, and in the aftermath of the 1992 Los Angeles civil unrest,[31] the essay drew attention to class divisions in the black community, especially the marginalization of the black poor. It also indirectly targeted the BCCC and underlined the debate over the freedom school program. The essay derided "traditional black politics" and the "civil rights politics" of black leaders, such as the BCCC, for ignoring the concerns of alienated black youth and for embracing strategies that were safe, that befitted a middle-class agenda, and that had no immediate or long-term impact.[32] It scolded these leaders for neglecting what the authors believed were more transformational forms of organizing:

> Building a cross-class multi-generational movement requires that we
> recognize and confront class and generational cleavages that divide the

African-American community in the 1990's. Organizing strategies which ignore or seek to work around these cleavages inevitable [*sic*] impede our efforts to build effective broad-based political support in the black community for the policies and programs that will solve the current crisis of black youth. . . . Working-class African-Americans have long recognized that traditional civil rights organizations have not seen them as integral to their political empowerment strategies. Rather than viewing poor and working class members of our community as potential agents for social change, middle-class led organizations too often see those who are poor and less educated as constituents to be served.[33]

These observations reflected what some leading activists in the BSLN perceived to be the inclination among the BCCC to privilege institutional leveraging practices over grassroots organizing. The inclination toward institutional leveraging, as Minkoff points out, is fairly common among movement and advocacy groups that seek an institutional "niche," or a stable resource base and access to political institutions and elites.[34] The shortcoming of this approach is that it will often result in the refutation of innovative organizing strategies or opposition to militant political action.

BSLN's influential activists feared that if a community or political organizing module was not included in the freedom school training and curriculum, then the program could become a service-based initiative that did little to challenge unequal power relations. They did not want the freedom schools to be a community service program (i.e., mentoring, tutoring, volunteerism, academic enrichment, etc.) that did little to agitate for structural change. They wanted it to raise critical issues concerning social justice, child poverty, and racial inequities, as well as heighten the political consciousness of the summer organizers and the youth who benefited from the program. Yet they also understood that financial and political elites preferred community service, rather than community organizing and even advocacy, because it did not call for systemic reform to institutional racism and poverty.

As part of its framing strategy, the BSLN frequently used the concept "service advocacy" to define their initiatives and mediate the tensions between activists and elites, who were favorable to either service or volunteer activities. Service advocacy attempts to synthesize service-related activism with community organizing and direct action. It attempts to link service such as tutoring and mentoring programs with oppositional politics and social change initiatives. Nicole Johnson, a freedom school site coordinator in Oakland and member of BSLN National Coordinating Committee, said a service advocacy approach can "provide you with access to folks" who could not advocate for themselves, which can "ultimately create a larger campaign then just service or just advocacy."[35] Social justice organizations have also utilized this activism to capture resources and withstand attacks from conservatives.[36]

The concern about service-related activism was further highlighted by BSLN allies who attended President Bill Clinton's Summer of Service training in June 1993. Summer of Service grew out of Clinton's campaign promise to develop a national youth opportunity corps that would resemble a contemporary New Deal–style Civilian Conservation Corps or VISTA program. This national program intended to replicate similar job corps and youth service programs that had already been established in some states. The college-aged young people who participated in Clinton's national youth opportunity corps were designated to work in different projects throughout the summer and school year, some of which included tutoring and teaching in urban schools, building houses for the homeless, and other community service programs. In exchange, they were eligible to receive financial and educational assistance for their work.[37]

Although Clinton's plan for a youth opportunity corps was well received within liberal circles, almost from the start, congressional Republicans opposed it. Clinton countered by initiating a pilot program, the Summer of Service, in 1993. Summer of Service was a precursor to the AmeriCorps program, which was the "programmatic centerpiece" of the National and Community Service Act of 1993.[38]

The Summer of Service of 1993 and the related AmeriCorps program provided resources to local organizations to hire staff support. Local groups involved in antipoverty work were eligible for assistance from AmeriCorps to pay for young staff to work in their programs throughout the year. Without these resources, it would have been difficult for many groups to sustain their programs. Within BSLN circles, many publicly praised the youth service initiative because it provided summer employment for young people. As a result of the BCCC's connections to the White House, the BSLN was allowed to send some of its staff members to lobby the Clinton administration on behalf of this program. When the Summer of Service and AmeriCorps programs were enacted in 1993, the BSLN and BCCC were then able to use the funds provided by these programs to help pay for some organizers to staff the freedom schools.

Notwithstanding these advantages, BSLN members raised concerns about the program's utility as a vehicle for social change and poverty reduction. These concerns were expressed at the national training session for the Summer of Service program held at San Francisco's Treasure Island. The session brought together one thousand young people from around the country, including BSLN freedom school organizers.

BSLN organizers, especially the New York freedom school contingent, criticized the Summer of Service program for its paternalism and the exclusion of blacks and Latinos at the senior staff level. Despite the fact that most of the participants were of color, AmeriCorps senior staff were mostly white and the training did not include any strategies for addressing systemic inequalities that debilitated poor communities of color. Toya Lillard and Adrianne Garden-Vazquez, an activist representing the Brooklyn-based youth program El Puente, shared these concerns in a rousing statement before the training participants. They stated, "We feel that it is inconsistent for a program whose participant base is 86% People of Color (POC) to have little or no representation at the decision-making level."[39] The statement reflected what often happens when people of color are excluded from designing projects that impact their own communities.

After the Summer of Service, Countryman and Sullivan levied their own criticisms toward the community service movement and the AmeriCorps program. Similar to Lillard and Garden-Vazquez's criticisms, their commentary charged the service community with two weaknesses: "1) the underrepresentation of young people of color and young people from working-class and poor backgrounds in the leadership of most of the nationally recognized service organizations; and 2) the failure to develop strategies that seek to solve the problems caused by persistent poverty, rather than just meeting the immediate needs of poor people."[40] A larger worry of the Summer of Service and Ameri-Corps programs was whether they (and similar programs) would lead to the demobilization of a potential base of young activists who were willing to embrace more radical alternatives to ameliorating poverty. Another worry was that the AmeriCorps program circumscribed social activism among young people by privileging organizations that did not agitate for social change.

Freedom Schools, 1994–1996

After the summer of 1994, many community organizing components of the freedom school curriculum that were present from 1992 to 1994 were taken out of the Training Institute's two-week training. A freedom school curriculum team was created, comprising BSLN and BCCC members, which was responsible for developing training sessions and curricula focusing on academic and cultural enrichment. The freedom school program began to look more like the CDF–Marlboro County's summer enrichment program and the age requirements for the participants in the freedom school program. Whereas the 1993 and 1994 Summer Freedom School program accepted youth under eighteen years of age, beginning in 1995 the participants could be no older than twelve.

Despite these changes, the freedom schools aided the BSLN's recruitment of young people. With the BCCC and CDF's backing, the BSLN opened freedom school sites in a dozen cities throughout the country. All the summer organizers were required to attend the BSLN's organizing school. As a result, about 150 college-aged students participated in the institute and freedom schools in the summer of 1993 and over 200 participated the following year. With the implementation of the freedom schools and the BSLN's expansion in 1993 and 1994, its national conference attracted about 400 attendees by 1994. The freedom school program also allowed the BSLN to recruit young people into its organization who were less politically sophisticated than some of the organization's leaders, but were attracted to the program's focus on children.[41] This gave the BSLN members an opportunity to politicize through the institute young people who otherwise may not have been introduced to community organizing.

Still, even though the freedom schools had many positive attributes, it faced several challenges in their first two years of operation. One challenge was coordinating freedom schools with local agencies, community organizations, and churches, which were required to help raise funds for the costs of the program and summer organizers. Because the costs of running a freedom school amounted to tens of thousands of dollars, they were generally limited only to communities and organizations that had the capacity and local support networks to run and help raise the funds for the program.[42] For instance, BSLN members debated with Edelman over the implementation of a freedom school program in Raleigh, North Carolina, in 1994. Although there was strong community interest, the local organizations and agencies did not have enough resources to establish one. Sullivan made an appeal to Edelman for additional monetary resources to support freedom school sites in Raleigh. Edelman, on the other hand, suggested that a community organization or agency's ability to raise the funds was demonstrative of its willingness to establish an effective program. Steven White intervened in what was a tense conversation between Edelman and Sullivan over the Raleigh site and said it was necessary to support the efforts of local groups in the city to establish freedom schools. White maintained that North Carolina was "one of the strongest places in terms of a student base and activities from the beginning of the project until now."[43] To not have a freedom school site, he argued, would seriously hinder its activities in the area.

Another concern was that, in some locales, the summer organizers received little assistance from sponsoring organizations or had to compete with entrenched organizations for the same children to participate in the program. In addition, the organizers were unprepared to deal with the emotional distress, violence, and abuse experienced by many children in the program.[44] Most of the organizers were college students or college-age young adults (under twenty-five years old), and the problems experienced by freedom school children required far greater attention from experienced health care professionals, social workers, and counselors.

A third problem was that at the end of the summer there were few resources dedicated to continuing local initiatives that had been jump-started a few months earlier in the communities that had freedom school sites. The BSLN did not adequately capitalize on the resource pool of college-age young people who were recruited into the program. Once the summer ended, many young people left their freedom school sites and were given little direction by BSLN's leadership on how to engage in related initiatives throughout the academic school year.

Although some freedom schools, such as those in Oakland, San Francisco, and Washington, D.C., had year-round after-school programs, most sites around the country closed down once the summer came to an end. Kim Davis, the site coordinator of the Norfolk, Virginia, freedom schools in 1994, said "that one of the main issues that the program overall had to really address was the continuity piece. It's one thing to bring in folks that could do effective summer programs. But it's another thing when everyone you bring has to leave."[45] She was disappointed with the absence of postsummer initiatives, especially after her freedom school participants initiated a voter education drive and letter writing campaign to secure reauthorization of the SFSP.

The BCCC and BSLN'S Antiviolence Campaign

One of the BCCC and BSLN's most important campaigns targeted gun violence in the 1990s. The campaign attempted to mobilize young people and local organizations to oppose gun violence through youth speak-outs, community forums, teach-ins, workshops, and protest marches. Another goal was to mobilize these constituencies to support gun control measures and oppose draconian crime policies.

From the mid-1980s to the mid-1990s, many black communities were ravaged by gun violence, and youth were among the hardest hit group. Katherine McFate commented, "What ha[d] changed is the age of the homicide victims and perpetrators,"[46] as firearm death rates among black youth increased dramatically during this period. Among blacks between the ages of fifteen and nineteen, firearm deaths increased from a little over 700 in 1985 to over 2,200 in 1993 (an increase of 214 percent), and for those between the ages of fifteen and twenty-four, gun-related homicide was the leading cause of death.[47]

The increase in gun violence occurred as many jobless and underemployed youth became involved in the culture of drug activity, particularly with the proliferation of crack cocaine. The communities with high levels of gun violence also had the highest rates of poverty, unemployment and underemployment. These communities were adversely impacted by the deindustrialization that began in the early 1970s, the loss of blue-collar skilled jobs, the tightening of the labor market, and the devolution policies and cutbacks in social welfare programs that became so prominent under the Reagan-Bush administrations.[48] Invariably, young people from impoverished and alienated communities were the most likely to fall prey to the drug culture and gun violence.

Another concern by the BCCC was the role that gun manufacturing industries played in contributing to this crisis. BCCC members were advised on this issue by the Violence Policy Center, a Washington, D.C., advocacy group that lobbies for the regulation of the firearms industry.[49] The marketing strategy of the major gun manufacturing industries was outlined by Josh Sugarmann and Kristen Rand in *Cease Fire: A Comprehensive Strategy to Reduce Firearms Violence*. The authors claimed that nonwhite young people were targeted by gun manufacturing industries in order to boost slumping gun sales after 1983: "Eventually it became clear that the slump [in gun sales] stemmed from saturation of the primary market of white males. . . . The 1983 handgun slump taught the industry that it could not take sales for granted and forced its members to rethink how they marketed their product. . . . The firearms industry decided to: Expand the market beyond white males with the new target markets being women and youth. A niche marketing plan was undertaken similar to that employed by cigarette and alcohol manufacturers."[50] The outcome of this marketing strategy was an increase in gun manufacturing and production, especially of high-caliber weapons that were bought and, in many instances, resold illegally on the street. For example, the production of nine millimeter handguns increased from 36,000 in 1975 to over 400,000 in 1989. By 1983, the demand for and production of nine millimeter handguns had actually reached a low point at 14,848, almost a 60 percent drop from the 1975 level, yet it peaked in 1994 when output of this weapon rose to almost 650,000.[51] Whether gun manufacturing industries intentionally targeted nonwhite youth for gun distribution, as Sugarmann and Rand contend, is debatable and perhaps will never be fully verified. Nonetheless, the point remains that the rise in gun production significantly contributed to the rise of illegal gun resales on the street. The combined increase of gun production and the participation of blacks in the drug culture contributed to the unprecedented increase of gun violence among black youth.

These trends convinced the CDF and BCCC to develop a strategy for reducing gun violence among youth, while connecting this effort to ameliorative juvenile justice policies. The BCCC devoted two of its constituency task forces to combating this epidemic. The BCCC's Juvenile and Family Court Judges Leadership Council, initially coordinated by Fulton County (Georgia) Juvenile Court judge Glenda Hatchett Johnson, concentrated on legal issues concerning children in the juvenile and child welfare systems.[52] The group's Anti-Violence Task Force (AVTF) originated out of the Anti-Violence Network that met at the BCCC's March 1993 conference. Attending the conference were "some 100 anti-violence experts—people who run community-based and grass roots violence prevention organizations, programmatic and policy experts who presented violence prevention curricula in the schools."[53] The AVTF comprised social workers, health care professionals, academicians, religious leaders, grassroots organizers, and policymakers. More than any other BCCC task force, it had a direct connection to grassroots organizations working in impoverished communities.

The antiviolence campaign was concerned about two other phenomena during this period. The first was the emergence of what some criminologists called the "super-predators" image, initially popularized by criminologist John Dilulio in an essay in the *Weekly Standard* titled "The Coming of the Super-Predators."[54] In the essay, he conjured images of menacing youth or bogeymen emerging in the United States, who were young, uncontrollable, committed to a life of crime, and on the verge of destroying the moral fabric of the United States. This characterization projected young offenders (presumably black males) as remorseless, hardened criminals who were responsible for widespread social mayhem that could be stopped only by zero-tolerance policies.[55] Social advocates, including the BCCC, contended that the "super-predators" characterization targeted youth of color and was reinforced by daily news reports that portrayed them as criminals. Furthermore, the "super-predators" image exacerbated racial resentment, prejudices, and fears about uncontrollable, violent black and Latino youth.

Some policies advanced as immediate solvents to the "super-predators" phenomenon were harsher prison sentences, putting more police officers on the street, and the death penalty for juveniles. Symptomatic of these policies was the congressional debate over the Omnibus Crime Bill in 1993 and 1994. Interestingly, the initial crime bill intended to set aside a large amount of funds for crime prevention measures in cities hard hit by crime.[56] Much of this came about through the lobbying efforts of groups such as the BCCC's AVTF. As early as 1993, the AVTF attended congressional hearings and convened meetings with Senators Christopher Dodd (D-CT) and Paul Simon (D-IL) and other government officials, lobbying them to include the "Ounce of Prevention Fund" in an early draft of the legislation. This provision intended to distribute funds to community groups to implement crime prevention programs.[57] Despite the lobbying, many of the social spending measures were excluded from the final version of the bill due to the opposition of Republicans and moderate Democrats.[58] To the dismay of social advocates, the final version of the 1994 Crime Bill (officially called the Violent Crime Control and Law Enforcement Act) included mandatory-minimum sentencing guidelines and funds for prison construction.[59]

In actuality, the Crime Bill symbolized an overall shift away from social spending and toward zero-tolerance policies that were first implemented at the state and local levels in the 1980s. The BSLN's allies opposed these measures as early as November 1992 at the Young Adult Leadership Meeting in Atlanta, Georgia. At this meeting, the Criminal Violence and Justice Working Group criticized U.S. drug policy for disproportionately targeting young blacks for imprisonment and police abuse. The group called for more judicious measures that reduced weapons proliferation, dedicated resources for crime prevention and youth development programs, and encouraged police officers to "reside in the communities in which they work."[60] It also approved organizing campaigns against media outlets that negatively characterized African Americans as criminals.

The BSLN mobilized opposition to the Crime Bill when it surfaced as a major issue leading up to the 1994 congressional elections. At the National Rainbow Coalition's three-day national summit in Washington, D.C., in January 1994, Errol James of the BSLN's National Coordinating Committee (NCC) and a member of the Harlem Writers Crew told the group that an urban policy agenda and jobs program could reduce gun violence.[61] At the summit, the Rainbow Coalition outlined a grassroots campaign to deter young people away from crime and violence by connecting them with family, church, and school institutions. Rev. Jesse Jackson promised to recruit college students to provide tutoring to those in jail and to initiate mentoring programs for youth at one hundred churches in one hundred cities.[62] Jackson then announced a

mobilization campaign against gun violence led by the Rainbow Coalition and other community groups on the anniversary of Dr. Martin
Luther King, Jr.'s assassination.

After the summit, the BSLN, in coordination with the BCCC,
launched its own National Day of Action Against Violence (NDAAV)
in over forty cities. The initiatives were held on April 4, 1994, the
twenty-sixth commemorative observance of King's assassination. The
day was chosen to highlight the importance of antiviolence direct
action campaigns (and the theme of King's commitment to nonviolent
direct action) in combating gun violence. The activities included youth
speak-outs, parent and community meetings, letter writing campaigns,
and informing the community about the importance of combating gun
violence and the adverse impact of the Crime Bill.[63] Notwithstanding
the NDAAV activities, the Crime Bill was passed with the inclusion of
draconian measures that negatively impacted poor black youth.

After the passage of the Crime Bill, the BCCC launched its Safe
Start *Cease the Fire!* initiative in seventeen cities. This public education
and media campaign was coordinated by Enola Aird, the BCCC's acting director and the former chair of the Commission on Children in
Connecticut. The initiative recruited religious leaders, child advocates,
grassroots leaders, and community-based groups for a media advocacy
campaign targeting commercial and cable television for public service
announcements about social consciousness, prevention programs, and
gun control measures.[64] Drawing from the work of Dr. Deborah Prothrow-Stith, a medical professional who worked in a Boston emergency
room during the height of youth violence, the campaign insisted that
violence was a public health issue.[65]

The BSLN organized another NDAAV in April 1995 and assisted
with the *Cease the Fire!* campaign. Malkia Lydia, an NCC member, joined the student advisory board for the Corporation for Public Broadcasting "to help launch a national media campaign in 1995
to reduce youth violence."[66] In North Carolina, BSLN members
were "invited to join the advisory board of the local public station
to plan a town meeting—to be broadcast live—on violence featur-
ing youths from around the state."[67] In 1996, the BSLN organized its
third NDAAV and merged this initiative with its voter mobilization
activities. As part of the NDAAV, BSLN members sponsored voter

education and registration drives in coordination with activists, fraternities and sororities, clubs, and other organizations. This effort blossomed into a coalition called Black Youth Vote, which had the "purpose of changing the way youth participate in society politically."[68] The BSLN's voter mobilization campaign encouraged young people to choose the "ballot over the bullet" and urged them to register and vote for candidates who supported their agenda of advocating for social prevention policies that helped to curb gun violence.[69]

BSLN activists also organized teach-ins, student gatherings on high school and college campuses, intergenerational mass meetings, heal-ins, and community forums on police brutality.[70] Midwest regional field organizer Naomi Walker organized a "Stop the Violence" conference attended by 150 high school students in Columbus, Ohio. At the conference the students developed an antiviolence agenda, which was then presented to city officials. In St. Paul, Minnesota, field organizer Kelli Doss organized a citywide candlelight vigil at a local church, and BSLN members coordinated a letter writing campaign to elected officials in North Carolina urging them to support gun control laws.[71] Similar activities occurred in two dozen cities throughout the country.

The BCCC and BSLN's antiviolence campaign helped to shape the dialogue in many communities concerning race, incarceration, and crime. The BCCC and BSLN received support from local activists who had been engaged in crime prevention initiatives long before both groups were formed. Thus, both groups had a credible network of indigenous activists from which they could draw. In New York, Geoffrey Canada of the prominent community-based group the Rheedlen Centers for Children and Families helped to coordinate antiviolence efforts. The BCCC received additional backing from Joe Marshall of the San Francisco–based Omega Boys Club, an antiviolence group that offers survival skills to impoverished youth. A total of 120 community organizers, social policy and health care experts, and social advocates assisted the campaign through the BCCC's AVTF. The BCCC and BSLN both agreed that antiviolence initiatives were necessary to curb the growing public health epidemics and the harsh criminal and juvenile justice polices that penalized black and Latino youths. The BSLN had ground troops to carry out the initiatives, while the BCCC offered social visibility to BSLN members through its media campaign, and by acquainting them with key government officials and social advocates who were critical to the antiviolence campaign.

By 1994, gun violence homicides among young blacks saw a slight decrease, and between 1995 and 1996, this number declined by almost 23 percent.[72] A number of factors contributed to this trend, including an expanding economy and a slowing demand for guns. However, it is important to underscore the efforts of numerous local organizations and activist networks as well as national groups, such as the BCCC/BSLN contingent, which also contributed to this declining trend.

The BSLN and Local-Level Organizing

Organizing local communities was the central focus of the BCCC and BSLN's antiviolence campaign. The BSLN members, in particular, served as the foot soldiers for carrying out this campaign. Because the BSLN had few monetary resources allocated to local-level organizing, their initiatives relied extensively on intangible resources such as the commitment, time, energy, and consciousness-raising activities of indigenous activists allied with the organization. These resources are useful for recruiting new members or allies, creating group solidarity, and bridging the interests of younger and older activists.[73]

Young people who participated in the BSLN's local organizing efforts were recruited into the organization through the Summer Freedom School program and regional meetings. Others belonged to indigenous organizations that joined forces with the BCCC and BSLN, and had jump-started antiviolence initiatives before the BSLN's campaign. In addition to the antiviolence initiatives, BSLN members were engaged in an impressive and often contentious array of activities throughout the United States. The last part of this chapter focuses on these activities in New York/Northeast region, the Southern region, and the Western region.

New York/Northeast Region

The BSLN had affiliates in Poughkeepsie, Harlem, and Brooklyn, New York. In Poughkeepsie, BSLN members established an affiliate at Vassar College. The chapter had a multiracial membership base of a dozen students who ran an after-school tutoring program in a nearby housing project.[74] They also developed an alliance with incarcerated persons at the Green Haven Correctional Facility, a maximum-security institution in Poughkeepsie. The incarcerated persons even raised over $900 for the BSLN's tutoring program.[75] The campus-prison alliance was actually formalized decades earlier with the creation of the Vassar Green Haven Prison Program. Africana studies professor Lawrence Mamiya was instrumental in building this program and bridging the divide between the campus and the prison.

The first freedom school in New York was established in 1993 in collaboration with the Rheedlen Centers for Children and Families. Rheedlen was a prominent youth advocacy group led by Geoffrey Canada, a superbly gifted organizer and advocate whose organization also served as BCCC's eastern regional office. These attributes helped to enhance the visibility of the Rheedlen Centers, creating a safe haven for young people in Harlem. Long after the BSLN's collapse, Canada gained national acclaim for creating the Harlem's Children Zone, a holistic community-based initiative that provides comprehensive educational, wrap-around, and preventive programs to neighborhood families and children. Children Zone established Canada as one of the country's dynamic urban educators.[76]

Although Canada was a significant figure inside of the BCCC's circle, he had complicated relationship with some BSLN members who believed he was overly protective of the Rheedlen Centers' autonomy. Tensions between Canada and BSLN members surfaced as early as the summer of 1993. After the BSLN's national staff selected the organizers for the four freedom school sites in Harlem, Canada expressed concern about having minimal input in the decisions considering that his organization offered space, administrative support, and facilitation for the program.[77] This sullied relations between Canada and some members of the national staff, which received several complaints from Harlem freedom school workers about their experiences with Canada. Despite this tension, the summer workers and the children who attended the freedom schools worked on the passage of the Family Preservation and Support Services Act of 1993, which provided funding for child welfare services and programs for at-risk youth.[78]

Another affiliate was the New York Metro chapter, located in Brooklyn. The political orientations of the affiliate were influenced by the Central Brooklyn Partnership (CBP), a grassroots organization founded in 1989 by Mark Griffith and Errol T. Louis located in the Bedford-Stuyvesant and Crown Heights areas of Brooklyn. A couple of years later, Griffith and Louis established an offshoot of the CBP called the Central Brooklyn Credit Union, an economic development institution that provided financial literacy to neighborhood residents. The credit union had 2,500 neighborhood investors and provided banking services and loans to its members.[79]

The BSLN's emergence in Central Brooklyn occurred at the time when conditions were ripe for activism. Two years before the Metro chapter's founding conference, in August 1991, civil unrest broke out in the Crown Height's section of Brooklyn, after a seven-year old Guyanese boy was killed by a car driven by a Hasidic Jewish scholar. After police officers released the driver, a group of blacks participated in a revenge killing of a visiting rabbinical student. The incidents sparked three days of civil unrest between the two groups in the Crown Heights neighborhood that resulted in scores of injured and arrested people.[80] Several New York Metro members were involved in the organizing efforts around the Crown Heights incident, including Mark Griffith, Errol Louis, and Sean Joe, a member of the Crown Heights Youth Collective.

CBP/Central Brooklyn Credit Union was a gathering place for young blacks politicized by the Crown Heights unrest, as well as BSLN members and other activists from the Bedford-Stuyvesant, Crown Heights, and Fort Greene sections of the borough. In 1993, Griffith and other activists organized the New York Metro chapter's founding conference at the Borough of Manhattan Community College. The BSLN's association to the CBP gave it a strong indigenous community organization that reinforced its local initiatives.

One project that gave the Metro chapter tremendous credibility was its Nia NuArts Liberation School. The school was the brainchild of BSLN member Dorothy Chavannes and became a mechanism for educating low-income children and politicizing young volunteers in the program.[81] The program had after-school and weekend components, and children from housing developments in the Central Brooklyn area were recruited into the program.

The Peoples' Community Feeding Program was another project of the Metro chapter. Marie Marthol worked closely with Kamau Franklin (aka Karl Franklin), as well as several students associated with Hunter College's Black Student Union, to start the program. Soon after the program was established, Marthol and Franklin joined the Metro chapter and worked closely with the CBP. This allowed them to continue the feeding program, which the BSLN took over and became "the foster parent of it kind of by default."[82] The feeding program was patterned after a similar project implemented by the African Descendants Awareness Movement, a Harlem-based organization that administered a feeding site in front of the Apollo Theater. Unlike the SFSP, which operated out of BSLN's freedom school sites, the program was coordinated and paid for through in-kind contributions from churches.[83]

The feeding program was a testament to the Metro chapter's organizing efforts and its attempt to "create standing programs," as Marthol recalled.[84] It helped the Metro chapter establish credibility among local activists and organizations, some of which were suspicious of the BSLN's attachment to the CDF and BCCC. Of note, the program challenged some of the young people who were used to intellectualizing about the ills facing low-income black communities to actually become engaged in a social change initiative.[85]

The Metro chapter consisted of two dozen committed volunteers. An additional group of young people, who were not part of the BSLN, worked closely with the organization through its feeding program and liberation school. The Metro chapter increased its visibility by developing alliances and coalitions with student and youth groups throughout New York City and on college campuses. For example, the Nia NuArts Liberation School grew out of a coalition between the Metro chapter, the Black Student Union of Hunter College, and the Network of Underground Artists. These organizations formed the Nia Youth Collective to develop the critical thinking and community organizing skills of young people.[86]

Azabache was another coalition that BSLN members joined in 1996. Cofounded by Lumumba Bandele, a respected organizer from the Manhattan Caribbean Cultural Center, Azabache attempted to address the concerns of black and Latino youth emerging out of the civil unrests in Crown Heights and Washington Heights.[87] The coalition represented groups throughout New York, including Alianza Dominicana of Washington Heights, the Malcolm X Grassroots Movement organization, the Student Power Network, El Puente of Brooklyn, and Harlem's Brotherhood organization.

While coalition building helped the Metro chapter create standing programs and establish credibility within activist circles, it uncovered sharp ideological differences that existed within the Metro chapter. These tensions manifested themselves in minor but peculiar ways. In Azabache, the group debated whether to invite young whites to join the organization.[88] Members of the Nia Youth Collective also debated the name of its alternative school. Some members wanted to name it the Nia NuArts "Freedom School." However, the organization's most radical members wanted to name it the Nia NuArts "Liberation School" after the Black Panther Party's alternative school. After much debate, the group decided on the "liberation" designation.

Some Metro chapter members, as well as others inside of the Nia Youth Collective, criticized the BSLN for having "reformist ideals" and for consisting of "bourgeois or semi-bourgeois students."[89] They pushed the BSLN to embrace a more radical orientation. Burrowes, who was appointed as the New York field organizer in 1995, recalled that there was constant discussion about whether the BSLN "should be hardline one way or the other" in terms of its ideological orientation.[90] Kamau Franklin was the most persistent on this issue and infused a revolutionary nationalist fervor within the affiliate. He wanted the BSLN to offer a more ardent criticism of capitalism and reformist approaches to social change. This was a challenge for the BSLN because many of its members lacked a radical ideological approach to community organizing.

The ideological tensions did not necessarily hinder the BSLN from establishing concrete programs, but they turned some of the young people away from participating in its initiatives. On the other hand, the ideological debates actually helped to separate those who were committed activists from those who generally talked about social and political action, but did not necessarily do the work. Marthol stated, "[The ideological debates] actually needed to happen and was helpful to us. . . . [They] helped us to sort our priorities; like why are we doing this. What's your motivation and what do you expect to come out of it. . . . It also, I think, kind of separated out people who were just ideologues and not necessarily ready to do all the work from those who may not have had their own political ideologies sorted out . . . but wanted to work with kids."[91] Interestingly, the ideological divisions in Brooklyn were tensions that BSLN activists tried to avoid at its founding conference and early organizational meetings. In Brooklyn, this was difficult to do because the BSLN members established several successful initiatives that brought together a diverse group of young people. Inevitably, this diversity was going to lead to some tensions.

As the Metro chapter established ties with local activists, it was faced with the pressures of balancing the larger national goals of its organization with the needs, concerns, and ideological underpinnings of its local constituents. In 1995, the BSLN began organizing around voter education in preparation for the 1996 election cycle. The campaign was part of the BSLN's Citizenship 2000 proposal developed by Jenice View, an expert in the pedagogy of popular education. This was "a basic civics and advocacy curriculum designed to encourage young adults (ages 18–30) to become active participants in the local and national decision-making process."[92] The BSLN's national program on voter registration/education received mixed results in Brooklyn. Some activists were apprehensive about engaging in a full-scale voter education and registration campaign because they believed that it might co-opt their more militant and radical elements. The Metro chapter activists were more concerned about finding ways to engage young people in a more radical transformation of the political system. Also, the decades-long experiences of dealing with neglectful politicians, many of whom were black, discouraged some Metro chapter activists from engaging in electioneering activities.

Other members of the Brooklyn affiliate welcomed the electoral work. Celena Green helped to coordinate the Metro chapter's voter education and registration campaign and set a goal of registering one thousand young people in the New York area.[93] Others organized against prospective mayor Rudy Giuliani's mayoral campaign in Brooklyn.[94] Still, the concerns over Citizenship 2000 pointed to the BSLN's difficulties with implementing a national agenda within a local affiliate like the Metro chapter. This local affiliate had an autonomous, indigenous constituency base that had already developed its own agenda and programs.

The strain between the BSLN's national agenda and New York constituency surfaced when the CDF announced its Stand for Children campaign in 1996 in opposition to the Welfare Reform Bill (Personal Responsibility and Work Opportunity Reconciliation Act of 1996). As discussed in the next chapter, the culmination of the Stand for Children mobilization campaign was a protest march in June 1996 consisting of children and child and youth advocates. Although it was led by the CDF, the BCCC and BSLN mobilized grassroots activists and organizers in support of the march.

While the Stand for Children mobilization campaign had good intentions, it forced the BSLN members to redirect their energies away from local initiatives and toward the CDF's efforts to combat welfare reform. In New York, Harlem BSLN activists backed the Stand for Children campaign because of their association with the Rheedlen Centers and its affiliation with the BCCC. However, in Brooklyn, the initiative was not well received by the Metro chapter and its allied groups. When the Stand for Children campaign began, the chapter had been assisting the National Congress of Puerto Ricans and other left-oriented groups, underground groups, and street gangs in organizing for Racial Justice Day (RJD), an annual event protesting police brutality and other issues related to racism and oppression. Leading up to an RJD meeting, Burrowes invited a representative from the Harlem affiliate to the discussion. Before the meeting, she informed the representative that RJD activists would be lukewarm to the CDF's Stand for Children. To RJD activists, the Stand for Children initiative had not gained credibility within their circles and any discussion of merging the two events could sully relations between the activists and the Metro chapter. Even so, the Harlem affiliate urged the RJD organizers to embrace the Stand for Children mobilization efforts. As a result, Burrowes recalled that event organizers "wouldn't even let us speak at Racial Justice Day even though we had organized several organizations to be there."[95] The Metro chapter was virtually excluded from playing a major role on the day of the event.

The Stand for Children campaign threatened the Metro chapter's autonomy, which was very much focused on "forging its own local identity [and] creating its own agenda, which was loosely connected with the national agenda."[96] It occurred right after Metro chapter activists had recently organized several hundred high school and college-age youth activists to attend the BSLN's national conference. In addition, the Stand campaign occurred when the women from the Metro chapter had recently formed a coalition with New York's prominent Zulu Nation and started a young girl/young women's collective called Sista II Sista.

By late 1996, the BSLN collapsed due to conflicts between its national leadership and the BCCC stemming partly from its lukewarm position toward the Stand for Children rally. Yet, even if the BSLN continued to remain active, its local efforts in New York would have been paralyzed by the agenda of its national apparatus. The Metro chapter also had difficulty raising the necessary resources to continue operating its programs in an effective manner. For example, the Nia NuArts Liberation School closed its doors in 1996, a little over a year after it was founded, because it ran out of money.

If the Metro chapter had continued to function effectively, it would have had to develop a strategy for raising funds to sustain programs over the long haul.[97] Franklin realized that raising money for movement activism is one of the most challenging responsibilities for advocates and organizations interested in social and political transformations. He stated that when organizing, one must think about "capturing resources early, as opposed to thinking the revolution per se is around the corner."[98] In other words, having a strategy for raising resources is important for social movements.

The Southern Region

North Carolina was a major stronghold for BSLN activities. The 1992 summer organizing initiative in North Carolina created a base of support among black college students in the region, and was a major reason why the state became the home of the BSLN's southern regional office. The BSLN's North Carolina membership comprised students from Duke University, from the University of North Carolina at Chapel Hill, and from historically black colleges and universities such as North Carolina Central University, North Carolina A&T University, and Shaw University.

In late 1993, Darriel Hoy was hired to coordinate activities in the southern regional office. The Yazoo City, Mississippi, native and Duke University graduate was one of the organization's most dedicated organizers. Before joining the BSLN in 1992, she worked on the Harvey

Gantt 1990 senatorial campaign and as an organizer with the North Carolina Student Rural Health Coalition. Hoy was also the area coordinator for the BSLN's North Carolina freedom school program in the summer of 1993, which had sites in Raleigh, Charlotte, and Durham.

Hoy's contribution to the BSLN's southern regional field activities was immeasurable. It refuted claims, often advanced by interest group scholars, that community and political activists are motivated by selective or personal economic incentives.[99] While this may apply to some activists, in the case of Hoy and the band of activists who assisted her in the southern activities, their motivation came from a passionate commitment to ameliorating oppressive conditions that affected the black community. For example, Dara Dillahunt, a recent graduate from North Carolina Central University, worked closely with Hoy when she coordinated the Raleigh freedom school in 1993. The program was located in the Walnut Terrace public housing complex, which was hit by the recent deaths of a mother and her child from carbon monoxide poisoning. The freedom school, with the assistance of BSLN activists, helped to revive the community in the aftermath of the tragedies.[100]

As the southern regional field organizer, Hoy brought an innate sensibility of how to develop the leadership skills of young blacks and then integrate them in on-the-ground campaigns. Regarding her typical workday, Hoy recalled,

> My general responsibilities were to organize. No two days were the same. We had all kinds of constituents to work with. . . . I worked initially and mainly with students—going on different college campuses, educating the students about the BSLN, providing training, and getting them involved with some of our campaigns that we had going. I worked with students in at least four or five states. . . . I would try to meet with student governments, try to find out who are the people on campus doing things even though they might not be the mainstream leaders. I would go and spend a day on campus just to try to check it and see how things might be directed. . . . I talked with professors, especially history professors, professors in political science, professors who might be into the movement. Then, [I would talk with] fraternities and sororities even though they were probably the most difficult people to work with. I would let them know about what we were trying to do and try to figure out what

were their issues on campus and what were they trying to accomplish. And, I would see how those blended together and how we could deliver training to them to move people on their campuses.[101]

Under Hoy's direction, the southern regional office coordinated several campaigns in North Carolina and throughout the southern region. Between July and October 1995, she convened local planning meetings with groups such as the Congregations Offering Preventative Education and the Durham Congregations in Action.[102] These meetings focused on the National Observance of Children's Sabbaths, another CDF initiative that encouraged "religious leaders and groups to work for children through education, hands-on service, and advocacy."[103] She also worked on the BCCC's Childhood Hunger Campaign. This campaign attempted "to mobilize freedom school host organizations, interns, college students who deliver youth service programs, and church congregations to [pressure] their Congress person, encouraging him or her to support the reauthorization of the summer food service program."[104] As part of the campaign, the southern regional field office formed an alliance with the Food Action Research Council, the North Carolina Hunger Network, and other statewide hunger networks. Together, these groups appealed to the U.S. Department of Agriculture to raise the nutritional value and quality of meals served through the SFSP. Through their efforts, this coalition helped to increase the enrollment of children in the program by 11 percent.[105]

Another campaign organized by the southern regional field office was its fight against the Balanced Budget Amendment in 1995, a provision that targeted welfare and social programs for children for budget cuts.[106] The CDF initiated the campaign and the BSLN constituents in Virginia and on five campuses in the North Carolina region assisted in this effort.[107]

Although Hoy's office was in Raleigh-Durham, North Carolina, she had an extensive network of students on at least twenty college and university campuses in the South.[108] In Norfolk, Virginia, in 1995, she and her assistant, Raymond Gavins, supported students with their NDAAV. At the University of Arkansas at Pine Bluff, a collective of students called upon Hoy for assistance with their antidiscrimination activities. And Hoy trained young activists from Tougaloo College in Mississippi who were organizing in response to the *Fordice* case. Many blacks believed the court ruling could lead to the dismantling of historically black colleges and universities.[109]

Similar to the New York Metro chapter, the BSLN southern regional office had difficulty balancing its local and state agendas with the BCCC and CDF's programs. This required Hoy to balance three roles, simultaneously, as the BSLN, BCCC, and CDF field organizer and representative and, at times, subordinate the BSLN's agenda in favor of advancing the CDF's programs. The southern regional office's rather close attachment to the CDF allowed the BSLN to build relationships with some state and local organizations that it otherwise might have shunned. However, the high priority given to BCCC and CDF's programs left little time for advancing the BSLN's initiatives in a more formalized manner, which Hoy described as "one of the most frustrating things" about the job.[110] This, in turn, diverted the BSLN southern regional staff away from addressing the concerns of its constituency, in exchange for pushing BCCC and CDF based programs like Children's Sabbath Day and the Stand for Children mobilization campaign.

One of the most successful campaigns involving BSLN activists in the southern region occurred in Edelman's birthplace of Marlboro County, South Carolina. Marlboro County was typical of nurturing southern communities dominated by a southern black Christian cultural ethic. It had what historian Robin Kelley called an "alternative culture emphasizing collectivist values, mutuality, and fellowship."[111] The BCCC's Marian David, a native of Marlboro County, said it was a place where "the models that I saw were just people always helping people."[112] In this sense, community activism and social uplift were organic within the black communities of Marlboro County.

While this portrait reflected the Marlboro County of Edelman and David's childhood, to a large extent, much had changed in the area since the 1950s and 1960s. Like in many southern rural communities, poverty persisted and illiteracy rates were high, as were teenage pregnancy and unemployment. To curb these problems, Edelman opened up a regional office in Marlboro County. The office probably had more institutional support than most CDF offices around the country because of its connection to Edelman. By 1994, the responsibilities for developing the freedom school curriculum were actually coordinated with the Marlboro County office. Within two years, the Marlboro County office gained nearly complete supervision over the design of the curriculum.

The CDF–Marlboro County office also sponsored a summer enrichment program that served four hundred children and teenagers and started a recreation program staffed by college students. It created another program targeting pregnant mothers, some of whom were teenagers, to help reduce the infant mortality rate. Another program, the Primary Enrichment Program, worked on improving the test scores of five- to eight-year-olds. Finally, the office operated the Educational Enrichment and Leadership Development project and a rites-of-passage program called Adventures in Excellence. Staffing these programs were some young people, many of whom were in high school and made up the nucleus of the office's Teenage Leadership Core.[113] Members of the group attended some of the BSLN's national freedom school training sessions and Advanced Service and Advocacy Workshops (ASAWs) in Clinton, Tennessee. By 1995, the loose coalition of young people in Marlboro County conducted training sessions for freedom school interns attending the EBCPTI.

James Young was perhaps the most dynamic student involved in BSLN activities. He first became involved in community activism in Bennettsville (located in Marlboro County) as a high school senior. Yet, his activism revolved around service initiatives and lacked any bearings toward political and movement activism. After he attended some workshops organized by the BSLN in 1995, Young's political transformation began to take place. At these workshops, some of the organization's influential leaders encouraged him to take on a leadership role in his community and inside of the BSLN. With the BSLN's influence, he transformed from a participant in Bennettsville's service programs into an influential organizer of a small band of young social and political activists in the area.

Near the end of 1995, Young, along with Picket Harrington and Cedric Harrison, two members of the Teenage Leadership Core who were affiliated with the BSLN, initiated a direct action campaign to get a community center in Bennettsville. Building a community center was important for these young people because they had no place to "hang out" other than local fast-food restaurants, despite the high youth unemployment rate in the county.[114] However, the city council, the newly elected mayor, and even some black residents voiced opposition to the community center. Instead, city officials proposed to build a prison in Marlboro County. Some believed the center would be too costly and increase taxes, while others believed the city's resources should go toward the prison.

Young and members of the Teenage Leadership Core attended the city council meetings to voice disapproval with their position.[115] Matthew Countryman, the former director of the EBCPTI, offered assistance to the organizing efforts, and a local church opened its doors for the students to hold planning meetings. Hoy traveled to Bennettsville to train the young people in direct action advocacy. She recalled, "While [the organizing effort] was going on, there were a lot of people, a lot of the black adults [politicians and ministers] in the community who blocked what they were doing and who were not supportive. . . . Everybody turned their back until things were over and then they were all well behind them."[116] Later, activities in Bennettsville received national attention as Teenage Leadership Core members were invited to speak on Black Entertainment Television's *Teen Summit*, which at the time was black America's most popular teen talk show. The television episode angered some longtime residents who believed the young activists embarrassed their town.

Although the young activists convinced city officials to vote on behalf of the center, it was never built because of bureaucratic inertia. Still, their organizing efforts brought negative attention to the mayor, who suffered a defeat in her reelection campaign. The initiative, moreover, earned Young a tremendous amount of respect inside of BSLN circles. In February 1996, he ran for a vacant office seat on the group's NCC on the theme of "people helping people." In this respect, he became the conscience of the coordinating committee.

Organizing on the West Coast

The BCCC/BSLN western regional offices were located in the San Francisco Bay Area and in Los Angeles, California. In the Bay Area, the western regional office coordinated activities in both Oakland and San Francisco. With the exception of the freedom schools in the Los Angeles area and one in San Diego, the BSLN did not have much of a presence in Southern California.[117]

Organizing in California was difficult for several reasons. First, the BSLN did not have a full-time regional coordinator until late 1995 when

Taj James was hired to coordinate its activities out of the Bay Area. Prior to this time, most of the initiatives in the San Francisco Bay Area were facilitated by the Urban Strategies Council, an Oakland-based advocacy organization led by Angela Glover Blackwell, which operated as the BCCC's western regional outlet. The Urban Strategies Council incubated the freedom school program in the Bay Area. Greg Hodge, a BSLN advisor and the BCCC's local initiatives coordinator, as well as Ifetayo Lawson, the Oakland freedom school coordinator in 1993 and 1994, handled much of the responsibilities for the freedom schools. Yet, this was one of their many responsibilities while on staff at the Urban Strategies Council.[118] Beyond the freedom school initiatives, there was little time to focus on other BSLN organizing initiatives in Oakland and San Francisco.

The BSLN had additional difficulties adjusting to the indigenous activist structure (organizations, activists, networks) in the Bay Area. Black indigenous organizations blossomed in the Bay Area as early as the mid-nineteenth century. Immediately, they took on the role of familial institutions for new migrants from the South and East Coast who left most of their families behind. As black social and political institutions evolved in the Bay Area throughout the twentieth century, they did not face the extremities of Jim Crow–style segregation as similar groups had faced in the South, and their activities were not moderated by political machines that curtailed activists on the East Coast. Thus, the black indigenous infrastructure evolved more independently of mainstream political institutions and white political elites than had been the norm in other places. This allowed Bay Area black communities to develop their own social and political institutions, which by some accounts paralleled or outnumbered white organizations.[119]

It was this autonomous activist structure that influenced the political orientations of BSLN members in the Bay Area. Thus, mobilizing students and youth in the area was a strenuous activity because many BSLN activists were attracted to local organizations that were somewhat wary of outside or national organizations. At the time, many of these groups used African-centered approaches or relied heavily on black nationalist appeals to rehabilitate noncollege black youth. Even before the creation of the BSLN, several prominent rites-of-passage and survival programs had already gained traction among black youth since the late 1980s. The Omega Boys Club was established in San Francisco and later opened up a chapter in Oakland. The organization mentored black youth from low-income black communities and juvenile detention centers. The Simba, Inc. organization in Oakland was another mentoring program for black adults and youth, as was the Black Family Institute's Hawk Foundation, an African-centered rites-of-passage program for black youth between the ages of twelve and seventeen.

The freedom schools were attractive to homegrown BSLN members and transplants who were imbued with a high level of race consciousness and who infused African-centered cultural practices inside of the overall freedom school program. Bay Area BSLN members placed a high premium on the freedom schools and recruited college and noncollege young people to staff them. The young activists molded the freedom schools as alternative educational institutions that could potentially evolve into abbreviated African-centered schools and rites-of-passage programs.

In Los Angeles, BSLN activists struggled to develop alliances with the area's indigenous activists. During the summers of 1993 and 1994, the BSLN operated freedom schools in Watts and South Central Los Angeles, although many of the summer organizers were not raised in the Los Angeles area and were unaccustomed to its social and political culture. Sean Greene, a native of New Haven, Connecticut, was assigned to work in Los Angeles. He said, "The [BSLN's direct action organizing] model was developed with the East Coast in mind and that just didn't work once we got to L.A."[120] He described Los Angeles as a place where there existed "a bunch of neighborhoods linked together," yet were "worlds apart," and where the lack of a central subway system in the vast geographical landscape of the area made organizing very difficult. BCCC member Reed Tuckson said the social isolation and economic marginalization of Los Angeles's impoverished community was further exacerbated by tensions between blacks and Latinos who were struggling for "crumbs at the bottom of the table."[121] BSLN members also described activists in Los Angeles as "turf conscious," and guarded about outsiders coming into their communities and competing for the same constituencies and resources. This is not necessarily unique to Los Angeles, but generally arises when outsiders parachute into communities without building relationships with indigenous activists.

Another challenge was the lack of resources and institutional support for activities in Los Angeles.[122] BSLN activists received minimal backing from the BCCC's local sponsoring agency, the Charles Drew Development Corporation. In contrast, the Bay Area BSLN affiliate received assistance from the Urban Strategies Council, several religious groups, and rites-of-passage and survival-skills-oriented organizations.

In 1995, the BSLN and BCCC began to build more sustainable relationships with BSLN members and local organizers in the western region. Several Los Angeles organizers attended the BSLN's ASAW "Community Organizing: Lessons of the 1960s Civil Rights Movement" at the Alex Haley Farm in Clinton, Tennessee. Included in the group were Tony Zepeda, a community organizer from South Central Los Angeles, and Tony Massengale of the Watts Wellness Promotion Violence Prevention Program, whose commentary at the beginning of the chapter indicates that community organizing is essential to movement building and accountability. The workshop allowed BSLN members to interact with several 1960s civil rights activists including David Dennis, formerly of the Congress of Racial Equality; Dorothy Cotton, former education director for the Southern Christian Leadership Conference; Judy Richardson of SNCC; and historians Howard Zinn and Clayborne Carson.

By late 1995, the trajectory of the BSLN's initiatives began to move in a different direction in the Bay Area. Western regional activists received a vote of confidence when BSLN activists from the New York Metro chapter urged the NCC and the BCCC to dedicate more resources to organizing initiatives on the West Coast. The Brooklyn affiliate submitted a proposal to the national staff requesting changes to the BSLN Constitution/Bylaws. This proposal scolded the national organization for its "east coast centeredness," and insisted that the BSLN must "function coast to coast and find ways to allow the entire country to participate and feel empowered."[123] A short time later, Taj James, a recent graduate from Stanford University, was brought in to head the western regional office. He had several unique qualities that were necessary to transforming the Bay Area's BSLN affiliate and shaping it into a more activist-oriented organization. First, he was a highly skilled organizer who willingly trained other young activists in social and political activism. Second, he understood the social and racial diversity of the Bay Area.

Given this context, it was essential for the BSLN to build up its traditional black base, while simultaneously forming alliances across racial and ethnic lines. By the mid-1990s, many Bay Area high schools were multiracial hotbeds that frequently experienced interracial violence between youth of color.[124] Furthermore, according to James, "Diversity in the Bay Area is one thing that makes doing organizing from a black student organization perspective interesting because if you really want to have an impact you have to effectively build coalitions across all kinds of communities. Whereas, in other parts of the country, that's not as much the case."[125] When James was hired as the western regional field organizer in December 1995, he worked hard to connect the work of the BSLN with that of other local organizations and student groups in California. He helped to organize young people to rally behind the Kid's First ballot initiative in Oakland, which designated "a fixed percentage of the city's annual budget for youth programs."[126] On May 15, 1996, the Bay Area affiliate cosponsored a Bay Area Youth Caucus meeting as part of Coleman for Children & Youth's Youth Making Change initiative. The purpose of the meeting was to discuss the possibility of organizing a youth coalition similar to Azabache in New York.[127] Another project that James set out to implement was to place a BSLN Local Coordinating Committee on every Bay Area college campus that had a significant black population within a three-year period.[128] However, this was never accomplished due to BSLN's collapse in late 1996.

Importantly, when James was hired, the Bay Area was undergoing a social and political transformation. Gentrification issues plagued several black communities in San Francisco and Oakland, where the BSLN initially opened up freedom school sites. Also, conservatives proposed several statewide ballot propositions between 1994 and 1996 that adversely affected black and Latino youth: Proposition 187, which targeted undocumented Latino immigrants and denied them from receiving social and educational services; Proposition 184, the "Three Strikes" crime bill, that proposed harsh prison sentences for those convicted of felonies and nonviolent offenses; and Proposition

209, the anti–affirmative action bill proposed in 1996. In March 1995, the BSLN dedicated an entire workshop at its national conference to discussing the implications of Proposition 187 in a session titled "Proposition 187 and Other Cultural Issues." The previous year, Gregory Hodge of the Urban Strategies Center organized a meeting at the West Oakland Community Center to discuss the racial impact of Proposition 184.[129] And in 1996, James organized college-age young people to combat Proposition 209, the anti–affirmative action ballot initiative.

Conclusion

This chapter examined the BSLN's grassroots initiatives with a focus on the Summer Freedom School program, the youth group's antiviolence initiative that was implemented in collaboration with the BCCC, and its local organizing projects. The chapter further highlighted the difficulty national organizations have implementing projects at the local level. This task is less strenuous if groups such as the BSLN and BCCC garner support from local activists and indigenous groups, as was the case with the freedom schools and antiviolence initiative.

Another important point is that many of the BSLN's initiatives were shaped by the nature of the political environment. As discussed by students of social movements, the political and economic environment has a tremendous influence on the type of activism or movement politics that is acceptable or embraced by rank-and-file constituencies.[130] The antiviolence initiative was attractive because the black community had been seriously impacted by youth violence. Also, crime prevention measures had already been carried out by local grassroots organizers before the BSLN and BCCC developed their antiviolence campaign.

The experiences of the BSLN's local affiliates in the different regions were indicative of how the local context shaped their trajectory of activism. These experiences accentuated the tensions within the movement infrastructure that circumscribed the BCCC, the CDF, and BSLN, and was wedded to indigenous activists. Whereas the relationship between these groups cultivated a positive intergenerational collaborative project in the antiviolence initiative and helped to sustain the freedom school program, it was at times harmful to its efforts at the local levels. It also threatened the BSLN's ability to develop autonomous local organizing structures.

Did the BSLN's mobilization and organizing initiatives have an impact in the communities that it targeted for direct action advocacy? The answer to this question varies and depends upon how one measures impact. In terms of helping to facilitate the passage or implementation of a major legislation such as the Crime Bill, the BSLN did not have an immediate impact. However, due to the BSLN's coordinated efforts with the BCCC, it was able to mobilize various communities in support of popular education and violence prevention programs.

In terms of the local level initiatives, the BSLN's impact was small, but no less important. In fact, it created new mobilization opportunities for young activists to participate in movement initiatives. In North Carolina, the BSLN worked with religious leaders and child advocacy organizations, established a presence on college campuses, and trained young people in social and political activism. Its organizing efforts were an extension of the indigenous organizational activity in North Carolina and contributed to the decades-old tradition of community organizing. In South Carolina, the BSLN politicized several young activists who may have otherwise been exposed only to service-related activism. In Brooklyn, the BSLN helped to start or, in the case of the Peoples' Community Feeding Program, take over programs that were coordinated by young people.

Despite the BSLN's demobilization in 1996, at least two New York Metro chapter programs continued to operate in the late 1990s: the Peoples' Community Feeding Program and the Sista II Sista program.[131] In the San Francisco Bay Area, the presence of the freedom school program allowed the BSLN to train dozens of homegrown activists. Taj James, the coordinator of the BSLN's West Coast affiliate, was also instrumental in mobilizing young people in opposition to California's Proposition 21 in 2000. As discussed earlier in the book, youth and child advocates believed this ballot proposition disproportionately harmed low-income youth of color. In 2000, James founded the Movement Strategy Center, one of the country's prominent incubators of social movement organizations.

The BSLN's organizing efforts reflected its mobilization capacity and ability to utilize creative organizing to expand its constituency and challenge various inequities. Yet, the constraints some of its leading activists faced inside of its movement infrastructure reflected difficulties with sustaining intergenerational alliances. The next chapter discusses in detail these difficulties, which hastened the demobilization of the BSLN and the disintegration of its ties to the BCCC and CDF.

7

The Collapse of the Black Student Leadership Network

> Our focus must shift from porno-organizing—quick events
> and disjointed activities which are mandated from the
> national level just to get bodies involved with BSLN but are
> incapable of being sustained on the local level—to develop-
> ing strategic campaigns that are identified and sustained by
> local leadership.
> —Darriel Hoy, Raymond Gavins, and Naomi Walker, 1995

During its short-lived tenure, the Black Student Leadership Network
(BSLN), with the assistance of the Children's Defense Fund (CDF)
and the Black Community Crusade for Children (BCCC), attempted
to build a mass-based social movement organization that mobilized
young people for social and political action. The three groups operated in the same movement infrastructure, which had linkages to social
advocates, local organizations and activists, and intellectuals throughout the country.

Movement infrastructures consist of diverse organizations that often
debate the optimum strategies that can advance their causes. They may
consist of groups or activists that have more resources and organizations than other groups internal to the infrastructures. As a result, it
is common for hierarchies and disputes to emerge among groups even
within the same movement infrastructures. These disputes may be race-
or class-oriented, or they may emerge over philosophical differences

between groups or disagreements over strategies, tactics, and the movement's priorities.[1] In the case of intergenerational movement infrastructures or networks with vibrant adult and youth wings, they can be shaped by generational cleavages.

The stability of movement infrastructures and deployment of creative organizing strategies are also affected by the leadership skills, styles, and commitment of movement bridge-builders. According to Morris and Staggenborg, social movement leaders "offer frames, tactics, and organizational vehicles that allow participants to construct a collective identity and participate in collective action at various levels."[2] These leadership approaches are further shaped by gender norms, personal biography, when and how activists join movements, and the division of labor inside of movement infrastructures. The quality, experiences, flexibility, and skills of bridge-builders then serve as heuristic devices that help them evaluate new opportunities for movement building, identify threats to movement infrastructures, target resources that can assist mobilization campaigns, and bring stability to movements during periods of crises.[3] These leadership characteristics may actually be more critical to shaping the stability of movement infrastructures and their use of creative organizing strategies than selective resources and politically favorable conditions.[4]

This chapter examines the intergroup tensions among the CDF, BCCC, and BSLN, as well as the intraorganizational tensions that existed inside of the BSLN. Despite the BSLN's early successes, by the end of 1994 and continuing to 1996, it faced several crises that destabilized the organization. The first crisis revolved around the mounting tensions between the BCCC and Steven White, the BSLN's director. These tensions eventually led to White's departure at the end of 1994. Further dissension surfaced between White and Lisa Y. Sullivan, one of the BSLN's most influential activists, after she was hired to coordinate the BSLN, BCCC, and CDF's field operations in 1994.

The second crisis occurred in 1995 when some of the organization's more influential members began to voice concerns about the BSLN's organizational shortcomings. Despite the local organizing campaigns, the BSLN still had not developed a comprehensive program beyond the Ella Baker Child Policy Training Institute (EBCPTI) and Summer Freedom School initiative. This greatly concerned the BSLN's National

Coordinating Committee (NCC) and regional staff, which subsequently set out to restructure the organization in 1995 and 1996. As indicated in the opening commentary by Hoy, Gavins, and Walker, BSLN's leadership cadre wanted to develop "strategic campaigns" that were "identified and sustained by local leadership." It believed the restructuring process would expand the organization's base beyond the freedom school participants and its college student constituency.

Last, there was increasing skepticism among BSLN members, particularly its leadership nucleus, about the commitment of the BCCC and CDF in supporting the youth formation's agenda and programs. Their skepticism increased after the CDF announced plans to launch the Stand for Children campaign in 1996 that targeted the welfare reform legislation deliberated by Congress at the time. Although the campaign had good intentions, it may have accentuated the challenges with institutional leveraging. The Stand For Children campaign neutralized the BSLN's program, which, in turn, encouraged its leaders to push for greater organizational autonomy. After the BCCC resisted the BSLN's attempts at exercising greater control over its agenda, the youth organization disbanded in August 1996.

The first part of this chapter discusses the internal debates that beset the BSLN in 1994 and 1995. The second part looks at how the BSLN reorganized itself and developed a political program that could potentially have a far-reaching impact in the 1990s had it been fully implemented. A discussion is then offered on the difficulties the BSLN faced in implementing its program in the final year of the organization's abbreviated history.

The BSLN and Intraorganizational Tensions

As indicated above, the first crisis revolved around the departure of the BSLN's national director, Steven White, at the end of 1994. White's exit from the BSLN was precipitated by his complex relationship with some BCCC members. The debates over the Summer Freedom School program, in part, pointed to the underlying tensions between White and BCCC's core leadership. As BSLN members staffed freedom schools in 1993 and 1994, White received numerous complaints from BSLN members around the country about the lack of support from locally based

sponsoring organizations. As these complaints came in, he communicated them to some BCCC and CDF staff members.[5]

Further concern emerged, as White remembered, when the training for the freedom school program, the EBCPTI, was consolidated
into one national training session in 1994. The previous year, in 1993,
the BSLN had two organizers' trainings, at Shaw University in Raleigh,
North Carolina, and Holy Names College in Oakland, California. Yet by
1994 the EBCPTI moved to Clinton, Tennessee, at the historic 127-acre
Alex Haley Farm, which the CDF purchased for $2.5 million.[6] Edelman
wanted Haley Farm to serve as a national training center for social justice organizing and leadership development.[7]

The training session for the Summer Freedom School program in
1994 was supposed to be a grand opening of sorts for the farm. Yet the
event was delayed because of logistical problems and the farm's poor
facilities. A few days before the training, the national staff transferred
the EBCPTI activities for the two hundred participants to neighboring
Knoxville College. Knoxville College, however, was ill-prepared to service the needs of the participants, and its dormitory facilities were in
shoddy condition. All of this confusion reflected poorly upon White,
who received most of the blame.[8]

Furthermore, in 1993, Matthew Countryman, then the director of the
EBCPTI, resigned to continue his graduate studies. After Countryman's
departure, White hired his own staff to run the freedom school training
without receiving the BCCC's formal approval. This action may have
caused some discomfort among BCCC members, particularly since he
hired staff who wanted to incorporate a community organizing and
advocacy curriculum in the freedom school training.[9]

In addition to these concerns, White believed his advocacy for the
BSLN was a continuing dilemma for both the BCCC and CDF. As he
explained, the BCCC had garnered a significant amount of attention
and "heightened internal power" inside of the CDF, and "What they
[CDF staff] knew about the BCCC was through the work of BSLN."[10]
He pushed for BSLN's initiatives on a day-to-day basis, and frequently
clashed with BCCC members and CDF staff.

Apart from the disagreements with White and core BCCC leaders
throughout 1994, Sullivan was hired as the organization's Field Division
director. She was brought in for her organizing skills and because of

Edelman's push "to integrate effectively all of our [CDF BCCC/BSLN] grassroots work into a cohesive field operation."[11] The position required monitoring the CDF's grassroots activities, working with the BCCC so that it could make strong connections with national and local organizations, and monitoring the BSLN's initiatives.

Prior to her entry into CDF's national headquarters, Sullivan had been involved in the EBCPTI and freedom schools, and assisted in developing the BSLN's constitution and bylaws. She also helped BSLN staff members build relationships with activists outside of the organization. The appointment placed her in a position to have a direct impact upon the organizing and outreach efforts of the CDF, BCCC, and BSLN.

Sullivan's new position within the CDF/BCCC/BSLN infrastructure also placed her in an administrative position directly above White. This did not sit well with some BSLN members, she later recalled, especially after she communicated to White that some BCCC members were critical of his work.[12] It is unclear whether these criticisms were directed at his job performance or if they stemmed from his advocacy of the BSLN's agenda within the CDF and BCCC infrastructure. Many of the sentiments within the BSLN point to the latter interpretation.

Nonetheless, after Sullivan relayed these criticisms, tensions surfaced between her and White. Some staff members at the national headquarters and other BSLN members believed Sullivan's appointment and communication of the BCCC's concerns to White were deliberate attempts to push him out as director. Moreover, they concluded that she was brought in as the "gatekeeper" for the BCCC, so that it could "manipulate the agenda" of the BSLN.[13]

Another concern was that Sullivan did not fully appreciate the struggles that White had undertaken advocating for the BSLN's agenda inside of the CDF's national headquarters. The BSLN was one of several competing interests inside of CDF vying for legitimacy, and White and other BSLN members routinely faced roadblocks pushing the BSLN's agenda through the CDF's bureaucracy. Helene Fisher, a BSLN member and the EBCPTI's director, stated, "We had already been within the CDF infrastructure. So we knew what walls were there, what battles, what glass ceilings, and whatever else that was there that prevented us from being able to do what was necessary in order to have it [the BSLN] be a real effective program from an organizing perspective, and from a programmatic perspective."[14] She attributed the Sullivan/White conflict to Sullivan's newcomer status inside of the CDF's organizational bureaucracy. Still, because of the tensions between White and the BCCC, he exited the organization at the end of 1994. Some BSLN members believed Sullivan did not support White or validate his stances inside of the BCCC/CDF infrastructure and blamed her for White's departure. These sentiments were strongly shared among the organization's young adult advisors and national staff.

Sullivan was partially blamed for White's departure despite the fact that she was the person most responsible for bringing him into the BSLN. During the BSLN's first six months in operation, she lobbied Edelman and the BSLN's interim Working Committee on behalf of his appointment as the organization's national director. Still, his departure was demoralizing for the BSLN staff inside of the CDF's national headquarters. The tensions between the two had the potential to fracture the organization because both were among the most well respected inside of the BSLN. The Sullivan/White conflict was also problematic since both were close friends up until the crisis, and had worked together on John Daniels's 1989 and 1991 mayoral campaigns in New Haven.

Notwithstanding these concerns, it is likely that Sullivan had nothing to do with White's departure. Some members of the BCCC may have wanted her to neutralize White, but this does not appear to have been her intention.[15] Instead, because of her strong convictions about community organizing, she urged for a reorganization of the BCCC— one that envisioned a more equitable relationship between the BCCC and BSLN. In the memo to the BCCC submitted in September 1996, she insisted on an organizational structure that would share decision making between the adults and young people. This included a move away from the BCCC's hierarchical organizational structure so that the BCCC and BSLN's staffing reflected a "multi-disciplinary, multi-generational movement." In essence, she pushed for "the replacement of organizational hierarchy with high-performance multi-generational work teams."[16] This emerged out of her belief in an intergenerational organizational structure and leadership model. Furthermore, the restructuring process that she proposed included a director or program assistant responsible for spearheading BSLN initiatives.

Regardless of Sullivan's intentions, there remained the belief among some members that she undermined White's position inside the BSLN, and that she was brought in to align the organization with the CDF and BCCC's programmatic objectives. One reason for this was that, up until late 1994, Sullivan resisted overtures by Edelman to be part of the national leadership staff that was centralized in the CDF's headquarters in Washington, D.C. Her appointment as the CDF Field Division director was indeed a surprise to BSLN's core leadership staff. Another reason why these allegations were directed toward Sullivan was that after White's departure, she inherited the position of BSLN's "acting director." Some took this to mean that her intentions, all along, had been to obtain more power inside of the CDF/BCCC/BSLN infrastructure.

Interestingly, Sullivan's job title never changed from "acting director" to "director," which should have signaled that she did not want to force White out of the organization. Although she carried out the responsibilities as acting director of the BSLN, she shared them with the other duties she performed for the BCCC and CDF. As early as September 1995, she claimed that her direct involvement in the BSLN as acting director would most likely cease once the BSLN carried out its goals of voter education and mobilization after the November 1996 elections.[17]

The conflict between White and Sullivan sent reverberations throughout the leadership ranks of the organization. Many described this conflict as did BSLN young adult advisor, Mark Griffith of the Central Brooklyn Partnership, who said, "it was like watching your parents go through a divorce."[18] The relationship between Sullivan and some BSLN members worsened after a leadership development meeting at the Haley Farm in February 1995. At the meeting, the young activists expressed concerns about White's departure and the perceived takeover of the Summer Freedom School program by the BCCC, which actually occurred before Sullivan's arrival. As a result of these concerns, Matthew Countryman and Richard Gray organized a meeting of BSLN members to discuss these changes. Sullivan was not invited to the meeting, but after finding out about it, she expressed her disappointments about being excluded. She believed much of the focus of the meeting was directed toward her conflict with White. Both Countryman and Gray apologized for the incident and insisted that she was not targeted for retribution.[19] Nonetheless, the relationship between Sullivan and the young adult advisors was never the same after this meeting.[20]

Some BSLN members believed the Sullivan/White dispute was exacerbated by several members of the BCCC who were interested in removing White as director of the BSLN.[21] These sentiments were prevalent, since at the time of the conflict, the BSLN was being increasingly "absorbed within the CDF infrastructure."[22] It is unclear whether the BCCC added fuel to this conflict. Relying solely upon this explanation, notwithstanding its possible validity, ignores the internal dynamics of the BSLN that were separate and apart from those of its adult organization.

The tension between White and Sullivan reflected the larger differences in their styles of leadership. White's leadership style in the BSLN was best described as that of an "internal advocate," which was a familiar role for him dating back to his work with Mayor Daniels in New Haven. He advocated aggressively on behalf of the BSLN's agenda within BCCC and CDF circles, but kept most of his disagreements with the parent groups to himself, thus preventing these issues from disrupting the BSLN's relationship with them. For this reason, White wore two hats: one that articulated the concerns of the BSLN constituency within BCCC and CDF circles and another that effectively balanced the agenda of the BCCC within the BSLN. Even after his unceremonious departure, some BSLN members called upon him for advice and consultation.[23]

While White was ingenious in balancing the BSLN's agenda within the BCCC, Sullivan's best attribute was as a movement bridge-builder in the mold of Ella Baker. She was the person most responsible for the BSLN's formation, and had been instrumental in guiding the BSLN toward a path of developing a comprehensive national program after she took over the reins as acting director in 1995 and 1996. After inheriting the position of acting director, she urged the BSLN to develop an Ella Baker Community Organizing National Training School to train young people in community organizing. She also contacted community organizers as well as child and youth advocates around the country to gain their support for the BSLN's creation of "Issue Clusters." The clusters intended to focus on pertinent policies such as "hunger, affirmative action, legislative redistricting, handgun violence, welfare reform and civic education."[24] With the exception of Countryman, the initial director of the BSLN's Training Institute, no one did more than Sullivan to institutionalize a theory of collective and democratic leadership within the organization. She was also responsible for promoting tolerance among students and youth for diverse viewpoints.[25] This was necessary, she believed, to mitigate the antidemocratic tendencies found even within progressive and radical movements.

Sullivan believed the animosities directed toward her were indicative of a much deeper tension about women leading an organization like the BSLN. After White's departure, she was not given a vote of confidence from some of her male peers inside the BSLN, nor was she approached by them to explain her position about the conflicts with White. She believed the fallout over her arrival at the CDF's national headquarters reflected "the kind of sexism that women always deal with when they're coming into realizing that their leadership is central to the process, and it offends the men around them."[26] She strongly believed that her dispute with White, and the lack of support she received from some members of the BSLN's leadership circle, underscored the unwillingness by some members to fully accept a woman in a prominent leadership position. These sentiments were further reinforced when she—not the BCCC or the organizational culture of the CDF—received most of the blame for White's departure.

It is difficult to conclude whether other BSLN members also believed sexism or gender hierarchy plagued the organization. Save the inclusionary gender language in the BSLN's constitution, the issues of sexism, women leadership, and gender hierarchy were not seriously discussed prior to 1994. Neither did any members on the BSLN's leadership staff author any position papers about sexism in the organization as had been done by several women activists inside SNCC.[27] There was some agreement among BSLN's women members that less noticeable, subtle forms of sexism existed in the organization, but they did not treat this with any serious concern. In addition to Sullivan, Nicole Burrowes, a leading BSLN organizer in Brooklyn, New York, maintained that she and other BSLN freedom school staff members experienced sexism while working for the Harlem freedom schools in 1993. Yet Burrowes's charges were directed toward BCCC allies and not BSLN staff, and there was sharp disagreement with this charge.[28]

Even though few women publicly spoke about sexism in the BSLN, Sullivan's sentiments should be taken seriously. If the BSLN reflected prior movement organizations such as SNCC and the Black Panther Party (BPP), it is likely that her claims were valid. Despite their progressive and radical orientations, women activists in SNCC and the BPP said gender hierarchies persisted in both organizations.[29] These criticisms helped to lay the foundation for second wave feminism, which in addition to being shaped by women in civil rights and black power organizations, was also propelled by lesser known groups such as Mothers Alone Working, Brooklyn's Sisterhood of Black Single Mothers, and the Mount Vernon/New Rochelle Group (also called the Pat Robinson Group).[30] These organizations advanced a framework for governance—a framework that was influenced by earlier feminist and women's rights movements—that attempted to institutionalize gender equity within the internal operations of their movement infrastructures.

Furthermore, sexism usually takes place not outside the boundaries of traditional leadership roles, but within the context of leadership and sociopolitical struggles. The reluctance to talk about sexism underscores a unique feature about gender relations inside of movement organizations.[31] Silence or anonymity may give some indication about the nature of gender hierarchy itself. For example, the initial claims about sexism in SNCC were written in a position paper that was signed anonymously. Such publicly stated claims often disrupt what appear to be democratically structured organizations. As a consequence, many women may fear reprisals for publicly making statements about sexism inside of such organizations.

Social movement organizations, despite their objectives of creating a more egalitarian society, often fail to fully confront their own internal contradictions about discriminatory patterns such as gender and class hierarchies within their organizations. This is an unfortunate circumstance since movement activists, perhaps more than any other activists, should take an aggressive stance toward confronting and combating such contradictions that appear to be afloat inside their organizations. This must be an ongoing exercise for movement activists and organizations since they attempt to shape public discourse about what a just society must look like.

Perhaps the internal organizational crises that plagued the BSLN in late 1994 and 1995 could have been avoided. Yet, these crises unmasked the larger difficulties that faced the BSLN's core leadership as it attempted to build a social movement organization. The fact of the matter is that the debates probably would have emerged sometime in the BSLN's life cycle, even if White had not left the organization. The status of the BSLN as the youth wing of the BCCC and its attachment to the CDF made it difficult to persevere along an antibureaucratic/ antihierarchical path. More important, the political fallout stemming from White's departure and his dispute with Sullivan challenged the BSLN's idealism. Internal crises generally plague most groups, but they can be especially harmful to youth formations that have fragile resource bases and tend to rely upon nonselective incentives to recruit and retain their members.

A Call for Organizational Transformation

The internal crises revealed another troubling pattern about the BSLN. The organization suffered from various weaknesses, both in terms of its infrastructure and in terms of projecting a political program that was relevant to black youth. Therefore, in order to become a more relevant organization, the BSLN needed a cohesive relationship with the BCCC, while simultaneously exercising control over its agenda. As a result of the crises that emerged at the end of 1994, BSLN members outlined some proposals that intended to strengthen its internal operations and develop a comprehensive program. These measures attempted to increase the strength of the BSLN's NCC and expand the organization's base beyond college students.

As mentioned above, in a meeting at the Haley Farm in February 1995, the BSLN's core leadership met separately to develop a memorandum articulating these concerns.[32] The caucus consisted of some of the BSLN's strongest field organizers, staff, young adult advisors, and NCC members. The caucus was clearly disturbed about White's exit from the BSLN and the organization's lack of autonomy. It concluded that the BSLN needed to be restructured in a way that provided it with greater control over its agenda. It wanted the BSLN to move beyond the boundaries of the freedom school and the Training Institute, a concern that was "crucial in terms of transforming the BSLN into a legitimate youth movement."[33] The group urged the BSLN's NCC to help facilitate the development of a "more concrete structure so as to solidify owner-ship of the BSLN."[34] Though Sullivan expressed disappointment for not being included in the meeting as the new acting director, she addressed these concerns a month later in another meeting at the Haley Farm. At the meeting, she distributed an internal memorandum to BSLN staff, advisors, and NCC members outlining her thoughts on how the BSLN could become a potent political force.

In the memorandum, she said the BSLN should serve as the van-guard youth organization for mobilizing voters, that it needed to expand its base of constituents, and encouraged building relationships with youth advocacy groups around the country.[35] She encouraged the group to develop its "strategic capacity to help Asian and Latino col-lege-students develop their networks and organizational infrastructure to address the local needs of children and families through service and advocacy."[36] Building alliances with Latino youth activists, in particu-lar, was extremely important because many communities where BSLN members operated, such as in the New York area, were in close proxim-ity to Latino neighborhoods or were mixed with blacks and Latinos.

As early as June 1993, El Puente, a Latino youth advocacy organization in Brooklyn, asked the BSLN if it could send its members to the EBCPTI organizers' session at Shaw University. Their participation allowed the BSLN to develop a relationship with Latino youth activists early in the organization's history. This relationship was further cemented by the coalition that the New York Metro chapter forged with El Puente, as well as other Puerto Rican and Dominican social and political activist groups, including Alianza Dominicana, the National Congress of Puerto Ricans, and the Young Lords. One of the most vocal proponents of strengthen-ing ties between black and Latino youth groups was Claudine "Candy" Taaffe, a Harlem native of Puerto Rican and West Indian ancestry and a founding BSLN member, who worked in the Summer Freedom School program in Los Angeles in 1993 and was elected to the NCC in 1995. Louis Negron, a Puerto Rican community organizer from the northern section of Oakland, California, also joined the BSLN in 1994 and saw his "membership as a way to bridge the gap between blacks and Latinos."[37] He was elected as the co-chair of the BSLN's NCC in 1994.

In April 1995, several field organizers issued perhaps the most comprehensive critique of the BSLN's internal functions and offered a plan for restructuring the organization. Darriel Hoy and Raymond Gavins of the southern regional office, along with Naomi Walker of the Midwest regional office, outlined these concerns, stating that it would be a mistake to refuse "to acknowledge the gravity of BSLN's shortcomings and instead chose to move forward with the hopes that our problems would just disappear."[38] Central to their concerns were the lack of an accountable organizational structure; the failure to involve the BSLN constituents and freedom school participants in long-term, on-the-ground advocacy campaigns; and the BSLN's failure to develop an effective communication structure between its leadership and constituents.

The three activists proposed an organizing project called One Thousand by Two Thousand, which intended to redirect the BSLN's energies toward grassroots organizing. The project had two major components. First, it intended to develop the local organizing capacity of the BSLN through a formalized recruitment policy and the establishment of local organizing committees around the country that targeted an additional one thousand members for recruitment into the organization by the year 2000. The second component of the project was directed toward developing a more activist-oriented NCC. This proposal set strict standards for NCC members: each NCC member had to be a registered voter, the individual had to volunteer twenty-five hours a month in BSLN activities (positions were unpaid), the individual had to establish a local base of twenty core members, and she or he had to assist with the leadership development of fifteen additional members. Additional recommendations urged NCC members to each register one thousand voters per year, to conduct monthly reading and discussion groups that focused on current political issues, to organize two advocacy campaigns, and to host a meeting with a local elected official or political candidate.[39]

Further support for the One Thousand by Two Thousand project's recommendations for reorganizing the BSLN came from Sullivan. She insisted that "the majority of [the BSLN's] attention must now focus on building a field apparatus that can sustain the growth and development of the Network."[40] She urged BSLN members to recruit new members into the organization's fold who had "credible organizing experience that extends beyond campus activism."[41] She then insisted upon a direct linkage between BSLN field staff and local BCCC initiatives. Additional pressures for reorganizing the BSLN came from the New York Metro chapter, which urged the NCC to "serve as the leadership body of BSLN" and give closer attention to recruitment efforts on the West Coast.[42]

These pressures led the BSLN field staff and NCC to endorse the creation of Local Coordinating Committees and to expand its constituency base beyond college students.[43] In 1995, the BSLN began to recruit young professionals, black fraternity and sorority members, and young black seminarians into the organization.[44] It also reached out to young community and grassroots leaders through its ASAW trainings at the Haley Farm.

In 1995 and 1996, the BSLN explored several other initiatives that complemented its focus on community organizing and political mobilization activities. Sean Joe, the newly elected co-chair of the NCC, as well as Taaffe, urged the BSLN to utilize technology and the Internet for community organizing ventures. The BSLN became a planning member of the National Youth Center Network, "an organization of youth service groups working together to explore Internet opportunities."[45] They emphasized the intersection of technology and politics, or the creation of what Joe called the "E-Field activist,"[46] long before the popularization of social media activism and online political mobilization in the 2000s.

After the BSLN's collapse, the utilization of diverse and decentralized media channels would become the norm for post–civil rights era activists. Whereas the sixties generation took advantage of the growth of television as a mass medium after World War II to expose the country to racial terrorism in the South, post–civil rights activists relied upon social media tools and new technologies to advance their agendas. These "digital Democrats" are more apt to use new technologies such as blogging and Facebook to promote political activities.[47] Along these lines, young activists use the same communication technologies as global justice activists that target financial institutions and structural adjustment programs in Western Europe, the Middle East, and Global South.[48] Yet, the BSLN began experimenting with decentralized technologies a few years before they were popularized by young activists in electoral and movement campaigns.

Beginning in 1995, the BSLN members threw their full weight behind voter education, mobilization, and registration. In April 1995, the

BSLN hosted a workshop on Voter Registration and Education in the Black Community at the Haley Farm. Several months later, the NCC distributed a working paper that outlined its goals for the upcoming year. The NCC indicated that a massive voter education, mobilization, and registration campaign would be at the top of the BSLN's agenda in preparation for the November 1996 presidential and congressional elections.[49] In the organization's quarterly newspaper, Leslie Watson-Davis, a founding member of the BSLN, urged the group to "take the lead to register blacks to vote in the 1996 elections."[50] By 1996, the BSLN helped to initiate the newly formed Black Youth Vote project, a coalition of national organizations dedicated to mobilizing young black voters across the country.

Citizenship 2000 was a major part of the BSLN's voter education and mobilization activities. This was a comprehensive grassroots, civic and electoral organizing campaign, developed by renown popular educator Jenice View, that augmented the BSLN's goals of voter mobilization. Under the banner of Citizenship 2000, the BSLN planned to recruit young people to engage their local communities in electoral politics.[51]

To expand its base among young blacks and Latinos for its Citizenship 2000 campaign, the BSLN targeted its upcoming conference for a massive mobilization effort.[52] The *alternative* conference was held in coordination with the CDF's annual meeting in Charlotte, North Carolina, from February 19 to 21, 1996. The BSLN's staff, field organizers, and NCC members implemented an organizing campaign to recruit young people to the conference. As a result of this recruitment drive, over twelve hundred black and Latino college and high school students and young community organizers attended the conference. This was compared to only three hundred participants the year before. The conference was a dynamic event with several workshops on community service, voter registration, and direct action organizing. Other workshops focused on environmental racism, the Latino student movement, childhood hunger, advocacy in the juvenile justice system, media advocacy, community organizing, technology and social action, and grassroots approaches to community development. The conclusion of the conference saw a mass rally of black and Latino students, youth, and young adults.[53]

The conference signaled the BSLN's move toward becoming a full-fledged student/youth movement organization. With the twelve hundred participants in attendance, along with the One Thousand by Two Thousand project, the Citizenship 2000 campaign, and Black Youth Vote project, the BSLN assembled the ingredients to have a major impact upon the 1996 elections.

The Demobilization of the Black Student Leadership Network

Between 1995 and 1996, the BSLN took significant steps toward reorganization and developing a comprehensive political program. Still, the tensions between the BSLN and BCCC/CDF had always existed, but they intensified after the BSLN began to reorganize and as the CDF, along with the BCCC's blessings, decided to carry out the Stand for Children mobilization. Stand for Children intended to arouse opposition to the welfare legislation that was under consideration by Congress and President Clinton. This legislation proposed to downsize the status of welfare in the United States, eliminate Aid to Families with Dependent Children, and, in the words of President Clinton, "end welfare as we know it."[54] It was widely believed by Washington political insiders that the Welfare Reform Bill would be signed into law sometime before the November elections.

Essentially, the Stand for Children was a scaled-down version of the Poor People's Campaign in 1968. It called for a mass rally on June 1, 1996, by families, child and social advocates, and youth activists to bring attention to the harmful impact of the legislation.[55] Though more than 3,700 organizations sponsored the Stand for Children campaign, the initiative was the brainchild of Marian Wright Edelman.[56] She was one of the first activists to advise Dr. Martin Luther King, Jr. to initiate a Poor People's Campaign in the nation's capital. Hence, one can interpret her push for the Stand for Children campaign as blossoming out of her long-held belief that marches and rallies of great magnitude were useful to bring attention to important social and political issues.[57] Edelman dedicated CDF's resources as well as its national and regional headquarters to the Stand mobilization.[58] Because of their connections to the CDF, the energies of the BCCC and BSLN were channeled into mobilizing for the campaign.

Interestingly, the Stand for Children rally was not part of the CDF's early mobilization activities targeting the welfare reforms. Instead, the CDF staff organized a letter writing campaign in which hundreds of thousands of postcards were sent to the White House. They organized thousands of call-ins to the president and held weekly candlelight vigils outside the White House. According to Lisa Simms, a field organizer with the CDF (she also doubled as a BSLN field team leader), this work was exhausting. "We turned the whole basement in CDF into a war room," she recalled, frequently requiring her to spend eleven- to twelve-hour days working on the welfare legislation.[59] The public announcement for the Stand rally in January 1996 actually caught her and others by surprise. It was announced only six months before the rally date of June 1, and just one month before the CDF conference and the BSLN's alternative gathering in February. Most of the BSLN's leading figures were unenthusiastic about the rally. They questioned the timing and available resources and feared that it would divert attention away from their initiatives.

Despite these concerns, the Stand for Children rally was a success. The mobilization efforts established ad hoc organizing structures in forty-six states called Children Action Teams and targeted ten states that had the poorest children for mobilization. The rally brought together over two hundred thousand young people, student and youth activists, and child and social advocates from around the country.[60] The campaign also laid the groundwork for the CDF to establish a permanent Stand for Children organization (Stand Action Center), headed by Jonah Edelman, that continued to advocate for children after the rally.

Despite Stand for Children's success, it adversely impacted BSLN's organizing activities. Because the BSLN and BCCC were wedded to the CDF, the relationship placed increasing pressure upon BSLN members to move the Stand mobilization campaign to the top of their agenda. The campaign sapped the energies of BSLN's officers, administrative staff, and allies, as well as delayed the implementation of the Citizenship 2000 campaign and the One Thousand by Two Thousand project. Although the BSLN was initially told that it would not be redirected to the Stand campaign, after its February 1996 conference, its members were pulled into the CDF initiative.

After the BSLN's energies were rechanneled toward the Stand for Children campaign, it had difficulty leveraging its base of twelve hundred black and Latino young activists who were recruited to its annual gathering in February 1996 to carry out its agenda.[61] Although to which extent is unclear, the success of the alternative conference may have prompted the CDF to rechannel the BSLN's energies toward Stand for Children, in an attempt to capitalize on the collective of young organizers that emerged from the conference. If the CDF's intentions were to utilize the BSLN's newfound mobilization capacity and resources, then this was probably to be expected. The CDF was in the biggest fight of its life. This struggle was not about organizational survival because the CDF had already gained an institutional niche and a presence in Washington's lobby circles. However, as the leading national advocacy organization on child welfare, the CDF had a lot to lose if the welfare legislation was implemented. Edelman had even more to lose if Clinton signed the welfare bill because Hillary Clinton was a former staff attorney for the CDF and Edelman had personal ties to the Clinton administration.

More than any other event, the Stand for Children campaign shed light on the BSLN and BCCC's fragile relationship. It revealed how little autonomy the BSLN had to carry out its own initiatives. Kim Davis, a BSLN member and former freedom school site coordinator who was hired by the national office in 1995, said "Stand [for Children] brought up a real big issue around who sets the agenda for the organization."[62] This created an additional burden for the BSLN's NCC, national staff, and field organizers since they had to help plan for the Stand initiative.

The Stand for Children campaign provoked tense discussions between BSLN and BCCC members about the youth organization's autonomy over its agenda. At these meetings, occurring from February through July 1996, the BSLN's core leaders argued that their agenda was neutralized by the Stand initiative. The NCC insisted that Stand "severely drained the BSLN organizers and resources" that were intended for Citizenship 2000 and voter mobilization initiatives, which were expected to have an impact on the November 1996 elections.[63]

In reality, the BSLN members were calling not necessarily for a complete break from the BCCC and CDF, but for some variation of semiautonomy. As argued by southern regional field organizer Darriel Hoy, the BSLN wanted to "be an autonomous organization that maintain[ed] a working relationship with BCCC and CDF."[64] Hence, BSLN members pushed for "a joint strategic planning process" in which they could be incorporated in a shared decision-making capacity into the BCCC and CDF's "planning, implementation, [and] evaluation process."[65] Despite the BSLN's insistence on some form of autonomy, its requests were turned down. With this refusal, the BSLN was forced to abandon its Citizenship 2000 initiative and other programs during the most critical stretch of the 1996 presidential and congressional elections.

BCCC eastern regional coordinator Geoffrey Canada insisted that the BSLN/BCCC conflict was more complex than the adult organization's refusal to grant its youth wing greater autonomy. He believed that had the BSLN won the support from the majority of the BCCC's Working Committee, which consisted of close to forty members, then it could have very well obtained the type of semiautonomy that it requested. However, if the BSLN's core leadership "could not produce those numbers of folks," then "they weren't going to be able to move an agenda."[66] Canada believed that the strong disagreements about the BCCC's hierarchical status were felt most strongly among the BSLN's core leadership, many of whom were staff members paid through the CDF's funds. Yet, the BSLN's rank-and-file members who volunteered their energies to the organization did not necessarily share these same sentiments.

The refusal to grant the BSLN some autonomy over its agenda was understandable given the multiple pressures confronting Edelman and the BCCC within the CDF hierarchy. Jessica Gordon Nembhard, an expert in black economic development who at one time served as the BCCC's acting deputy director, hinted that some CDF staff were concerned that Edelman was spending too much energy and resources on the BCCC and, subsequently, the BSLN. She believed there was never a real "demarcation between the two groups," or agreement between the BCCC and BSLN about their separate and overlapping tasks.[67] Moreover, parent organizations rarely relinquish control over their youth counterparts. In many cases, these types of relations often are built around unequal relationships, in which the parent organization sets the agenda even over the objections of its youth wing.[68] Thus, it was easy to understand why the BCCC wanted the BSLN's agenda to play a secondary role within the CDF/BCCC organizational structure. For instance, Canada said the BCCC and CDF consisted of individuals who had spent decades amassing resources and building organizations to support their work.[69] Accordingly, it would have been detrimental for them to risk losing control over their resources even if it minimized the role of the BSLN. In a similar analysis, Angela Glover Blackwell stated that "the BSLN just wanted more control and wanted to do what it wanted to do . . . and I think it was legitimate . . . but [it] wasn't legitimate with the dollars they [BSLN members] were raising . . . out of the office of CDF . . . with the money that Marian [Wright Edelman] was raising out of the CDF for the BCCC."[70] In essence, the Stand for Children campaign revealed an undeniable and unavoidable reality.

There were several reasons why the BSLN pushed for more semiautonomy. First, it received votes of confidence for autonomy from some BCCC members. As early as July 1994, Otis Johnson, the BCCC's local initiatives coordinator, insisted that the BSLN's shortcomings stemmed from its structural position in the BCCC and CDF, which placed constraints on the youth organization. He urged the BCCC to support the BSLN's efforts at "building a student movement that provide[d] semi-autonomy for the students but gives the support and protection of BCCC/CDF."[71] Other BSLN allies shared similar sentiments such as Kent Amos of the Washington, D.C., Urban Family Institute, Tony Massengale, a prominent South Central Los Angeles organizer who joined the BCCC in 1995, and Judge Glenda Hatchett Johnson, former chair of the BCCC's Juvenile and Family Court Judges Working Committee.[72] In addition, the BSLN's leadership had to be accountable to the twelve hundred delegates who attended its 1996 annual conference and approved the Citizenship 2000 project and other BSLN initiatives.[73] "The tensions between remaining accountable to a constituency while being an organization within an organization has created tremendous tensions that did not lend themselves to answers," the NCC wrote in a memorandum circulated inside BSLN and BCCC circles.[74] If the BSLN leadership core subordinated its own agenda in favor of the BCCC and CDF's initiatives, this may have disrupted its relationships with its various constituencies and delegates who ratified its agenda at the 1996 conference.

Weary of the debates on the BSLN's autonomy and the rigid organizational structure of the CDF office, BSLN paid staff members resigned in the summer of 1996. Because of these disputes, the finances allocated to the BSLN were frozen, some staff members responsible for assisting the student/youth organization were removed, and the BSLN canceled a training session that focused on mobilizing students at black colleges and universities for the election cycle.[75] Afterward, the BSLN's NCC resigned in protest, which led to the eventual demobilization and collapse of the organization.

The BSLN could have continued to operate within the CDF/BCCC infrastructure. It had its largest constituency ever, and a year before the Stand for Children initiative, it secured $1.6 million in funds to support organizing initiatives from 1995 to 1999.[76] Yet, these funds targeted the BSLN's reorganization initiatives in 1995 and 1996. Had the BSLN continued to operate within the confines of the CDF/BCCC infrastructure, it would have had to scale back its agenda at the expense of the BCCC and CDF programs. Furthermore, the BSLN may have been an expendable organization since the CDF had already made plans to incubate and support the independent formation of its new Stand for Children organizational affiliate.

Conclusion

Between 1991 and 1996, the BSLN operated as a national-level or federated organization that had strong ties to local activists and young organizers. Yet, the BSLN's demobilization in 1996 was a missed opportunity for the young activists involved in the organization and its parent organizations, the CDF and BCCC. These groups—or the leadership cadres in the organizations—were unable to agree upon a collective decision-making strategy for mobilizing black students and young people of the post–civil rights generation.

Despite the BSLN's turn toward creative organizing, as indicative of its One Thousand by Two Thousand and Citizenship 2000 projects, it was never able to overcome the institutional leveraging of some activists inside its movement infrastructure. This was exhibited as early as 1993 when its leadership cadre debated the content of the Summer Freedom School program. The Stand for Children campaign, though it had good intentions, also defused the BSLN energies and agenda.

Notwithstanding the BSLN's criticisms of the BCCC and CDF's influential leaders, they recognized the value of their parent groups in contributing the time, resources, and expertise to the youth initiative. This effort, though lasting only six years (1991–96), provided an avenue for young people to participate in movement activities. Marian Wright Edelman was instrumental in "creating a context" for this to take place.[77] Moreover, in the last three decades, very few national figures have dedicated more time, energy, and resources than Edelman toward reducing child poverty and directing their organization's resources to support grassroots and antipoverty initiatives targeting young blacks.

Still, the collapse of the CDF/BCCC/BSLN relationship pointed to the failure of liberals and progressives to effectively construct a grassroots movement for social change in the 1990s. It was indicative of the inability of entrenched black leaders to link their resources with young activists in order to engage in a transformational movement to challenge the frontal assault on poor blacks. Taj James, the BSLN's western regional field organizer, drew a comparison between the CDF/BCCC/BSLN experience and the conservative movement's ability to unite behind a political program at this time: "[Conservatives] link together their media institutions, their politicians, their foundations, their grassroots organizations, and their think tanks. They're not all one organization. But, they're able at times to say we have strategic objectives we want to accomplish—how can we mobilize our resources strategically to get that done."[78] Unfortunately, the CDF/BCCC/BSLN relationship never materialized into this kind of oppositional movement alliance.

Ironically, the BSLN's demobilization occurred at a time when the CDF experienced its biggest setback since the organization was founded in the early 1970s. Simultaneous with the BSLN's collapse, President Clinton signed into law the Welfare Reform Bill in August 1996 despite the Stand for Children rally. It was a sobering event for CDF and many BCCC members, some of whom were strong allies to Clinton. Edelman stated that the bill was "the biggest betrayal of the children and the poor" in twenty-five years.[79] Dr. Robert Peterkin, who helped to coordinate the group's outreach to black school superintendents, said Clinton's retreat on health care, along with the welfare and crime bills, "only solidified the belief that the black community had to do something for itself . . . because you can't count on friends, you can't count on Clinton."[80] After the signing of the bill, Peter Edelman, Marian Wright Edelman's husband, resigned in protest from his position as the assistant secretary for planning and development in the Clinton administration's Department of Health and Human Services.[81]

Had the BSLN continued to operate and been given autonomy over its agenda, it had the potential to merge young community and street organizers, college students, graduate and professional students, and fraternity and sorority members into a loose-knit organization. This type of formation could have had a significant impact on grassroots social and political mobilization in low-income communities. It could have served as a countervailing force to the conservative movement in the post–civil rights era.

After the BSLN's demobilization, its former members made two attempts to revitalize what was left of the organization. In September 1996, the first meeting was organized by the BSLN's influential young adult advisor, Richard Gray, in Wareham, Massachusetts. Unfortunately, little came from this meeting. The second meeting occurred in April 1998 at Vassar College and had Sullivan's imprimatur. The Vassar Gathering, as it was called, gave impetus to a new organization that was formed a year after the meeting, in 1999, called Building Local Organizing Communities (BLOC). Organized by former BSLN members Taj James, Claudine Taaffe, and Lisa Simms, BLOC pulled together a multiracial network of youth and young adult community organizers from around the country to provide institutional support for local youth-based initiatives. Yet this initiative was also short-lived and collapsed within a few years.

The remaining chapters examine intergenerational activism after the collapse of the BSLN. One of the major initiatives addressed by the BSLN, BCCC, and CDF was the disproportionate confinement of blacks and Latinos in the juvenile justice system. By the early 2000s, a collection of localized campaigns composed of a multiracial constituency of activists, advocates, and community workers attempted to address racial disparities and abuse in the juvenile justice system. Reflecting a theme of the antiviolence work that occurred in the 1990s, these groups also attempted to advance initiatives that reduced the participation of low-income black youth in the drug culture and criminal activities.

PART III

8

Reclaiming Our Youth

Policing and Protesting Juvenile Injustice

Look at this way—either you're going to be raped at Tallulah
or else you're going to be fighting every day.
—Grover Arbuthnot, 2004[1]

Grover Arbuthnot was twenty-one years old when he was shot and killed in New Orleans, Louisiana. Like many youth in the city, he grew up poor, having spent most of his formative years in the St. Thomas public housing development. While still in his teens, he was arrested for armed robbery and was sent to the Swanson Correctional Center for Youth (also called the Tallulah Correctional Center for Youth). Tallulah exemplified the harsh realities of the U.S. juvenile justice system. Shortly after opening its doors in 1994, the private facility earned a reputation as one of the country's worst maximum-security youth detention centers. Juveniles were the regular targets of physical abuses by prison guards; overcrowding contributed to numerous fights and rapes in the facility; the youth were not properly educated; adequate mental health counseling was not available to the youth; and for young people such as Arbuthnot, there were no meaningful aftercare programs to prevent recidivism.

When recounting the experiences of his nearly four years in Tallulah, Arbuthnot recalled seeing "guards busting [youth's] heads open with walkie talkies and kids stripped naked and stuck into cold, concrete-and-metal lockdown cells."[2] Brenda Brue, whose son spent two years in Tallulah, remembered similar experiences. "These children," she said, "are abused by guards who are supposedly there to care for them. Guards beat on the children, sell them drugs and have sex with them."[3] In 1995, Tallulah was investigated by the well-respected Human Rights Watch, which issued a report titled *Children in Confinement in Louisiana.* The report detailed the civil and human rights abuses in Tallulah and three other youth prisons (East Baton Rouge, Bridge City, and Monroe) in the state.[4] Three years later, Senator Paul Wellstone of Minnesota led a delegation of a dozen health care professionals on a visit to the facility to probe rumors of maltreatment. In the same year, the U.S. Department of Justice and the Juvenile Justice Project of Louisiana (JJPL) filed separate lawsuits accusing Tallulah of civil rights violations. After numerous legislative hearings, investigations, and protests, juvenile justice advocates and community activists succeeded in forcing the state legislature to close Tallulah in 2004. The decision was an important victory for activists concerned about reforming the juvenile justice system.

The Tallulah story, the work of juvenile justice advocates, and Arbuthnot's unfortunate death underscore several concerns regarding the treatment of at-risk youth with histories in the criminal justice system. Although child advocates initially envisioned the juvenile justice system as a rehabilitative institution,[5] in the post–civil rights era, the country's juvenile justice system has become more punitive and ill equipped to respond to the modern realities facing impoverished youth victimized by drugs, violence, and abuse. David Utter, the cofounder of JJPL, explained how institutional racism exacerbates the maltreatment of black youth in the juvenile justice system in Louisiana. He said, "I don't think there is any question that the juvenile justice system policy that was developed from 1990 forward, which is the time I know best, could not have happened without institutional racism, without slavery, and without Louisiana's larger prison industrial complex."[6] Many young blacks whose fate was influenced by Tallulah, and similarly situated youth around the country, were disproportionately targeted by law enforcement agencies. Reflecting on the intersection of race and incarceration in Maryland, Maceo Hallmon of the East Baltimore Youth & Family Services and former president of the Maryland Juvenile Justice Coalition (MJJC), said "the deeper you get in the juvenile justice system, the darker that system becomes."[7] During the 1990s and early 2000s, black youth received longer sentences than their white counterparts, even when charged for the same offenses, and were disproportionately locked up in secure detention centers. They also had inadequate and sometimes nonexistent legal representation during the adjudication and postdisposition phases in juvenile courts. And, there was a greater likelihood that black youth would have their cases transferred to (adult) criminal courts (this process is called waivers).[8]

In reviewing the activities of juvenile justice advocates and activists, or what I refer to as the juvenile justice reform movement (JJRM), this chapter examines their attempts to deinstitutionalize and decriminalize the juvenile justice system. The JJRM is a decentralized collection of localized campaigns that galvanized social justice activists in the 1990s and 2000s. Unlike the BSLN and the movement initiatives of the 1960s, yet similar to the anti-apartheid movement of the 1980s, JJRM networks were multiracial and multisectoral in terms of the occupational backgrounds of their primary activists and movement bridge-builders. These networks comprised grassroots activists and community organizers; institutional activists, policymakers, and legal advocates; members of think tanks and academicians; youth workers and organizers; mentoring and prevention organizations; and street bureaucrats such as social workers, educators, school counselors, probation officers, and rehabilitation and mental health counselors.

The JJRM has focused on an assortment of issues: expanding constitutional protections for youth offenders, democratizing procedural issues in the juvenile justice system, advocating for aftercare and mentoring programs, and protesting zero-tolerance policies and the growth of youth prisons.[9] Movement activists are also concerned about reducing racial disparities and the overrepresentation of racial minority youth in the juvenile justice system, or what is generally referred to as disproportionate minority contact and confinement.[10]

JJRM's diverse infrastructure makes it an unusual site for locating youth movement activism. In contrast to the movement campaigns discussed throughout the book, many JJRM movement bridge-builders are adults, are well educated, and are fixated on policymaking and legal advocacy. With the exception of JJRM activists in New York City and the San Francisco Bay Area, jurisdictions with vibrant youth organizing cultures, JJRM activists were not overly influenced by community organizing or direct action orientations. Even the street and youth workers who gravitated to JJRM campaigns were mostly involved in service-related activities and mentoring programs instead of social justice initiatives reinforced by an oppositional political ethos. Therefore, a "youth" movement culture was less visible in JJRM activities outside of jurisdictions with strong histories of youth organizing.

Despite these concerns, I place JJRM within the discussion of youth movement activism and intergenerational politics because the status of marginalized youth in relation to the juvenile justice system alerted social justice and civil rights activists about regressive policies impacting poor communities. Much of the literature on youth activism implies a unidirectional level of influence, in which movement networks or adult activists ignite young people to participate in movement activities. However, movement activism can entail a reciprocal exchange that allows young people or their social predicament to propel activism among adults. Young people serve as the canary in the mine. Their social predicament or status alerts others—and in this case, adults or activists disengaged from movement-building activities—about the harmful impact of regressive policies, and the need to do something about them. Throughout this book, I refer to this as positionality, which is a creative organizing strategy that allows movement bridge-builders to highlight urgent problems about issues typically ignored by influential allies outside of their networks. Many incarcerated youth during this period, as Arbuthnot indicates, faced horrific abuses in the juvenile justice system that alarmed civil rights and social justice activists. By underscoring these abuses, movement bridge-builders and young people provided a context for adult activists, including the parents of incarcerated youth, to participate in movement campaigns.

Black youth (and their social status) were central to the JJRM's organizing efforts because of the racial hierarchies in the juvenile justice system. The Youth Law Center's Building Blocks for Youth initiative, a national youth advocacy group, tracked disproportionate minority contact patterns in the late 1990s. It found that blacks with no prior admissions were six times more likely than whites to be incarcerated for similar offenses. Among youth convicted of violent offenses, the average length of incarceration was 193 days for whites, 254 for blacks, and 305 for Latino youth.[11] For drug offenses, blacks were forty-eight times more likely than whites to be sentenced to juvenile detention,[12] and more likely to have their cases waived to criminal courts.[13] Some criminologists attributed these problems to the "differential involvement" of black and Latino youth in serious criminal activities,[14] while others argued that white youth were given preferential treatment in the system.[15] Regardless of the varying explanations, racial hierarchies were embedded in the juvenile justice system. These phenomena sparked a wave of JJRM campaigns in the late 1990s and early 2000s, and black youth were central to these efforts. These campaigns were funded by philanthropic foundations specializing in youth advocacy and juvenile justice, including the Surdna Foundation, the Open Society Institute, and the Annie E. Casey Foundation.

The remainder of this chapter focuses specifically on how social justice networks and youth activists created a movement infrastructure that targeted juvenile justice inequities from 1998 to 2005. This movement infrastructure created a safe space for marginal youth and youth workers to become engaged in social activism. It shifted the debate about youth offenders from punitive to rehabilitative treatment and exposed the entrenched racism in the juvenile justice system. It also developed the leadership capacity of parents and relatives of incarcerated youth. The next section provides a closer look at the entrenched problems in the juvenile justice system. Afterward, I look closely at JJRM campaigns in Louisiana, Maryland, and New York.

Social Control, Youth, and Juvenile Justice

There is not a unified juvenile justice system, but fifty-one systems, one for each state and the District of Columbia. Management of these systems can be difficult because they tend to be divided into local units, which are "delivered through county courts and local probation offices and state correctional agencies and private service providers—each with its own rules and idiosyncrasies."[16] Because each state has dominion over its system, punitive and ameliorative reforms tend to bubble up from the

states and influence federal statutes. For example, states have the authority to set age limits for prosecuting juveniles as adults; and they have
jurisdiction over punishable crimes, the length of detention, and the
construction of youth prisons.[17] Some states even allow for juvenile court
proceedings to be unsealed, and others have implemented "blended sentencing" measures that integrate juvenile and adult sentences.[18]

The juvenile justice system became a focal point for activists in the
1990s, largely in response to the spread of punitive state policies and the
expansion of youth prisons during this period. JJRM activists were distressed at the congressional debate over zero-tolerance national policies
such as the Violent Crime Control and Law Enforcement Act of 1994,
the Violent Youth Predator Act of 1996, and the Consequences for Juvenile Offenders Act of 1999. JJRM activists argued that these measures
reinforced racial and class hierarchies. They also believed the problems
in the juvenile justice system were reflective of a larger metanarrative
about the role of the government and its relationship to working-poor
youth, youth of color, and their families.

JJRM activists believed zero-tolerance policies had the effect of turning the juvenile justice system into a social control agency, or what
McCarthy, McPhail, and Crist refer to as a public order management system (POMS). A POMS is an institutional or bureaucratic arrangement
that manages real or perceived threats, whether they are politically or
society based.[19] POMSs are "institutional templates" fashioned to "confront a variety of public order threats, including sport victory celebrations
and large religious gatherings as well as political protests [and juvenile
crime]."[20] Thus, POMSs have been interpreted as bolstering disciplin-
ary institutions such as prisons and juvenile justice systems that penalize
marginalized communities and regulate various forms of opposition.

I accept the authors' interpretation of POMS, with minor modifica-
tions. First, it is not that unusual for some members of the aggrieved
communities to embrace "get-tough" measures that are endorsed by
conservatives and deemed as bringing order to society. An assessment of neighborhood association meetings in high-crime areas would
probably reveal that frustrated residents support youth curfews, harsh
prison sentences for offenders, and police crackdowns on drug dealers.
Consequently, in order to offset support for punitive policies among
these residents, JJRM activists have had to advance community-based,

anticrime initiatives that mitigate risk behavior and reduce the participation of at-risk youth in the juvenile justice system. This can help to
undermine the support among some aggrieved communities for punitive crime measures.

Second, I give special attention to the notion that long-standing
racial and socioeconomic hierarchies are reinforced by POMSs. As
discussed earlier in the chapter, the overrepresentation of minority
youth in the juvenile justice system has been a major concern among
JJRM advocates. Some scholars contend that black and Latino at-risk
youth have been used as cannon fodder to advance conservative partisan agendas.[21] Barry Feld states that the juvenile justice system tran-
sitioned from a rehabilitative agency that disproportionately impacted
white ethnic immigrant groups to a punitive one that adversely affected
blacks and other racial minority groups. This occurred concurrently
with the rise of the militant phases of the civil rights and new social
movements. In fact, long before the explosion of juvenile crime, there
was an attempt by public officials to reinstitutionalize the juvenile court
system under the adult criminal justice system.[22] Feld insists that this
was championed by conservative forces that wanted to penalize young
people who were involved in civil disobedience, counterculture activities, and other forms of "deviant" behavior that did not conform to
established social and political norms. Conservatives pushed for correc-
tive measures, not necessarily because of enormously high crime rates,
but in order to undermine the due process revolution of the 1960s, and
because this push was part of the southern strategy that was used to win
over racially conservative whites. Conservatives sought to redefine, in
somewhat more subtle terms, the image of black youth, as unmanage-
able and engaged in lawlessness.[23]

The juvenile justice system's racial hierarchy was exacerbated by the
mainstream media's coverage of urban youth.[24] Mendel states that the
media coverage "exerted a powerful influence on the juvenile crime
debate during the 1990s, and it remains today the pivotal ingredient in
the public's understanding of crime issues."[25] We Interrupt This Message,
a prominent media advocacy group, sponsored several media studies
in the past decade that measured the coverage of youth of color by major
news organizations. The studies found media coverage of black and
Latino youth tended to focus on their involvement in criminal activities,

with little mention of their participation in politics, civic life, education, sports, and recreation.[26] Poverty and unemployment as underlying causes of risky behavior, however, received scant attention by the news organizations. The racialized news coverage persisted despite evidence that juvenile arrests and violent crimes spiraled downward from 1993 to 2001.[27]

Racial disparity in the juvenile justice system was debated by Congress when it reauthorized the Juvenile Justice Delinquency and Prevention Act in 1988. It was also debated in 1992 when Congress persuaded states to develop remedies for reducing disproportionate minority confinement in their juvenile justice systems.[28] Through the Civil Rights of Institutionalized Persons Act (CRIPA) of 1980 (it was reauthorized in 1997) and the Violent Crime Control and Law Enforcement Act of 1994, juvenile justice and child advocates were successful in leveraging the federal government to investigate abuses in youth prisons. CRIPA gives the Department of Justice "the statutory authority to protect institutionalized persons,"[29] including juveniles in detention centers and secure facilities. Between 1980 and 1998, the Justice Department investigated eighty-eight juvenile facilities for civil rights abuses due to CRIPA.[30] The Violent Crime Control and Law Enforcement Act of 1994 gave the Justice Department additional powers to file civil lawsuits against youth prisons.[31]

Despite the importance of these policies, they did little to reshape the relationship between racial minorities and the system, primarily because the laws were enacted at the same time states began to implement their own zero-tolerance policies. These laws also did little to mitigate the differential treatment of young girls and women, as well as gay and lesbian youth. By the late 1990s, the incarceration rate of females grew at a faster rate than that of males.[32] In the study of Maryland's juvenile justice system, *Maryland: An Assessment of Access to Counsel and Quality Representation in Delinquency Proceedings*, the authors discovered that "Girls are often discriminated against by judges, probation and detention workers," and many have histories of sexual abuse.[33] A team of researchers commissioned by the Gay Youth Project of the Urban Justice Center in New York City further revealed that lesbian, gay, bisexual, and transgendered (LGBT) youth suffered from maltreatment in New York's juvenile facilities. They were the targets of verbal and physical harassment, and "the professionals [judges, attorneys, and social workers] working with LGBT youth generally lack[ed] expertise and training in sexual orientation and gender identity issues."[34] Kenyon Farrow worked with LGBT youth in New York City shortly before his appointment as the regional coordinator of the New Orleans–based Critical Resistance South. He found that homeless LGBT youth, most of whom were black or Latino, were the overwhelming targets of zero-tolerance policies in New York City.[35] What all of these findings suggest is that preexisting chauvinisms and hierarchies are reinforced by POMS institutions such as the juvenile justice system.

JJRM activists attempted to ameliorate the punitive dimension of the juvenile justice system through lobbying, protests, and public education campaigns. Yet, their most successful efforts occurred when they alerted policymakers, activists, and advocates outside of their networks about the harmful impact of zero-tolerance policies. This strategy of positionality allowed JJRM coalitions to disrupt the implementation of zero-tolerance policies that adversely affected black youth. Policy interference occurs when movement actors use strategies and tactics designed to interfere or disrupt the implementation of draconian policies. JJRM activists also used a strategy of appropriation as they sought to convince indigenous networks and activists outside of their networks to support their causes. For example, JJRM activists used this strategy to develop cross-movement linkages between movement groups concerned about juvenile justice issues and public education funding. The most successful uses of appropriation targeted the parents and adult relatives of incarcerated youth and placed them at the forefront of JJRM activities.

The remainder of this chapter assesses three statewide juvenile justice campaigns in Louisiana (pre–Hurricane Katrina in 2005), Maryland, and New York. The three campaigns benefited from the guidance of the Juvenile Detention Alternatives Initiative (JDAI) coordinated by the Annie E. Casey Foundation's Bart Lubow. At its height, the JDAI worked in seventy-five jurisdictions in nineteen states.[36] Its guiding principles included the development of state and local coalitions that would lead juvenile justice reform activities; the formation of working or executive committees within the coalitions that would implement the coalition's programs; data collection demonstrating abuses and racial disparities in the juvenile justice system, and solutions for remedying these problems; and the implementation of an action plan that would achieve the coalition's objectives.[37] Most JDAI-inspired efforts sought cooperation from public officials, even from those presumably hostile to social justice policies. This approach produced results in most cases, but in others such as New York City under the leadership of Mayor Rudy Giuliani's administration in the 1990s, public officials rejected the JDAI's assistance.[38] Still, because the JJRM campaigns were tied to JDAI's guiding principles and networks, they all supported similar policies. These included aftercare and preventative programs, the decommissioning or downsizing of notorious youth prisons, and civil rights protections for incarcerated youth.

The Louisiana Juvenile Justice Reform Movement

Louisiana, more than any other state, epitomized the crisis in the juvenile justice system in the 1990s and early 2000s. The state had one of the highest youth incarceration rates in the country. Blacks made up the overwhelming majority of the state's juvenile justice system—80 percent of juveniles in detention in 2003, despite composing only 39 percent of the state's youth population. Of incarcerated youth, 75 percent were jailed for nonviolent offenses, and in some Louisiana parishes (counties), 90 percent of the youth entered juvenile court without legal representation.[39]

If Louisiana was symbolic of the problems in the country's juvenile justice system, then the epicenter of the crisis was the Tallulah Correctional Center for Youth. As exemplified in the JJPL-sponsored documentary *Tallulah,* the youth facility reflected how POMSs such as the juvenile justice system are bolstered by partisan and progrowth interests. The system was controlled by Richard Stalder, who, in addition to residing over Tallulah for a short time, was the former head of the Department of Public Safety and Corrections. JJRM activists viewed Stalder as a relic of the Jim Crow South, its racial conservatism and feudalistic past. He used his position as the chief functionary of the state's criminal and juvenile justice systems to dole out funds, political patronage, and jobs to friends.[40] Stalder's reputation among JJRM activists was best explained by Utter, JJPL's cofounder:

> The people that support him [Stalder] have markedly different views about a white person who commits a crime and black person who

commits a crime. It's nothing they will ever say, but you tell me how you can have documented proof of injuries, such as twenty-eight children sent to the hospital in twenty days, the first twenty days in August 1996. . . . If those children were white, if those children were my kids—you know, white middle-class kids—there would have been an absolute uproar. And Stalder would have been fired and that place [Tallulah] would have been shut down and reform would have happened immediately. But not only did none of that happen, but it continued on for five years.[41]

By the late 1990s, advocates and community activists began to mobilize opposition to the state's justice system, with the JJPL being one of the lead organizations spearheading the campaign. Opening its doors in 1997, two years after Human Rights Watch issued its scathing report of the state's youth facilities, the JJPL immediately offered legal representation and postdisposition services for youth offenders.

In addition to documenting the abuses in Louisiana's youth prisons, the JJPL organized family members of incarcerated youth, which led to the formation of an affiliate organization called Families and Friends of Louisiana's Incarcerated Children (FFLIC) in 2000. Mostly composed of black women,[42] FFLIC's mission was to create "a better life for all of Louisiana's youth, especially those who are involved, or at risk of becoming involved in the juvenile justice system."[43] Interestingly, FFLIC's emergence was somewhat accidental. When the JJPL opened its doors, its executive assistant, Gina Womack, would routinely take phone calls from parents of incarcerated youth. Parents would request assistance because they were afraid to seek help from their families or churches due to potential ostracism. Soon thereafter, Womack informed Utter about these conversations, and both agreed to create FFLIC so that parents of incarcerated youth could be at the forefront of their initiatives. Womack was then hired as the group's statewide community organizer.

During FFLIC's early years, Avis Brock, a parent, was hired to organize other parents. Initially, as Womack recalls, the group began as a network for relatives of incarcerated youth and allowed parents to congregate and share stories in a safe space. In its first year the group met in Baton Rouge, but due to logistical challenges, the meeting location was changed to New Orleans. Monthly meetings were also hosted by parents in Lake Charles, located in southwestern Louisiana.[44]

Before Hurricane Katrina struck the Gulf Coast in 2005, FFLIC had 75 to 100 active members and close to 20 or 30 people who regularly attended meetings. Overall, FFLIC had about 450 parents in its database. When JJPL was established, its chief advocates visited youth detention centers to interview youth. These contacts provided an avenue for JJPL to have access to their parents and relatives. Thus, as Womack remembers, when FFLIC was created "we would be able to contact the parents of the kids we visited."[45] After earning a respectable reputation and garnering media attention, FFLIC recruited parents through word of mouth, visits to public housing developments, and outreach efforts at the courthouse.

Although FFLIC started out as an outgrowth of the JJPL's advocacy initiatives, it evolved into a full-fledged community organizing group. Adults composed the membership base, but most of them were driven to activism because of the adverse treatment of their family members. FFLIC reflected an innovative method in contemporary community organizing that embraces intergenerational relationship building, but from a parent-centered perspective. For example, the Sankofa Community Outreach and Restoration Center in Chicago, an action and support group for parents of the incarcerated, used a parent-centered organizing approach. Another example was the Community Organizing and Family Issues (COFI) organization in Chicago. In the 1990s COFI was established on the belief that "parents, as leaders of families, are a great untapped source of community leadership." By 2000, over one thousand parents, many from low-income communities, were trained in COFI's "development organizing" strategy sessions.[46]

Interestingly, FFLIC belied the myth that low-income black parents are uniquely pathological and divorced from political participation. In recent years, this cohort has been demonized for purportedly nurturing a culture of anti-intellectualism, failure, and dysfunction in the black community. This narrative reflects what political scientist Cathy Cohen calls the "secondary marginalization" by respectable blacks who attack the black poor and youth as pathological, deny them community recognition, and downplay the importance of structural and racial inequalities.[47] Comedian Bill Cosby and journalist Juan Williams insisted that the failures of blacks are wedded to their lack of personal responsibility instead of structural inequalities such as racism and poverty. Black women, who disproportionately head families in low-income and high-crime communities, were implicitly linked—in the case of Bill Cosby's speech commemorating the fiftieth anniversary of *Brown v. Board of Education* case in 2004, explicitly linked—to this narrative.[48] However, FFLIC offered a counternarrative as Xochitl Bervera, another FFLIC organizer, discovered in her work with the parents. She stated, "I think the most interesting thing is we're working with majority, low-income communities where quality of life is really bad. What is consistently startling—maybe it's only startling because the counter message is always 'these are throw-away kids, these are families that don't care about those kids'—is how much these parents are so committed, not just to their children, but to [all] children."[49] In September 2001, FFLIC organized a mock jazz funeral of the Tallulah youth facility as part of the campaign by the JJPL and other advocacy groups. The funeral, re-created in the New Orleans cultural tradition, symbolized the group's belief that Tallulah needed to close.

The JJPL and FFLIC also documented the experiences of young people in the facility through interviews and testimonials, and presented these concerns before the state's legislature. On May 7, 2002, they traveled to the state capitol for a grassroots lobbying session and testified at a historic hearing before the Senate Judiciary Committee.[50] JJPL and FFLIC were also successful at creating a "firewall," or separation of responsibilities, between the Office of Youth Services and the Department of Corrections.[51] This was important because Louisiana was one of few states where the adult corrections department ran juvenile justice services and programs.

In 2003, Louisiana's reform movement achieved a monumental victory when the legislature enacted the Juvenile Justice Act of 2003. This legislation mandated the closure of Tallulah; required greater cooperation between government agencies that came into close contact with children and youth; reestablished the Children's Cabinet and created a Children's Cabinet Research Council; and established the Implementation Commission, which supervised the implementation of the statute's major provisions.[52] Two years before the law was passed, the state legislature, upon the insistence of Louisiana's chief justice, Paul Calogero, created the Juvenile Justice Commission and Ad Hoc Juvenile Advisory Board. Immediately, the commission began to hold hearings around the state. Public officials, advocacy groups, juveniles, and organizations such as FFLIC were all invited to testify and offer recommendations for reforms.[53] Other groups engaged in the lobbying efforts, including the Effective Coalition for Juvenile Justice, Louisiana Appleseed, the Metropolitan Crime Commission of New Orleans, and the YouWho Coalition.

A challenge facing Louisiana's JJRM was linking its efforts, such as closing Tallulah, with community-based strategies that attempt to divert at-risk youth from entry and reentry into the juvenile justice system. This required a critical examination of poverty-reduction policies that could perhaps reduce the risks of incarceration. New Orleans activists believed that impoverished neighborhoods were death traps for black youth. The city's illiteracy and school drop-out rates were among the highest in the country, and its low-wage tourist economy intensified racial and class divisions. Consequently, many youth were drawn to the drug culture in order to compensate for a poor education and low-wage jobs. These public health hazards produced a violent mix, in which poor youth were not only susceptible to transitioning into the juvenile justice system, but also equally vulnerable to becoming victims of crime and violence.

In 2004, JJPL created an aftercare program to provide "meaningful, supportive and coordinated services for youth upon their release from juvenile prisons."[54] Officially called the Youth Empowerment Project (YEP), the initiative was created by Melissa Sawyer, the YEP's executive director who initially worked with the JJPL's postdisposition project; Rebecca Kendig, the executive director of case management services for the project; and staff attorney Angela Conyers. YEP attempted to reduce the risk factors of incarcerated youth by developing "individual case plans," which "ensure that services are coordinated and are provided in a meaningful manner to youths transitioning home from juvenile prisons."[55] The plan was similar to the individualized education programs (IEPs) that public schools must administer for each of their special education students. YEP consisted of six phases, beginning before a youth was released from detention to several years after being released. The project materialized after several youth in JJPL's postdisposition program, including Grover Arbuthnot, were killed after leaving detention.[56]

Additional efforts to link policy reforms with community-based prevention programs were developed by other activists and grassroots organizations. Corlita Mahr, a former organizer with the JJPL, worked with a coalition of organizers, advocates, and policymakers on a comprehensive strategy that attempted to bring together programs and providers from multiple agencies and departments: mental health services, human services, the education department, the child welfare system, and the juvenile justice system. These departments were balkanized, rarely shared data on at-risk children, and were not engaged in cross-agency collaborations. Mahr said, "People ha[d] actually been sitting down around tables from different areas and saying [that] we need to have common assessment tools. That hasn't happened before."[57] The collaborations were formalized into a proposal by the Louisiana's Youth Enhanced Services (YES) for Mental Health, a group of mental health consumers and workers, advocates, and social service providers who created a child mental health initiative. The initiative intended to "develop a comprehensive community based system of care for children with a serious emotional disturbance."[58] Ideally the initiative would have synthesized or connected the aforementioned agencies under one umbrella agency or department. It is an example of interest convergence because it would create a large safety net for young people who were serviced by multiple service agencies.

The Maryland Juvenile Justice Reform Movement

Similar to the Louisiana campaign, Maryland's juvenile justice initiatives focused initially on shutting down or downsizing maximum-security youth facilities in the state. The first facility targeted by the JJRM activists was Cheltenham youth detention center, the state's oldest youth prison.[59] Originally built in 1872 as a reformatory school for "colored children," the detention center earned a tough reputation for its overcrowded population and callous treatment of detainees. A 2003–2004 Department of Justice investigation into Cheltenham uncovered what many advocates had been saying for years—that the youth facility, along with another youth prison in the state called Charles H. Hickey, Jr., violated federal civil rights laws such as CRIPA.[60] Similar to the situation at Louisiana's Tallulah prison, beatings, rape, violence, and abuse by guards were common at these facilities.[61]

Cheltenham's civil rights abuses underscored the salience of race in the juvenile justice system because it was viewed as a symbol of the state's Jim Crow past. Initially, the reform initiatives were coordinated by the Maryland Campaign to Close Cheltenham, which was formed after local media uncovered racial disparities in the juvenile justice system. The campaign evolved into the MJJC in 1997.[62]

Gregory Perkins, an East Baltimore minister and the former head of Baltimore's Interdenominational Ministerial Alliance, was a leading figure in the early phase of the campaign, and eventually served on a statewide commission created to draw up proposals for reforming the juvenile justice system. Although state officials did not allow him to visit Cheltenham, youth and parents who were familiar with the facility told him horror stories of the facility. About one hundred youth were packed into "cottages" that were supposed to hold only twenty-five offenders. Because of overcrowding, Perkins said, "There [were] not enough bathrooms, so many young men [had to go the bathroom] in the cells . . . [where] the staff pour[ed] bleach—you talk about a filthy, overcrowded, violent environment for the children."[63] The Justice Department investigation also revealed that physically and mentally disabled youth were neglected and mistreated in the prisons.

Once the MJJC was formalized, it became the state's leading advocacy organization on juvenile justice reform. Its membership base was drawn from grassroots organizations, policymakers, juvenile justice advocates, and youth workers. Its host agency was the Advocates for Children and Youth in Baltimore. The MJJC had several committees, including the Legislative Policy Committee and a Best Practices Committee, which looked at community-based prevention programs that reduced recidivism.[64]

The MJJC's interest in highlighting abuses in juvenile facilities extended beyond the treatment of youth at Cheltenham and Hickey. In 2004, Maryland's Office of the Independent Juvenile Justice Monitor found disarray at the Baltimore City Juvenile Justice Center. It uncovered inadequate staffing, infrastructure dangers, inappropriate housing, and poor services at the detention center.[65] Additional abuses were found in the Waxler School for Girls and the Alfred D. Noyes Children's Center in Rockville, Maryland. The public outcry from these abuses eventually led to the closure of Hickey in 2005 and forced the Maryland legislature to create a Joint Oversight Committee on the Department of Juvenile Services.[66]

The MJJC and juvenile justice advocates lobbied for several statutes that attempted to overhaul the entire juvenile justice system. The bills proposed updating the state's diversionary and aftercare programs; ensured that juveniles were given due process in the courts; provided regulatory guidelines for mental health and hygiene services for juvenile offenders; and called for the creation of a Subcabinet Coordinating Council on Juvenile Delinquency Prevention and Diversion Program.[67] The MJJC also worked closely with several legislators to draft a bill that provided more funding for diversionary programs targeting troubled youth.[68]

A controversial proposal embraced by the MJJC recommended moving the supervision of the independent monitor—the agency that investigated abuses in the juvenile justice system—from the governor's office to the state attorney general's office.[69] Another bill would have "forced Department of Juvenile Justice staff to appear before a judge when there are delays in providing youths with court-ordered treatment services."[70] The first measure underscored a systemic problem in the juvenile justice system, which was the shortage of state-funded treatment, aftercare, and diversionary programs for youth. This was particularly the case in Baltimore, where eight thousand youth were arrested annually as of the late 1990s, yet the juvenile justice system had just one diversionary program for the city's youth.[71] The second statute underscored the politics of POMSs. Then governor Bob Ehrlich insisted, as a major campaign issue in 2002, that he would reform the juvenile justice system. In late 2005, he closed the Hickey facility, but he disappointed JJRM activists when he considered a proposal to transfer the facility's youth to out-of-state prisons in Iowa, Pennsylvania, and Texas. He also wanted to maintain control over the independent monitor's office. Many feared that he was trying to control the monitor's office, especially since he was up for reelection in 2006.

Between October 2004 and April 2005, with the assistance of Cameron Miles, the MJJC's community outreach coordinator, the coalition held monthly meetings with high-profile public officials to discuss juvenile justice activists. These officials included Thomas V. "Mike" Miller, president of the Maryland Senate, Nancy S. Forster, Maryland's public defender, Delegate Norman H. Conway of the House Appropriations Committee, Senator Brian E. Frosh, chairman of the Judicial Committee, and Patricia Jessamy, the state attorney for Baltimore. In addition, the

MJJC mobilized community activists and youth, mainly from Baltimore, on trips to the state capitol in Annapolis to lobby legislators, and worked closely with Democrat Bobby Zirkin, a delegate representing Baltimore County. On January 17, 2005, JJRM activists organized a rally called Justice Monday at the state capitol to highlight the abuses in youth prisons.

On March 17, 2005, the MJJC organized another lobbying session to pressure state senators to approve legislation that would fund diversionary and prevention programs. Laura Hinds, the deputy director of the Advocates for Children and Youth, urged the Senate Finance Committee to give close attention to the "front end on the juvenile justice system" that would deter young people from criminal activities. She said that as many as fifty thousand youth had been referred to the state's Department of Juvenile Services in the previous year, but there was "not an array of community-based services" to assist them. She and others believed that the state should redistribute its spending from youth prisons to prevention programs.[72] Additional testimonies came from Miles, parents and youth who had contact with the juvenile justice system, and representatives from grassroots organizations such as Danté Wilson, the founder of Reclaiming Our Children and Community Projects, Inc., a Southwest Baltimore youth development group that provided comprehensive services to at-risk youth. He believed the privatization of systems of care services, such as mental health programs, created an institutional pathology that perpetuated the crises of at-risk youth and their families in Baltimore.[73] Nonprofit groups that received contracts to assist at-risk youth were more interested in recycling them through their systems, for profiteering purposes, instead of transitioning them out of systems of care institutions.

Despite these efforts and to the disappointment of JJRM advocates, Governor Ehrlich vetoed the measure to remove the supervision of the independent monitor's office outside of his control. However, due to the MJJC's pressures, he retained the popular, independent monitor and asked the Maryland Department of Education to expand educational services to incarcerated youth.

An overlooked and underappreciated dimension of the juvenile justice and criminal justice arenas is the work by JJRM activists to link policy-based reform initiatives with grassroots strategies that are used to combat crime and divert youth from jail. Similar to New

Orleans, Baltimore has been devastated by deindustrialization and an entrenched, multigenerational drug culture.[74] These phenomena presented an interesting challenge for juvenile advocates in Maryland. Even though they have to reform the system through policy change, they were also determined to prevent youth from participating in crime and violence, which leads to their participation in the system.

In 2004 and 2005, organizations and advocates affiliated with the MJJC made extensive efforts to offer community-based responses to at-risk youth. Cameron Miles created a youth program called Mentoring Male Teens in the Hood in 1996, which mentored youth, ages eight to eighteen. He also had a mentoring program in the Gay Detention Center, Baltimore's $60 million juvenile facility. In the mid-2000s, Miles emerged as a leading figure and perhaps most passionate voice for juvenile justice reform. After serving more than four years in prison, he attended and graduated from Coppin State University. Through personal connections, he eventually worked on a local political campaign and later became involved in juvenile justice activism. By 2005, 140 youth were enrolled in his mentoring program.[75] Miles's activist orientation reflects what scholar-activist Shawn Ginwright calls a "radical healing" approach to community building and social justice. Radical healing integrates self-development, critical pedagogy and knowledge of African and African American history, mentoring, and rites-of-passage programs to build the leadership capacity and self-esteem of at-risk youth. Ginwright has used this holistic approach to create safe spaces for youth to discuss social justice issues, inequality, and antiviolence approaches.[76] As the MJJC's outreach coordinator, Miles has been successful in developing a similar holistic approach. He bridged the interests of community activists and professional advocates, who, notwithstanding their commitment to reform, were often divorced from the day-to-day realities of low-income and working-class black youth and families.

Another prominent figure was Maceo Hallmon, an East Baltimore social advocate who served as president of the MJJC during its early years. Hallmon was critical of the coalition's attention to policy change at the state level and what he believed was its inattention to grassroots organizing in the city's low-income communities. He pushed for a greater "connection between the coalition and community,"[77] and for blacks to have greater input in the policy development stage of juvenile justice reforms.

Kimberly Armstrong of Northeast Baltimore was another well-respected figure in the coalition. Recruited by Miles, who mentored her son after he served a one-year sentence in the Hickey facility, Armstrong was a city bus driver, but she quit her job to give more attention to her troubled son. She eventually became the interim codirector of the MJJC and formed her own youth program for girls called Just 4 Me Mentoring.

Unfortunately, her activism was not enough to save her sixteen-year-old son, who was murdered in September 2004.[78] The death struck a nerve in the JJRM community because of Armstrong's public role in the movement. Despite the incident, she believed her son was indirectly responsible for recruiting her into movement activism. She said, "My son was murdered. I don't know why, I don't know who [murdered my son] . . . without him, I would not even be doing this [activism]. Maybe his purpose was to bring me into *my* purpose. I am nothing like I used to be. I used to be quiet . . . I was the typical person, going to work, coming home. I used to let people intimidate me, but not anymore."[79] Furthermore, psychologist and Johns Hopkins University professor Lauren Abramson founded the Community Conferencing Center in Baltimore. Modeled after a conflict resolution initiative in Maori, New Zealand, the Community Conference Center resolves disputes by bringing together all parties involved in a conflict—the offenders, the victims of crimes, families, and communities—in order to repair damages that may have been incurred from crimes or confrontations. These conflict mediation meetings, officially called "community conferences," are mediated by trained facilitators. Since the mid-1990s, over four thousand people have participated in community conferences, and hundreds of young people have been diverted from the juvenile justice system.[80]

Earlier in the chapter, I stated that the JJRM has used the strategy of appropriation to develop an interest convergence between different movements or activists groups. This strategy is exemplified in the work of Miles, Armstrong, Wilson, Abramson, and the other activists. All were intent on synthesizing demands for systemic changes in the juvenile justice system with community-based antiviolence activities. They believed that crime prevention programs, for example, mentoring programs, diversion programs, and mutual aid initiatives, were central to the overall strategy for reducing the overrepresentation of black youth in the juvenile justice system.

New York City and Justice for Youth

Whereas adult-led and legal advocacy groups coordinated the JJRM campaigns in Louisiana and Maryland, New York City's juvenile justice campaign was fueled by youth activists, community organizers, and street workers. The Youth Force of the South Bronx was one the most prominent youth-based organizations involved in JJRM activities in the 1990s. Youth Force was founded by thirteen activists, but its orientation was profoundly shaped by Kim McGillicuddy, a respected organizer with deep roots working in low-income black and Latino communities. In addition to its media study of *New York Times* coverage of black and Latino youth discussed earlier in the book, the Youth Force created the Community Justice Center to provide legal education, job and education referrals, and counseling for young people going through the judicial system.[81] It also formed a Youth Court in 1998 that offered prevention programs for impoverished youth before closing its doors in late 2003.[82]

Youth Force's work was similar to that of Clifford Shaw, a University of Chicago sociologist who investigated juvenile crime in the 1930s. Shaw established the Chicago Area Project, a community organization program that "attempted to prevent delinquency at the local level as well as more punitive treatment of serious and violent offenders."[83] He concluded that political, structural, and societal problems contributed to juvenile delinquency and abuse in the system. Thus, if reformers democratized the juvenile court without addressing stereotypes about delinquent behavior, as well as the root causes of poverty and public health dilemmas, he believed they would fall short of reforming the juvenile justice system. Similar to Shaw, the Youth Force used community organizing practices to ameliorate inequities in the system and to combat poverty and violence. In addition to juvenile justice, Youth Force engaged in tenant organizing and developed a "Street University" that trained youth in organizing and advocacy work.[84] It established the Ujima Project in the Spofford Juvenile Center (now called the Bridges Juvenile Center), the city's worse juvenile facility at the time. This program brought together youth offenders to formulate strategies for improving the conditions in Spofford.

Many organizers affiliated with the group had been incarcerated in juvenile detention centers and were introduced to social justice issues and trained as community organizers by the group. For example, Andre Holder grew up in a Brooklyn public housing development and began selling drugs in his early teens. After spending time in juvenile facilities and group homes, including a brief period in Riker's Island, he joined Youth Force as a teenager and worked with its youth court initiative. (New York law allows young people between the ages of sixteen and nineteen to be transferred into Rikers.) He eventually became a full-fledged organizer working with several groups on juvenile justice reform.[85]

Youth Force's most innovative project was the Democracy Multiplied Zone (DMZ). This was a geographically designated area in the South Bronx delineated by neighborhood boundaries that functioned as a safe zone for youth where they could receive targeted developmental resources.[86] The DMZ was similar to the increasingly popular Harm Free Zone (HFZ) initiative celebrated by criminal and juvenile justice activists such as Tamika Middleton, the former regional coordinator of Critical Resistance South. She believed HFZ (and similar initiatives such as the DMZ) are organizing models that allow aggrieved communities to "feel safe enough to reduce the reliance or eliminate the reliance on the police [for public safety]."[87] Although the Youth Force's organizing initiatives raised the political consciousness of poor youth in New York City, after the election of Mayor Rudy Giuliani in 1994, he instituted several zero-tolerance policies that set back juvenile justice reforms in the city.

In addition, the Prison Moratorium Project (PMP) was established in 1995 by a coalition of activists from New York City and Chicago. Its first initiative, Education, Not Incarceration, pushed to redirect the state's budget expenditures away from prisons and toward higher education. Kate Rhee, PMP's first full-time staff person, admitted that this "was a tough sell," mainly because prison expansion was not a viable issue, even for many social justice activists.[88] Hence, one of the challenges was convincing potential allies that criminal justice reform is linked to education, welfare, and other issues.

The PMP's efforts were aided by a Justice Policy Institute study drawing the connection between public education funding and expenditures for prison construction. Afterward, PMP activists developed an alliance with students from the State University of the New York (SUNY) campuses in Upstate New York who were concerned about the rising cost of public education. They used the report to frame the antiprison move-ment as fundamental to the education reform and, as a result, encour-aged SUNY students to join their campaign. The students then pres-sured the state legislature to redirect the budget expenditures to higher education programs.[89]

In the early 2000s, PMP served as a movement center for youth activists. It initiated No More Youth Jails in 2001 to protest a proposal to spend $65 million of New York's capital budget for the expansion of the city's juvenile detention system.[90] The Justice 4 Youth Coalition, a col-lection of seventy-five to one hundred youth activists, many of whom were formerly incarcerated, was an outgrowth of the PMP's initiatives. The youth activists were placed "at the forefront" of the campaign. Rhee said that a fundamental flaw in the juvenile and criminal justice arenas was that criminologists, advocates, and professionals were typically the spokespersons for the JJRM. Yet this campaign was very much about "revamping the field of expertise" to include youth impacted by zero-tolerance measures. After holding community meetings and staging protests, the coalition succeeded in convincing the city to remove $53 million of the $65 million from the capital budget.

Another target was the closure of the Spofford youth prison. Similar to Tallulah and Cheltenham, Spofford symbolized New York's nefarious juvenile justice system, which disproportionately impacted blacks and Latinos.[91] Mishi Faruqee, the director of the Correctional Association of New York's Juvenile Justice Project, wrote, "While African Americans and Latinos make up less than two-thirds of the city's youth popula-tion, they comprise more than 95 percent of the young people at Spof-ford. Moreover, over half of the young people incarcerated at Spofford come from just 15 neighborhoods—the same communities that have the highest rates of poverty, substandard housing and under-performing schools in the city."[92] Several JJRM organizers interviewed for this study that spent time in Spofford said violence was rampant in the facility. Pamanicka "Chino" Hardin, a former youth organizer with the Justice 4 Youth Coalition, was incarcerated in Spofford for six months during her midteenage years. She described Spofford as "a very dreary place" in which the "staff were very mean or very serious and like the other pris-oners, were intimidating."[93] She said, "So when I entered into Spofford [New York City youth detention center] one of the biggest things that disgusted me wasn't so much how the building itself was like chicken pens or that the staff were very mean or very serious and like the other prisoners, were intimidating. But it was [Spofford's] smell . . . I think the morgue smells better than the smell at Spofford. It was like the smell of death." She said that unequal gender relations, patriarchy, and homophobia were embedded in the youth facility. The mostly male staff made the girl inmates "put on a jumpsuit, with sneakers, underwear and stuff that other people had worn, so it wasn't really sanitary." She also remembered attempts by male prisoners who escaped from their cells to assault female inmates. Hardin's story is a familiar tale. Arrested seventeen times before twenty years old, she came from a poor Brooklyn neighborhood. Like many youth, she ended up at the Rikers Island at age sixteen, shortly after leaving Spofford.

Finally, it is important to note that New York's advocates, like those in Louisiana and Maryland, pushed for a comprehensive approach to reforming the juvenile justice system. Juvenile justice reform was problematic in New York because city officials rejected attempts by national policymakers to reform the juvenile justice system. As mentioned earlier in this chapter, Bart Lubow of the Annie E. Casey Foundation developed an innovative model for reforming juvenile justice systems that was initially adopted by the city. However, Mayor Giuliani rejected it when he came into office.[94]

Mishi Faruqee, in her testimony before the city council's Committee on Public Safety and Juvenile Justice Committee, urged the city to "develop a comprehensive plan for a continuum of community-based services that include alternatives to court, alternatives to detention, aftercare, family support and youth development programs."[95] She and other advocates proposed forming a Juvenile Justice Coordinating Committee that would be tasked with developing a master plan for achieving several objectives: reducing juvenile crime and detention, expanding the city's Department of Probation's Alternative to Detention Program, funding nonprofit agencies to deliver aftercare and prevention programs, and reducing Family Court caseloads.[96]

In addition, Faruqee created the Each One, Teach One Leadership Program in 2004 that drew upon the experiences of Youth Force and the Justice 4 Youth Coalition. Sheldon Petgrave, a young activist raised in Queens, New York, was hired as the training coordinator for the program, which prepared youth to take the lead in advancing the JJRM's social justice claims. It used a community organizing approach to "enable young people to learn about the juvenile justice system and how juvenile justice laws and policies affect them."[97] The participants were required to participate in a twelve- to fifteen-week leadership training program that introduced them to social movement building and grassroots organizing. Thomas Mims, a youth activist placed with the Juvenile Justice Project as part of an aftercare program, helped to write some of the curricula for Each One, Teach One despite being in his late teens. He drafted curricula for sessions on the Attica uprising, the Black Panther Party, and youth-police interactions.[98] The program also educated the youth about the challenges confronting LGBT youth in detention, trained them on how to get laws passed and how to evaluate a city budget, and even taught them how to negotiate peace treaties between rival gangs.

Conclusion

This chapter examined several JJRM campaigns in the late 1990s and early 2000s. In recent decades, the U.S. juvenile justice systems have shifted from rehabilitative institutions to punitive and social control agencies. Because each state has jurisdiction over its juvenile justice system, federalism allows state officials to mold juvenile policies to fit the partisan agendas in their jurisdictions. Accordingly, juvenile justice systems and the success of juvenile justice reforms must be evaluated on a state-by-state basis.

This chapter reinforced the viewpoint that movements can help remedy inequalities and are instrumental to democratizing a society as well as a system (the juvenile justice system) that is resilient to change. As a decentralized movement, the JJRM has won some victories by using strategies such as positionality, framing, and appropriation. These victories included the closure of Tallulah and the enactment of the Juvenile Justice Reform Act of 2003 in Louisiana, the downsizing of the Cheltenham and closure of Hickey in Maryland, and the cancellation of millions of dollars in New York City's capital budget that were initially targeted for the expansion of youth prisons.

Despite these victories, the JJRM still has a long way to go. Reforms are slow to come by, and many states and localities continue to implement zero-tolerance policies that have a disproportionate impact on poor youth and youth of color. Furthermore, despite federal mandates encouraging states to reduce racial disparities in their systems, disproportionate minority confinement is still a major problem. Females, LGBT youth, and undocumented immigrants face an additional set of problems during their transition in and out of the juvenile justice system.

Moreover, JJRM activists were faced with the unique challenge of developing comprehensive approaches that address inequalities in the juvenile justice system, while simultaneously deterring young people from trouble on the street. The next chapter shifts attention to black youth participation in the labor movement. Though labor and juvenile justice reform are two different spheres of movement building, they were both shaped by similar and equally devastating political and economic contexts. Joblessness, the loss of industrial jobs, and social and political alienation plagued the communities targeted by both JJRM and labor activists. Chapter 9 explores these issues in great detail as well as focuses on the intersection of race, class, and generational politics in the labor movement.

9

We Are Labor Too

[Union Summer] interns have changed a lot. People have
ownership of [labor] campaigns and really identify with
struggle.
—Renaye Manley, Chicago, June 25, 1996

When John Sweeney was elected president of the American Federation
of Labor and Congress of Industrial Organizations (AFL-CIO) in 1995,
labor movement progressives hoped his election would help recruit
young people, women, and people of color into an aging and politically impotent labor movement. After his election, he began to implement many reforms within the AFL-CIO hierarchy that were first pronounced through his New Voices platform. This included the doubling
of minority and women appointments to the AFL-CIO's fifty-three-
member board and the creation of the Union Summer program, an initiative that recruited hundreds of college-age young people as frontline
organizers for locally based labor campaigns.

Modeled after the Student Nonviolent Coordinating Committee
(SNCC) and Council of Federated Organizations freedom summer in
Mississippi in 1964, Union Summer attempted to create a movement
infrastructure for young people to cut their teeth in labor movement

activities.[1] It was actually one of several initiatives during this period that gave young people an opportunity to identify with the labor movement, as explained by Renaye Manley, a field staff member with the Chicago-based Union Summer program in 1996. Other initiatives included Jobs with Justice's Student Labor Action Coalition and United Students Against Sweatshops, both of which coordinated successful living wage campaigns at various colleges and universities.[2]

This chapter examines the labor movement's recruitment of young people, particularly African Americans, in support of economic justice initiatives. Movement bridge-builders in the labor movement attempted to strategically link framing strategies with organizing and the cultural work of local unions and community-labor coalitions. They relied upon indigenous activists and groups to create an interest convergence between local labor activists, workers, and students who were recruited into the labor movement. Labor and workers' rights activists also focused on intergenerational movement activism in order to shift the labor movement away from institutional leveraging, or efforts by old-guard laborites to channel labor's resources inside of established bureaucratic and political institutions.

I focus attention on the period from 1989 to 2005. This period experienced the expansion of global capitalism, the continuing decline of the industrial and manufacturing sectors, and the imposition of free trade agreements. These phenomena were injurious to low-wage workers in the United States and the Global South. This period also experienced the AFL-CIO presidencies of Lane Kirkland and Thomas Donahue, two labor leaders tied to the moderate orientations and institutional leveraging of George Meany whose reign as the AFL-CIO president lasted almost twenty-five years. The creation of the AFL-CIO's Organizing Institute (OI) in 1989 and Union Summer in 1996, as well as Sweeney's presidential election and reelection in 1995 and 2005, were attempts to repudiate the politics and organizing approaches of labor's old guard. During this period, the Service Employees International Union (SEIU), the Union of Needle Trades, Industrial, and Textile Employees (UNITE), and the Hotel and Restaurant Employees (HERE) also increased their outreach activities to black, Latino, and immigrant workers.

The first section of the chapter offers a brief discussion of race, class, and politics in the post–civil rights era. I am primarily concerned with assessing the material conditions and political contexts shaping post–civil rights black America, which, I argue, required more diverse or alternative strategies for recruiting and organizing young blacks into the labor movement. The second section focuses on contemporary labor organizing initiatives, primarily the status of young blacks in the AFL-CIO's Union Summer campaign and the overall relationship between labor and the post–civil rights generation.

Race, Class, and Generational Politics

The Union Summer campaign and the attempts by AFL-CIO activists to create a movement infrastructure for labor activism among blacks and young people of color are given special consideration in this chapter. Yet black participation in labor movement and economic justice initiatives was profoundly shaped by several phenomena, beginning in the early 1970s, that devastated working-class and working poor communities: deindustrialization and the shift from a manufacturing to a service-based economy and the suburbanization of metropolitan America that left many poor and working-class blacks isolated away from major employment opportunities.[3]

The deindustrialization of the American Rust Belt and central cities on the West Coast led to the reverse migration of blacks to southern states between 2000 and 2010. By the end of the decade, nearly 60 percent of blacks lived in the South and 40 percent of the resettlement population was between twenty and forty years of age. Most blacks moved to Georgia, Florida, Texas, and North Carolina.[4] These resettlement states were generally hostile toward workers' rights and lacked the strong union cultures that existed in the North and on the West Coast.

The socioeconomic conditions of working-class blacks worsened after the ascendancy of the conservative right in American politics, as exhibited by the Ronald Reagan and George H. W. Bush presidencies. These presidencies downsized many social welfare and safety net programs for working-class and even middle-income communities.[5] Despite this trend, in the 1980s Republicans made significant inroads in appealing to some union members and moderate Midwesterners who made up the emerging coalition of "Reagan Democrats."[6] In response to this phenomenon, moderate and conservative Democrats (under the

leadership of groups like the Democratic Leadership Council and the
Blue Dog coalition) successfully marginalized the New Deal/left coalition of the party. As Carl Boggs notes, "By the 1990s this coalition had
broken down, giving way to a collection of narrow, sectoral interests
working to push the [Democratic] party toward the 'dynamic middle'
and away from a politics of struggle."[7] These trends ushered in cutbacks
to social safety net and social welfare programs championed by African
Americans, labor, and left-of-center Democrats.

In the early 1990s, the North American Free Trade Agreement
(NAFTA) was passed and signed into law by President Bill Clinton
over the objections of key black labor leaders such as the Coalition of
Black Trade Unionists (CBTU).[8] Disillusionment also spread throughout the ranks of labor after the Republican Party takeover of Congress.
These events, along with the inability of key labor leaders to adjust
to the changing political economy, raised serious concerns about the
continued influence of the AFL-CIO and black labor groups. Another
problem in the 1980s and 1990s was the outsourcing and privatization
of public sector jobs held by blacks in municipalities such as custodial
services, public works, and transportation jobs.[9] Consequently, many
blacks and Latinos in the public sector workforce were forced to compete for a smaller number of municipal jobs that paid relatively lower
wages than they had in previous decades (when adjusting for inflation).

These phenomena contributed to the precipitous decline of union
membership in the 1980s and 1990s to just below 12 percent of the private sector workforce.[10] Yet this decline was aided by the suppression of
union activity and federal court decisions that chipped away at workers'
rights claims.[11] Antiunion forces intensified their opposition to labor
organizing. For instance, shortly after the AFL-CIO initiated the Union
Summer campaign, the Wessels & Pautch law firm even created an
antiunion manual circulated to companies, outlining twenty strategies
companies could utilize to counter the 1996 Union Summer offensive.[12]

The changes in the political economy, the conservative ascendancy,
the retrenchment of social welfare policies, and municipal downsizing
measures altered the makeup of black America at the end of the twentieth century. They marginalized working-class/working-poor blacks
and reduced the availability of stable, well-paid union jobs. Historian
Michael Honey discovered that older black labor activists in Memphis,

many of whom participated in the 1968 sanitation workers' strike, despaired about the loss of union jobs in the city and its impact on young blacks. In his 1989 interview with Evelyn Bates, a retired union member and organizer at the Firestone plant in Memphis, she stated,

> There's no jobs out there for young people today. You have as many col-
> lege students walking around as you have children that haven't been to
> college, 'cause they can't find nothing to do. *Blacks cannot find nothing*
> *to do here.* So what good is an education if you can't get a job, what's the
> use of going? And I guess that's the way the youngsters is looking at it.
> If the youngsters would just realize that this dope and stuff that's going
> on is nothing but killing them and keeping them from getting good jobs
> and a good education. But they don't seem to realize. Young people get
> trapped in that.[13]

The political and economic marginalization of the poorest blacks further exaggerated the sense of social and community alienation of those
living in the most economically distressed neighborhoods.[14] In their
study of urban poverty, Cohen and Dawson concluded that blacks living in the most impoverished neighborhoods in postindustrial communities generally had the weakest attachments to community institutions
and associations. These conditions were similar to those experienced
by working-poor blacks living in southern rural communities targeted
by labor organizers in the 1990s and 2000s. Patrick Scott, the southern
regional coordinator of the AFL-CIO's OI, became a labor organizer just
after graduating from Morehouse College in the mid-1990s. Yet his first
experience observing exploitative conditions at a work site occurred
while he was still in college, when his brother, also a labor organizer,
took him on a site visit to a textile plant in central Georgia. "I hadn't
seen anything like it before. . . . [The mostly black workers] worked
under horrendous conditions," he recalled.[15] His portrait was similar to
the discussion in the second chapter of James Jackson's close encounters
with black women working in the tobacco factory near his childhood
home. Both experiences, despite being separated by six decades, were
transformative moments in the lives of the young men.

The marginalization of the black working class occurred concurrently with the growth of the black middle class as a result of the gains

and opportunities produced by the civil rights movement.[16] While many middle-class blacks have access to educational institutions, good jobs, and comfortable lifestyles, others have been subject to living in communities with rampant public health crises, unemployment and underemployment, and social alienation. Ironically, the opportunities afforded to middle-class or college-educated blacks have made it increasingly difficult to attract this cohort to movements.[17] Seasoned labor organizer and activist Bill Fletcher stated, "The more disconcerting problem which they [labor organizers] have encountered is the prevailing ideology on many of these campuses: instead of encouraging activism, [black] students are encouraged toward entrepreneurialism."[18] Some argue that this has intensified class divisions in the black community even among young blacks of the post–civil rights generation.[19]

These phenomena underscored tensions among black activists groups and intellectuals, dating back to the 1960s and 1970s, about what cohort of black youth (college-educated or working-class blacks) should be the main targets for recruitment into progressive movement infrastructures. Many young activists influenced by Marxist-Leninist approaches said working-class youth should be the focus of movement-building activities.[20] As some SNCC members moved toward radicalism, the organization's executive secretary, James Forman, argued that while students brought with them certain technical skills, they lacked the enthusiasm to create a revolutionary organization because of their middle-class bias.[21] By 1972, Student Organization for Black Unity also questioned the utility of positioning college students at the forefront of the movement.[22]

On the other hand, former SNCC chairperson Kwame Ture (aka Stokely Carmichael), the founder and leader of the radical-left All African People's Revolutionary Party, maintained that it was important to organize *students* because they "have a really important responsibility" to confront the most serious problems facing blacks.[23] He believed the revolutionary fervor was already present among the black masses (poor and working class), and it was the student population or the emergent intelligentsia that needed to be convinced of the importance of engaging in transformational social movements.[24]

A third viewpoint, expressed by Huey Newton, founder and chairperson of the Black Panther Party, contended that movement infrastructures needed to focus their energies on mobilizing alienated and underemployed/unemployed ghetto youth, or the lumpen proletariat. He believed technological advancements, deindustrialization, and the loss of blue-collar skilled jobs would reduce the import of the black working class, who would "become unemployables or lumpen [proletariats]." Because of this outcome, he urged the Panthers to organize urban poor youth or "brothers [and sisters] off the block," including those involved in illegitimate or criminal activities.[25]

Fletcher expressed some sentiment for this last viewpoint. As early as 1995, he scolded young labor activists for focusing on boycotting Chinese goods, while ignoring the problems affecting America's low-income and urban youth. He believed organized labor needed to experiment with new strategies that addressed the contemporary realities of young people and the largely underemployed and unemployable blacks under severe strain from the changing political economy. The unemployment councils of the 1930s was one example that caught his attention. He also believed organized labor needed to reach out to gang members and train them for the skilled trades.[26]

Another perspective, argued by Tannock and Flocks, insists that the mobilization of youth should not be confined to the so-called lumpen proletariat, the young union member, or middle-class college students. They claim that "most of the young workers we see in our daily lives, however, are actually in their late teens and early twenties. These youth are often working to pay rent, cover personal expenses, help out their parents or support their children, all the while trying to get ahead in the world."[27] According to the authors, many of these young people attend community colleges part-time or full-time, but work full-time jobs, which often subject them to daily forms of racism, discrimination, and sexism. Cameron Barron, a seasoned labor organizer and researcher, said there were discussions inside the AFL-CIO about mobilizing this constituency, but there was not much emphasis "paid to community colleges as there were to larger universities."[28] He argued that community-labor coalitions, connecting labor struggles to community and cultural work in the black community, and reaching out to community colleges and vocational schools could provide a pathway for young blacks to participate in labor and workers' rights initiatives.

The Origins of Union Summer

The previous section offered a context for evaluating labor and workers' rights activism in the post–civil rights and postindustrial period. From the late 1980s through the 1990s, progressives inside of the labor movement attempted to reenergize the AFL-CIO. As mentioned above, Sweeney's New Voices platform attempted to increase the AFL-CIO's membership base through outreach activities to people of color, youth, and women. Sweeney was the former SEIU president in New York, where he earned a reputation as a bruising organizer. Prior to his election victory, the AFL-CIO had no strategies for organizing young blacks. Longtime president Lane Kirkland, who led the organization from 1979 to 1995, had little interest in grassroots, social movement unionism.

Though Sweeney's election is generally viewed as a point of departure from the AFL-CIO's orthodoxy under Kirkland, labor activists lobbied for racial inclusion and youth participation several years prior to his arrival. In 1989, these activists created the OI, which became the primary vehicle for recruiting young people and training them in the techniques of labor organizing. The OI's creation was a direct consequence of the decline of union membership, the collapsing industrial base, and the "perception of labor" as weak compared to corporate power.[29] The belief that "unions didn't care about [immigrants, women, and people of color]" and the perception among progressives who "didn't see labor as progressive or relevant to the social problems going on" led to the formation of OI. Thus, perceptions of racial and gender marginalization encouraged some AFL-CIO staff members to create a youth and young adult arm that could place young people, women, and people of color at the forefront of union activism. The United Food and Commercial Workers, American Federation of State, County and Municipal Employees, United Brotherhood of Carpenters, and SEIU were identified as the most student/youth-friendly unions that could host OI members.

Still, this push for inclusion in 1989 did not lead to an influx of blacks, Latinos, and women into the AFL-CIO's affiliates. In 1992, Susan Eaton authored the report *Union Leadership Development in the 1990s and Beyond*, in which she wrote that labor's inflexible bureaucracy and unwillingness to expand its membership base to women and racial minorities contributed to its declining influence.[30] A year later, OI leaders expressed continued disappointment with exclusionary practices inside labor and said there was a need to "speak up against personal [and] institutional racism, sexism, and insensitivities" encountered during organizing apprenticeships.[31] These pressures may have contributed to the underlying support for Sweeney, especially since he promised to recruit young people as well as black and Latino labor organizers into influential leadership positions.

After Sweeney's election, he dedicated millions of dollars to reorganizing the AFL-CIO's Organizing Department. He wanted the department to "to jump-start massive campaigns that [might] bring tens of thousands of new, mostly young workers into unions."[32] OI's three-day training workshop continued to be a staple of the department's recruitment of young blacks, Latinos, and Asians who composed 25 percent of the participants from January to December 1996.[33] Union Summer, a labor organizing internship, was then born in 1996 in order to recruit young people into the labor movement. Andy Levin, a thirty-five-year-old labor organizer, was selected to lead Union Summer during its early years, and the AFL-CIO leveraged resources from local unions and community-labor coalitions to assist the program.

In its first year of operation, Union Summer developed an extensive recruitment process. Applicants to the Union Summer program were evaluated on a seven-point scale that measured their motivation, leadership, people skills, desires to work long hours and relocate for the internship, maturity, strategic thinking, and flexibility.[34] Of the 3,500 applicants for the Union Summer program in 1996, 42 percent had parents who were in unions.[35] About 1,000 (of the 3,500) young people were placed in internships with twenty-seven unions and community-labor coalitions around the country.

Union Summer work was strenuous and required interns to carry out multiple activities.[36] In the early years of the program, interns worked in three-week waves or blitz campaigns often for seven-day work weeks. In 1996, interns at the Charleston, South Carolina, site joined forces with the Carolina Alliance for Fair Employment to organize black housekeepers and service workers at hotels—or what was termed "plantation resorts"—in Hilton Head, St. Helena Island, Daufuskie Island, and Charleston.[37] Their efforts helped unionize one hundred hotel workers into the International Union of Operating Engineers (IUOE). A typical work schedule was described in a midsummer report authored by the South Carolina field staff:

> The days have been hectic, and our nights . . . well let's just say a good night sleep has become a luxury. What keeps us waking up every morning (besides the morning calls and relentless door knocking) is that thought that hundreds of workers of the so-called "plantation resorts" have experienced far worse suffering than the lack of sleep. We have seen their haggard faces as they board crowded buses to work long hours for meager wages without benefits and job security. . . . With all the injustice around us, even our truest desires do not seem worthwhile. So we wake up early in the morning (sometimes as early as 3:00 AM) to protest, organize, and help educate the people of South Carolina about the process of forming Unions.[38]

Similar Union Summer initiatives occurred at the twenty-six other sites around the country. In Akron, Ohio, union summer organizers assisted with the creation of a poor people's advocacy group.[39] Interns in Detroit worked closely with four unions (IUOE, AFSCME, Carpenters, and UFCW) to organize workers at hospitals, group homes, drug stores, and Cracker Barrel.[40] St. Louis interns gathered over twenty thousand petitions for a living wage referendum, and Los Angeles interns working with HERE Local 814 handed out one thousand petitions at Camachos Restaurant, which led to the rehiring of "all workers whose status was disputed."[41] In Nashville, the "Nashville Ten," which consisted of mostly white students between the ages of eighteen and twenty-one, helped to organize sixteen protests for workers at Bridgestone-owned MasterCare garages.

Blacks made up two-thirds of the interns at the Miami location in 1996. The group conducted eighty house visits to rally support for a UNITE-led nursing home campaign, and assisted with a boycott of the *Miami Herald*. In the first half of the summer, interns visited fifty-five drug stores asking them not to sell mushrooms from Quincy Farms, where the United Farm Workers led a unionization campaign.[42] Leslie Moody, the field staff leader of the Denver site, organized a picket of over forty stores in support of a UFCW boycott. The Denver activists also conducted door-to-door outreach with the grassroots organization ACORN, petitioned four hundred workers in support of several union campaigns, contacted two hundred fifty janitors at Denver Tech Center, rallied four hundred protestors at the *Denver Post*, and contacted five hundred city workers in support of an AFSCME collective bargaining campaign.[43] Union Summer's intense work schedule, long hours, and multitasking were staples that remained in the program long after its embryonic stage.

The Union Summer field staff intentionally targeted black students for recruitment during the nascent stage of the program by extending the "historically black colleges [and universities] recruitment" plan to Union Summer. The plan was developed in the early stages of the OI program. Blacks made up 20 percent of the Union Summer interns in 1996 and half of the interns were racial minorities (blacks, Latinos, and Asians). Of the participants, 60 percent were women.[44] Although Union Summer reduced the overall number of students recruited into the

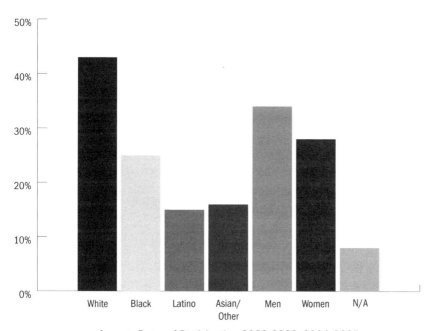

Average Rates of Participation 2000-2002, 2004-2005

Chart 9.1. Participation Rates in the AFL-CIO's Union Summer Program

program in the early 2000s, it still maintained a good record of targeting college-age blacks. In the early 2000s, the AFL-CIO appointed Patrick Scott, a well-respected organizer, to lead the Atlanta southern regional office's organizing initiatives. He made concerted efforts to recruit black students from black colleges and universities in the South.[45] Chart 9.1 outlines demographic data for the Union Summer program from 2000 to 2005. A majority of the participants (58 percent) were women. Blacks made up the largest racial minority, averaging 25 percent of the summer interns over this period. Overall, people of color (blacks, Latinos, and Asians) made up over 50 percent of the summer interns.

A prevailing argument throughout this book is that creative organizing can help movement infrastructures circumvent the constraints of institutional leveraging. Strategic framing was widely used to encourage black groups to support Union Summer initiatives, which in turn helped recruit blacks into the Union Summer program. Norman Hill, a labor leader with the A. Philip Randolph Institute (APRI), enthusiastically endorsed the program and wrote in 1996 that "blacks have as much at stake in [Union Summer] as they had in the Freedom Summer of 32 years ago." He believed that because the collapsing industrial sector "has had a devastating impact on black workers," "black Americans, disproportionately poor, stand to gain most" from Union Summer and similar initiatives.[46] From his perspective, Union Summer could be used to connect college-age blacks to workers' rights struggles.

Local labor activists, in their requests to the national office for Union Summer interns, used framing to bridge the interests of their constituents and youth who could assist their campaigns. These activists highlighted the horrific conditions facing low-wage workers as a rationale for seeking support, but also drew attention to the transformative experiences that young people could gain through their participation in workers' rights campaigns at their sites. The United Farm Workers (UFW), which organized strawberry workers in California's Central Coast (Salinas, Watsonville, and Santa Cruz), believed this initiative could give students a close look at the appalling workplace conditions of their workers. The UFW emphasized that "the conditions of strawberry workers and their families in the field [are] depressive and unhuman [sic] since they are exposed to deadly pesticides, they work long hours, with miserable [pay], and the housing for the farmworkers is deplorable."[47] The report provided a context for understanding the occupational hazards facing low-wage workers.

Although many blacks in Union Summer were college students with no experience in labor organizing campaigns,[48] there were some exceptions. Raised in a union family, Tanza Coursey was encouraged to apply for Union Summer after participating in a living wage campaign on campus. Felicia Porchia also joined Union Summer following her work with a union campaign at Fresno State University, and after working with the SEIU organizing health care workers at Queens of Angels Hospital in Los Angeles. These pre–Union Summer activities led her to believe that unions and workers' rights campaigns can drastically improve the lives of the workers. Other students such as Rikkia Graham were actively engaged in nonunion initiatives before participation in Union Summer in 2002. Prior to Union Summer, she was involved in community service, voter registration, and direct action activities.[49]

Overall, the Union Summer campaign was part of a larger push to bring awareness to college students, young blacks, and others about economic justice issues. Audrey Walton participated in Union Summer program in 2002 while still a college student and was recruited to the program through her African American studies course at Ohio State University. She worked with the SEIU local in Columbus, Ohio, organizing janitors in the city and neighboring suburbs. This entailed "mapping out the buildings" and determining who owns them, the pay scales of the janitors, and how many employees worked there. She recalled spending a lot of time examining wealth disparities and their impact of the political economy on workers.[50]

Race, Class, and Gender in Union Summer

Although the AFL-CIO's Union Summer and OI programs actively recruited young blacks into the labor movement, these outreach efforts faced many challenges. First, the location of Union Summer interns was fragmented in the early years of the program. Levin explained this problem in a 1996 memorandum to field staff titled "What's After Union Summer."[51] He said that black and white students were unevenly distributed in sites throughout the country because of late planning. This resulted in sites that had mostly white interns—for example, the

Nashville location had only one person of color out of ten interns—while others, such as the Miami location, had mostly black interns or other people of color. Another problem was that Union Summer fell short of its recruitment goals for reaching nonstudents. Only 13 percent of the interns were non–college students, whereas the initial goal was to have them make up half of the Union Summer appointments.

In addition, the screening of applicants was centralized under one or two field staff, thus prompting Levin to say that the job was "the equivalent of a director of a small college admissions program" and designed to fail.[52] He said that some interns were ill prepared to work in an intensive organizing campaign. In the early summer of 1996, he drafted a memorandum to field staff asking them to explain to the interns that "this is an organizing internship, not a vacation. You will have a full, seven-day-a-week schedule. The effort will involve many long days of gritty organizing work."[53] He recommended a scaled-down program in 1997, perhaps no more than two to three hundred interns and four full-time application screeners. He later urged the AFL-CIO to consider developing a Youth Labor Action Center to address these concerns.

Another problem was that Union Summer was overly bureaucratic and oriented from the top down. As a result, the Union Summer field staff tried to re-create a culture of union activism and get young people to adopt it, despite the fact that many had little knowledge of labor movement history. Unlike the student and youth groups discussed throughout the book, there is no evidence that Union Summer had a national coordinating committee or decision-making process involving young people beyond the national and field staff that implemented the project. Groups such as the Black Student Leadership Network, SNCC, and Southern Negro Youth Congress had three tiers of leadership: a national staff, a field staff or leadership team, and a coordinating committee. Organizing decisions as well as strategies for mediating internal conflicts were adjudicated through a dialogic exchange involving all three tiers of leadership. Yet, Union Summer had only national and field staffs.

Some observers criticized Union Summer for failing to cultivate a metanarrative critique of economic exploitation among black interns. In her exhaustive treatment of the 1996 Union Summer campaign, Bunnage applauded the 1996 Union Summer's recruitment of young people of color. Yet, she found that class consciousness was more salient among white and Latino summer interns than among blacks. African American summer organizers were the least likely of all the groups (blacks, whites, Latinos, Asians, gays/lesbians) to conceptualize union activism in social movement language,[54] and the least likely to say Union Summer impacted them personally and professionally.[55] Epstein also argues that while Union Summer appropriately emphasized racial and gender diversity, its focus on college students marginalized class consciousness and the recruitment of working-class young adults into the program. She concluded that many students had little knowledge of labor relations and worker-management struggles.[56]

These studies focus on Union Summer in its early stage, mainly its first year of operation in 1996. Yet in my interviews of black participants in Union Summer—field staff and interns who participated in the program in the early 2000s—I found that race, class, and generational analyses were interwoven in their analyses of the program. Dorian Warren contends that labor organizing is a dialectical process in which multiple identities (race, gender, sexual orientation) inform class struggles and class struggles shape identity-based grievances. Too often, he writes, scholars create a "false dichotomy between the politics of recognition and redistribution."[57] The above-mentioned criticisms of Union Summer interpreted identity-based claims as separate from class politics, but for black organizers, the two grievances (identity and class) intersected.

More than anything, Union Summer was a pedagogical tool that allowed students and young adults to test the waters of grassroots activism. For example, Desiree Wilkins participated in the Union Summer 2002 and worked with AFSCME in Newark, New Jersey, organizing workers at home health care agencies. She joined Union Summer to "diversify" her experiences after hearing a labor recruiter speak to her class at Ohio State University. Sylvia Brown was the former president of her local union, the Communication Workers of America. She participated in the OI and Union Summer and was a strong supporter of the AFL-CIO's intergenerational outreach activities. Yet, she claimed these activities were "middle-class," or were carried out as if the organizers understood poor blacks without really understanding their day-to-day experiences.[58]

Rather than rejecting anticapitalist critiques of capitalism and exploitation, blacks in Union Summer may have been expressing apprehension about the program's organizing approaches. Union Summer's early years focused on blitz campaigns that drowned interns in seven-day work weeks. Labor scholar Daisy Rooks calls this a "cowboy mentality" that has adversely affected labor organizing activities.[59] Cameron Barron argued that organized labor overvalued the cowboy mentality at the expense of appreciating a different kind of organizing culture that may have resonated among young blacks:

> The biggest obstacle is the very nature of how campaigns are run. You have people living out of suitcases for long periods of time in order to run campaigns. I think that model was effective at a certain period in history when you had production plants which literally contained thousands of people. . . . The workforce is not as concentrated as it once was . . . that model needs to have people who know things about the community in which they are trying to organize. . . . I think black organizers would gravitate to that kind of model. . . . I ran into too many [black] students who said that they didn't want to be away from home . . . that is a fundamental thing that needs to happen . . . [changing the] the whole model of how organizing is done.[60]

Barron's sentiments seem to indicate that the relational organizing approach most commonly associated with Ella Baker could help sow stronger ties between organized labor and unskilled, nonunionized blacks.[61] This organizing approach emphasizes reflection; relationship building among organizers, indigenous networks, and workers; and developing the leadership capacity so that workers, themselves, take the lead in transformative movement campaigns. But, this model takes time and cannot be implemented in blitz campaigns.

Another organizing model, the Youth and Student Network Initiative, was created by Bill Fletcher in 2003. At the time, the former SEIU labor leader was the president of TransAfrica Forum. The youth network intended to lobby against sweatshop exploitation in Africa and the Caribbean, but little is known about its impact after Fletcher departed the organization in 2006.

The SEIU also advanced innovative models of organizing young blacks. In 2001 SEIU's 32BJ Youth Brigade, composed of a multiracial contingent of youth and young adults, organized janitors in Newark,

New Jersey. Most of the participants were "the children of workers" involved in "intra-class solidarity."[62] Two years later, the SEIU established the Generation S program. The initiative evolved out of a proposal by several blacks such as Rahman Muhammad, an SEIU organizer in Newark, who wanted to educate young workers about union organizing, collective bargaining, technology, and campaign communications.[63] The short-lived program targeted young and mostly black and Latino workers under thirty years of age from SEIU's more than three hundred local unions.

Conclusion

The title of this chapter, "We Are Labor Too," indicates that young black organizers assisting economic justice and labor campaigns, as well as young black workers and union members, are essential to revitalizing labor movement struggles. In all of the youth-based initiatives discussed in this book, organizing young blacks into labor unions and workers' associations is perhaps the most difficult task. Though young blacks have a historical tie to economic justice claims—as exhibited with the Southern Negro Youth Congress in the 1930s and 1940s—labor movement activism is more complicated than the previous intergenerational struggles described earlier in this book. Synthesizing race and class grievances is a challenge by itself, but doing so in an era in which a sizeable number of blacks are excluded from a stable workforce complicates the matter. Global restructuring and the privatization ethos emerging out of late capitalism have also isolated low-income black youth from gainful employment opportunities. This neoliberal shift has been augmented by a respectability discourse that blames marginalized black youth for social ills, crime and violence, and poverty, thus allowing lawmakers to legitimize cutbacks in social safety net programs for underresourced communities.[64]

In examining race and generational politics in post–civil rights labor activities, with a specific focus on Union Summer, I contend that creative organizing can be used to educate and inject young blacks in labor activities. These strategies must consider targeting non-college-age young blacks and those living in working-class/working-poor communities who are subject to the most severe forms of economic injustices.

They must also replace the blitz organizing model used in the early stages of Union Summer with models such as the relational approach championed by Baker and her philosophical progeny.

Furthermore, mainline black labor groups and workers' rights networks must commit the requisite resources toward reenergizing support for economic justice struggles among young blacks. These groups have been largely ineffective in mobilizing a new generation of black workers. The CBTU and APRI, the two most well-known black labor groups, increased their outreach efforts to young blacks, with the former group establishing a Youth Committee in 1997. These efforts had little impact in most communities, although veteran black labor activists, all of whom were active with these groups at the time of this study, commended the CBTU and APRI for providing leadership training, voter education, and electioneering activities.[65] Yet, the activists said there has been a noticeable absence of young people at the groups' gatherings and an urgent need for mentoring programs targeting young black workers.

Conclusion

Instead of spending time worrying about what established leaders are thinking and aren't doing, we had better start getting over the fear of change, and do something ourselves before those young behind us start calling our generation out for being trifling, no good, out of touch, and ineffective.
—Lisa Y. Sullivan, October 14, 1996

Five years after the collapse of the Black Student Leadership Network (BSLN), Lisa Y. Sullivan, the organization's cofounder and most visible member, passed away from an unexpected illness. Her death was a shocking blow to many young activists who viewed her as both a mentor and a rising young leader who symbolized the hopes and dreams of the post–civil rights generation. As a student of African American politics and social movements, Sullivan believed, perhaps too optimistically, that she could bridge the interests of young and older activists in black America and in social justice circles around a common agenda that addressed the unique conditions facing low-income communities of color.

Yet after nearly two decades working with grassroots youth organizations, Sullivan began to develop a sharp critique of the internal operations of youth-oriented activist circles in the black community. In October 1996, she authored a letter to young black activists titled "On Leadership: An Open Letter to the Next Generation of Black Leaders."

As suggested in her commentary at the beginning of this chapter, the letter reflected her thoughts about intergenerational relations in black activist circles and the direction of movement activism at the end of the twentieth century. While acknowledging the toxicity of generational tensions in black activist circles, she asserted that they were less about age, "but rather a function of the social, cultural, historical, and psychological differences that separate the generations." For young activists concerned with addressing the "socioeconomic chaos" and oppression of the black poor, she believed that "our energy and focus needs to shift to developing and critiquing our own leadership." She urged young blacks to avoid the trap of generational criticisms of older black leaders, however attractive or true they might be. Instead, she pushed them to value "collective leadership and ordinary citizen participation," and to take risks in advancing transformative strategies that can effectively address the crises in their communities.

In many respects, Sullivan's comments mirrored the sentiments of James Jackson that were discussed in the second chapter. In his 1931 speech, "The World beyond the Campus," the teenage radical urged his classmates to move beyond their middle-class predilections and inject themselves in transformational resistance campaigns. Sullivan's comments also reflected the concerns of young activists in the American Federation of Labor–Congress of Industrial Organizations (AFL-CIO) in 1989 as well as black labor activists inside of the Service Employment International Union (SEIU) in the early 2000s, as both groups believed their organizations needed to implement innovative strategies to reach young people and particularly young people of color. For the AFL-CIO, this led to the creation of the Organizing Institute and later Union Summer, and the development of a recruitment strategy designed specifically to reach students at black colleges and universities. In 2003, the SEIU also created Generation S, which attempted to introduce mostly young black and Latino union members to workers' rights concerns, community-labor coalitions, and progressive electoral campaigns. These concerns also resonated among the multiracial contingent of advocates who worked on behalf of youth exiting the nation's juvenile justice systems. Advocates from the Juvenile Justice Project of Louisiana successfully advanced measures to reform the juvenile justice system and assist at-risk youth in the adjudication process. Yet they were forced to buttress their approaches with antiviolence and community intervention initiatives after several of their constituents were killed in street-level violence.

The experiences of these organizations, networks, activists, and advocates underscore a significant concern of post–civil rights generation activists and adult activists working in youth-oriented networks and movement infrastructures. Notwithstanding the generational tensions that plague both transformational and contained movement campaigns, young activists should not invest their energy in resolving a complex and seemingly never-ending debate about tensions between younger and older activists. Rather, it is imperative for them to consider whether generational tensions are reflective of deeper grievances about the trajectory of social movements and black politics. These grievances may be intraracial class divisions, disputes over access to resources, philosophical differences over strategies and tactics, concerns about political co-optation and institutional leveraging, and power struggles inside of movement infrastructures. More important, young activists should invest in organizing strategies that can ameliorate the despair in marginalized and underresourced communities.

The young people who are the central focus of this book were anchored in black-led movement infrastructures as well as multiracial network-affiliated groups working on issues that were particularly relevant to low-income and working-class blacks. The initiatives discussed in this book—the Free South Africa Movement, the New Haven youth movement, BSLN, the labor movement and Union Summer, and the juvenile justice reform movement (JJRM)—were coordinated by movement infrastructures and bridge-builders who connected indigenous activists with policymakers and advocates. They were further shaped by the models of organizing and movement frames advanced by earlier student and youth formations such as the Southern Negro Youth Congress (SNYC), the Student Nonviolent Coordinating Committee (SNCC), and the Student Organization for Black Unity (SOBU).

A major theme of this book is that youth-oriented transformational movements—high-risk initiatives that are diffuse and have a long-term impact on political culture—have been episodic in the post–civil rights era. Most contemporary initiatives have been contained or relatively low-risk, have been short-lived, and have had difficulty spreading beyond their initial locale or infrastructure. Notwithstanding these difficulties, young activists and their adult allies have expanded the opportunity structure of movement activism among young people. This has occurred with the assistance of movement bridge-builders, or leading activists, advocates, and grassroots organizers who use innovative strategies and tactics to propel initiatives. In addition, movement bridge-builders help to mobilize the resources to sustain these activities and solidify linkages among youth activists, indigenous leaders and community networks, and adult or established leaders.

Interestingly, movement bridge-builders have created opportunities for movement activism among adults. Generally, youth activism is viewed as unidirectional in which adults cultivate young people for activism. However, youth activism has a bidirectional character as well in which adults can propel or coordinate youth activities, but youth activists can encourage adults to support movement activities. At the very least, youth activists can alert adults to public health hazards affecting young people and marginalized communities. This occurred in the JJRM campaigns in Maryland and Louisiana. The adverse conditions of youth in detention actually fueled movement activism of working-class families whose children were adversely impacted by this crisis.

I contend that the amelioration of systemic and persistent inequities will require a revitalization of the transformational energy of social movements and that young people and activist networks are essential to this endeavor. These inequities cannot be resolved by electoral politics, by itself, especially given the increasingly influential role of corporate and big money interests in electioneering activities. Neither is institutional leveraging able to address these phenomena given the moderating influences of the U.S. political system. What is needed is a new politics of engagement rooted in transformational activism and augmented by movement infrastructures and bridge-builders, which understand how to build alliances and bridge differences between competing groups, and when to take advantage of political opportunities.

Yet revitalizing movement activism, especially among young blacks, will require movement bridge-builders to address four dilemmas that have perplexed social movements since the protest cycle of the 1960s: (1) the mobilization of resources that can sustain long-term grassroots campaigns, or what I call the resource/support dilemma; (2) the privileging by some grassroots activists and advocates of institutional leveraging practices over high-risk strategies; (3) the dexterity of movement bridge-builders and indigenous activists and their ability to take advantage of favorable political contexts; and (4) the advancement of creative organizing strategies and tactics that can mobilize marginalized, noncollege black youth and young adults living in poor communities. As described below, these dilemmas are clouded by the fact that youth groups operate in diverse movement infrastructures that force them to negotiate with adult allies, advocates, funding agencies, and indigenous activists.

Student/Youth Activism and the Resource/Support Dilemma

As young activists mobilize members of an aggrieved population, they must figure out how to marshal the resources necessary to facilitate such social movement-building activities. Members of an aggrieved population, particularly the cohorts within the group who have little social visibility and the least access to institutional power, tend to have few resources to fund and facilitate social movement activities. As a result, youth groups with few resources often seek out patrons who can help support their activities. For intergenerational or cross-sector initiatives, this can lead to a patron-client relationship between two groups.[1] Organizations that play the role of patrons will search for clients (or youth) who can recruit members to their organizations or give them legitimacy, loyalty, and support. Such was the case of the AFL-CIO's recruitment of young people through the Union Summer program. Union Summer injected young people into labor campaigns, but it also augmented the organized labor's agenda. It gave the AFL-CIO intangible resources (time, commitment, and energy) that hastened the spread of the "New Voices" campaign after Sweeney's election.

Unfortunately, patron-client relations such as parent/youth formations can create conflicts between the two groups in a movement infrastructure. The main conflict is the unequal exchange of resources or differences in power between the parent and youth groups,[2] especially if parent organizations have institutional ties and relationships with political elites. Under this circumstance, youth groups may view their parents as moderating influences or devices of social control, hence restraining the militant enthusiasm of young activists.

It is fairly common for youth formations to *willingly* engage in patron-client relations, as exemplified with the BSLN and the Children's Defense Fund/Black Community Crusade for Children (BCCC) as well as the SNYC and groups affiliated with the Communist Party. Patrons or parent groups tend to have more resources or greater access to resources, technical expertise, and valuable experience in social and political activities, all of which are useful to youth-oriented movement formations. Accordingly, youth groups may form relations with adult patrons who have shared grievances, as long as the parent groups provide the requisite resources to sustain long-term mobilization activities. Due to the lack of resources and political experience, it is likely that young activists and movement bridge-builders working with youth formations will continue to engage in relationships that are defined by patron-client bonds in order to facilitate their involvement in social movement activities. However, these bonds will lead to tensions whenever adult and youth groups have ideological or philosophical disagreements and their agendas do not mesh.

Movement infrastructures characterized by parent-youth formations are further tested by changes in the political context such as electoral shifts or even international events as exhibited in the case of the SNYC in the 1940s. Contextual changes may convince parent formations to change their goals or strategies in order to survive these transitions. If this occurs, then it will have a demonstrative impact on youth formations that are allied with them. It can increase or decrease the likelihood that youth groups will receive support from their adult counterparts for transformational or militant activities.

Complicating matters is that the resource base of youth-oriented movements has changed since the 1960s and 1970s. In the first wave of movement activism in the 1930s, black youth groups relied on a mix of private donations and contributions from left and labor organizations. Private donors and philanthropic foundations also poured money into civil rights groups in the 1950s and 1960s. In the post–civil rights era, with the exception of a few groups, most of the financial resources that support movement campaigns, paid staff, and organizational continuity come from philanthropic foundations. Undergirding these campaigns is a nonprofit sector that must comply with a complex set of rules and regulations.

Considering the challenges associated with the resource/support dilemma, it is imperative that parent and youth formations develop meaningful and productive kinships. The SNYC was able to experience some success because it received substantial support from the Communist Party and its affiliates, which backed its efforts to mobilize blacks in the south. Likewise, the CDF/BCCC/BSLN alliance showed promise early on, particularly in 1992, because these organizations shared similar goals and objectives. If younger activists form relationships with older activists, it is important for the young people to have the independence or semiautonomy to develop political programs.

Institutional Leveraging and Elite Mobilization

A second dilemma confronting young activists relates to the utility of institutional leveraging strategies used by grassroots and advocacy groups. Institutional leveraging is the byproduct of political incorporation.[3] Grassroots activists have been attractive to institutional leveraging practices in the post–civil rights era as the U.S. political system has become better prepared to withstand militant political activities and other forms of organized resistance.[4]

Institutional leveraging and the containment of youth-based movements and black youth militancy have been partially influenced by the development of a professional, black middle-class leadership apparatus in the post–civil rights era.[5] This leadership apparatus privileges elite, top-down patterns of mobilization and agitation over bottom-up efforts that seek to mobilize aggrieved communities and make extensive demands upon the political system. As pointed out in chapters 5 to 7, the BCCC had difficulties transcending its elite and institutionalized status even though some of its members were grassroots activists. The BCCC's inability to transcend its status was acknowledged by the BSLN's leading activists, including Matthew Countryman, the influential director of the Ella Baker Child Policy Training Institute. He explained, "The other thing is we [BSLN's core leadership] really thought it [the BCCC] was going to get beyond the black professional class. In retrospect, there was never any sign that it was going to do that. . . . There was never any work to expand beyond this kind of new professional elite."[6] Even some JJRM activists tended to privilege institutionalized leveraging practices over transformational movement activities. This is partially due to the changing political environment in the past forty years, which, as Minkoff argues, has forced many groups to advance less confrontational and moderate approaches to social change.[7] These practices, however, can be detrimental to grassroots groups that operate within the same movement infrastructures yet promote confrontational strategies to social change.

Political Context and Indigenous Resources

A third dilemma confronting young activists and movement networks is whether they can take advantage of mobilization opportunities created by a changing social and political context, and whether they can effectively appropriate or utilize indigenous resources to facilitate opportunities for young people to participate in movement activities. Despite the fact that institutional leveraging and exaggerated public health epidemics have mitigated youth militancy, minor changes in the larger political environment can create enough weak spots or openings in the political system, such that they give rise to situations in which young people are more inclined to participate or support social movements.[8]

Consequently, activists and organizations involved in social and political change initiatives will frequently be presented with some openings for broader mobilization even if the contextual changes or shifts are minor. In other words, despite the fact that broad changes or shifts in the environment may not take place, minor changes can nonetheless create the necessary conditions for transformational patterns of mobilization. Such was the case of the New Haven youth movement, where conditions were ripe for the type of social and political activism that had unfolded in the area. The city had an alienated and impoverished black population who had been ignored by many black leaders who were institutionalized in the Democratic Party machinery. However, there was a small cadre of black leaders who were willing to distance themselves, at least temporarily, from the party machinery, and aligned themselves with the interests of young people. Young blacks politicized by worsening police-community relations further believed that the election of a black mayor could address racial profiling. A new mayor had the power to appoint a new and more community-friendly police chief. All of these factors created opportunities for social and political mobilization in New Haven during the late 1980s.

As movement bridge-builders coordinate movement infrastructures and take advantage of favorable political contexts, they need the active participation of indigenous activists and networks. The experiences of SNCC and SOBU illustrate that youth activists, by themselves, cannot propel a movement or stitch together movement infrastructures without the effective use of indigenous groups and adult activists. Another example is the AFL-CIO's Union Summer program, which drew upon the energies of local labor leaders and community-labor coalitions. The important point is that bridge-builders will be given some mobilization opportunities due to routine openings and weak spots in the political system. If these groups can effectively utilize the enormous resource capacity of indigenous groups, then they can convert potential mobilization opportunities into popular mobilization campaigns.

The World beyond the Campus

Finally, transformational movements must draw upon the energies of marginalized youth and young adults isolated from colleges and universities. This can be accomplished by focusing on the daily forms of oppression experienced by them and their families. Earlier in the book, I argued that creative organizing can activate the latent energies of adult activists and advocates by focusing on the maltreatment of poor youth and the persistent and systemic inequalities affecting their families. I refer to this as positionality because it elevates the plight of poor black youth to such a critical position that professionals, adult activists, and civil rights groups are compelled to advance ameliorative solutions to the crises affecting them. Political scientist Cathy Cohen says young blacks living in the poorest communities experience a "secondary marginalization" or dual form of discrimination.[9] This occurs when the life circumstances of poor blacks are adversely affected by institutional inequities as well as a social stigma pronounced by political conservatives and even the black middle-class who view them as unworthy, a stain on the civil rights legacy, and responsible for the so-called failings of black America.

Considering the stigma attached to poor youth, their exclusion from equal educational and economic opportunities, and their propensity to fall prey to incarceration and criminal activities, transformational movements must develop strategies for mobilizing noncollege black youth. This concerned was expressed by the SNYC in the 1930s, by the SOBU in the 1970s, and by Bill Fletcher, a radical intellectual and labor activist, in the 1990s. But still, most civil rights groups as well as the coterie of liberal-progressive formations (labor, environmental, juvenile justice reform, child advocacy) have no real plan for organizing noncollege youth situated in economically distressed communities. Even the BSLN concentrated heavily on students rather than noncollege youth, despite the pressures by leaders within the organization to reach out and mobilize young people outside of the university environs. As explained by Sean Joe, the co-chair of the BSLN's National Coordinating Committee, "When you talk about the young people on the street, they're not involved in the discussion that the BSLN and BCCC are involved in. They're not involved, because we are not targeting them. We're using the plight of young people as a platform for a discussion about them, but our talking, our energies, and our resources are not really addressing their issues or seeking out their voices."[10] Organizing young people who are not part of the university setting is a far more difficult task than organizing college students. Noncollege, poor youth tend to have more financial and family commitments and economic burdens than do even the most distressed college students. Still, it is essential for social movement organizations to cultivate low-income youth (and their families) since they are the targets of the most repressive social policies.

Study Design and Methodology

This book uses a multiple-case study approach to assess youth-based participation in social movements. The research covers three waves of movement activism: the 1930s to 1940s, the 1950s to 1970s, and the 1990s to 2000s. The Free South Africa Movement took place in the 1980s and bridged the second and third waves of youth activism. This book draws extensively from qualitative sources, including rarely used archival data and interviews of eighty-one activists.

Location and Status of the Archives and Collection File

The archival data were drawn from two repositories. First, I relied on archival data preserved at official libraries and research centers and in oral histories and documentation catalogues. The second repository consists of archival sources that have not been officially catalogued at a research center. I refer to these sources as *collection files*. They comprise organizational records, memorandums, membership data, emails, newsletters, and internal deliberations of the Black Student Leadership Network (BSLN) and Black Community Crusade for Children (BCCC) as well as the juvenile justice reform movement (JJRM). Below is a description of the archival data.

American Federation of Labor and Congress of Industrial Organization (AFL-CIO) Union Summer Program, George Meany Memorial Archives, National Labor College, Silver Spring, MD (accessed in 2011). These files were used for the analysis in chapter 9. I had to receive special permission from the AFL-CIO's Secretary-Treasurer's Office to survey the archives because they had not been officially "processed" or catalogued at the time of this study.

Black Student Leadership Network/Black Community Crusade for Children Collection (BSLN/BCCC) File. These files detail the activities of the BSLN and BCCC and were analyzed in chapters 5 through 7 (collected from 1999 to 2001). The records were collected during the interview stage with the leaders of these organizations. I also used a snowball method in which organizational records were obtained through recommendations from interviewees. Finally, I was actively involved in the BSLN's Summer Freedom School program from 1993 to 1996, thus giving me access to a limited amount of records.

Civil Rights Documentation Project Vertical File Collection, Moorland-Spingarn Library, Manuscripts Division, Howard University, Washington, D.C. (accessed in 1999–2000). This collection documents the activities of the Student Nonviolent Coordinating Committee (SNCC) and the Child Development Group of Mississippi and was analyzed in chapter 3.

The Ed Strong Papers, Moorland-Spingarn Research Center, Howard University, Washington, D.C. (accessed in 1999–2000). Ed Strong was a prominent youth organizer in the 1930s and 1940s. He was one of the founding members of the Southern Negro Youth Congress, and was the first chairperson of the National Negro Congress's Youth Continuations Committees. The papers assisted with chapter 2's examination of the Southern Negro Youth Congress (SNYC).

The Federal Bureau of Investigation, Southern Negro Youth Congress, #100-HQ-6548 (accessed in 1999). These records document the Federal Bureau of Investigation's monitoring of the SNYC (see chapter 2). They were obtained through a Freedom of Information Act Request.

Juvenile Justice Reform Movement Collection File (collected from 2004 to 2005). This collection file examines the JJRM's initiatives and was analyzed in chapter 8. The data were gathered during four visits with JJRM coalitions: Baltimore and Annapolis, Maryland (2004 and 2005), New Orleans, Louisiana (2005), and New York City (2004).

The Papers of the National Negro Congress, Library of Congress, Washington, D.C. (accessed in 1999–2000). These papers were helpful in explaining the origins of the SNYC (see chapter 2), which was birthed from the National Negro Congress's Youth Council.

Ralph J. Bunche Oral History Collection, Civil Rights Documentation Project, Moorland-Spingarn Research Center, Howard University, Washington, D.C. (accessed in 1999–2000). This repository documents the activities of young blacks prior to World War II. This was examined in chapter 2.

The Records of the National Urban League, Library of Congress, Washington, D.C. (accessed in 2011). This data source covers the activities of the National Urban League and its allied organizations from the post–World War I period (see chapter 2) to the 1970s.

Student Nonviolent Coordinating Committee (SNCC) Papers, Howard University, Washington, D.C. (accessed in 1999–2000). These papers pertain to SNCC's activities and were examined in chapter 3.

Interview Methodology and Biographies of Interviewees

Eighty-one activists and advocates were interviewed either in person or by telephone between 1999 and 2005. The interview protocol was approved by the Institutional Review Boards at Howard University, the University of Illinois at Champaign-Urbana, Williams College, and Middle Tennessee State University.

A life-cycle, semistructured method was used for the interviews. The method was designed to gather the following information: (1) the personal biographies of the interviewees, including their own introduction to movement activism; (2) the strategies, tactics, and policy objectives guiding their organizations or coalitions; (3) the internal makeup and decision-making processes of their organizations or coalitions; and (4) the intergenerational collaborative work of their groups.

With the exception of a handful of subjects involved in labor union initiatives (see chapter 9), all the interviewees held influential positions or were prominent voices in their respective movement infrastructures. Most were identified through primary and secondary research such as newsletters, organizational minutes and memorandums, organizational websites, and newspaper articles. Some people were identified through a snowball method in which their names were generated through recommendations from other interviewees. As mentioned earlier, a select number of interviewees in chapter 9 did not hold significant leadership positions. Yet these were interns in the AFL-CIO's Union Summer program in 2002. The names and contact information of the summer interns were obtained from AFL-CIO staff. Below are abbreviated biographies of the interviewees that highlight their positions, roles, and responsibilities during the time periods under study.

Abbreviated Biographies of Interviewees

Lauren Abramson	Founder of the Community Conferencing Center in Baltimore, MD
Enola Aird	Acting director of the Black Community Crusade for Children and the chair of the Commission on Children in Connecticut
Phillip Allen	Summer intern with the AFL-CIO's Union Summer program
Kimberly Armstrong	Interim codirector of the Maryland Juvenile Justice Project
Cameron Barron	Prominent labor activist and educator
Tim Black	Longtime activist from Chicago, IL
Angela Glover Blackwell	Executive director of the Urban Strategies Council in Council and founder/president of PolicyLink
Xochitl Bervera	Codirector of Friends and Families of Louisiana's Incarcerated Children and cofounder of Safe Streets/Strong Communities in Louisiana
Drema Brown	Member of the Freedom School Curriculum Committee for the Black Student Leadership Network
Sylvia Brown	Former president of her local union (Communication Workers of America) and participant in the AFL-CIO's Union Summer program
Nicole Burrowes	New York State field organizer for the Black Student Leadership Network and founding member of Sista II Sista Freedom School for Young Women of Color
Geoffrey Canada	President of the Rheedlen Centers for Children and Families in Harlem, NY and president/chief executive officer of the Harlem Children's Zone
Kia Chatmon	Freedom School Program assistant at the Children's Defense Fund
Crandall Choice	Summer intern with the AFL-CIO Union Summer program
Milton Coleman	Former editor of the *African World* and member of the Student Organization for Black Unity
Angela Conyers	Staff attorney at the Juvenile Justice Project of Louisiana and cofounder of the Youth Empowerment Project in New Orleans
Matthew Countryman	Prominent activist in the anti-apartheid movement and director of the Black Student Leadership Network's Ella Baker Child Policy Training Institute
Tanza Coursey	Summer intern with the AFL-CIO's Union Summer program
Marian David	Director of the freedom schools for the Children's Defense Fund
Kim Davis	Site coordinator of the Norfolk freedom schools; co-coordinator of the Black Student Leadership Network Conference in 1996; and field assistant at the Children's Defense Fund

Scott X Esdaile	Prominent activist in New Haven, CT
Kenyon Farrow	Southern regional coordinator for Critical Resistance South
Mishi Faruqee	Director of the Correctional Association of New York's Juvenile Justice Project and founder of the Each One, Teach One Leadership Program
Helene Fisher	Area coordinator of the Washington, D.C., freedom schools and director of the Ella Baker Child Policy Training Institute
Bill Fletcher	Education director and assistant to the president of the AFL-CIO and president of TransAfrica Forum
Andrea Foggy	Freedom school site coordinator in Oakland and San Francisco, CA
Patricia Ford	Executive vice president of the Service Employees International Union and special assistant to the president for civic affairs of the Metropolitan Washington Council, AFL-CIO
Kamua "Karl" Franklin	Cofounder of the Peoples' Community Feeding Program and prominent member of the Black Student Leadership Network's New York Metro chapter
Raymond Gavins	Field intern with the Black Student Leadership Network
Rikkia Graham	Summer intern with the AFL-CIO Union Summer program
Richard Gray	Co–executive director for the National Coalition of Advocates for Students and a young adult advisor to the Black Student Leadership Network
Sean Greene	Community organizer and participant in the Los Angeles freedom schools and the Black Student Leadership Network's first organizing initiative in North Carolina
Mark Winston Griffith	Executive director, cofounder, and chairperson of the Board of Directors of the Central Brooklyn Partnership, and an advisor to the Black Student Leadership Network
Maceo Hallman	Former president of the Maryland Juvenile Justice Coalition and director of the East Baltimore Community Center
Chino Hardin	Youth organizer with the Justice 4 Youth Coalition in New York City
Channing Hawkins	Coordinator of the Service Employees International Union's Generation S Program
Gregory Hodge	Advisor to the Black Student Leadership Network and the Black Community Crusade's local initiatives coordinator
Andre Holder	Youth organizer with Youth Force of the South Bronx and the Juvenile Justice Project
Darriel Hoy	Southern regional field organizer for the Black Student Leadership Network

Esther Cooper Jackson	Former member and executive secretary of the Southern Negro Youth Congress
James Jackson	Prominent activist with the Southern Negro Youth Congress
Taj James	Western regional field organizer for the Black Student Leadership Network
Keith Jennings	Prominent activist in the anti-apartheid movement, a principal leader in the Progressive Black Student Alliance, and advisor to the Black Student Leadership Network
Sean Joe	Co-chair of the Black Student Leadership Network's National Coordinating Committee
Nelson Johnson	National chairperson for the Student Organization for Black Unity
Nicole Johnson	Co-chair of the Black Student Leadership Network's National Coordinating Committee and freedom school site coordinator in Oakland, CA
Kasey Jones	Cofounder and field organizer with the Black Student Leadership Network
Malikah J. Kelly	Youth organizer with the Juvenile Justice Project at the Correctional Association of New York
Malkia Lydia	Member of the Black Student Leadership Network's National Coordinating Committee and member of the Student Advisory Board for the Corporation for Public Broadcasting
Corlita Mahr	Statewide community liaison for the Juvenile Justice Project of Louisiana
Marie Marthol	Cofounder of the Peoples' Community Feeding Program and prominent member of the Black Student Leadership Network's New York Metro chapter
Lolita McDavid	Executive director, Greater Cleveland Office of the Children's Defense
Sarah McKenzie	Executive director of the AFL-CIO Organizing Institute and director of recruitment and screening at the AFL-CIO
Tamika Middleton	Southern regional coordinator for Critical Resistance South
Cameron Miles	Community outreach coordinator of the Maryland Juvenile Justice Project
Thomas Mims	Youth organizer with the Juvenile Justice Project at the Correctional Association of New York
Steve A. Minter	Executive director of the Cleveland Foundation and member of the Black Community Crusade Steering Committee
Jessica Gordon Nembhard	Acting deputy director for the Black Community Crusade for Children

Anita Patterson	Chair of the National Women's Committee for the Coalition of Black Trade Unionists
Gregory Perkins	President of the Interdenominational Ministerial Alliance in Baltimore, MD
Robert Peterkin	Director of the Urban Superintendents Program at the Harvard Graduate School of Education and member of the Black Community Crusade for Children's Steering Committee
Sheldon Petgrave	Training coordinator for the Each One, Teach One Program sponsored by the Correctional Association of New York's Juvenile Justice Project
Felicia Porchia	Summer intern with the AFL-CIO Union Summer program
Deborah Prothrow-Stith	Former commissioner of public health for the Commonwealth of Massachusetts and member of the Black Community Crusade for Children Working Committee and Anti-Violence Task Force
Kate Rhee	Director of the Prison Moratorium Project in Brooklyn, NY
Barbara Sabol	Administrator/commissioner of the New York City Human Resources Administration and chair of the Black Community Crusade's Human Services Committee
Melissa Sawyer	Advocate at the Juvenile Justice Project of Louisiana as well as cofounder and executive director of the Youth Empowerment Project in New Orleans
Patrick Scott	Southern regional coordinator of the AFL-CIO Organizing Institute
Lisa Simms	Senior field organizer/special projects coordinator at the Children's Defense Fund and Black Student Leadership Network field team leader
Stacy Smith	Executive director of Communities Organized to Improve Life, Inc. in Baltimore, MD
Lisa Y. Sullivan	Advisor to the New Haven NAACP Youth Council, cofounder of the Black Student Leadership Network, and director of the Field Division at the Children's Defense Fund
Claudine "Candy" Taffe	Founding member of the Black Student Leadership Network and member of the organization's National Coordinating Committee
Reed Tuckson	Former president of Charles Drew University in Los Angeles and executive vice president and chief of medical affairs at United-Health Group
David Utter	Cofounder and director of the Juvenile Justice Project of Louisiana
Jason Walker	Freedom school coordinator for the Black Student Leadership Network and Children's Defense Fund
Audrey Walton	Summer intern with the AFL-CIO Union Summer program

Steven White	Campaign manager for John Daniels's 1989 mayoral election and director of the Black Student Leadership Network
Desiree Wilkens	Summer intern with the AFL-CIO Union Summer program
Danté Wilson	Founder of Reclaiming Our Children and Community Projects, Inc. in Baltimore, MD
Gina Womack	Cofounder and executive director of the Families and Friends of Louisiana's Incarcerated Children
James Young	Member of the Teenage Leadership Core in Marlboro County, SC and member of the Black Student Leadership Network National Coordinating Committee

Profiles of Principal Organizations and Networks

Name	Years in operation	Organization type
AFL-CIO Union Summer	1996–present	Network-affiliated
Black Student Leadership Network	1991–96	Multigenerational
Free South Africa Movement	1980s	Network-affiliated
Justice 4 Youth & Juvenile Justice Project at the Correctional Association of New York	2000s	Multigenerational & network-affiliated
Juvenile Justice Project of Louisiana	1990s–2000s	Network-affiliated
Maryland Juvenile Justice Coalition	1990s–2000s	Network-affiliated
New Haven Youth Movement	1980s	Youth-led
Progressive Black Student Association	1980s	Youth-led
Southern Negro Youth Congress	1937–49	Youth-led
Student Nonviolent Coordinating Committee	1960s	Youth-led
Student Organization for Black Unity & Youth Organization for Black Unity	1969–75	Youth-led

NOTES

1. Debra C. Minkoff, *Organizing for Equality: The Evolution of Women's and Racial-Ethnic Organizations in America, 1955–1985* (New Brunswick, NJ: Rutgers University Press, 1995).
2. George T. Crane, "Collective Identity, Symbolic Mobilization, and Student Protest in Nanjing, China, 1988–1989," *Comparative Politics* 26, no. 4 (July 1994): 400.
3. Joyce A. Hanson, *Mary McLeod Bethune and Black Women's Political Activism* (Columbia: University of Missouri Press, 2003).
4. Cathy Cohen, *Democracy Remixed: Black Youth and the Future of American Politics* (Oxford: Oxford University Press, 2010); Jennifer Tilton, *Dangerous or Endangered? Race and the Politics of Youth in Urban America* (New York: New York University Press, 2010), 9; Lester K. Spence, *Stare in the Darkness: The Limits of Hip-Hop and Black Politics* (Minneapolis: University of Minnesota Press, 2011).
5. For a rebuttal of the postracial argument, see Robert Staples, "The Post Racial Presidency: The Myths of a Nation and Its People," *Journal of African American Studies* 14, no. 1 (March 2010): 128–144.
6. Dominque Apollon, *Don't Call Them "Post-Racial": Millennials' Attitudes on Race, Racism and Key Systems in Our Society* (Oakland, CA: Applied Research Center, 2012), 2, 21.
7. Rinku Sen, "Race and Occupy Wall Street," *Nation* (October 26, 2011), http://www.thenation.com/article/164212/race-and-occupy-wall-street# (accessed August 22, 2012).
8. Daniel HoSang, "Youth and Community Organizing Today" (New York: Funders' Collaborative on Youth Organizing Occasional Paper Series on Youth Organizing, 2003), 7; Kay E. Sherwood and Julie Dressner, *Youth Organizing: A New Generation of Social Activism* (Philadelphia: Public/Private Ventures, 2004), 27–48.
9. Jason Seawright and John Gerring, "Case Selection Techniques in Case Study Research: A Menu of Qualitative and Quantitative Options," *Political Research Quarterly* 61, no. 2 (June 2008): 301.
10. Jo Freeman, "Model for Analyzing the Strategic Options of Social Movement Organizations," in *Social Movements of the Sixties and Seventies*, ed. Jo Freeman (New York: Longman, 1983), 207.
11. Sidney Tarrow, *Power in Movement: Social Movements, Collective Action and Politics* (New York: Cambridge University Press, 1994), 86.
12. Judith Taylor, "Organizational Elaboration as Social Movement Tactic: A Case Study of Strategic Leadership in the First US School-Sponsored

Program for Gay and Lesbian Youth," *Social Movement Studies* 6, no. 3 (December 2007): 311–326.

13. Frances Fox Piven and Richard A. Cloward, *Poor People's Movements: Why They Succeed, How They Fail* (New York: Vintage, 1979 [1977]).

NOTES TO CHAPTER 1

1. Youth Force, *In Between the Lines: How the New York Times Frames Youth* (New York: We Interrupt This Message, 2001); Youth Media Council, *Speaking for Ourselves: A Youth Assessment of Local News Coverage* (San Francisco: We Interrupt This Message, 2002).

2. Evelyn Nieves, "California Voters in Conservative Initiatives," *New York Times* (March 12, 2000): 2; Carl Nolte, "Bay Area Voters Are State's Contrarians," *San Francisco Chronicle* (March 10, 2000): A17.

3. Andrea Simpson, *The Tie That Binds: Identity and Political Attitudes in the Post-Civil Rights Generation* (New York: New York University Press, 1998), 3.

4. Kenneth T. Andrews, "Social Movements and Policy Implementation: The Mississippi Civil Rights Movement and the War Poverty, 1965–1971," *American Sociological Review* 66 (February 2001): 75–76.

5. Holloway Sparks, "Dissident Citizenship: Democratic Theory, Political Courage, and Activist Women," *Hypatia* 12, no. 4 (Fall 1997): 74–110; also see John Lofland, *Social Movement Organizations: Guide to Research on Insurgent Realities* (New York: Aldine, 1996), 3.

6. See Adolph Reed, Jr., "Demobilization in the New Black Political Regime: Ideological Capitulation and Radical Failure in the Postsegregation Era," in *The Bubbling Cauldron: Race, Ethnicity, and the Urban Crisis*, ed. Michael Peter Smith and Joe R. Feagin (Minneapolis: University of Minnesota Press, 1995), 182–208; Robert C. Smith, *We Have No Leaders: African Americans in the Post-Civil Rights Era* (Albany: State University of New York Press, 1996); Cedric Johnson, *Revolutionaries to Race Leaders: Black Power and the Making of African American Politics* (Minneapolis: University of Minnesota Press, 2007).

7. My description of transformational and contained movements is similar to McAdam, Tarrow, and Tilly's discussion of "transgressive" and "contained" contention. See Doug McAdam, Sidney Tarrow, and Charles Tilly, *Dynamics of Contention* (New York: Cambridge University Press, 2001), 7–8.

8. Minkoff, *Organizing for Equality*.

9. Charles Payne, *I've Got the Light of Freedom: The Organizing Tradition and the Mississippi Freedom Struggle* (Berkeley: University of California Press, 1995). Also see Ronald W. Walters and Robert C. Smith, *African American Leadership* (Albany: State University of New York Press, 1999), 235.

10. Jo Freeman, "Resource Mobilization and Strategy: A Model for Analyzing Social Movement Organization Actions," in *Dynamics of Social Movements*, ed. Mayer N. Zald and John D. McCarthy (New York: Longman, 1983), 172.

11. See Mancur Olson, *Logic of Collective Action* (Cambridge, MA: Harvard University Press, 1965), 5–9, 131–135, 161; Seymour Lipset, *Rebellion in the University* (Boston: Little, Brown, 1971), 34–46.

12. Dennis Chong, *Collective Action and the Civil Rights Movement* (Chicago: University of Chicago Press, 1991).

13. Aldon D. Morris, "Birmingham Confrontation Reconsidered: An Analysis of the Dynamics and Tactics of Mobilization," *American Sociological Review* 58 (October 1993): 621–636.

14. Karl Mannheim, "The Sociological Problem of Generations," in *Studies in Social Movements: A Social Psychological Perspective*, ed. Barry McLaughlin (New York: Free Press, 1969 [1951]), 352–369. Also see Alan B. Spitzer, "The Historical Problem of Generations," *American Historical Review* 78, no. 5 (December 1973): 1361–1362; Karl Mannheim, "The Sociology of Knowledge," in *Ideology & Utopia: An Introduction to the Sociology of Knowledge* (San Diego, CA: Harcourt Brace, 1985 [1936]), 270.

15. Young Wisdom Project of the Movement Strategy Center, *Making Space, Making Change: Profiles of Youth-Led and Youth-Driven Organizations* (Oakland, CA: Movement Strategy Center, 2004), 11.

16. Clarence Lang, "Political/Economic Restructuring and the Tasks of Radical Black Youth," *Black Scholar* 28, nos. 3–4 (Fall–Winter 1998): 30–38; Jacinda Fairholm, "Seeking Justice for All," *Alternatives Journal* 24, no. 3 (Summer 1998): 9.

17. Jennifer L. O'Donoghue, Benjamin Kirshner, and Milbrey W. McLaughlin, "Introduction: Moving Youth Participation Forward," *New Directions for Youth Development: Theory, Practice Research, and Youth Participation* 96 (February 2003): 15–26.

18. Mannheim, "Sociological Problem of Generations," 362.

19. Simpson, *Tie That Binds*; Walter W. Stafford, "The National Urban League Survey: Black America's Under-35 Generation," in *The State of Black America*, ed. Lee A. Daniels (Washington, D.C.: National Urban League, 2001); Celeste M. Watkins, "A Tale of Two Classes: The Socio-economic Divide among Black Americans Under 35," in *The State of Black America*, ed. Lee A. Daniels (Washington, D.C.: National Urban League, 2001), 67–85; and David A. Bositus, *Diverging Generations: The Transformation of African American Policy Views* (Washington, D.C.: Joint Center for Political and Economic Studies, 2001).

20. Bakari Kitwana, *The Hip-Hop Generation: Young Blacks and the Crisis in African-American Culture* (New York: Basic Civitas Books, 2002).

21. David Plotke, "What's So New about New Social Movements," in *Social Movements: Critiques, Concepts, Case-Studies*, ed. Stanford Lyman (New York: New York University Press, 1995), 127.

22. For a gender-based critique of Karl Mannheim's concept of political generations, see Beth E. Schneider, "Political Generations and the Contemporary Women's Movement," *Sociological Inquiry* 58 (Winter 1988): 4–21.

23. Dominique Apollon, *Millennials, Activism and Race* (Oakland, CA: Applied Research Center, 2012), 5.

24. Johanna Wyn and Rob White, *Rethinking Youth* (London: Sage, 1997), 15.

25. Lisa García Bedolla, *Fluid Borders: Latino Power, Identity, and Politics in Los Angeles* (Berkeley: University of California Press, 2005).

26. Nancy Whittier, "Political Generations, Micro-cohorts, and the Transformation of Social Movements," *American Sociological Review* 62, no. 5 (October 1997): 762.

27. Peter Edelman, "American Government and Politics of Youth," in *A Century of Juvenile Justice*, ed. Margaret K. Rosenheim et al. (Chicago: University of Chicago Press, 2002), 310–315.

28. E. Franklin Frazier, *Negro Youth at the Crossways: Their Personality Development in the Middle States* (New York: Schocken Books, 1967 [1940]), 168–176 and Charles S. Johnson, *Growing Up in the Black Belt: Negro Youth in the Rural South* (New York: Schocken Books, 1941).

29. This is discussed in a number of works: Clayborne Carson, *In Struggle: SNCC and the Black Awakening of the 1960s* (Cambridge, MA: Harvard University Press, 1981); Payne, *I've Got the Light of Freedom*; and Jennifer Frost, *"An Interracial Movement of the Poor": Community Organizing and the New Left in the 1960s* (New York: New York University Press, 2001); Young Wisdom Project of the Movement Strategy Center, *Making Space, Making Change*, 11.

30. For a discussion of patron-client relations, see James C. Scott, "Patron-Client Relations and Political Change in Southeast Asia," *American Political Science Review* 66, no. 1 (1972): 92; Laura Guasti, "Peru: Clientelism and Internal Control," in *Friends, Followers and Factions: A Reader in Political Clientelism*, ed. Steffen W. Schmidt et al (Berkeley: University of California Press, 1977), 422–438; Martin Kilson, "Political Change in the Negro Ghetto, 1900–1940s," in *Key Issues in the Afro-American Experience*, vol. 2, ed. Nathan I. Huggins, Martin Kilson, and Daniel M. Fox (New York: Harcourt Brace Jovanovich, 1971), 171–174.

31. Christine Kelly, *Tangled Up in Red, White, and Blue: New Social Movements in America* (Lanham, MD: Rowman & Littlefield, 2001), chap. 5.

32. Carson, *In Struggle*, 21.

33. Ibid., 19–24.

34. Barbara Ransby, *Ella Baker and the Black Freedom Movement: A Radical Democratic Vision* (Chapel Hill: University of North Carolina Press, 2003), 245.

35. This was revealed to me at SNCC's forty-year anniversary conference in April 2000 in Raleigh, North Carolina, in an informal discussion with James Lawson, the nonviolence activist-theoretician and advisor to the Nashville student group that contributed the most committed members to SNCC's initial organizational base. Furthermore, I have had several discussions with Lawson about this topic, and specifically King's role at SNCC's founding conference, during his time as a lecturer at Vanderbilt University from 2006 to 2010 and as an advisor to the Nonviolence Resistance and Social Justice Committee in Nashville. King also

experienced his own difficulties working in the South and competing with the NAACP, which was wary of the SCLC because both organizations competed for a similar church-based constituency. See Piven and Cloward, *Poor People's Movements*, 222; and Taylor Branch, *Parting the Waters: America in the King Years 1954–1963* (New York: Touchstone, 1988), 222, 264–265.

36. Tricia Rose, *Black Noise: Rap Music and Black Culture in Contemporary America* (Wesleyan, CT: University Press of New England, 1994); Michael Eric Dyson, *Know What I Mean? Reflections on Hip-Hop* (New York: Basic Civitas Books, 2007); S. Craig Watkins, *Hip Hop Matters: Politics, Pop Culture, and the Struggle for the Soul of a Movement* (Boston: Beacon, 2006); Nelson George, *Hip-Hop America* (New York: Penguin, 2005); Jeff Chang, *Can't Stop Won't Stop: A History of the Hip-Hop Generation* (New York: Picador, 2005); Robin D. G. Kelley, *Race Rebels: Culture, Politics, and the Black Working Class* (New York: Free Press, 1996), chap. 8; Andreana Clay, *The Hip-Hop Generation Fights Back: Youth, Activism, and Post–Civil Rights Politics* (New York: New York University Press, 2012), 104.

37. Tamika Middleton, interview by Sekou M. Franklin, July 15, 2004. Middleton was the regional coordinator of Critical Resistance South, a criminal justice reform organization based in New Orleans. This assessment is based on her accounts of the conference.

38. To protest California's Proposition 21 in 2000, Riley organized mobile rallies where "flatbed trucks with loudspeakers drove through Oakland and other city streets with local hip-hop stars on the mic [microphone], educating about the impact of Prop 21." See Youth Force Coalition, *Schools Not Jails: A Report on the Northern California Youth Movement Against Proposition 21* (San Francisco, April 2000), 8.

39. Murray Forman, "'Hood Work: Hip-Hop, Youth Advocacy, and Model Citizenry," *Communication, Culture & Critique* 6 (2013): 244–257.

40. Aisha Durham, Brittney C. Cooper, and Susana M. Morris, "The Stage Hip-Hop Feminism Built: A New Directions," *Signs* 38, no. 3 (Spring 2013): 721–737.

41. Yvonne Bynoe, *Stand and Deliver: Political Activism, Leadership, and Hip-Culture* (Berkeley, CA: Soft Skull Press, 2004), 20.

42. Spence, *Stare in the Darkness*, 15–17. Also, for a discussion of authenticity in hip-hop, see Jeffrey O. G. Ogbar, *Hip-Hop Revolution: The Culture and Politics of Rap* (Lawrence: University of Kansas Press, 2007).

43. Spence, *Stare in the Darkness*, 126–127.

44. Kurt Schock, *Unarmed Insurrections: People Power Movements in Nondemocracies* (Minneapolis: University of Minnesota Press, 2004), 35.

45. John Krinsky and Ellen Reese, "Forging and Sustaining Labor-Community Coalitions: Workfare Justice in Three Cities," *Sociological Forum* 21, no. 4 (December 2006): 625.

46. Sherwood and Dressner, *Youth Organizing*, 27–48; HoSang, "Youth and Community Organizing Today," 7.

47. Russell L. Curtis and Louis A. Zurcher, "Stable Resources of Protest Movements: The Multi-organizational Field," *Social Forces 52, no. 1* (1973): 53–61.

48. See the following studies for a discussion of mobilizing structures: Dieter Rucht, "Movement Allies, Adversaries, and Third Parties," in *The Blackwell Companion to Social Movements*, ed. David A. Snow and Sarah A. Soule (Oxford: Blackwell, 2003), http://www.blackwellreference.com/subscriber/ tocnode?id=g9780631226697_chunk_g97806312266979 (accessed June 28, 2012); Steven Buechler, *Women's Movement in the United States: Women Suffrage, Equal Rights, and Beyond* (New Brunswick, NJ: Rutgers University Press, 1990); Suzanne Staggenborg, "Social Movement Communities and Cycles of Protest: The Emergence and Maintenance of a Local Women's Movement," *Social Problems* 45, no. 2 (May 1998): 108–204; Kevin Djo Everett, "Professionalization and Protest: Changes in the Social Movement Sector, 1961–1983," *Social Forces* 70, no. 4 (June 1992): 957–975; Mayer N. Zald and John D. McCarthy. "Social Movement Industries: Competition and Conflict," in *Social Movements in an Organizational Society*, ed. Mayer N. Zald and John D. McCarthy (New Brunswick, NJ: Transactions, 1987), 161–180; LISTEN, Inc., "An Emerging Model for Working with Youth" (New York: Funders' Collaborative on Youth Organizing Occasional Paper Series on Youth Organizing No. 1, 2003), 19.

49. Andrews, "Social Movements and Policy Implementation, 76.

50. Rucht, "Movement Allies, Adversaries, and Third Parties."

51. Ibid.

52. Tilton, *Dangerous or Endangered?*, 200–202.

53. Sherwood and Dressner, *Youth Organizing*; Julie Quiroz-Martinez, Diana Pei Wu, and Kristen Zimmerman, *ReGeneration: Young People Shaping Environmental Justice* (Oakland, CA: Movement Strategy Center, 2005), 48–55.

54. Andrews, "Social Movements and Policy Implementation," 79; Payne, *I've Got the Light of Freedom*; John Dittmer, *Local People: The Struggle for Civil Rights in Mississippi* (Urbana: University of Illinois Press, 1995).

55. Zald and McCarthy, "Social Movement Industries."

56. Dara Z. Strolovitch, *Affirmative Advocacy: Race, Class, and Gender in Interest Group Politics* (Chicago: University of Chicago Press, 2007), 8.

57. Ibid., 78–79.

58. Cathy Cohen, *The Boundaries of Blackness: AIDS and the Breakdown of Black Politics* (Chicago: University of Chicago Press, 1999).

59. Verta Taylor, "Gender and Social Movements: Gender Processes in Women's Self-Help Movements," *Gender & Society* 13 (1999): 8–33; Mary Margaret Fonow, "Protest Engendered: The Participation of Women in the 1985 Wheeling-Pittsburgh Steel Strike," *Gender & Society* 12, no. 6 (December 1998):710–728.

60. Aaronette M. White, "All the Men Are Fighting for Freedom, All the Women Are Morning Their Men, but Some of Us Carried Guns: A Race-Gendered Analysis of Fanon's Psychological Perspectives on War," *Signs: Journal of Women in Culture and Society* 32, no. 4 (2007): 857–884.

61. Herbert Haines, *Black Radicals and the Civil Rights Mainstream, 1954–1970* (Knoxville: University of Tennessee Press, 1988), 84–88; Doug McAdam, *Political Process and the Development of Black Insurgency, 1930–1970* (Chicago: University of Chicago Press, 1985), chap. 8.

62. Suzanne Staggenborg, "The Consequences of Professionalization and Formalization in the Pro-Choice Movement," *American Sociological Review* 53 (August 1988): 590.

63. McCarthy, Britt, and Wolfson, cited in Minkoff, *Organizing for Equality*, 12.

64. Minkoff, *Organizing for Equality*, 12–13; Bishwapriya Sanyal, "NGOs' Self-Defeating Quest for Autonomy," *Annals of the American Academy of Political and Social Science* 554 (November 1997): 30; Joel A. C. Baum and Christine Oliver, "Institutional Linkages and Organizational Mortality," *Administrative Science Quarterly* 36, no. 2 (June 1991): 187–219; Joseph Craig Jenkins and Craig M. Eckert, "Channeling Black Insurgency: Elite Patronage and Professional Social Movement Organizations," *American Sociological Quarterly* 51, no. 6 (December 1986): 812–829; Gary T. Marx, "External Efforts to Damage or Facilitate Social Movements: Some Patrons, Explanations, Outcomes, and Complications," in *The Dynamics of Social Movements: Resource Mobilization, Social Control, and Tactics*, ed. Mayer N. Zald and John D. McCarthy (Cambridge, MA: Winthrop, 1979).

65. Everett, "Professionalization and Protest."

66. This type of organizational behavior is called isomorphism. See Paul DiMaggio and Walter R. Powell, "The Iron Cage Revisited: Institutional Isomorphism and Collective Rationality in Organizational Fields," *American Sociological Review* 48 (April 1983): 147–160; John W. Meyer and Brian Rowan, "Institutionalized Organizations: Formal Structure as Myth and Ceremony," *American Sociological Review* 83, no. 2 (1977): 340–363.

67. G. William Domhoff, "The Role of Nonprofits in American Social Conflict," *American Behavioral Scientist* 52, no. 7 (March 2009): 966.

68. Debra C. Minkoff, "From Service Provision to Institutional Advocacy: The Shifting Legitimacy of Organizational Forms" *Social Forces* 72, no. 4 (June 1994): 943–969.

69. Apollon, *Millennials, Activism and Race*, 10.

70. J. L. Cohen, cited in John J. Chin, "The Limits and Potential of Nonprofit Organizations in Participatory Planning: A Case Study of the New York HIV Planning Council," *Journal of Urban Affairs* 31, no. 4 (2009): 455.

71. Kenneth T. Andrews and Bob Edwards, "Advocacy Organizations in the U.S. Political Process," *Annual Review of Sociology* 30 (2004): 498.

72. Hasan Kwame Jeffries, *Bloody Lowndes: Civil Rights and Black Power in Alabama's Black Belt* (New York: New York University Press, 2009), 212–245.

73. E. J. Dionne, Jr., *Why Americans Hate Politics* (New York: Simon & Schuster, 1991); David Chalmers, *And the Crooked Places Made Straight: The Struggle for Social Change in the 1960s* (Baltimore, MD: Johns Hopkins University Press, 1996), 141.

74. See Tom Hayden's comments in Cheryl Lynn Greenberg, *A Circle of Trust: Remembering SNCC* (New Brunswick, NJ: Rutgers University Press, 1998), 33.

75. Winston A. Grady-Willis, "The Black Panther Party: State Repression and Political Prisoners," in *The Black Panther Party [Reconsidered]*, ed. Charles E. Jones (Baltimore, MD: Black Classic Press, 1998), 369–375; McAdam, *Political Process*, chap. 8.

76. Melvin L. Oliver and Thomas M. Shapiro, *Black Wealth/White Wealth: A New Perspective on Racial Inequality* (New York: Routledge, 1995), 65; John P. Blair and Rudy H. Fitchtenbaum, "Changing Black Employment Patterns," in *The Metropolis in Black and White: Place, Power, and Polarization*, ed. George C. Galster and Edward W. Hill (New Brunswick, NJ: Rutgers University, Center for Urban Policy Research, 1992), 77; William Julius Wilson, *When Work Disappears: The New World of the Urban Poor* (New York: Knopf, 1996).

77. Michael C. Dawson, *Behind the Mule: Race and Class in African-American Politics* (Princeton, NJ: Princeton University Press, 1994), 29–33; Martin Carnoy, *Faded Dreams: The Politics and Economics of Race in America* (Cambridge: Cambridge University Press, 1994), 61, 145–147; Gerald David Jaynes and Robin M. Williams, Jr., eds., *Common Destiny: Blacks and American Society* (Washington, D.C.: National Academies Press, 1989), 338–339; Jack Douglass, "The Growing Importance of Youth and College Students in American Society," in *Youth: Divergent Perspectives*, ed. Peter K. Manning (New York: John Wiley, 1973), 46–50; Lisa Y. Sullivan, "Beyond Nostalgia: Notes on Black Student Activism," *Socialist Review* 20, no. 4 (October–December): 21–28; see Lang, "Political/Economic Restructuring," 32–33; Luke Tripp, "The Political Views of Black Students during the Reagan Era," *Black Scholar* 22, no. 3 (Summer 1992): 45–51.

78. Philip G. Altbach and Robert Cohen, "American Student Activism: The Post-Sixties Transformation," *Journal of Higher Education* 61, no. 1 (January–February 1990): 34; Bruce Hare, "Structural Inequality and the Endangered Status of Black Youth," *Journal of Negro Education* 56, no. 1 (1987); Lani Guinier, "No Two Seats: The Elusive Quest for Political Equality," *Virginia Law Review* 77, no. 8 (November 1991): 1423n31; Hanes Walton, *When the Marching Stopped: The Politics of Civil Rights Regulatory Agencies* (Albany: State University of New York Press, 1988), 187; Reed, "Demobilization in the New Black Political Regime."

79. Reed, "Demobilization in the New Black Political Regime," 185.

80. Robert C. Smith, "Black Power and the Transformation from Protest to Politics," *Political Science Quarterly* 96, no. 3 (Autumn 1981): 437.

81. For more discussion on this, see Greenburg, *Circle of Trust*, 39–60.

82. Shawn Ginwright, Pedro Noguero, and Julio Cammorato, *Beyond Resistance! Youth Activism and Community Change: New Democratic Possibilities for Practice and Policy for America's Youth* (New York: Routledge, 2006); Barry N. Checkoway and Lorraine M. Gutiérrez, "Youth Participation and Community Change," *Journal of Community Practice* 14, nos. 1–2 (2006): 1–9; Melvin Delgado and Lee

Staples, *Youth-Led Community Organizing: Theory and Action* (New York: Oxford University Press, 2007).

83. Todd C. Shaw, *Now Is the Time! Detroit Black Politics and Grassroots Activism* (Durham, NC: Duke University Press, 2009), 18–30.

84. Marshall Ganz, "Resources and Resourcefulness: Strategic Capacity in the Unionization of California Agriculture, 1959–1966," *American Journal of Sociology* 105 (January 2000): 1019; also see Marshall Ganz, *Why David Sometimes Wins: Leadership, Organization, and Strategy in the California Farmworker Movement* (New York: Oxford University Press, 2009).

85. Doug McAdam, "Tactical Innovation and the Pace of Insurgency," *American Sociological Review* 48 (December 1983): 735–754.

86. Tera Hunter, *To 'Joy My Freedom: Southern Black Women's Lives and Labors After the Civil War* (Cambridge, MA: Harvard University Press, 1997), chap. 4.

87. James C. Scott, *Domination and the Arts of Resistance* (New Haven, CT: Yale University Press, 1990); Robin D. G. Kelley; "'We Are Not What We Seem': Rethinking Black Working-Class Opposition in the Jim Crow South," *Journal of American History* 80, no. 1 (June 1993): 75–112; Paul Ortiz, *Emancipation Betrayed: The Hidden History of Black Organizing and White Violence in Florida from Reconstruction to the Bloody Election of 1920* (Berkeley: University of California Press, 2005); Josee Johnston, "Pedagogical Guerillas, Armed Democrats, and Revolutionary Counterpublics: Examining Paradox in the Zapatista Uprising in Chiapas Mexico," *Theory and Society* 29, no. 4 (August 2000): 463–505; Victor Montejo, *Voices from Exile: Violence and Survival in Modern Maya History* (Lawton: University of Oklahoma Press, 1999).

88. Belinda Robnett, "African-American Women in the Civil Rights Movement, 1954–1965: Gender, Leadership, and Micromobilization," *American Journal of Sociology* 101, no. 6 (May 1996): 1661–1693.

89. David A. Snow and Robert D. Benford, "Master Frames and Cycles of Protest," in *Frontiers in Social Movement Theory*, ed. Aldon Morris and C. McClurg Mueller (New Haven, CT: Yale University Press, 1992), 137.

90. Takis S. Pappas, "Political Leadership and the Emergence of Radical Mass Movements in Democracy," *Comparative Political Studies* 41, no. 8 (August 2008): 1122.

91. David A. Snow and Robert D. Benford, "Ideology, Frame Resonance, and Participant Mobilization," in *International Social Movement Research: From Structure to Action*, ed. Bert Klandermans, Hanspeter Kreisi, and Sidney Tarrow (Greenwich, CT: JAI, 1988), 197–218.

92. Robert P. Moses and Charlie Cobb, Jr., "Organizing Algebra: The Need to Voice a Demand," *Social Policy* 31, no. 4 (Summer 2001): 8.

93. Aldon Morris, "Black Southern Student Sit-In Movement: An Analysis of Internal Organization," *American Sociological Review* 46, no. 6 (1981): 744–767; Aldon Morris, *The Origins of the Civil Rights Movement: Black Communities Organizing for Change* (New York: Free Press, 1984); Minion K. C. Morrison, *Black Political*

Mobilization: Leadership, Power, and Mass Behavior (Albany: State University of New York Press, 1987).

94. Carol Conell and Kim Voss, "Formal Organization and the Fate of Social Movements: Craft Associations and Class Alliance in the Knights of Labor," *American Sociological Review* 55, no. 2 (April 1990): 255.

95. David Garrow, *Bearing the Cross: Martin Luther King, Jr. and the Southern Christian Leadership Conference* (New York: Vintage, 1988 [1986]), 240–245.

96. McAdam, Tarrow, and Tilly, *Dynamics of Contention*, 45–47.

97. Ibid., 334.

98. For a description of the "canary in the mine" and racial justice, See Lani Guinier and Gerald Torres, *The Miner's Canary: Enlisting Race, Resisting Power, Transforming Democracy* (Cambridge, MA: Harvard University Press, 2002).

99. Marco G. Giugni, "Was It Worth the Effort? The Outcomes and Consequences of Social Movements," *Annual Review of Sociology* 98 (1998): 371–393.

100. Rucht, "Movement Allies, Adversaries, and Third Parties."

101. Aldon D. Morris and Suzanne Staggenborg, "Leadership in Social Movements," in *The Blackwell Companion to Social Movements*, ed. David A. Snow, Sarah A. Soule, and Hanspeter Kriesi (Oxford: Blackwell, 2003), http://www.blackwellreference.com/subscriber/tocnode?id=g9780631226697_chunk_g97806312266979 (accessed June 28, 2012); Hahrie Han, et al. "The Relationship of Leadership Quality to the Political Presence of Civic Associations," *Perspectives on Politics* 9, no. 1 (March 2011): 45–59.

NOTES TO CHAPTER 2

1. Esther Cooper Jackson, *This Is My Husband: Fighter for His People, Political Refugee* (Brooklyn, NY: National Committee to Defend Negro Leadership, 1953), 17; James Jackson, interview by Sekou M. Franklin, May 16, 2000.

2. James Jackson, interview.

3. John Lovell, Jr., "Youth Programs of Negro Improvement," *Journal of Negro Education* 9, no. 3 (July 1940): 379–387.

4. Raymond Wolters, *The New Negro on Campus: Black College Rebellions of the 1920s* (Princeton, NJ: Princeton University Press, 1975); St. Claire Drake, interview by Robert E. Martin, July 28, 1969, 46–47, Ralph J. Bunche Oral History Collection, Civil Rights Documentation Project, Moorland-Spingarn Research Center, Howard University, Washington, D.C.

5. Genna Rae McNeil, "Youth Initiative in the African American Struggle for Racial Justice and Constitutional Rights: The City-Wide Young People's Forum of Baltimore, 1931–1941," in *African Americans and the Living Constitution*, ed. John Hope Franklin and Genna Rae McNeil (Washington, D.C.: Smithsonian Institution Press), 58–62.

6. Ibid., 59–74.

7. Ransby, *Ella Baker and the Black Freedom Movement*, 82–91.

8. Harvard Sitkoff, *A New Deal For Blacks: The Emergence of Civil Rights as a National Issue. Volume 1: The Depression Decade* (New York: Oxford University Press, 1978), 47–57; Ira Katznelson, *When Affirmative Action Was White: An Untold History of Racial Inequality in Twentieth Century America* (New York: Norton, 2005); Michael S. Holmes, "The New Deal and Georgia's Black Youth," *Journal of Southern History* 38, no. 3 (August 1972): 443–460.

9. Resolution No. 72, authored by Delegate Jordan W. Chambers, Railway Coach Cleaners No. 16088, St. Louis, Missouri, from the 41st Annual Convention of the American Federation of Labor, Denver, CO, June 13–25, 1921, Box I: F87, Records of the National Urban League, Library of Congress, Manuscript Division, Washington, D.C.

10. Letter to five black legislators of the 54th General Assembly of Illinois, authored by 27 black labor leaders, May 29, 1925, Box I: F87, Records of the National Urban League.

11. "Labor Unions Excluding the Negro," Labor Union Surveys, Working Papers, Box I: F87–F89, Records of the National Urban League.

12. Early Survey Files, Labor Union Survey, Box I: F87–F89, Records of the National Urban League.

13. A similar call was made by black activists a decade earlier and led to the formation of the short-lived Negro Sanhedrin movement. See C. Alvin Hughes, "The Negro Sanhedrin Movement," *Journal of Negro History* 69, no. 1 (1984): 3–4.

14. Lawrence S. Wittner, "The National Negro Congress: A Reassessment," *American Quarterly* 22, no. 4 (1970): 885.

15. Daniel Bell, *Marxian Socialism in the United States* (Princeton, NJ: Princeton University Press, 1952 [1967]).

16. Ibid., 143–145.

17. Ibid., 143.

18. Wittner, "National Negro Congress," 887–889.

19. "Report of the Youth Section of the National Negro Congress," February 14–16, 1937, p. 37, Reel 2, Part I, Papers of the National Negro Congress, Library of Congress, Manuscript Division, Washington, D.C.

20. Ibid.

21. Johnetta Richards, "The Southern Negro Youth Congress: A History" (Doctoral dissertation, University of Cincinnati, 1987), 20.

22. Azinna Nwafor, "The Revolutionary as Historian: Padmore and Pan-Africanism. A Critical Introduction to George Padmore: Pan-Africanism or Communism," in *Pan-Africanism or Communism*, by George Padmore (Garden City, NY: Doubleday, 1971), xxvi–xxvii. Nwafor suggests that the Communist Party patterned much of its recruitment plans after the Garvey movement. For another discussion of the Communist Party's recruitment of southern Blacks and its belief in self-determination, see Ed Strong, "The Influence of the Socialist and Communist Parties on the American Negro," 167-1, 167-2,

Ed Strong Papers, Moorland-Spingarn Research Center, Howard University, Washington, D.C.

23. C. L. R. James, "The Historical Development of the Negroes in American Society," in *C.L.R. James on the "Negro Question,"* ed. Scott McLemee (Jackson: University Press of Mississippi, 1996), 74; also see Wilson Record, *The Negro and the Communist Party* (New York: Atheneum, 1971 [1951]), 54–61. Record claims that the CP's emphasis on "collective security" actually caused it to give less attention to the black predicament.

24. "Report of Committee on Permanent Organization," Reel 2, Part I, 29, Papers of the National Negro Congress; also see "The Southern Negro Youth Congress," 3, 167-1, Ed Strong Papers.

25. "Congress Background," 2, Reel 2, Part I, Papers of the National Negro Congress.

26. For a description of the SNYC's organizational structure, see C. Alvin Hughes, "We Demand Our Rights: The Southern Negro Youth Congress, 1937–1949," *Phylon* 48, no. 1 (1984): 39–41.

27. Robert Cohen, *When the Old Left Was Young: Student Radicals and America's First Mass Student Movement, 1929–1941* (New York: Oxford University Press, 1993), 219–220.

28. Marian Thompson Wright, "Negro Youth and the Federal Emergency Programs: CCC and NYA," *Journal of Negro Education* 9, no. 3 (1940): 397–407.

29. B. Joyce Ross, "Mary McLeod Bethune and the National Youth Administration: A Case Study of Power Relationships in the Black Cabinet of Franklin D. Roosevelt," *Journal of Negro History* 60, no. 1 (January 1975): 12.

30. Christopher E. Linsin, "Something More Than a Creed: Mary McLeod Bethune's Aim of Integrated Autonomy as Director of Negro Affairs," *Florida Historical Society* 72, no. 1 (Summer 1997): 29.

31. See Frazier, *Negro Youth at the Crossways*; Johnson, *Growing Up in the Black Belt*; Jesse Atwood, *Thus Be Their Destiny: The Personality Development of Negro Youth in Their Communities* (Washington, D.C.: American Council on Education, 1941); Ira De Reid, *In a Minor Key: Negro Youth in Story and Fact* (Westport, CT: Greenwood, 1971 [1940]); Allison Davis and John Dollard, *Children of Bondage: The Personality Development of Negro Youth in the Urban South* (Washington, D.C.: American Council on Education, 1946).

32. Drake, interview, 46–47.

33. Raymond Wolters, *Negroes and the Great Depression: The Problem of Economic Recovery* (Westport, CT: Greenwood, 1970), 280.

34. Irene Diggs, "The Amenia Conferences: A Neglected Aspect of the Afro-American Struggle," *Freedomways* 13, no. 2 (1973): 130.

35. Ibid., 131–133.

36. Drake, interview; also see Wilson Record, *Race and Radicalism: The NAACP and the Communist Party* (Ithaca, NY: Cornell University Press, 1964), 97.

37. Mark Naison, *Communists in Harlem during the Depression* (Urbana: University of Illinois Press, 1973), 200.

38. Sitkoff, *New Deal for Blacks*, 260.

39. NAACP Youth Council News, "We Build Together a World of Justice, Freedom, Equality," *Crisis* 44, no. 7 (July 1937): 217.

40. Walter White, "The Youth Council of the N.A.A.C.P.," *Crisis* 44, no. 7 (July 1937): 215.

41. "Resolutions," 1937, Reel 2, Part I, Papers of the National Negro Congress.

42. Leo Wolman, "The Turning Point in American Labor Policy," *Political Science Quarterly* 55, no. 2 (June 1940): 161–175.

43. Hughes, "We Demand Our Rights," 45–46. For an excellent account of the Richmond tobacco strike, see Erik S. Gellman, *Death Blow to Jim Crow: The National Negro Congress and the Rise of Militant Civil Rights* (Chapel Hill: University of North Carolina Press), chap. 2.

44. James Jackson, interview.

45. Ibid.

46. "Southern Negro Youth Congress, Report of the Executive Secretary," December 13, 1943, Papers of the National Negro Congress.

47. "A Request to the George Marshall Labor Fund for a Grant-In/AID of Two Thousand Dollars to the Southern Negro Youth Congress for the Purpose of Establishing in the City of Birmingham, Alabama a Labor School Project," 1941, 5, 167-1, 167-2, Ed Strong Papers.

48. Ibid.

49. Ibid.

50. "S.N.Y.C. News," October 1940, 4, 167-1, 167-2, Ed Strong Papers.

51. Cohen, *When the Old Left Was Young*, 224.

52. Ibid.

53. Chana Kai Lee, *For Freedom's Sake: The Life of Fannie Lou Hamer* (Urbana: University of Illinois Press, 1999).

54. "Southern Negro Youth Congress, Report of the Executive Secretary."

55. "Proceedings of the Youth Leadership Seminar," 167-1, 167-2, Ed Strong Papers.

56. Esther Jackson (also referred to as Esther Cooper Jackson), interview by Sekou M. Franklin, May 16, 2000.

57. Ibid.

58. Ibid.

59. Cohen, *When the Old Left Was Young*, 221.

60. Record, *Negro and the Communist Party*, 301.

61. Wolters, *Negroes and the Great Depression*, 469.

62. Wittner, "National Negro Congress," 887.

63. Wolters, *Negroes and the Great Depression*, 295.

64. Randolph, quoted in Wittner, "National Negro Congress," 900.

65. Naison, *Communists in Harlem During the Depression*, 169.

66. Letter from Edward E. Strong to John Davis, December 20, 1940, 167-1, 167-2, Ed Strong Papers.

67. "S.N.Y.C. News," October 1940, 1, 3.

68. Branch, *Parting the Waters*, 170–171.

69. Letter from Louis Burnham to Edward E. Strong, December 1, 1941, 1, 167-1, 167-2, Ed Strong Papers.

70. "Youth Congress Issues Call for Fifth Conference," February 18, 1942, 167-1, 167-2, Ed Strong Papers.

71. Esther Cooper Jackson, interview.

72. Ibid.

73. Tim Black (Chicago-based activist from the 1940s to the present), interview by Sekou M. Franklin, March 13, 1999.

74. Southern Negro Youth Congress, #100-HQ-6548, Part 2, August 13, 1947, Federal Bureau of Investigation Files, U.S. Department of Justice, Washington, D.C..

75. Bunche, quoted in Gunnar Myrdal, *The American Dilemma* (New York: Harper & Row, 1944 [1962] 818-819).

76. Robin D. G. Kelley, *Hammer and Hoe: Alabama Communists during the Great Depression* (Chapel Hill: University of North Carolina Press, 1990).

77. Esther Jackson, interview.

78. Augusta V. [Strong] Jackson, "Southern Youth's Proud Heritage, No. 1, 1964," in *Freedomways Reader: Prophets in Their Own Country*, ed. Esther Cooper Jackson and Constance Pohl (Boulder, CO: Westview Press, 2000), 19.

79. Augusta V. [Strong] Jackson, "Southern Youth Marches Forward," *Crisis* 45, no. 6 (June 1938): 170.

80. Ibid.

81. Ibid.

82. Southern Negro Youth Congress, #100-HQ-6548, Part I, "Undeveloped Leads," 28–30, Federal Bureau of Investigation Files.

83. Hughes, "We Demand Our Rights," 48–49. One of these churches was the Sixteenth Street Baptist Church, which two decades later, experienced the horrific bombing of four young girls.

84. Richards, "Southern Negro Youth Congress," 48.

NOTES TO CHAPTER 3

1. Ella Baker, interview by John Britton, June 19, 1968, 29–30, Ralph J. Bunche Oral History Collection.

2. Gloria Richardson, interview by John Britton, October 11, 1967, 32, Ralph J. Bunche Oral History Collection.

3. Ibid., 1. According to SNCC's archives, its initial members were in strong support of having a southern-based leadership cadre to lead the organization, at least during its early development.

4. "Recommendations: Passed by the Student Nonviolent Coordinating Committee," October 14–16, 1960, p. 2, Reel 1, Student Nonviolent Coordinating Committee (SNCC) Papers, Howard University, Washington, D.C.

5. Ibid.

6. Greenberg, *Circle of Trust*, 61.

7. Carson, *In Struggle*, 118–119; James Forman, *The Making of Black Revolutionaries* (Seattle: University of Washington Press, 1997 [1972]), 452.

8. Dittmer, *Local People*, 208–211; Carson, *In Struggle*, 112–114.

9. Forman, *Making of Black Revolutionaries*, xiv–xvi.

10. For a more extensive look at the hundreds of letters sent to the SNCC office by patrons indicating their refusal to provide any more financial contributions to the organization, see the SNCC Papers.

11. Dittmer, *Local People*, 273.

12. Forman, *Making of Black Revolutionaries*, 390.

13. Ibid., 392.

14. Ibid., 388.

15. Ibid., 388.

16. Baker, interview by Britton.

17. Payne, *I've Got the Light of Freedom*, 339.

18. Forman in Greenburg, *Circle of Trust*, 40–41. For an extensive discussion on the debates over the Voter Education Project (VEP), see Forman, *Making of Black Revolutionaries*, 266–269.

19. Dittmer, *Local People*, 119–120.

20. Ibid., 368. For an extensive account of the CDGM, see Polly Greenburg, *Devil Has Slippery Shoes: A Biased Biography of the Maximum Feasible Poor Parent Participation* (Washington, D.C.: Youth Policy Institute, 1990 [1969].

21. Dittmer, *Local People*, 371.

22. "Fact Sheet" of the Child Development Group of Mississippi, 159-2, Folder 18, Civil Rights Documentation Project Vertical File Collection, Moorland-Spingarn Library, Manuscripts Division, Howard University, Washington, D.C.

23. Dittmer, *Local People*, 369–371. For a more complete discussion of the federal government's fear of Black Power advocates controlling CDGM programs, see "Accusations and Answers," Child Development Group of Mississippi, 159-2, Folder 18, Civil Rights Documentation Project Vertical File Collection.

24. Jenkins and Eckert, "Channeling Black Insurgency," 816.

25. Taylor, "Organizational Elaboration as Social Movement Tactic," 312.

26. "Central Committee of SNCC," Baltimore, MD, October 28–30, p. 9, Reel 3, SNCC Papers.

27. Clarence Lang, *Grassroots at the Gateway: Class Politics and the Black Freedom Struggle in St. Louis, 1936–75* (Ann Arbor: University of Michigan Press, 2009), 208.

28. Carson, *In Struggle*, 294.

29. Kenneth S. Jolly, *Black Liberation in the Midwest: The Struggle in St. Louis, Missouri, 1964–1970* (New York: Routledge, 2006), 158–159; Lang, *Grassroots at the Gateway*, 223.

30. Martha Biondi, *The Black Revolution on Campus* (Berkeley: University of California Press, 2012), 2–3.

31. Claude W. Barnes, Jr., "Bullet Holes in the Wall: Reflections on the Dudley/A&T Student Revolt of May 1969," in *American National and State Government: An African American View of the Return of Redemptionist Politics*, ed. Claude W. Barnes, Samuel A. Moseley, and James D. Steele (Dubuque, IA: Kendall/Hunt, 1997), 193.

32. Ibid., 197.

33. Ibid.

34. Ibid., 197–198.

35. Nelson Johnson in Hubert Canfield, "Who Will You Work For?," *African World* (September 4, 1971): 5.

36. SOBU News Service, "The Elections," *African World* 1, no. 3 (November 21, 1970): 3.

37. SOBU News Service, "SOBU Explains National Program," *African World* 1, no. 1 (October 17, 1970).

38. Milton Coleman, "N.C. Independent Black Political Party Formed," *African World* 11, no. 5 (December 11, 1971): 1, 9.

39. YOBU News Service, "Building the Black Assembly," *African World* 2, no. 30 (September 30, 1972): 3.

40. Smith, *We Have No Leaders*.

41. Johnson, *Revolutionaries to Race Leaders*, 98–101.

42. William Chafe, *Civilities and Civil Rights: Greensboro, North Carolina and The Black Struggle for Freedom* (New York: Oxford University Press, 1980), 338.

43. Ibid.

44. Barnes, "Bullet Holes in the Wall," 194; Jelani Favors, "North Carolina A&T Black Power Activists and the Student Organization for Black Unity," in *Rebellion in Black & White: Southern Student Activism in the 1960s*, ed. Robert Cohen and David J. Snyder (Baltimore, MD: Johns Hopkins University Press, 2013), 270.

45. For greater clarity on the meaning of black nationalism and Pan-African socialism, see Padmore, *Pan-Africanism or Communism*, xix; Ronald W. Walters, *Pan-Africanism in the African Diaspora: An Analysis of Modern Afrocentric Political Movements* (Detroit, MI: Wayne State University, 1993), 46–68; and John Bracey, Jr., "Black Nationalism since Garvey," in Huggins, Kilson, and Fox, *Key Issues in the Afro-American Experience,* 259–279.

46. Johnson, *Revolutionaries to Race Leaders*, 137–138.

47. Jim Grant and Milton Coleman, "Day of Solidarity to Save Black Schools," *African World* 11, no. 3 (November 13, 1971): 1x.

48. SOBU News Service, "North Carolina Youth Organization for Black Unity Purpose and Program," *African World* 11, no. 3 (November 13, 1971): 4X; SOBU

News Service, "N.C. YOBU Shows Growth," *African World* 2, no. 15 (May 9, 1972): 5.

49. Fanon Che Wilkins, "In the Belly of the Beast: Black Power, Anti-Imperialism, and the African Liberation Solidarity Movement, 1968–1975" (Doctoral dissertation, New York University, 2001).

50. Ibid.

51. Ibid., 201.

52. Milton Coleman, interview by Sekou M. Franklin, August 3, 2000; Nelson Johnson, interview by Sekou M. Franklin, August 6, 2000.

53. Wilkins, "In the Belly of the Beast," 204.

54. YOBU News Service, "YOBU Unites Students and Community," *African World* 3, no. 10 (March 3, 1973): 12.

55. Walters and Smith, *African American Leadership*, 131.

56. Nelson Johnson, interview.

57. Coleman, interview.

58. Nelson Johnson, interview.

59. Chafe, *Civilities and Civil Rights*, 312.

60. In the early 1970s, each year the ALSC organized an African Liberation Day, which was a series of mass rallies held across the nation. See Walters, *Pan-Africanism in the African Diaspora*, 71; Johnson, Revolutionaries to *Race Leaders*, chap. 4.

61. Walters, *Pan-Africanism in the African Diaspora*, chap. 2.

62. Ibid., 235–250.

63. Sarah A. Soule, "The Student Divestment Movement in the United States and Tactical Diffusion: The Shantytown Protest," *Social Forces* 75, no. 3 (March 1997): 857–858.

64. Keith Jennings, interview by Sekou M. Franklin, August 30, 1999.

65. Matthew Countryman, "Lessons of the Divestment Drive," *Nation* (March 26, 1988): 408–409.

66. Jennings, interview.

67. Ibid.

68. Matthew Countryman, interview by Sekou M. Franklin, September 13, 2000.

69. Dona Richards, "Reports on the Beginnings of the African Project," n.d., 159-14, Civil Rights Documentation Project Vertical File Collection.

70. Jennings, interview.

71. Countryman, "Lessons of the Divestment Drive," 408.

72. Ibid., 407–408.

73. Countryman, interview.

74. Countryman, "Lessons of the Divestment Drive," 409.

75. Ibid., 408–409.

76. Ibid., 408.

77. Ibid., 408–409.

78. Frances Fox Piven and Richard A. Cloward, *The New Class War: Reagan's Attack on the Welfare State and Its Consequences* (New York: Pantheon, 1982).

79. Some of these court cases were *City of Richmond v. J.A. Croson Co.* (1989), *Fire-fighters v. Stotts* (1984), *Wards Cove Packing Company Co. v. Antonio* (1989), and *Wygant v. Jackson Board of Education* (1986).

80. B. Drummond Ayres, Jr., "Protest at Howard U. Brings a Surprising Review," *New York Times* (March 16, 1989): A26; Robert Thomson, "Howard Board Sets Emergency Meeting on Student Unrest," *Washington Post* (March 15, 1989): C1.

NOTES TO CHAPTER 4

1. Lisa Y. Sullivan, interview by Sekou M. Franklin, May 3, 2000.

2. William Finnegan, "A Reporter at Large: Out There—II," *New Yorker* (September 17, 1990): 68.

3. Demetrios Caraley, "Washington Abandons the Cities," *Political Science Quarterly* 107, no. 1 (Spring 1992): 12.

4. See Peter Dreier, John Mollenkopf, and Todd Swanstrom, *Place Matters: Metropolitics for the Twenty-First Century* (Lawrence: University Press of Kansas, 2001).

5. Manning Marable, *Race, Reform, and Rebellion: The Second Reconstruction in Black America, 1945–1990*, rev. 2nd ed. (Jackson: University Press of Mississippi, 1991), 191, 218; Lisa Y. Sullivan, "Hip-Hop Nation: The Undeveloped Social Capital of Black Urban America," *National Civic Review* 86, no. 3 (Fall 1997): 235–243; and Dreier, Mollenkopf, and Swanstrom, *Place Matters*.

6. Douglas W. Rae, *City: Urbanism and Its End* (New Haven, CT: Yale University Press, 2004), 362.

7. Moses and Cobb, "Organizing Algebra," 8.

8. In my readings, I found different projections of the budget deficit in 1990. One estimate put it at $12 million, but Mayor John Daniels put the number at $11.7 million. Another estimate put the budget gap at around $38 million. Regardless, the budget deficit suggests that New Haven was in a state of fiscal shock during this period. In fact, in 1990, Moody's Investors Service and Standard & Poor's, two bond rating agencies, lowered New Haven's bond rating due to "the rapid weakening of the city's financial position." See Robert A. Hamilton, "Tight Budgets Force Towns to Cut Costs," *New York Times* (February 18, 1990): 1; James Barron, "Yale to Pay Millions in New Municipal Fees," *New York Times* (April 3, 1990): 1; and Associated Press, "New Haven's Bond Rating Is Downgraded by Moody's," *New York Times* (June 28, 1990): B2.

9. Stephanie Simon, "Yale Pledges $1.5M to City, Easing Town-Gown Relations," *Boston Globe* (April 8, 1990), 74.

10. Department of Health for the City of New Haven, *New Haven 1989 Annual Report of Vital Statistics* (New Haven, CT, 1990).

11. "O'Neil Rejects Using Troops in Drug Fight," *New York Times* (May 6, 1989): 30.

12. Brooks Moriarty, "NAACP Mourns Slayed Youths," *Yale Daily News* (February 2, 1989): 3.

13. "Activists Mount Vital, Tough Mission," *New Haven Register* (August 2, 1989): 8.

14. Scot X Esdaile, interview by Sekou M. Franklin, February 27, 2003.

15. William Finnegan, "A Reporter at Large: Out There—I," *New Yorker* (September 10, 1990): 75–76; Sullivan, interview.

16. Jennings, interview.

17. Sullivan, interview.

18. Ibid.

19. Joseph N. Boyce, "Grass-Roots Quest: More Blacks Embrace Self-Help Programs to Fight Urban Ills," *Wall Street Journal* (July 26, 1990): A11.

20. Sullivan, interview.

21. Adrienne C. Hedgespeth, "Service Planned for Blacks Slain over Drugs," *New Haven Register* (January 29, 1989): A9.

22. Rob Gurwitt, "A Younger Generation of Black Politicians Challenges Its Leaders," *Governing* (February 1990): 32.

23. Esdaile, interview.

24. See Kathryn A. McDermott, *Controlling Public Education: Localism versus Equity* (Lawrence: University Press of Kansas, 1999).

25. Wayne A. Santoro and Gail M. McGuire, "Social Movement Insiders: The Impact of Institutional Activists on Affirmative Action and Comparable Worth Policies," *Social Problems* 44, no. 4 (November 1997): 506.

26. Sullivan, interview.

27. Kim S. Hirsh, "Activists Urging City Students to Walk Out over School Funds," *New Haven Register* (May 1988): 1.

28. African-American Youth Congress/NAACP Youth Council et al., "An Open Letter to Mayor Biagio DiLieto," *New Haven Independent* (December 8, 1988): 28.

29. Ibid., 28.

30. Michael A. Jefferson et al. "City Power Structure Gets Touchy When Black Students Stand Up to Racism," *New Haven Register* (May 11, 1988): 17.

31. Yohuru Williams, "No Haven: Civil Rights, Black Power, and Black Panthers in New Haven, Connecticut, 1956–1971" (Doctoral dissertation, Howard University, Washington, D.C., 1998), 115–140.

32. Ibid., 7.

33. Ibid., 153.

34. Steven White, interview by Sekou M. Franklin, March 3, 2000; Finnegan, "Reporter at Large: Out There—II," 64.

35. Marpessa Dawn Outlaw and Matthew Countryman, "The Autobiography of Deidre Bailey: Thoughts on Malcolm X and Black Youth," in *Malcolm X in Our Own Image*, ed. Joe Woods (New York: St. Martin's, 1992), 236.

36. Sullivan, interview.

37. Robert A. Dahl, *Who Governs? Democracy and Power in an American City* (New Haven, CT: Yale University Press, 1979 [1961].

38. Mary E. Summers and Phillip Klinker, "The Daniels Election in New Haven and the Failure of the Deracialization Hypothesis," *Urban Affairs Quarterly* 27, no. 2 (December 1991): 206.

39. Ibid., 208.

40. Outlaw and Countryman, "Autobiography of Deidre Bailey," 233.

41. Summers and Klinker, "Daniels Election in New Haven," 208.

42. White, interview.

43. Sullivan, interview.

44. Sullivan, interview; White, interview.

45. Adrienne C. Hedgespeth, "Black Women Set Goals for Posts on City Boards," *New Haven Register* (November 3, 1989): 5.

46. Some of the funds for the voter registration efforts came from Youth Action, a left-oriented national student activist organization that operated during the 1980s. Matthew Countryman, a former divestment student activist at Yale University and an organizer with Youth Action, convinced the group to disseminate funds to the New Haven youth voter registration efforts. Countryman, interview.

47. Sullivan, interview.

48. Lee, *For Freedom's Sake*, 63.

49. Summers and Klinker, "The Daniels Election in New Haven and the Failure of the Deracialization Hypothesis"; Josh Kovner, "State Voter Registration Dips," *New Haven Register* (November 2, 1989): 6.

50. Outlaw and Countryman, "Autobiography of Deidre Bailey," 237.

51. In New Haven, mayoral elections are staggered every two years, instead of every four years. Daniels was elected for a second term, 1991–1993.

52. K. D. Codish, "The New Haven Police Academy: Putting a Sacred Cow Out to Pasture," *Police Chief* (November 1996): 40–41.

53. Ibid.

54. Douglas Rae, "Making Life Work in Crowded Places," *Urban Affairs Review* 41, no. 3 (January 2006): 274; White, interview.

55. John P. Elwood, "Rethinking Government Participation in Urban Renewal: Neighborhood Revitalization in New Haven," *Yale Law & Policy Review* 12, no. 1 (1994): 145–147.

56. Rae, "Making Life Work in Crowded Places," 284–286.

NOTES TO CHAPTER 5

1. Manning Marable, "Toward a Renaissance of Progressive Black Politics," in *Speaking Truth to Power: Essays on Race, Resistance, and Radicalism* (Boulder, CO: Westview, 1992), 78.

2. Joseph McCormick, II and Sekou M. Franklin, "Expressions of Racial Consciousness in the African American Community: Data from the Million Man March," in *Blacks and Multiracial Politics in America*, ed. Yvette M. Alex-Assenoh and Lawrence J. Hanks (New York: New York University Press, 2000), 317–319.

3. Morris, "Birmingham Confrontation Reconsidered."

4. Lipset, *Rebellion in the University*, 34–46.

5. Mark Winston Griffith, interview by Sekou M. Franklin, April 5, 2000.

6. Marian Wright Edelman, "Remarks by Marian Wright Edelman, President of the Children's Defense Fund at the Howard University" (Washington, D.C.: Children's Defense Fund, May 12, 1990), BSLN/BCCC Collection File.

7. Garrow, *Bearing the Cross*, 576–578.

8. Mickey Kaus, "The Godmother: What's Wrong with Marian Wright Edelman," *New Republic* 208, no. 7 (February 15, 1993): 21–25.

9. Black Community Crusade for Children, *Progress and Peril: Black Children in America* (Washington, D.C.: Children's Defense Fund, 1993), see description on the inside cover of the book titled *About CDF*.

10. Children's Defense Fund, "Children's Defense Fund Interim Report to the Van Ameringen Foundation, Inc. Black Community Leadership Training, March 1, 1990–December 1990" (1991): 1, BSLN/BCCC Collection File.

11. Edelman, "Remarks by Marian Wright Edelman."

12. Children's Defense Fund, "Children's Defense Fund Interim Report."

13. Ibid.

14. Sullivan, interview.

15. Andrea Maneulita Payne, "One Step Forward," *City Limits* 21, no. 4 (April 1996): 8.

16. See Kasey Jones, interview by Sekou M. Franklin, June 17, 2000.

17. Marian Wright Edelman, letter to Bellagio participants, December 5, 1990, 7, BSLN/BCCC Collection File.

18. Ibid., 7, 9.

19. See memorandum titled "The Bellagio Black Leadership Meeting for Children and Their Families," Children's Defense Fund (n.d.), BSLN/BCCC Collection File.

20. Reed Tuckson, interview by Sekou M. Franklin, February 11, 2002.

21. Barbara Sabol, interview by Sekou M. Franklin, January 29, 2002.

22. Enola Aird, interview by Sekou M. Franklin, January 25, 2002.

23. Steve Minter, interview by Sekou M. Franklin, January 18, 2002.

24. Otis Johnson, "The Black Community Crusade for Children: Building a National Movement" (Concept paper, July 20, 1994): 2, BSLN/BCCC Collection File.

25. Black Community Crusade for Children, "What You Can Do to See That No Child Is Left Behind and That Every Child Has a Healthy Start, a Head Start, a Fair Start, and a Moral Start in Life" (n.d.), 1–17, BSLN/BCCC Collection File.

26. Johnson, "Black Community Crusade for Children."

27. Black Community Crusade for Children, "What You Can Do."

28. By 1996, the BCCC had opened up several other regional offices, including another Midwestern office in Cincinnati, Ohio, a southern regional office in Jackson, Mississippi, and another office in St. Paul, Minnesota.

29. Lolita McDavid, interview by Sekou M. Franklin, December 12, 2001.

30. Black Community Crusade for Children, "Summary of the Black Community Crusade for Children Regional Offices and Constituency Group Meetings," 9, BSLN/BCCC Collection File.

31. Sullivan, interview.

32. Ibid.

33. Matthew Countryman, letter to Marian Wright Edelman, July 24, 1991, BSLN/ BCCC Collection File.

34. Ibid.

35. Jones, interview; Malkia Lydia, interview by Sekou M. Franklin, November 2, 1999.

36. Atwater had previously served as Strom Thurmond's chief political strategist in his 1970 senatorial campaign, as the deputy campaign manager for Ronald Reagan, as George Bush's campaign manager, and also as chairperson of the Republican National Committee. He was also largely responsible for orchestrating and reinvigorating the southern strategy of courting white southerners by making implicit racist appeals to them. See Thomas Byrne Edsall with Mary D. Edsall, *Chain Reaction: The Impact of Race, Rights, and Taxes on American Politics* (New York: Norton, 1991), 144–145, 220–223.

37. Jennings, interview.

38. Jeffery D. Robinson, "Black College Student Group Proposal," submitted by the Working Committee to the Children's Defense Fund, July 23, 1991, BSLN/BCCC Collection File; Kasey Jones, memo to black leadership meeting participants, "Meeting Follow-Up," July 29, 1991, BSLN/BCCC Collection File.

39. Children's Defense Fund, "Biographical Sketches of Black Student Leadership Meeting Participants," June 1991, BSLN/BCCC Collection File.

40. Richard Gray, interview by Sekou M. Franklin, March 15, 2000.

41. Ibid.

42. Wendy Battles, "Black Students Take Lead in Empowering Children," letter of draft of article sent to Steven White, April 14, 1992, BSLN/BCCC Collection File.

43. Matt Neufeld, "Students Take Time to Paint, Canvass Artful Volunteers Aid Communities," *Washington Times* (September 21, 1992): B3.

44. Jones, interview.

45. Sean Greene, interview by Sekou M. Franklin, April 11, 2000.

46. Ibid.

47. White, interview.

48. Black Student Leadership Network, *Black Student Leadership Network House Party Manual* (Washington, D.C.: Children's Defense Fund, 1995), BSLN/BCCC Collection File.

49. Black Student Leadership Network Staff, "The Black Student Leadership Network 1991–1996," 1996, 38, BSLN/BCCC Collection File.

50. Black Student Leadership Network, "Steering Committee Reports," *We Speak! A Voice of African-American Youth* 1, no. 2 (Winter 1992–1993): 4, BSLN/BCCC Collection File.

51. Gray, interview.

52. Black Student Leadership Network, "Constitution/Bylaws of the Black Student Leadership Network," 1993, BSLN/BCCC Collection File. According to the BSLN archives, the organization made no distinction between the constitution and the bylaws.

53. Belinda Robnett, *How Long? How Long? African American Women in the Struggle for Civil Rights* (New York: Oxford University Press, 1997), 191.

54. Joshua Gamson, "Messages of Exclusion: Gender, Movements, and Symbolic Boundaries," *Gender & Society* 11, no. 2 (April 1997): 178–183.

55. Verta Taylor and Nancy E. Whittier, "Collective Identity in Social Movement Communities: Lesbian Feminist Mobilization," in *Frontiers in Social Movement Theory*, ed. Aldon D. Morris and Carol McClurg Mueller (New Haven, CT: Yale University Press, 1992), 104–129.

56. Ransby, *Ella Baker and the Black Freedom Movement*; Charles M. Payne, "Ella Baker and Models of Social Change," *Journal of Women in Culture and Society* 14, no. 4 (1989): 885–899.

57. Carol Mueller, "Ella Baker and the Origins of 'Participatory Democracy,'" in *Women in the Civil Rights Movement: Trailblazers and Torchbearers, 1941–1965*, ed. Vicki L. Crawford, Jacqueline Anne Rouse, and Barbara Woods (Brooklyn, NY: Carlson, 1990), 52.

58. Black Student Leadership Network, "Black Student Leadership Network's— Midwest Academy Training Sessions," prepared by the Ella Baker Child Policy Training Institute, Washington, D.C., May 12–15, 1994, 4–5, BSLN/BCCC Collection File.

59. Countryman, interview.

60. Marian Wright Edelman, "Freedom Schools," memorandum, September 9, 1991, BSLN/BCCC Collection File.

61. Ibid.

62. Michele N.-K. Collison, "Network of Black Students Hopes to Create a New Generation of Civil Rights Leaders," *Chronicle of Higher Education* 39, no. 6 (September 30, 1992): A28.

63. Ibid., A29.

64. Ibid.

65. Ibid., A29.

66. Nicole Burrowes, interview by Sekou M. Franklin, May 2, 2000; Collison, "Network of Black Students," A29.

67. Burrowes, interview.

68. Collison, "Network of Black Students," A29.

69. Greene, interview.

70. Darriel Hoy, interview by Sekou M. Franklin, September 9, 2000.

71. Countryman, interview; Gray, interview.

72. Countryman, interview.

73. Ibid.

74. Black Community Crusade for Children, "What You Can Do."

75. Johnson, "Black Community Crusade for Children," 8–9.

76. See Black Community Crusade for Children, "Summary of the Black Community Crusade for Children Regional Offices and Constituency Group Meetings," 13.

77. Johnson, "Black Community Crusade for Children," 9.

78. Black Student Leadership Network, "Regional Reports: Atlanta," *We Speak! A Voice of African-American Youth* 1, no. 2 (Winter 1992–1993): 6, BSLN/BCCC Collection File.

79. See African American Leadership Young Adult Working Group, "Progressive Economic Development in Black America: Models of Self-Help," minutes of Economic Development Workshop, November 20, 1992, Atlanta, GA, 1–3, BSLN/BCCC Collection File; notes for meeting on November 20–22, 1992, Atlanta, GA, 1–8, BSLN/BCCC Collection File; African American Leadership Young Adult Working Group, "Summary of Proceedings/Working Group," Criminal Justice and Violence Working Group (Bruce Bennett, Donna Daniels, Malik Edwards, Gregory Hodge, Reverend Bernice King, Allen Martin, and Gilda Williams), January 15, 1993, Atlanta, GA, 1–3, BSLN/BCCC Collection File.

80. African American Leadership Young Adult Working Group, Young Adult Conference Working Paper on Health Care, Health Care Committee: Carole Joyner, Marty Rodgers, Matthew Countryman, submitted by Matthew Countryman, BSLN/BCCC Collection File.

81. African American Leadership Young Adult Working Group, "Paper on Social, Economic, and Political Empowerment," submitted by the Empowerment Working Group: Kim Freeman, Keith Jennings, Lisa Y. Sullivan, and Steven White, BSLN/BCCC Collection File.

82. Ibid., 3.

83. Some of the attendees to the Amenia Conference included E. Franklin Frazier, Abram Harris, and Ralph Bunche.

84. Jennings, interview.

85. Ibid.

86. Countryman, interview.

NOTES TO CHAPTER 6

1. Black Community Crusade for Children, "Tony Massengale: Organizing as a Tool for Change," *Necessary: News of the Black Community Crusade for Children* 2, no. 4 (Spring 1995): 8–9, BSLN/BCCC Collection File. Tony Massengale is a prominent South Central Los Angeles organizer who joined the Black Community Crusade for Children in 1995. At the time, he was the assistant director at the Community Youth Gang Services Project in Los Angeles and founder of Community CANDO and the Center for Civic Capacity Building.

2. See Robnett, "African-American Women in the Civil Rights Movement," 1667.

3. Francesca Polletta, "Free Spaces in Collective Action," *Theory and Society* 28 (1999): 1–38; Francesca Polletta, "The Structural Context of Novel Rights Claims: Southern Civil Rights Organizing, 1961–1966," *Law & Society Review* 34, no. 2 (2000): 383, 402.

4. Daniel J. Sherman, "Disruption or Convention? A Process-based Explanation of Divergent Repertoires of Contention among Opponents to Low-level Radioactive Waste Disposal Sites," *Social Movement Studies* 7, no. 3 (December 2000): 265–280; John Stolle-McAllister, "Local Social Movements and Mesoamerican Cultural Resistance and Adaptation," *Social Movement Studies* 6, no. 2 (September 2007): 161–175.

5. Jo Reger, "Organizational Dynamics and Construction of Multiple Feminist Identities in the National Organization for Women," *Gender and Society* 16, no. 5 (October 2002): 725.

6. BSLN organizers also worked diligently in other areas throughout the country: Naomi Walker, the Midwest regional field organizer coordinated activities in Ohio; Kelli Doss, another Midwest regional organizer, coordinated the Minnesota-based activities; and Deidre Proctor was responsible for BSLN initiatives in the Mid-Atlantic region (Washington, D.C., Delaware, and New Jersey), primarily in the organization's later years. Due to the lack of data, this study does not give detailed attention to their laborious work in these areas.

7. C. Alvin Hughes, "A New Agenda for the South: The Role and Influence of the Highlander Folk School, 1953–1961," *Phylon* 46, no. 3 (1985): 245; also see Charles M. Payne and Carol Sills Strickland, eds., *Teach Freedom: Education for Liberation in the African-American Tradition* (New York: Teachers College Press, 2008).

8. Some argue that the freedom school concept was developed by Boston educator and community activist Noel Day in 1963. He established a freedom school in Boston to serve students who were going to miss school after the Massachusetts freedom movement organized a one-day school boycott in the early sixties. Although little has been written about it, given Charlie Cobb's Boston-area roots, he may have been influenced by the activities of Noel Day. See Paul Lauter and Dan Perlstein, "Introduction," *Radical Teacher*, no. 40 (Fall 1991 [1964]): 2.

9. Ibid., 4.

10. Len Holt, *The Summer That Didn't End: the Story of the Mississippi Civil Rights Project in 1964* (New York: De Capo Press, 1992), 317; Bruce Watson, *Freedom Summer: The Savage Season That Made Mississippi Burn and Made America a Democracy* (New York: Viking, 2010). Also see Doug McAdam, *Freedom Summer* (New York: Oxford University Press, 1988).

11. Edelman, "Freedom Schools."

12. David Von Drehle, "Eager Advocates of Change Are Told to Await New Clinton Team's Results," *Washington Post* (December 14, 1992): A4.

13. Bill Clinton and Al Gore, *Putting People First: How We Can All Change America* (New York: Times Books, 1992).

14. See Adolph Reed, Jr., ed., *Without Justice for All: The New Liberalism and Our Retreat from Racial Equality* (Boulder, CO: Westview, 2001).

15. Blackwell, interview.

16. Countryman, interview. This conversation was confirmed through an informal (not recorded) interview by Roger Wilkins.

17. Darold Johnson and Darriel Hoy, "1994 Freedom Schools Feed Children and Empower Parents," *We Speak! A Voice of African American Youth* 1, no. 3 (Spring 1994): 1, BSLN/BCCC Collection File.

18. Ibid.

19. Blackwell, interview.

20. Black Community Crusade for Children, "Summary of the Black Community Crusade for Children Regional Offices and Constituency Group Meetings," 27.

21. Ibid., 22.

22. Ibid., 27.

23. Comer in Black Community Crusade for Children, "Summary of the Black Community Crusade for Children Regional Offices and Constituency Group Meetings," 27.

24. Ibid., 26.

25. White, interview.

26. Countryman, interview.

27. Ibid.

28. Helene Fisher, interview by Sekou M. Franklin, August 16, 1999.

29. Helene Fisher, "Ella Baker Small Group Notes at the Haley Farm," memorandum, December 20, 1993, 2–3, BSLN/BCCC Collection File.

30. Ibid.

31. The Los Angeles civil unrest occurred in the aftermath of the acquittal of four officers who, along with other Simi Valley, California, officers, were caught on videotape in the brutal beating of Rodney King in 1991.

32. Steven White, Lisa Y. Sullivan, and Matthew Countryman, "Building a Cross-Class, Multi-Generational Movement for Black Children," *We Speak! A Voice of African-American Youth*" (Winter 1992–1993), 6–7, BSLN/BCCC Collection File; Countryman, interview.

33. White, Sullivan, and Countryman, "Building a Cross-Class, Multi-Generational Movement for Black Children," 1.

34. Minkoff, *Organizing for Equality*.

35. Nicole Johnson, interview by Sekou M. Franklin, April 12, 1999.

36. Minkoff, *Organizing for Equality*.

37. Catherine Milton, "National Service: Secret Weapon in the Fight Against Crime," *Public Management* 76, no. 7 (July 1994): 6–10.

38. Ibid.

39. Toya Lillard and Adrianne Garden-Vazquez, "Excerpts from a Statement Delivered by Toya Lillard of the Harlem Freedom Schools and Adrianne Garden-Vazquez of El Puente at the Summer of Service Training Sessions," *Freedom News* 1 (July 9, 1993): 2, BSLN/BCCC Collection File; see Lisa Y. Sullivan and Matthew Countryman, "From the Director's Chair," *Freedom News* 1 (July 9, 1993): 1, BSLN/BCCC Collection File.

40. Matthew Countryman and Lisa Y. Sullivan, "National *Service*: Don't Do For, Do With," *Social Policy* 24, no. 1 (Fall 1993): 29.

41. Andrea Foggy, interview by Sekou M. Franklin, January 31, 2000; Kia Chatmon, interview by Sekou M. Franklin, August 17, 2000.

42. A review of several cities that housed freedom schools placed the costs as ranging from $43,000 to $73,000 depending on the number of freedom school sites and interns in a city, housing costs for the interns, and additional expenses for volunteers.

43. Black Student Leadership Network and the Black Community Crusade for Children, audiotaped conference call, March 3, 1994, BSLN/BCCC Collection File.

44. Jason Walker, interview by Sekou M. Franklin, March 16, 2000.

45. Kim Davis, interview by Sekou M. Franklin, April 24, 2000.

46. Katherine McFate, "Urban Violence: Drugs, Gangs, and Juveniles," mimeograph, 1991, 4, BSLN/BCCC Collection File.

47. Black Community Crusade for Children, "Saving Our Children from the Violence: The Ounce of Prevention," *Necessary: News of the Black Community Crusade for Children* 2, no. 3 (Summer 1994): 6, BSLN/BCCC Collection File.

48. Carnoy, *Faded Dreams*; Wilson, *When Work Disappears*; and Piven and Cloward, *New Class War*.

49. Geoffrey Canada, *Fist, Stick, Knife, Gun: A Personal History of Violence in America* (Boston: Beacon, 1995), 123.

50. Sugarmann and Rand, quoted in ibid., 123.

51. Violence Policy Center, *Firearms Production in America: 1975–1997—A State-by-State Breakdown* (Washington, D.C.: Violence Policy Center, 2000), 14–15. Data for this study were taken from the Bureau of Alcohol, Tobacco, and Firearms, Firearms Production Data.

52. Black Community Crusade for Children, "Summary of the Black Community Crusade for Children Regional Offices and Constituency Group Meetings," 30.

53. Black Community Crusade for Children, "A Gathering of Leaders," *Necessary: News of the Black Community Crusade for Children* (Spring 1993): 3, BSLN/BCCC Collection File.

54. John J. Dilulio, Jr., "The Coming of the Super-Predators," *Weekly Standard* 11, no. 1 (November 27, 1995): 23–28.

55. Franklin D. Gilliam, Jr. and Shanto Iyengar, "The Superpredator Script," *Nieman Reports* 52, no. 4 (Winter 1998): 45–51; Craig Donegan, "The Issues," *Congressional Quarterly* 6, no. 10 (March 15, 1996): 219–220.

56. Robert Singh, *The Congressional Black Caucus: Racial Politics in the U.S. Congress* (Thousand Oaks, CA: Sage, 1998), 183–185; and Mylan Denerstein, "Fighting Crime and Violence—The Buck Starts Here," *We Speak! Voice of African American Youth* 1, no. 3 (Spring 1994): 4, BSLN/BCCC Collection File.

57. Canada, *Fist, Stick, Knife, Gun*, 1995; Denerstein, "Fighting Crime and Violence," 4.

58. Clarence Lusane, "Congratulations, It's a Crime Bill," *CovertAction*, no. 50 (Fall 1994): 16.

59. David Masci, "$30 Billion Anti-crime Bill Heads to Clinton's Desk," *Congressional Quarterly Weekly Report* 52, no. 34 (August 27, 1994): 2488–2493.

60. Criminal Justice and Violence Working Group position paper, submitted by Greg Hodge (referencing Donna Daniels, Malik Edwards, Rev. Bernice King, Allen Martin, and Gilda Williams), January 15, 1993, 3, BSLN/BCCC Collection File.

61. For more information about the Harlem Writers Crew, see Terry Williams and William Kornblum, *The Uptown Kids: Struggle and Hope in the Projects* (New York: Putnam, 1994).

62. Liz Atwood, "Schmoke Backs Anti-crime Package but Sees Merit in Alternatives," *Baltimore Sun* (January 9, 1994): 3A; Deborah Barfield, "Black Violence Conference Ends with Hope, Proposal," *Philadelphia Inquirer* (January 9, 1994): A04.

63. Some of these cities were Oakland, CA; Cincinnati, OH; Columbus, OH; East Lansing, MI; Chicago, IL; Poughkeepsie, NY; New Haven, CT; Boston, MA; Harlem, NY; North Hampton, MA; Montgomery County, MD; Washington, D.C.; New Brunswick, NJ; Austin, TX; and Chapel Hill and Raleigh, NC. See Black Student Leadership Network, *A National Day of Action Against Violence: A Campaign for Life* (Washington, D.C.: Black Student Leadership Network, n.d.), 4, BSLN/BCCC Collection File.

64. Aird, interview; Lisa Y. Sullivan, "BSLN Kicks Off Youth Anti-violence Campaign," *We Speak! A Voice of African American Youth* 2, no. 4 (Winter 1994): 1, BSLN/BCCC Collection File.

65. Deborah Prothrow-Stith, interview by Sekou M. Franklin, January 23, 2002. Also see Deborah Prothrow-Stith with Michael Weismann, *Deadly Consequences* (New York: HarperCollins, 1991).

66. Sullivan, "BSLN Kicks Off Youth Anti-violence Campaign," 1.

67. Ibid.

68. Black Student Leadership Network Staff, "Black Student Leadership Network 1991–1996," 37.

69. Ibid., 34.

70. These NDAAV activities occurred in Cambridge and Springfield, MA; New Haven, CT; Wilmington, DE; San Francisco, Oakland, and San Jose, CA; Baltimore, MD; Washington, D.C.; Raleigh and Durham, NC; Bennettsville, SC; New York City and Poughkeepsie, NY; Boston, MA; and Cincinnati, OH. See Darriel Hoy, "Second Annual Day of Action Against Violence Keeps Dr. King's

Legacy Alive," *We Speak! A Voice of African American Youth* 4, no. 2 (Summer 1995): 4, BSLN/BCCC Collection File.

71. Ibid.

72. James Alan Fox and Marianne W. Zawitz, *Homicide Trends in the U.S.* (Washington, D.C.: U.S. Department of Justice, Bureau of Justice Statistics, 2000), 56–63.

73. Eric L. Hirsch, "Sacrifice for the Cause: Group Processes, Recruitment, and Commitment in a Student Social Movement," *American Sociological Review* 55 (April 1990): 244–245.

74. Davis, interview.

75. Ashindi Maxton, "Prisoners Raise Money for Black Student Leadership Network," *Miscellany News* (April 28, 1995): 6.

76. Paul Tough, *Whatever It Takes: Geoffrey Canada's Quest to Change Harlem and America* (Orlando, FL: Houghton Mifflin Harcourt, 2009).

77. Burrowes, interview; Geoffrey Canada, interview by Sekou M. Franklin, January 4, 2001.

78. Deidre Bailey, "Harlem, NY," *We Speak! A Voice of African-American Youth* Special Edition (Summer 1993): 1, BSLN/BCCC Collection File.

79. Mark Winston Griffith, "The Confessions of a Community Organizing Banker," *We Speak! A Voice of African American Youth* 2, no. 4 (Winter 1994): 8, BSLN/BCCC Collection File.

80. Todd S. Purdum, "Dinkins Calls for Healing in Brooklyn," *New York Times* (August 26, 1991): B1; John Kifner, "Youth Indicted in Fatal Stabbing," *New York Times* (August 27, 1991): A1.

81. Marie Monique Marthol, interview by Sekou M. Franklin, May 22, 2000.

82. Ibid.

83. Payne, "One Step Forward," 8.

84. Marthol, interview.

85. Marie Monique Marthol, "BSLN New York Metro Chapter Is on the Move," *We Speak! A Voice of African American Youth* 2, no. 4 (Winter 1994): 9, BSLN/BCCC Collection File.

86. Ibid.

87. Kierna Mayo Dawsey, "Azabache," *City Limits* (February 1996): 29, BSLN/BCCC Collection File.

88. Burrowes, interview; Marthol, interview.

89. Marthol, interview.

90. Burrowes, interview.

91. Marthol, interview.

92. Black Student Leadership Network, "BSLN Targets Voter Education for 1996," *We Speak! A Voice of African American Youth* 4, no. 3 (Fall 1995), BSLN/BCCC Collection File: 1; Jenice View, *Citizenship 2000: A Civic Education Curriculum for Mobilizing Communities Trainers Guide* (Washington, D.C.: View Associates, February 1996), BSLN/BCCC Collection File.

93. Black Student Leadership Network Staff, "Black Student Leadership Network 1991–1996," 24.

94. Burrowes, interview.

95. Ibid.

96. Marthol, interview.

97. Payne, "One Step Forward," 8.

98. Kamua Franklin, interview by Sekou M. Franklin, May 23, 2000.

99. Olson, *Logic of Collective Action*, 5–9, 131–135.

100. Pamela Babcock, "Freedom School Helps Salvage Summer," *News & Observer* (August 10, 1993): B1, B5.

101. Hoy, interview.

102. Darriel Hoy, "Quarterly Field Briefing," memorandum, October 27, 1995, BSLN/BCCC Collection File; Raymond Gavins, interview by Sekou M. Franklin, April 18, 2000.

103. Black Community Crusade for Children, "Children's Sabbaths: Awakening the Spirit on Behalf of Our Children," *Necessary: News of the Black Community Crusade for Children* 2, no. 1 (Summer 1994): 14, BSLN/BCCC Collection File.

104. Darriel Hoy, "BSLN History Project," 1996, BSLN/BCCC Collection File.

105. Ibid.

106. Ibid.

107. Ibid.; Hoy, interview.

108. This projection was drawn from the following sources: Hoy, "BSLN History Project"; Black Student Leadership Network, National Database, 1996, BSLN/BCCC Collection File; Black Student Leadership Network Staff, "Black Student Leadership Network 1991–1996"; Hoy, "Quarterly Field Briefing"; Darriel Hoy, "Inventory of Meetings and Activities in the Southern Region, July 17–October 27, 1995," 1995, BSLN/BCCC Collection File.

109. Christopher M. Brown, II and Robert M. Hendrickson, "Public Historically Black Colleges at the Crossroads," *Journal for a Just & Caring Education* 3, no. 1 (January 1997): 95–113.

110. Hoy, interview.

111. Kelley, "'We Are Not What We Seem,'" 79.

112. Marian David, interview by Sekou M. Franklin, May 1, 2000.

113. Ibid.

114. Hoy, interview.

115. James Young, interview by Sekou M. Franklin, April 7, 2000.

116. Hoy, interview.

117. This analysis of BSLN's West Coast activities are also informed by the author's own experiences working with the BSLN's Oakland, California, Summer Freedom School program from 1993 to 1996.

118. Ifetayo Lawson, letter to Sekou M. Franklin, May 2, 2000.

119. Delores Nason McBroome, *African Americans in California's East Bay 1850–1963* (New York: Garland, 1993); Douglas Henry Daniels, *Pioneer Urbanites: A Social*

and Cultural History of Black San Francisco (Berkeley: University of California Press, 1980).

120. Greene, interview.

121. Tuckson, interview.

122. Claudine Taaffe, interview; April 24, 1999; Gavins, interview; Greene, interview.

123. New York Metro Chapter, "Proposed Changes to the Constitution/Bylaws of the Black Student Leadership Network," March 24, 1995, 3, BSLN/BCCC Collection File.

124. Clay, *Hip-Hop Generation Fights Back*, 55.

125. Taj James, interview by Sekou M. Franklin, August 15, 1999.

126. Black Student Leadership Network Staff, "Black Student Leadership Network 1991–1996," 33.

127. Ibid., 32.

128. Taj James, "Vision-Guided Action Planning Circle," February 26, 1996, 3, BSLN/BCCC Collection File.

129. The author was present at this meeting.

130. McAdam, *Political Process*.

131. Burrowes, interview.

NOTES TO CHAPTER 7

1. Strolovitch, *Affirmative Advocacy*.

2. Morris and Staggenborg, "Leadership in Social Movements."

3. Ganz, "Resources and Resourcefulness"; Kelsy Kretchsmer and David S. Meyer, "Platform Leadership: Cultivating Support for a Public Profile," *American Behavioral Scientist* 50, no. 10 (June 2007): 1395–1412; Clifford Bob and Sharon Erickson Nepstad, "Kill a Leader, Murder a Movement? Leadership and Assassination in Social Movements," *American Behavioral Scientist* 50, no. 10 (June 2007): 1370–1394; Ganz, *Why David Sometimes Wins*, chap. 5, "The Great Delano Grape Strike (1965–1966)"; Taylor, "Organizational Elaboration as Social Movement Tactic," 312.

4. Han et al. "Relationship of Leadership Quality to the Political Presence of Civic Associations."

5. White, interview.

6. Marian Wright Edelman, "A School for Life, Character, and Leadership Development," memorandum, March 21, 1994, BSLN/BCCC Collection File.

7. Edelman wanted the Haley Farm to be a contemporary Highlander Folk School. Established by Myles Horton, the Highlander Folk School was one of the most important institutions for training civil rights and labor activists from the 1930s to the 1960. See Hughes, "New Agenda for the South."

8. White, interview.

9. Ibid.

10. Ibid.

11. Marian Wright Edelman, "Field Staff," memorandum, November 16, 1994, BSLN/BCCC Collection File.

12. Sullivan, interview.

13. Lisa Y. Sullivan, "Further Restructuring of BSLN and Future Staffing Issues," September 6, 1995, BSLN/BCCC Collection File.

14. Fisher, interview.

15. Sullivan, interview.

16. Sullivan, "Further Restructuring of BSLN and Future Staffing Issues."

17. Ibid.

18. Griffith, interview.

19. Countryman, interview.

20. Ibid.

21. Hoy, interview.

22. Fisher, interview.

23. Hoy, interview.

24. Lisa Y. Sullivan, "1995–1996 Mobilization Agenda," memorandum, August 9, 1995, BSLN/BCCC Collection File.

25. Countryman, interview.

26. Sullivan, interview.

27. Carson, *In Struggle*, 147.

28. Burrowes, interview; and Canada, interview.

29. Carson, *In Struggle*, 147–148; Tracye Matthews, "'No One Ever Asks What a Man's Role in the Revolution Is': Gender and the Politics of the Black Panther Party, 1966–1971," in *The Black Panther Party [Reconsidered]*, ed. Charles E. Jones (Baltimore, MD: Black Classic Press, 1998), 281–293.

30. Rosalyn Baxandall, "Re-visioning the Women's Liberation Movement's Narrative: Early Second Wave African American," *Feminist Studies* 27, no. 1 (Spring 2001): 225–245.

31. Gamson, "Messages of Exclusion," 194.

32. According to an internal memorandum, the participants at this meeting were Darriel Hoy, Kasey Jones, Jason Walker, Mark Griffith, Matthew Countryman, Raymond Gavins, Richard Gray, Deidre Bailey, Farah Griffin, Nicole Johnson, Sean Greene, and Naomi Walker.

33. Raymond T. Gavins, "Direction of the BSLN," February 6, 1995, BSLN/BCCC Collection File.

34. Ibid.

35. Lisa Y. Sullivan, "BSLN National Coordinating Committee, Staff, and Advisors," memorandum, March 6, 1995, BSLN/BCCC Collection File.

36. Ibid.

37. Louis Enrique Negron, "A Latino Voice from the Crowd," *Freedom News* 1, no. 3 (July 22, 1994): 3, BSLN/BCCC Collection File.

38. Darriel Hoy, Raymond T. Gavins, and Naomi Walker, "One Thousand by Two Thousand: Training, Organizing, and Galvanizing a New Generation of African Americans for Power in the Twenty-First Century," April 1995, 1–10, BSLN/BCCC Collection File.

39. Ibid.

40. Lisa Y. Sullivan, "Significance of Field Organizing and the Future Growth and Development of BSLN," July 24, 1995, BSLN/BCCC Collection File.

41. Ibid.

42. New York Metro Chapter of the Black Student Leadership Network, "Proposed Changes to the Constitutions/Bylaws of the Black Student Leadership Network," 1995, BSLN/BCCC Collection File.

43. Lisa Y. Sullivan, "BSLN to Go Local in 1996," *We Speak! A Voice of African American Youth* 3, no. 4 (Winter 1995): 2, BSLN/BCCC Collection File.

44. Thomas Bowen and Adolphus Lacey, "Mobilization of Black Seminarians and Young Black Pastors for Haley Farm Meeting," memorandum, May 10, 1996, BSLN/BCCC Collection File.

45. Karen Blair Thompson, "BSLN Builds Partnership with LEAP to Go On-Line," *We Speak! A Voice of African-American Youth* 3, no. 4 (Winter 1995): 5, BSLN/BCCC Collection File.

46. Sean Joe, "Technology and Its Impact on Field Organizing and the Future of BSLN," memorandum, August 26, 1995, BSLN/BCCC Collection File.

47. Cohen, *Democracy Remixed*, 181–189.

48. Jeffrey Scott Juris and Geoffrey Henri Pleyers, "Alter-activism: Emerging Cultures of Participation among Young Global Justice Activists," *Journal of Youth Studies* 12, no. 1 (February 2009): 57–75.

49. Black Student Leadership Network National Coordinating Committee "Putting Form to Function: A Call for Increased Infrastructure, Training and Accountability to Leave No Child Behind," BSLN Working Paper, July 7, 1995, BSLN/BCCC Collection File.

50. Leslie Watson-Davis, "Organize to Vote!," *We Speak! A Voice of African American Youth* 4, no. 2 (Summer 1995): 6, BSLN/BCCC Collection File.

51. Lisa Y. Sullivan, "Response to Citizenship 2000 Planning Memorandum," memorandum, August 28, 1995, BSLN/BCCC Collection File. Also see View, *Citizenship 2000.*

52. C. J. Clemons, "Black-Student Leadership Networking in Charlotte," *Charlotte Observer* (February 10, 1996): 1C.

53. Black Student Leadership Network, "1996 Black Student Leadership Network Conference Debriefing Report," 1996, BSLN/BCCC Collection File.

54. Martin Gilens, *Why Americans Hate Welfare: Race, Media, and the Politics of Antipoverty Policy* (Chicago: University of Chicago Press, 1999).

55. Marc Peyser and Thomas Rosentiel, "She's Taking Her Stand," *Newsweek* 127, no. 24 (June 10, 1996): 32; Betty Friedan, "Children's Crusade," *New Yorker* 72, no. 14 (June 3, 1996): 5–6.

56. Jonah Edelman, "Interview," *Dallas Morning News* (March 23, 1997): 1J.

57. See Garrow, *Bearing the Cross*, 576, 578.

58. Lisa Simms, interview by Sekou M. Franklin, May 8, 2000.

59. Ibid.

60. Peyser and Rosentiel, "She's Taking Her Stand," 32.

61. Drema Brown, interview by Sekou M. Franklin, April 19, 2000.

62. Davis, interview.

63. National Coordinating Committee of the Black Student Leadership Network, "Redefining and Recreating the Strategic Whole," memorandum, August 29, 1996, BSLN/BCCC Collection File.

64. Darriel Hoy, "Recommendations for a New Vision and Structure for the Black Student Leadership Network," memorandum, October 10, 1996, BSLN/BCCC Collection File.

65. Black Student Leadership Network National Coordinating Committee, "Facing Today's Leadership Challenges with Integrity and Humility," June 12, 1996, BSLN/BCCC Collection File.

66. Canada, interview.

67. Jessica Gordon Nembhard, interview by Sekou M. Franklin, January 30, 2002.

68. Ibid.

69. Canada, interview.

70. Angela Glover Blackwell, interview by Sekou M. Franklin, August 13, 1999.

71. Johnson, "Black Community Crusade for Children," 12.

72. Black Student Leadership Network, "Next Step Retreat Notes," October 1996, 3, BSLN/BCCC Collection File.

73. Young, interview.

74. National Coordinating Committee of the Black Student Leadership Network, "Redefining and Recreating the Strategic Whole."

75. Marian Wright Edelman, "Evaluation and Integration of CDF/BCCC/BSLN Activities and Efficient and Accountable Use of Resources," August 12, 1996, BSLN/BCCC Collection File; National Coordinating Committee of the Black Student Leadership Network, "Redefining and Recreating the Strategic Whole."

76. Lisa Y. Sullivan, "Multi-year Funding for BSLN," memorandum, July 24, 1995, BSLN/BCCC Collection File.

77. Gray, interview.

78. James, interview.

79. Ann Scales, "Clinton to Sign Welfare Bill into Law," *Boston Globe* (August 22, 1996): A23.

80. Robert Peterkin, interview by Sekou M. Franklin, December 12, 2001.

81. See Peter Edelman, "The Worst Thing Bill Clinton Has Done," *Atlantic Monthly* 279, no. 3 (March 1997).

NOTES TO CHAPTER 8

1. Katy Reckdahl, "Interrupted," *Gambit Weekly* 24, no. 81 (July 13, 2004): 22.

2. Ibid.

3. Brenda Brue, quoted in Xochitl Bervera, "The Death of Tallulah Prison," *Color-Lines* 7, no. 2 (Summer 2004): 26.

4. Human Rights Watch Children's Rights Project, *Children in Confinement in Louisiana* (New York: Human Rights Watch, October 1995).

5. David S. Tanehaus, *Juvenile Justice in the Making* (Oxford: Oxford University Press, 2004).

6. David Utter, interview by Sekou M. Franklin, July 14, 2004.

7. Maceo Hallmon, interview by Sekou M. Franklin, July 21, 2004.

8. Eleanor Hinton Hoyt, Vincent Schiraldi, Brenda V. Smith, and Jason Ziedenberg, *Pathways to Juvenile Detention Reform: Reducing Racial Disparities in Juvenile Detention* (Baltimore, MD: Annie E. Casey Foundation, 2002); Eileen Poe and Michael A. Jones, *And Justice for Some: Differential Treatment of Minority Youth in the Justice System* (Washington, D.C.: Youth Law Center's Building Blocks for Youth Initiative, April 2000); and Robert Gangi, Vincent Schiraldi, and Jason Ziedenberg, "New York State of Mind? Higher Education vs. Prison Funding in the Empire State, 1988–1998" (New York: Justice Policy Institute/Correctional Association of New York, 1998); Youth Force Coalition, *Schools Not Jails*.

9. Gangi, Schiraldi, and Ziedenberg, "New York State of Mind?"; Mike Males and Dan Macallair, *The Color of Justice: An Analysis of Juvenile Adult Court Transfers in California* (Washington, D.C.: Coalition for Juvenile Justice, January 2000).

10. Disproportionate minority contact occurs in all stages of the juvenile justice system, including intake, adjudication, disposition, confinement, and particularly waiver decisions. See Poe and Jones, *And Justice for Some*; Karen B. Shepard, "Understanding Disproportionate Minority Confinement," *Corrections Today* 57, no. 3 (June 1995): 114; Vincent Schiraldi and Mark Soler, "The Will of the People? The Public's Opinion of the Violent and Repeat Juvenile Offender Act of 1997," *Crime and Delinquency* 44, no. 4 (October 1998): 590.

11. Poe and Jones, *And Justice for Some*.

12. Ibid.

13. Ibid., 13.

14. Paul E. Tracy, *Decision-Making and Juvenile Justice: An Analysis of Bias in Case Proceedings* (Westport, CT: Praeger, 2005), 11–15.

15. Poe and Jones, *And Justice for Some*; Males and Macallair, *Color of Justice*.

16. Richard A. Mendel, *Less Hype, More Help: Reducing Juvenile Crime, What Works—and What Doesn't* (Washington, D.C.: American Youth Policy Forum, 2000), 47.

17. Barry C. Feld, *Bad Kids: Race and the Transformation of the Juvenile Court* (New York: Oxford University Press, 1999); Denise Casamento Musser, "Public Access to Juvenile Records in Kansas," *Corrections Today* 63, no. 3 (June 2001): 112–113.

18. Suzanne Cavanaugh and David Teasley, *Juvenile Justice Act Reauthorization: The Current Debate* (Washington, D.C.: CRS Report for Congress, February 5, 1998), 13.

19. John D. McCarthy, Clark McPhail, and John Crist, "The Emergence and Diffusion of Public Order Management Systems: Protest Cycles and Police Response,"

in *Globalization and Social Movements*, ed. Pierre Hamel et al. (New York: Palgrave, 2001), 72.

20. Ibid.

21. Marion Orr, "Congress, Race, and Anticrime Policy," in *Black and Multiracial Politics in America*, ed. Yvette M. Alex-Assenoh and Lawrence J. Hanks (New York: New York University Press, 2000), 225–256; Henry A. Giroux, "Mis/education and Zero Tolerance: Disposable Youth and the Politics of Domestic Militarization," *Boundary 2* 28, no. 3 (Fall 2001): 61–94.

22. Barry C. Feld, "Race, Politics, and Juvenile Justice: The Warren Court and the Conservative 'Backlash,'" *Minnesota Law Review* 87, no. 144 (May 2003): 1447–1578.

23. Ibid.

24. Lori Dorfman and Vincent Schiraldi, *Off Balance: Youth, Race and Crime in the News* (Washington, D.C.: Building Blocks for Youth, April 2001).

25. Mendel, *Less Hype, More Help*, 30.

26. Youth Force, *In Between the Lines*; Youth Media Council, *Speaking for Ourselves*. An additional study was conducted by We Interrupt This Message, called *Soundbites and Cellblocks: An Analysis of the Juvenile Justice Media Debate & A Case Study of California's Proposition 21* (San Francisco: We Interrupt This Message, 2001).

27. Howard N. Snyder, "Juvenile Arrests 2001," *Juvenile Justice Bulletin* (Washington, D.C.: Office of Juvenile Justice and Delinquency Prevention, December 2003).

28. Howard N. Snyder and Melissa Sickmund, "Juvenile Justice System Structure and Process," in *Essential Readings in Juvenile Justice*, ed. David L. Parry (Upper Saddle River, NJ: Pearson, 2005), 6.

29. Patricia Puritz and Mary Ann Scali, "Civil Rights of Institutionalized Persons: CRIPA Can Be Used to Eliminate Unlawful Conditions of Confinement in Juvenile Facilities," *Corrections Today* 60, no. 5 (August 1998): 80; Patricia Puritz and Mary Ann Scali, "Beyond the Walls: Improving Conditions of Confinement for Youth in Custody" (Washington, D.C.: American Bar Association/Juvenile Justice Center, January 1998), 2–6.

30. Puritz and Scali, "Civil Rights of Institutionalized Persons," 80.

31. Ibid. This was the one of the few strong points, from the standpoint of the JJRM, of the Violent Crime and Control Act of 1994. The major disappointment of the act was a provision that allowed thirteen-year-olds to be prosecuted in federal courts for possessing a firearm while committing violent crime.

32. U.S. Department of Justice, "Investing in Girls: A Twenty-First Century Strategy," *Journal of the Office of Juvenile Justice and Delinquency Prevention* 6, no. 1 (October 1999): 3–4.

33. Elizabeth Cumming et al., *Maryland: An Assessment of Access to Counsel and Quality Representation in Delinquency Proceedings* (Washington, D.C.: American Bar Association, Juvenile Justice Center, and Mid-Atlantic Juvenile Defender Center, April 2003).

34. Randi Feinstein et al., *Justice for All? A Report on Lesbian, Gay, Bisexual and Transgendered Youth in the New York Juvenile Justice System* (New York: Urban Justice Center, 2001).

35. Kenyon Farrow, interview by Sekou M. Franklin, July 14, 2004.

36. Jason Ziedenberg, *Models for Change: Building Momentum for Juvenile Justice Reform* (Washington, D.C.: Justice Policy Institute, December 2006), 5.

37. Kathleen Feely, *Pathways to Juvenile Detention Reform: Collaboration and Leadership in Juvenile Detention Reform* (Baltimore, MD: Annie E. Casey Foundation, 1999).

38. Mishi Faruqee, interview by Sekou M. Franklin, July 22, 2004.

39. Juvenile Justice Project of Louisiana, *Juvenile Justice Reform Factbook for Louisiana's Leaders* (New Orleans: Louisiana Appleseed, November 2003), 6–11.

40. Gabrielle Celeste et al. "Just Shut It Down: Bringing Down a Prison while Building a Movement," in *No Turning Back: Promising Approaches to Reducing Racial and Ethnic Disparities Affecting Youth of Color in the Justice System* (Washington, D.C.: Building Blocks for Youth, October 2005), 69–77.

41. Utter, interview.

42. Xochitl Bervera, interview by Sekou M. Franklin, July 14, 2004.

43. FFLIC New Parent Orientation Handbook, "FFLIC Mission and Governing By-Laws," n.d., JJRM Collection File.

44. Gina Womack, interview by Sekou M. Franklin, August 25, 2004.

45. Ibid.

46. Ellen Schumer and Susan O'Donnell, "Turning Parents into Strong Community Leaders," *Shelterforce Online* (November/December 2000): 4, http://www.shelterforce.com/online/issues/114/schumerodonnell.html (accessed November 24, 2013).

47. Cohen, *Democracy Remixed*, 28.

48. See Juan Williams, *Enough: The Phony Leaders, Dead-End Movements, and Culture of Failure That Are Undermining Black America—and What We Can Do about It* (New York: Crown, 2006). For a critique of Cosby and Williams, see Johnson, *Revolutionaries to Race Leaders*, 223–225.

49. Bervera, interview.

50. Avis Brock, "Families of Jailed Youths Want Tallulah Closed," *Times-Picayune* (May 6, 2002): B-4. Brock was the chairwoman of New Orleans's FFLIC chapter.

51. Juvenile Justice Project of Louisiana, http://www.jjpl.org/FamilyAndCommunityResources/FamiliesAndFriends/familiesandfriends.html (accessed May 1, 2008).

52. Ibid., 20–21.

53. Casey Strategic Consulting Group for the Joint Legislative Juvenile Justice Commission, *Reducing Incarceration in Louisiana* (Baltimore, MD: Annie E. Casey Foundation, February 2003), 7.

54. Juvenile Justice Project of Louisiana, "Youth Empowerment Project Case Management Protocol," n.d., 2, JJRM Collection File; Juvenile Justice Project of

Louisiana, "Youth Empowerment Project (Post-Disposition Project)," July 2004, JJRM Collection File.

55. Ibid.

56. Angela Conyers, interview by Sekou M. Franklin, July 14, 2004; Melissa Sawyer, interview by Sekou M. Franklin, July 14, 2004.

57. Corlita Mahr, interview by Sekou M. Franklin, July 15, 2004.

58. Louisiana YES, "Comprehensive Community Mental Health Services for Children and Adolescents with Serious Emotional Disturbances and Their Families," proposal to the Department of Health and Human Services Center for Mental Health Services for the Child Mental Health Services (CMHS) Initiative RFA No. SM-03-009 by the Louisiana Department of Health and Hospitals Louisiana Office of Mental Health, August 3, 2003, JJRM Collection File.

59. Mark Soler, *Public Opinion on Youth, Crime and Race: A Guide for Advocates* (Washington, D.C.: Youth Law Center's Building Blocks for Youth Initiative, October 2001), 27.

60. R. Alexander Acosta (assistant attorney general), "Investigation of the Cheltenham Youth Facility in Cheltenham, Maryland, and the Charles H. Hickey, Jr. School in Baltimore, Maryland," addressed to Governor Robert L. Ehrlich, Jr., April 9, 2004, JJRM Collection File.

61. At a meeting in Baltimore, organized by the Maryland Juvenile Justice Coalition, one youth—probably fifteen or sixteen years old—told the activists in attendance with a tone of distress that "nothing is going to change; state officials are still going to send us back to jail to get raped." This illustrated the type of despair that exists in places like Cheltenham, Hickey, and other juvenile facilities in the state of Maryland. Baltimore, MD, July 20, 2004.

62. Heather Ford, "Coordinated Efforts: The Maryland Campaign to Close Cheltenham," in *No Turning Back*, 54.

63. Greg Perkins, interview by Sekou M. Franklin, July 20, 2004.

64. Maryland Juvenile Justice Coalition, meeting minutes, October 20, 2004, JJRM Collection File.

65. Maryland Juvenile Justice Coalition, "New Report Details Life Threatening Conditions at Baltimore City Juvenile Justice Center," meeting minutes, September 13, 2004, JJRM Collection File.

66. *Washington Post* Editorial Board, "Trouble for Troubled Youth," *Washington Post* (April 9, 2005): A22.

67. Copies of House Bill 1303 (February 11, 2005) and Senate Bill 616 (February 4, 2005), Maryland General Assembly.

68. Maryland Juvenile Justice Coalition, meeting minutes, November 18, 2004, JJRM Collection File.

69. Greg Garland, "Advocates Call Vetoes of Two Juvenile Justice Bills 'Moving Backward,'" *Baltimore Sun* (May 21, 2005), 3.

70. Ibid.

71. Lauren Abramson and David B. Moore, "Transforming Conflict in the Inner City Community Conferencing in Baltimore," *Contemporary Justice Review* 4, nos. 3–4 (2001): 325.

72. Maryland General Assembly, Senate Finance Committee Hearings on SB 773 [Audio] (Department of Legislative Services, March 17, 2005). The Community Conferencing Center, Reclaim Our Children and Community Projects, Inc., On Our Shoulders, a West Baltimore youth mentoring program founded by Ray Cook, B-Spirit, a Baltimore youth organization, and the Just 4 Me Mentoring program also testified at the hearing.

73. Danté Wilson, interview by Sekou M. Franklin, July 21, 2004.

74. Stacy Smith, interview by Sekou M. Franklin, June 4, 2005.

75. Cameron Miles, interview by Sekou M. Franklin, July 27, 2004.

76. Shawn A. Ginwright, *Black Youth Rising: Activism & Radical Healing in Urban America* (New York: Teacher's College Press, 2010).

77. Hallmon, interview.

78. Ray Davis, "Mother's Efforts Aren't Enough to Save Her Son," *Baltimore Sun* (September 29, 2004), http://articles.baltimoresun.com/2004-09-29/news/0409290178_1_juvenile-homicide-juvenile-justice-juvenile-records (accessed March 2008).

79. Kimberly Armstrong, interview by Sekou M. Franklin, June 2, 2005.

80. Lauren Abramson, "Letter from the Founder and Director," *Peacing It Together* 1, no. 1 (December 2003): 1; Lauren Abramson, interview by Sekou M. Franklin, June 2, 2005; Lauren Abramson and David B. Moore, "The Psychology of Community Conferencing," in *Restorative Justice: Repairing Communities through Restorative Justice*, ed. John G. Perry (Lanham, MD: American Counseling Association, 2002), 123–140.

81. Barry Checkoway, Lisa Figueroa, and Katie Richards-Schuster, "Democracy Multiplied in an Urban Neighborhood: Youth Force in the South Bronx," *Children, Youth and Environments* 13, no. 2 (2003): 1–19.

82. Kezia Parsons, "Trial Size," *City Limits* 23, no. 7 (September/October 1998): 5.

83. Tanehaus, *Juvenile Justice in the Making*, 139.

84. Julia Burgess, "Youth Involvement Can Be the Key to Community Development," *Community Youth Development* 1, no. 1 (Winter 2000), http://www.cydjournal.org/2000Winter/burgess.html (accessed May 18, 2011).

85. Andre Holder, interview by Sekou M. Franklin, July 22, 2004.

86. Checkoway, Figueroa, and Richards-Schuster, "Democracy Multiplied in an Urban Neighborhood." One such project is the Harlem Children's Zone, a twenty-four-block area developed by Geoffrey Canada of the Rheedlen Centers for Children and Families. See Tough, *Whatever It Takes*; and Critical Resistance, "Harm Free Zone Proposal," April 12, 2004, JJRM Collection File.

87. Middleton, interview by Franklin.

88. Kate Rhee, interview by Sekou M. Franklin, August 5, 2004.

89. Ibid.

90. Valerie McDowell, "Justice for Youth Coalition: No More Youth Jails Campaign," in *No Turning Back*, 59; Hilary Russ, "Making Change: Two Turntables and a Megaphone," *City Limits* 27, no. 10 (December 2002): 32–33; Mishi Faruqee, *Rethinking Juvenile Detention in New York City: A Report by the Juvenile Justice Project of the Correctional Association of New York* (New York: Correctional Association of New York, March 2002).

91. Malikah J. Kelly, interview by Sekou M. Franklin, July 22, 2004; also see Malikah J. Kelly, *Broken Promises, Broken System: 10 Reasons New York City Should Close the Spofford Youth Jail* (New York: Correctional Association of New York, March 2004).

92. Mishi Faruqee, "Close Spofford Youth Jail to Save Money and Lives," *Newsday* (June 11, 2003), http://www.newsday.com/close-spofford-youth-jail-to-save-money-and-lives-1.491267 (accessed March 1, 2008).

93. Chino Hardin, interview by Sekou M. Franklin, July 22, 2004.

94. Faruqee, interview.

95. Mishi Faruqee, testimony before the New York City Council Committee on Public Safety and the Juvenile Justice Subcommittee, March 6, 2003, 3, JJRM Collection File.

96. Faruqee, *Rethinking Juvenile Detention in New York City*, ii-iii.

97. Juvenile Justice Project, "Each One, Teach One JJP, Leadership Program Facilitation Guide," n.d., JJRM Collection File; Sheldon Petgrave, interview by Sekou M. Franklin, July 23, 2004.

98. Thomas Mims, interview by Sekou M. Franklin, July 22, 2004.

NOTES TO CHAPTER 9

1. Jeremy Brecher and Tim Costello, "A New Labor Movement in the Shell of the Old?," in *The Transformation of U.S. Unions: Voices, Visions, and Strategies from the Grassroots*, ed. Ray M. Tillman and Michael S. Cummings (Boulder, CO: Lynne Rienner, 1999), 9–26; Harold Meyerson, "Organize or Die," *American Prospect* 14, no. 8 (September 1, 2003): 39–42.

2. Charlie Eaton, "Student Unionism and Sustaining Student Power," *Social Text* 20, no. 1 (Spring 2002): 51–60; Kevin Mattson, "The Academic Labor Movement: Understanding Its Origins and Current Challenges," *Social Policy* 30, no. 4 (Summer 2000): 4–10; and Lisa Featherstone, *Students Against Sweatshops: The Making of a Movement* (New York: Verso, 2002).

3. Wilson, *When Work Disappears*; William Julius Wilson, "The Economic Plight of Inner-City Black Males," in *Against the Wall: Poor, Young, Black, and Male*, ed. Elijah Anderson (Philadelphia: University of Pennsylvania Press, 2008), 60.

4. John Sullivan, "African Americans Moving South—and to the Suburbs," *Race, Poverty & the Environment* 18, no. 2 (2011): 16–19; Chris Kromm, "Black Belt Power: African Americans Come Back South, Change Political Landscape," *Race, Poverty & the Environment* 18, no. 2 (2011): 17.

5. Dawson, *Behind the Mule*, 29–33; Carnoy, *Faded Dreams*; Piven and Cloward, *New Class War*; Richard P. Nathan, Fred C. Doolittle, and Associates, *The Consequences of Cuts: The Effects of the Reagan Domestic Program on State and Local Governments* (Princeton, NJ: Princeton Urban and Regional Research Center, 1983), 23–88.

6. Michael H. Gottesman, "Union Summer: A Reawakened Interest in the Law of Labor?," *Supreme Court Review* (Annual 1996), 285–329; Kenneth Jost, "Labor Movement's Future," *CQ Researcher* 6, no. 24 (June 28, 1996): 562–565.

7. Carl Boggs, *The End of Politics: Corporate Power and the Decline of the Public Sphere* (New York: Guilford, 2000), 27.

8. Anita Patterson, interview by Sekou M. Franklin, March, 6, 2002.

9. Andy Merrifield, "The Urbanization of Labor: Living-Wage Activism in the American City," *Social Text* 18, no. 1 (Spring 2000): 31–54. For an excellent analysis of outsourcing, see Jane Williams, "Restructuring Labor's Identity: The Justice for Janitors Campaign in Washington, D.C.," in *The Transformation of U.S. Unions: Voices, Visions, and Strategies from the Grassroots*, ed. Ray M. Tillman and Michael S. Cummings (Boulder, CO: Lynne Rienner, 1999), 204–208.

10. Barry T. Hirsch and David A. McPherson, "Union Coverage and Membership Database, 'Metropolitan Area' 1986–2010 Data," http://www.unionstats.com (accessed October 2010).

11. Gottesman, "Union Summer," 285–287; Teague Orgeman, "Principles and Power: The AFL-CIO Under John Sweeney" (Unpublished manuscript, Williams College, Williamstown, MA, August 2002).

12. Wessel & Pautch, P.C., "Do's and Don'ts for Supervisors: Legal Information to Help You during a Union Organizing Campaign," in *Employer's Guide to Defending Against Union Summer*, 1996, George Meany Memorial Archives, National Labor College, Silver Spring, MD.

13. Evelyn Bates in Michael Honey, *Black Workers Remember: An Oral History of Segregation, Unionism, and the Freedom Struggle* (Berkeley: University of California Press, 1999).

14. Cathy J. Cohen and Michael C. Dawson, "Neighborhood Poverty and African American Politics," *American Political Science Review* 87, no. 2 (June 1993): 293; William Wilson, *When Work Disappears*.

15. Patrick Scott, interview by Sekou M. Franklin, June 19, 2003.

16. Oliver and Shapiro, *Black Wealth/White Wealth*, 65; Blair and Fitchtenbaum, "Changing Black Employment Patterns," 77.

17. Robert C. Smith, "Politics Is Not Enough: The Institutionalization of the African American Freedom Movement," in *From Exclusion to Inclusion: The Long Struggle for African American Political Power*, ed. Linda Williams and Ralph Gomes (Westport, CT: Praeger, 1992), 119.

18. Bill Fletcher, "Calling All Black Organizers," November 22, 1999, http://www.hartford-hwp.com/archives/45a/277.html (accessed April 2004).

19. Simpson, *Tie That Binds*; Stafford, "National Urban League Survey"; Watkins, "Tale of Two Classes"; Bositus, *Diverging Generations*; Smith, "Politics Is Not Enough," 119.

20. V. I. Lenin, *What Is to Be Done? Burning Questions of Our Movement* (New York: International, 1969), 85–88. Also, for a discussion of the challenges with mobilizing working-class youth, see Forman, *Making of Black Revolutionaries*, 413–415.

21. Forman, *Making of Black Revolutionaries*, 413–415.

22. YOBU News Service, "YOBU Unites Students and Community," 12.

23. Kwame Ture, "Kwame Ture Address, University of Massachusetts, April 14, 1997," reprinted in *Black Scholar* 27, nos. 3–4 (Fall–Winter 1997): 24. Ture claims that the inspiration for the All African People's Revolutionary Party (AAPRP) came from Kwame Nkrumah, the former president of Ghana, and President Sekou Toure of Guinea, in the late 1960s. The formal announcement of the AAPRP in the United States, however, came from Ture in November 1972. See Peter Noel, "Soul on Ice," *Village Voice* (November 24, 1998): 66; and YOBU News Service, "Carmichael Announces New Political Party," *African World* (November 11, 1972): 15.

24. Ture, "Kwame Ture Address," 30.

25. Chris Booker, "Lumpenization: A Critical Error of the Black Panther Party," in *The Black Panther Party*, ed. Charles E. Jones (Baltimore, MD: Black Classic Press, 1998), 345–346; also see Toni Morrison, ed., *To Die for the People: The Writings of Huey P. Newton* (New York: Writers and Readers, 1995 [1972]), 27–29.

26. Bill Fletcher, "From Gang Members to Union Members?," *Dollars & Sense*, no. 200 (July–August 1995).

27. Stuart Tannock and Sara Flocks, "'I Know What It's Like to Struggle': The Working Lives of Young Students in an Urban Community College," *Labor Studies Journal* 28, no. 1 (Spring 2003): 2.

28. Cameron Barron, interview by Sekou M. Franklin, June 27, 2003.

29. "Organizing Institute Notes," AFL-CIO Organizing Institute, 1989–1990, Collection RG98-002, Series 3, File 5/11, George Meany Memorial Archives.

30. Susan C. Eaton, *Union Leadership Development in the 1990s and Beyond: A Report with Recommendations*, June 1992, George Meany Memorial Archives.

31. " Organizing Institute Notes."

32. Margaret Hornblower, "Labor's Youth Brigade," *Time* 148, no. 4 (July 15, 1996): 44–45; Gottesman, "Union Summer." Overall, the AFL-CIO committed to these organizing efforts about $20 million, some of which was used for the Union Summer program.

33. "Spon/Unsponsored at Non-targeted 3-Day Trainings (Jan.–Dec. 1996)," Organizing Institute to O.I. D.C., p. 3. AFL-CIO Organizing Institute, 1989–1990, Collection RG98-002, Series 3, File 5/11, George Meany Memorial Archives.

34. "Campus Recruitment: Potential Applicant Interview Form," Union Summer, George Meany Memorial Archives.

35. "Preliminary Summary: Union Summer Statistics & Accomplishments," 1996, Union Summer, George Meany Memorial Archives.

36. Audrey Walton, interview by Sekou M. Franklin, July 22, 2003.

37. "Union Summer South Carolina Update," July 13, 1996; "Union Summer South Carolina Update," June 22, 1996; and "Union Summer South Carolina Update," July 29 [sic], 1996, all in Union Summer, George Meany Memorial Archives.

38. "Union Summer South Carolina Update," July 29 [sic], 1996.

39. Marc Cooper, "The Boys and Girls of (Union) Summer," *Nation* (August 12, 1996): 18–20; Hornblower, "Labor's Youth Brigade."

40. "Union Summer Detroit!!," Union Summer, George Meany Memorial Archives.

41. "Union Summer Statistics & Accomplishments," Preliminary Summary, Union Summer, George Meany Memorial Archives.

42. "June Union Summer Waves," preliminary and informal assessment, 6/28/96, Union Summer, George Meany Memorial Archives.

43. "June 1996 Denver" (Memorandum), Union Summer, George Meany Memorial Archives.

44. Cooper, "Boys and Girls of (Union) Summer"; Jost, "Labor Movement's Future."

45. Phillip Allen, interview by Sekou M. Franklin, August 23, 2003.

46. Norman Hill, "Union Summer and Black Workers," June 1996, Union Summer, George Meany Memorial Archives.

47. *La Fruta Del Diablo (The Devil's Fruit)*, Union Summer at Watsonville, 1996, Union Summer, George Meany Memorial Archives.

48. This analysis is drawn from my interviews with former student activists in Union Summer, particularly those who participated in the program within the past several years: Desiree Wilkens, interview by Sekou M. Franklin, July 14, 2003; Tanza Coursey, interview by Sekou M. Franklin, May 28, 2003; Felicia Porchia, interview by Sekou M. Franklin, June 2, 2003; Rikkia Graham, interview by Sekou M. Franklin, May 28, 2003; Walton, interview; Sylvia Brown, interview by Sekou M. Franklin, May 28, 2003; and Crandall Choice, interview by Sekou M. Franklin, June 30, 2003.

49. Graham, interview.

50. Walton, interview.

51. Andy Levin, "What's After Union Summer—Old Goals, New Data, Proposals for the Future, and Background Materials to Prompt Discussion at Our Retreat," memorandum to OD staff, August 20, 1996, Union Summer, George Meany Memorial Archives.

52. Ibid.

53. Andy Levin, "Communicating with Union Summer Applicants," memorandum to Carol C., Bonnie O., Marsena W., Susan B., Jonathan S., Lisa F., and Chris L., June 7, 1996, Union Summer, George Meany Memorial Archives.

54. Leslie Allison Brunnage, "Labor Movement Revitalization and Youth Participation: Cross-Demographic Alliances, Conflict, and Campaign Progress in the First Year of Union Summer" (Doctoral dissertation, University of California, Irvine, 2005), 217.

55. Ibid., 236.

56. Laura Epstein, "On Behalf of Labor: Middle-Class Labor Activism in the 20th Century" (Bachelor's thesis, Wesleyan University, Middleton, CT, 2009).

57. Dorian Warren, "A New Labor Movement for a New Century? The Incorporation of Marginalized Workers in U.S. Unions" (Doctoral dissertation, Yale University, New Haven, CT, December 2005), 77.

58. Sylvia Brown, interview.

59. Daisy Rooks, "The Cowboy Mentality: Organizers and Occupational Commitment in the New Labor Movement," *Labor Studies Journal* 28, no. 3 (Fall 2003): 37.

60. Barron, interview.

61. Ransby, *Ella Baker and the Black Freedom Movement*, chap. 12.

62. Max Mishler, in Rachel Haut, Natalie Kelly, and Max Mishler, "Youth Activism in the Labor Movement: 3 Perspectives," *New Labor Forum* 18, no. 1 (Winter 2009): 107.

63. Channing Hawkins, interview by Sekou M. Franklin, June 26, 2003.

64. Rose M. Brewer, "A Critical Sociology of African Americans, the U.S. Welfare State, and Neoliberalism in the Era of Corporate Globalization," in *Race and Ethnicity: Across Time, Space and Discipline*, ed. Rodney Coates (Leiden, Netherlands: Brill, 2004), 117–133.

65. Patricia Ford, interview by Sekou M. Franklin, August 20, 2003; Patterson, interview; Sarah McKenzie, interview by Sekou M. Franklin, September 4, 2003; Scott, interview; Bill Fletcher, interview by Sekou M. Franklin, July 10, 2003.

NOTES TO THE CONCLUSION

1. For a discussion of patron-clientelism, see the following: Scott, "Patron-Client Relations," 92; Guasti, "Peru"; and S. N. Eisenstadt and Louis Roniger, "Patron-Client Relations as a Model of Structuring Social Exchange," *Comparative Studies in Society and History* 22, no. 1 (1980): 44n3.

2. Eisenstadt and Roniger, "Patron-Client Relations," 52; Guasti, "Peru," 423, 422–424.

3. Bert Landry, *The New Black Middle Class* (Berkeley: University of California Press, 1987).

4. Smith, *We Have No Leaders*; David S. Meyers and Sidney Tarrow, "A Movement Society: Contentious Politics for a New Century," in *The Social Movement Society*, ed. David S. Meyer and Sidney Tarrow (Lanham, MD: Rowman & Littlefield, 1998), 1–28.

5. Reed, "Demobilization in the New Black Political Regime."

6. Countryman, interview.

7. Minkoff, *Organizing for Equality*.

8. Peter K. Eisenger, "The Conditions of Protest Behavior in American Cities," *American Political Science Review* 67 (March 1973): 11–28.

9. Cohen, *Democracy Remixed*.

10. Sean Joe, "Bridging the Gap: A Place for Everyone at the Table," *Necessary: News of the Black Community Crusade for Children* 3, no. 3 (Winter 1996): 12.

Abramson, Lauren. "Letter from the Founder and Director." *Peacing It Together* 1, no. 1 (December 2003): 1.

Abramson, Lauren and David B. Moore. "The Psychology of Community Conferencing." Pp. 123–140 in *Restorative Justice: Repairing Communities through Restorative Justice*, ed. John G. Perry. Lanham, MD: American Counseling Association, 2002.

———. "Transforming Conflict in the Inner City Community Conferencing in Baltimore." *Contemporary Justice Review* 4, nos. 3–4 (2001): 321–340.

"Activists Mount Vital, Tough Mission." *New Haven Register* (August 2, 1989): 8.

African-American Youth Congress/NAACP Youth Council et al. "An Open Letter to Mayor Biagio DiLieto." *New Haven Independent* (December 8, 1988): 28.

Akom, A. A. "Critical Hip Hop Pedagogy as a Form of Liberatory Praxis." *Equity & Excellence in Education* 42, no. 1 (2009): 52–66.

Altbach, Philip G. and Robert Cohen. "American Student Activism: The Post-Sixties Transformation." *Journal of Higher Education* 61, no. 1 (January–February 1990): 32–49.

Andrews, Kenneth T. "Social Movements and Policy Implementation: The Mississippi Civil Rights Movement and the War Poverty, 1965–1971." *American Sociological Review* 66 (February 2001): 71–95.

Andrews, Kenneth T. and Bob Edwards. "Advocacy Organizations in the U.S. Political Process." *Annual Review of Sociology* 30 (2004): 479–506.

Apollon, Dominique. *Don't Call Them "Post-Racial": Millennials' Attitudes on Race, Racism and Key Systems in Our Society*. Oakland, CA: Applied Research Center, 2012.

———. *Millennials, Activism and Race*. Oakland, CA: Applied Research Center, 2012.

Associated Press. "New Haven's Bond Rating Is Downgraded by Moody's." *New York Times* (June 28, 1990): B2.

Atwood, Jesse. *Thus Be Their Destiny: The Personality Development of Negro Youth in Their Communities*. Washington, D.C.: American Council on Education, 1941.

Atwood, Liz. "Schmoke Backs Anti-crime Package but Sees Merit in Alternatives Too." *Baltimore Sun* (January 9, 1994): 3A.

Ayres, B. Drummond Jr. "Protest at Howard U. Brings a Surprising Review." *New York Times* (March 16, 1989): A26.

Babcock, Pamela. "Freedom School Helps Salvage Summer." *News & Observer* (August 10, 1993): B1, B5.

Ballivían, Rocio Ramírez and Linda Herrera. "Schools of the Street: Hip-Hop as Youth Pedagogy in Bolivia." *International Journal of Critical Pedagogy* 4, no. 1 (2012): 172–184.

Barfield, Deborah. "Black Violence Conference Ends with Hope, Proposal." *Philadelphia Inquirer* (January 9, 1994): A04.

Barnes, Claude W., Jr. "Bullet Holes in the Wall: Reflections on the Dudley/A&T Student Revolt of May 1969." Pp. 193–201 in *American National and State Government: An African American View of the Return of Redemptionist Politics*, ed. Claude W. Barnes, Samuel A. Moseley, and James D. Steele. Dubuque, IA: Kendall/Hunt, 1997.

Barron, James. "Yale to Pay Millions in New Municipal Fees." *New York Times* (April 3, 1990): 1.

Baum, Joel A. C. and Christine Oliver. "Institutional Linkages and Organizational Mortality." *Administrative Science Quarterly* 36, no. 2 (June 1991): 187–219.

Baxandall, Rosalyn. "Re-visioning the Women's Liberation Movement's Narrative: Early Second Wave African American." *Feminist Studies* 27, no. 1 (Spring 2001): 225–245.

Bedolla, Lisa García. *Fluid Borders: Latino Power, Identity, and Politics in Los Angeles.* Berkeley: University of California Press, 2005.

Bell, Daniel. *Marxian Socialism in the United States.* Princeton, NJ: Princeton University Press, 1952 [1967].

Bervera, Xochitl. "The Death of Tallulah Prison." *ColorLines* 7, no. 2 (Summer 2004): 26–28.

Biondi, Martha. *The Black Revolution on Campus.* Berkeley: University of California Press, 2012.

Black Community Crusade for Children. *Progress and Peril: Black Children in America.* Washington, D.C.: Children's Defense Fund, 1993.

Blair, John P. and Rudy H. Fichtenbaum. "Changing Black Employment Patterns." Pp. 72–92 in *The Metropolis in Black and White: Place, Power, and Polarization*, ed. George C. Galster and Edward W. Hill. New Brunswick, NJ: Rutgers University, Center for Urban Policy Research, 1992.

Bob, Clifford and Sharon Erickson Nepstad. "Kill a Leader, Murder a Movement? Leadership and Assassination in Social Movements." *American Behavioral Scientist* 50, no. 10 (June 2007): 1370–1394.

Boggs, Carl. *The End of Politics: Corporate Power and the Decline of the Public Sphere.* New York: Guilford, 2000.

Booker, Chris. "Lumpenization: A Critical Error of the Black Panther Party." Pp. 337–362, in *The Black Panther Party*, ed. Charles E. Jones. Baltimore, MD: Black Classic Press, 1998.

Bositus, David A. *Diverging Generations: The Transformation of African American Policy Views.* Washington, D.C.: Joint Center for Political and Economic Studies, 2001.

Boyce, Joseph N. "Grass-Roots Quest: More Blacks Embrace Self-Help Programs to Fight Urban Ills." *Wall Street Journal* (July 26, 1990): A1, A11.

Bracey, John, Jr. "Black Nationalism since Garvey." Pp. 259–279 in *Key Issues in the Afro-American Experience*, vol. 2, ed. Nathan I. Huggins, Martin Kilson, and Daniel M. Fox. New York: Harcourt Brace Jovanovich, 1971.

Branch, Taylor. *Parting the Waters: America in the King Years 1954–1963.* New York: Touchstone, 1988.

Brecher, Jeremy and Tim Costello. "A New Labor Movement in the Shell of the Old?" Pp. 9–26 in *The Transformation of U.S. Unions: Voices, Visions, and Strategies from the Grassroots*, ed. Ray M. Tillman and Michael S. Cummings. Boulder, CO: Lynne Rienner, 1999.

Brewer, Rose M. "A Critical Sociology of African Americans, the U.S. Welfare State, and Neoliberalism in the Era of Corporate Globalization." Pp. 117–133 in *Race and Ethnicity: Across Time, Space and Discipline*, ed. Rodney Coates. Leiden, Netherlands: Brill, 2004.

Brock, Avis. "Families of Jailed Youths Want Tallulah Closed." *Times-Picayune* (May 6, 2002): B-4.

Brown, Christopher M., II and Robert M. Hendrickson. "Public Historically Black Colleges at the Crossroads." *Journal for a Just & Caring Education* 3, no. 1 (January 1997): 95–113.

Brunnage, Leslie Allison. "Labor Movement Revitalization and Youth Participation: Cross-Demographic Alliances, Conflict, and Campaign Progress in the First Year of Union Summer." Doctoral dissertation, University of California, Irvine, 2005.

Buechler, Steven. *Women's Movement in the United States: Women Suffrage, Equal Rights, and Beyond*. New Brunswick, NJ: Rutgers University Press, 1990.

Burgess, Julia. "Youth Involvement Can Be the Key to Community Development." *Community Youth Development* 1, no. 1 (Winter 2000). http://www.cydjournal. org/2000Winter/burgess.html (accessed May 18, 2011).

Bynoe, Yvonne. *Stand and Deliver: Political Activism, Leadership, and Hip-Culture*. Berkeley, CA: Soft Skull Press, 2004.

Canada, Geoffrey. *Fist, Stick, Knife, Gun: A Personal History of Violence in America*. Boston: Beacon, 1995.

Canfield, Hubert. "Who Will You Work For?" *African World* (September 4, 1971): 5.

Caraley, Demetrios. "Washington Abandons the Cities." *Political Science Quarterly* 107, no. 1 (Spring 1992): 1–30.

Carnoy, Martin. *Faded Dreams: The Politics and Economics of Race in America*. Cambridge: Cambridge University Press, 1994.

Carson, Clayborne. *In Struggle: SNCC and the Black Awakening of the 1960s*. Cambridge, MA: Harvard University Press, 1981.

Casey Strategic Consulting Group for the Joint Legislative Juvenile Justice Commission. *Reducing Incarceration in Louisiana*. Baltimore, MD: Annie E. Casey Foundation, February 2003.

Cavanaugh, Suzanne and David Teasley. *Juvenile Justice Act Reauthorization: The Current Debate*. Washington, D.C.: CRS Report for Congress, February 5, 1998.

Celeste, Gabrielle, et al. "Just Shut It Down: Bringing Down a Prison while Building a Movement." Pp. 69–77 in *No Turning Back: Promising Approaches to Reducing Racial and Ethnic Disparities Affecting Youth of Color in the Justice System*. Washington, D.C.: Building Blocks for Youth, October 2005.

Chafe, William. *Civilities and Civil Rights: Greensboro, North Carolina and the Black Struggle for Freedom*. New York: Oxford University Press, 1980.

Chalmers, David. *And the Crooked Places Made Straight: The Struggle for Social Change in the 1960s*. Baltimore, MD: Johns Hopkins University Press, 1996.

Chang, Jeff. *Can't Stop Won't Stop: A History of the Hip-Hop Generation*. New York: Picador, 2005.

Checkoway, Barry N., Lisa Figueroa, and Katie Richards-Schuster. "Democracy Multiplied in an Urban Neighborhood: Youth Force in the South Bronx." *Children, Youth and Environments* 13, no. 2 (2003): 1–19.

Checkoway, Barry N. and Lorraine M. Gutiérrez. "Youth Participation and Community Change." *Journal of Community Practice* 14, nos. 1–2 (2006): 1–9.

Chin, John J. "The Limits and Potential of Nonprofit Organizations in Participatory Planning: A Case Study of the New York HIV Planning Council." *Journal of Urban Affairs* 31, no. 4 (2009): 431–460.

Chong, Dennis. *Collective Action and the Civil Rights Movement*. Chicago: University of Chicago Press, 1991.

Clay, Andreana. *The Hip-Hop Generation Fights Back: Youth, Activism, and Post–Civil Rights Politics*. New York: New York University Press, 2012.

Clemons, C. J. "Black-Student Leadership Networking in Charlotte." *Charlotte Observer* (February 10, 1996): 1C, 5C.

Clinton, Bill and Al Gore. *Putting People First: How We Can All Change America*. New York: Times Books, 1992.

Codish, K. D. "The New Haven Police Academy: Putting a Sacred Cow Out to Pasture." *Police Chief* (November 1996): 40–44.

Cohen, Cathy. *The Boundaries of Blackness: AIDS and the Breakdown of Black Politics*. Chicago: University of Chicago Press, 1999.

———. *Democracy Remixed: Black Youth and the Future of American Politics*. Oxford: Oxford University Press, 2010.

Cohen, Cathy J. and Michael C. Dawson. "Neighborhood Poverty and African American Politics." *American Political Science Review* 87, no. 2 (June 1993): 286–302.

Cohen, Robert. *When the Old Left Was Young: Student Radicals and America's First Mass Student Movement, 1929–1941*. New York: Oxford University Press, 1993.

Coleman, Milton. "N.C. Independent Black Political Party Formed." *African World* 11, no. 5 (December 11, 1971): 1, 9.

Collison, Michele N.-K. "Network of Black Students Hopes to Create a New Generation of Civil Rights Leaders." *Chronicle of Higher Education* 39, no. 6 (September 30, 1992): A28–A29.

Conell, Carol and Kim Voss. "Formal Organization and the Fate of Social Movements: Craft Associations and Class Alliance in the Knights of Labor." *American Sociological Review* 55, no. 2 (April 1990): 255–269.

Cooper, Marc. "The Boys and Girls of (Union) Summer." *Nation* (August 12, 1996): 18–20.

Countryman, Matthew. "Lessons of the Divestment Drive." *Nation* (March 26, 1988): 406–409.

Countryman, Matthew and Lisa Y. Sullivan. "National *Service*: Don't Do For, Do *With*." *Social Policy* 24, no. 1 (Fall 1993): 29–34.

Crane, George T. "Collective Identity, Symbolic Mobilization, and Student Protest in Nanjing, China, 1988–1989." *Comparative Politics* 26, no. 4 (July 1994): 400.

Cumming, Elizabeth, et al. *Maryland: An Assessment of Access to Counsel and Quality Representation in Delinquency Proceeding.* Washington, D.C.: American Bar Association, Juvenile Justice Center, and Mid-Atlantic Juvenile Defender Center, April 2003.

Curtis, Russell L. and Louis A. Zurcher. "Stable Resources of Protest Movements: The Multi-organizational Field." *Social Forces* 52, no. 1 (1973): 53–61.

Dahl, Robert A. *Who Governs? Democracy and Power in an American City.* New Haven, CT: Yale University Press, 1979 [1961].

Daniels, Douglas Henry. *Pioneer Urbanites: A Social and Cultural History of Black San Francisco.* Berkeley: University of California Press, 1980.

Davis, Allison and John Dollard. *Children of Bondage: The Personality Development of Negro Youth in the Urban South.* Washington, D.C.: American Council on Education, 1946.

Davis, Ray. "Mother's Efforts Aren't Enough to Save Her Son." *Baltimore Sun* (September 29, 2004). http://articles.baltimoresun.com/2004-09-29/news/0409290178_1_juvenile-homicide-juvenile-justice-juvenile-records (accessed March 2008).

Dawson, Michael C. *Behind the Mule: Race and Class in African-American Politics.* Princeton, NJ: Princeton University Press, 1994.

De Reid, Ira. *In a Minor Key: Negro Youth in Story and Fact.* Westport, CT: Greenwood, 1971 [1940].

Delgado, Melvin and Lee Staples. *Youth-Led Community Organizing: Theory and Action.* New York: Oxford University Press, 2007.

Department of Health for the City of New Haven. *New Haven 1989 Annual Report of Vital Statistics.* New Haven, CT, 1990.

Diggs, Irene. "The Amenia Conferences: A Neglected Aspect of the Afro-American Struggle." *Freedomways* 13, no. 2 (1973): 117 134.

Dilulio, John J., Jr. "The Coming of the Super-Predators." *Weekly Standard* 11, no. 1 (November 27, 1995): 23–28.

DiMaggio, Paul and Walter R. Powell. "The Iron Cage Revisited: Institutional Isomorphism and Collective Rationality in Organizational Fields." *American Sociological Review* 48 (April 1983): 147–160.

Dionne, E. J., Jr. *Why Americans Hate Politics.* New York: Simon & Schuster, 1991.

Dittmer, John. *Local People: The Struggle for Civil Rights in Mississippi.* Urbana: University of Illinois Press, 1995.

Domhoff, G. William. "The Role of Nonprofits in American Social Conflict." *American Behavioral Scientist* 52, no. 7 (March 2009): 955–973.

Donegan, Craig. "The Issues." *Congressional Quarterly* 6, no. 10 (March 15, 1996): 219–226.

Dorfman, Lori and Vincent Schiraldi. *Off Balance: Youth, Race and Crime in the News*. Washington, D.C.: Building Blocks for Youth, April 2001.

Douglass, Jack. "The Growing Importance of Youth and College Students in American Society." Pp. 45–58 in *Youth: Divergent Perspectives*, ed. Peter K. Manning. New York: John Wiley, 1973.

Drake, St. Claire. "Introduction to the 1967 Edition." Pp. v–xvii in *Negro Youth at the Crossways: Their Personality Development in the Middle States*, by E. Franklin Frazier. New York: Schocken Books, 1967 [1940].

Dreier, Peter, John Mollenkopf, and Todd Swanstrom. *Place Matters: Metropolitics for the Twenty-First Century*. Lawrence: University Press of Kansas, 2001.

Durham, Aisha, Brittney C. Cooper, and Susana M. Morris. "The Stage Hip-Hop Feminism Built: A New Directions." *Signs* 38, no. 3 (Spring 2013): 721–737.

Dyson, Michael Eric. *Know What I Mean? Reflections on Hip-Hop*. New York: Basic Civitas Books, 2007.

Eaton, Charlie. "Student Unionism and Sustaining Student Power." *Social Text* 20, no. 1 (Spring 2002): 51–60.

Edelman, Jonah. "Interview." *Dallas Morning News* (March 23, 1997): 1J.

Edelman, Peter. "American Government and Politics of Youth." Pp. 310–338 in *A Century of Juvenile Justice*, ed. Margaret K. Rosenheim et al. Chicago: University of Chicago Press, 2002.

———. "The Worst Thing Bill Clinton Has Done." *Atlantic Monthly* 279, no. 3 (March 1997): 43–58.

Edsall, Thomas Byrne and Mary D. Edsall. *Chain Reaction: The Impact of Race, Rights, and Taxes on American Politics*. New York: Norton, 1991.

Eisenger, Peter K. "The Conditions of Protest Behavior in American Cities." *American Political Science Review* 67 (March 1973): 11–28.

Eisenstadt, S. N. and Louis Roniger. "Patron-Client Relations as a Model of Structuring Social Exchange." *Comparative Studies in Society and History* 22, no. 1 (1980): 42–77.

Elwood, John P. "Rethinking Government Participation in Urban Renewal: Neighborhood Revitalization in New Haven." *Yale Law & Policy Review* 12, no. 1 (1994): 138–183.

Epstein, Laura. "On Behalf of Labor: Middle-Class Labor Activism in the 20th Century." Bachelor's thesis, Wesleyan University, Middleton, CT, 2009.

Everett, Kevin Djo. "Professionalization and Protest: Changes in the Social Movement Sector, 1961–1983." *Social Forces* 70, no. 4 (June 1992): 957–975.

Fairholm, Jacinda. "Seeking Justice for All." *Alternatives Journal* 24, no. 3 (Summer 1998): 9.

Family and Friends of Louisiana's Incarcerated Children. "Organizational Description." http://www.jjpl.org/FamilyAndCommunityResources/FamiliesAndFriends/familiesandfriends.html (accessed March 2008).

Faruqee, Mishi. "Close Spofford Youth Jail to Save Money and Lives." *Newsday* (June 11, 2003). http://www.newsday.com/close-spofford-youth-jail-to-save-money-and-lives-1.491267 (accessed March 1, 2008).

———. *Rethinking Juvenile Detention in New York City: A Report by the Juvenile Justice Project of the Correctional Association of New York*. New York: Correctional Association of New York, March 2002.

Favors, Jelani. "North Carolina A&T Black Power Activists and the Student Organization for Black Unity." Pp. 255–277 in *Rebellion in Black & White: Southern Student Activism in the 1960s*, ed. Robert Cohen and David J. Snyder. Baltimore, MD: Johns Hopkins University Press, 2013.

Featherstone, Lisa. *Students Against Sweatshops: The Making of a Movement*. New York: Verso, 2002.

Feely, Kathleen. *Pathways to Juvenile Detention Reform: Collaboration and Leadership in Juvenile Detention Reform*. Baltimore, MD: Annie E. Casey Foundation, 1999.

Feinstein, Randi, et al. *Justice for All? A Report on Lesbian, Gay, Bisexual and Transgendered Youth in the New York Juvenile Justice System*. New York: Urban Justice Center, 2001.

Feld, Barry C. *Bad Kids: Race and the Transformation of the Juvenile Court*. New York: Oxford University Press, 1999.

———. "Race, Politics, and Juvenile Justice: The Warren Court and the Conservative 'Backlash.'" *Minnesota Law Review* 87, no. 144 (May 2003): 1447–1578.

Fendrich, James Max. *Ideal Citizens: The Legacy of the Civil Rights Movement*. Albany: State University of New York Press, 1993.

Finnegan, William. "A Reporter at Large: Out There—I." *New Yorker* (September 10, 1990): 51–86.

———. "A Reporter at Large: Out There—II." *New Yorker* (September 17, 1990): 60–90.

Fletcher, Bill. "Calling All Black Organizers." November 22, 1999. http://www.hartford-hwp.com/archives/45a/277.html (accessed April 2004).

———. "From Gang Members to Union Members?" *Dollars & Sense*, no. 200 (July–August 1995): 24–25.

Fonow, Mary Margaret. "Protest Engendered: The Participation of Women in the 1985 Wheeling-Pittsburgh Steel Strike." *Gender & Society* 12, no. 6 (December 1998): 710–728.

Ford, Heather. "Coordinated Efforts: The Maryland Campaign to Close Cheltenham." Pp. 52–57 in *No Turning Back: Promising Approaches to Reducing Racial and Ethnic Disparities Affecting Youth of Color in the Justice System*. Washington, D.C.: Building Blocks for Youth, October 2005.

Forman, James. *The Making of Black Revolutionaries*. Seattle: University of Washington Press, 1997 [1972].

Forman, Murray. "'Hood Work: Hip-Hop, Youth Advocacy, and Model Citizenry." *Communication, Culture & Critique* 6 (2013): 244–257.

Fox, James Alan and Marianne W. Zawitz. *Homicide Trends in the U.S.* Washington, D.C.: U.S. Department of Justice, Bureau of Justice Statistics, 2000.

Franklin, Sekou M. "Black Organizational Development and the Black Student Leadership Network." *National Political Science Review* 8 (2001): 206–220.

Frazier, E. Franklin. *Negro Youth at the Crossways: Their Personality Development in the Middle States*. New York: Schocken Books, 1967 [1940].

Freeman, Jo. "Model for Analyzing the Strategic Options of Social Movement Organizations." P. 207 in *Social Movements of the Sixties and Seventies*, ed. Jo Freeman. New York: Longman, 1983.

———. "Resource Mobilization and Strategy: A Model for Analyzing Social Movement Organization Actions." Pp. 167–189 in *Dynamics of Social Movements*, ed. Mayer N. Zald and John D. McCarthy. New York: Longman, 1983.

Friedan, Betty. "Children's Crusade." *New Yorker* 72, no. 14 (June 3, 1996): 5–6.

Frost, Jennifer. *"An Interracial Movement of the Poor": Community Organizing and the New Left in the 1960s*. New York: New York University Press, 2001.

Gamson, Joshua. "Messages of Exclusion: Gender, Movements, and Symbolic Boundaries." *Gender & Society* 11, no. 2 (April 1997): 178–199.

Gangi, Robert, Vincent Schiraldi, and Jason Ziedenberg. "New York State of Mind? Higher Education vs. Prison Funding in the Empire State, 1988–1998." New York: Justice Policy Institute/Correctional Association of New York, 1998.

Ganz, Marshall. "Resources and Resourcefulness: Strategic Capacity in the Unionization of California Agriculture, 1959–1966." *American Journal of Sociology* 105 (January 2000): 1019–1044.

———. *Why David Sometimes Wins: Leadership, Organization, and Strategy in the California Farmworker Movement*. New York: Oxford University Press, 2009.

Garland, Greg. "Advocates Call Vetoes of Two Juvenile Justice Bills 'Moving Backward.'" *Baltimore Sun* (May 21, 2005): 3.

Garrow, David. *Bearing the Cross: Martin Luther King, Jr. and the Southern Christian Leadership Conference*. New York: Vintage, 1988 [1986].

Gellman, Erik S. *Death Blow to Jim Crow: The National Negro Congress and the Rise of Militant Civil Rights*. Chapel Hill: University of North Carolina Press, 2012.

George, Nelson. *Hip-Hop America*. New York: Penguin, 2005.

Gilens, Martin. *Why Americans Hate Welfare: Race, Media, and the Politics of Antipoverty Policy*. Chicago: University of Chicago Press, 1999.

Gilliam, Franklin D., Jr. and Shanto Iyengar. "The Superpredator Script." *Nieman Reports* 52, no. 4 (Winter 1998): 45–51.

Ginwright, Shawn A. *Black Youth Rising: Activism & Radical Healing in Urban America*. New York: Teacher's College Press, 2010.

Ginwright, Shawn, Pedro Noguero, and Julio Cammorato. *Beyond Resistance! Youth Activism and Community Change: New Democratic Possibilities for Practice and Policy for America's Youth*. New York: Routledge, 2006.

Giroux, Henry A. "Mis/education and Zero Tolerance: Disposable Youth and the Politics of Domestic Militarization." *Boundary 2* 28, no. 3 (Fall 2001): 61–94.

Giugni, Marco G. "Was It Worth the Effort? The Outcomes and Consequences of Social Movements." *Annual Review of Sociology* 98 (1998): 371–393.

Gottesman, Michael H. "Union Summer: A Reawakened Interest in the Law of Labor?" *Supreme Court Review* (Annual 1996): 285–329.

Grady-Willis, Winston A. "The Black Panther Party: State Repression and Political Prisoners." Pp. 363–389 in *The Black Panther Party [Reconsidered]*, ed. Charles E. Jones. Baltimore, MD: Black Classic Press, 1998.

Grant, Jim and Milton Coleman. "Day of Solidarity to Save Black Schools." *African World* 11, no. 3x (November 13, 1971): 1x.

Greenberg, Cheryl, ed. *A Circle of Trust: Remembering SNCC*. New Brunswick, NJ: Rutgers University Press, 1998.

Greenburg, Polly. *Devil Has Slippery Shoes: A Biased Biography of the Maximum Feasible Poor Parent Participation*. Washington, D.C.: Youth Policy Institute, 1990 [1969].

Guasti, Laura. "Peru: Clientelism and Internal Control." Pp. 422–438 in *Friends, Followers and Factions: A Reader in Political Clientelism*, ed. Steffen W. Schmidt et al. Berkeley: University of California Press, 1977.

Guinier, Lani. "No Two Seats: The Elusive Quest for Political Equality." *Virginia Law Review* 77, no. 8 (November 1991): 1413–1514.

Guinier, Lani and Gerald Torres. *The Miner's Canary: Enlisting Race, Resisting Power, Transforming Democracy*. Cambridge, MA: Harvard University Press, 2002.

Gurwitt, Rob. "A Younger Generation of Black Politicians Challenges Its Leaders." *Governing* (February 1990): 29–33.

Hahrie Han, et al. "The Relationship of Leadership Quality to the Political Presence of Civic Associations." *Perspectives on Politics* 9, no. 1 (March 2011): 45–59.

Haines, Herbert. *Black Radicals and the Civil Rights Mainstream, 1954–1970*. Knoxville: University of Tennessee Press, 1988.

Hamilton, Robert A. "Tight Budgets Force Towns to Cut Costs." *New York Times* (February 18, 1990): 1.

Hanson, Joyce A. *Mary McLeod Bethune and Black Women's Political Activism*. Columbia: University of Missouri Press, 2003.

Hare, Bruce. "Structural Inequality and the Endangered Status of Black Youth." *Journal of Negro Education* 56, no. 1 (1987): 100–110.

Haut, Rachel, Natalie Kelly, and Max Mishler. "Youth Activism in the Labor Movement: 3 Perspectives." *New Labor Forum* 18, no. 1 (Winter 2009): 98–107.

Hedgespeth, Adrienne C. "Black Women Set Goals for Posts on City Boards." *New Haven Register* (November 3, 1989): 5.

———. "Service Planned for Blacks Slain over Drugs." *New Haven Register* (January 29, 1989): A3, A9.

Hirsch, Barry T. and David A. McPherson. "Union Coverage and Membership Database, 'Metropolitan Area' 1986–2010 Data." http://www.unionstats.com (accessed October 2010).

Hirsch, Eric L. "Sacrifice for the Cause: Group Processes, Recruitment, and Commitment in a Student Social Movement." *American Sociological Review* 55 (April 1990): 244–245.

Hirsh, Kim S. "Activists Urging City Students to Walk Out over School Funds." *New Haven Register* (May 1988): 1.

Holmes, Michael S. "The New Deal and Georgia's Black Youth." *Journal of Southern History* 38, no. 3 (August 1972): 443–460.

Holt, Len. *The Summer That Didn't End: The Story of the Mississippi Civil Rights Project in 1964.* New York: De Capo Press, 1992.

Honey, Michael. *Black Workers Remember: An Oral History of Segregation, Unionism, and the Freedom Struggle.* Berkeley: University of California Press, 1999.

Hornblower, Margaret. "Labor's Youth Brigade." *Time* 148, no. 4 (July 15, 1996): 44–45.

HoSang, Daniel. "Youth and Community Organizing Today." New York: Funders' Collaborative on Youth Organizing Occasional Paper Series on Youth Organizing, 2003.

Hoyt, Eleanor Hinton, Vincent Schiraldi, Brenda V. Smith, and Jason Ziedenberg. *Pathways to Juvenile Detention Reform: Reducing Racial Disparities in Juvenile Detention.* Baltimore, MD: Annie E. Casey Foundation, 2002.

Hughes, C. Alvin. "The Negro Sanhedrin Movement." *Journal of Negro History* 69, no. 1 (1984): 1–13.

———. "A New Agenda for the South: The Role and Influence of the Highlander Folk School, 1953–1961." *Phylon* 46, no. 3 (1985): 242–250.

———. "We Demand Our Rights: The Southern Negro Youth Congress, 1937–1949." *Phylon* 48, no. 1 (1987): 38–50.

Human Rights Watch Children's Rights Project. *Children in Confinement in Louisiana.* New York: Human Rights Watch, October 1995.

Hunter, Tera. *To 'Joy My Freedom: Southern Black Women's Lives and Labors after the Civil War.* Cambridge, MA: Harvard University Press, 1997.

Jackson, Esther Cooper. *This Is My Husband: Fighter for His People, Political Refugee.* Brooklyn, NY: National Committee to Defend Negro Leadership, 1953.

James, C. L. R. "The Historical Development of the Negroes in American Society." Pp. 63–89 in *C.L.R. James on the "Negro Question,"* ed. Scott McLemee. Jackson: University Press of Mississippi, 1996.

Jaynes, Gerald David and Robin M. Williams, Jr., eds. *Common Destiny: Blacks and American Society.* Washington, D.C.: National Academies Press, 1989.

Jefferson, Michael A., et al. "City Power Structure Gets Touchy When Black Students Stand Up to Racism." *New Haven Register* (May 11, 1988): 17.

Jeffries, Hasan Kwame. *Bloody Lowndes: Civil Rights and Black Power in Alabama's Black Belt.* New York: New York University Press, 2009.

Jenkins, Joseph Craig and Craig M. Eckert. "Channeling Black Insurgency: Elite Patronage and Professional Social Movement Organizations." *American Sociological Quarterly* 51, no. 6 (December 1986): 812–829.

Joe, Sean. "Bridging the Gap: A Place for Everyone at the Table." *Necessary: News of the Black Community Crusade for Children* 3, no. 3 (Winter 1996): 12.

Johnson, Cedric. *Revolutionaries to Race Leaders: Black Power and the Making of African American Politics.* Minneapolis: University of Minnesota Press, 2007.

Johnson, Charles S. *Growing Up in the Black Belt: Negro Youth in the Rural South.* New York: Schocken Books, 1941.

Johnston, Josee. "Pedagogical Guerillas, Armed Democrats, and Revolutionary Counterpublics: Examining Paradox in the Zapatista Uprising in Chiapas Mexico." *Theory and Society* 29, no. 4 (August 2000): 463–505.

Jolly, Kenneth S. *Black Liberation in the Midwest: The Struggle in St. Louis, Missouri, 1964–1970.* New York: Routledge, 2006.

Jost, Kenneth. "Labor Movement's Future." *CQ Researcher* 6, no. 24 (June 28, 1996): 562–565.

Juris, Jeffrey Scott and Geoffrey Henri Pleyers. "Alter-activism: Emerging Cultures of Participation among Young Global Justice Activists." *Journal of Youth Studies* 12, no. 1 (February 2009): 57–75.

Juvenile Justice Project of Louisiana. *Juvenile Justice Reform Factbook for Louisiana's Leaders.* New Orleans: Louisiana Appleseed, November 2003.

Katznelson, Ira. *When Affirmative Action Was White: An Untold History of Racial Inequality in Twentieth Century America.* New York: Norton, 2005.

Kaus, Mickey. "The Godmother: What's Wrong with Marian Wright Edelman." *New Republic* 208, no. 7 (February 15, 1993): 21–25.

Kelley, Robin D. G. *Hammer and Hoe: Alabama Communists during the Great Depression.* Chapel Hill: University of North Carolina Press, 1990.

———. *Race Rebels: Culture, Politics, and the Black Working Class.* New York: Free Press, 1996.

———. "'We Are Not What We Seem': Rethinking Black Working-Class Opposition in the Jim Crow South." *Journal of American History* 80, no. 1 (June 1993): 75–112.

Kelly, Christine. *Tangled Up in Red, White, and Blue: New Social Movements in America.* Lanham, MD: Rowman & Littlefield, 2001.

Kelly, Malikah J. *Broken Promises, Broken System: 10 Reasons New York City Should Close the Spofford Youth Jail.* New York: Correctional Association of New York, March 2004.

Kifner, John. "Youth Indicted in Fatal Stabbing." *New York Times* (August 27, 1991): A1.

Kilson, Martin. "Political Change in the Negro Ghetto, 1900–1940s." Pp. 167–192 in *Key Issues in the Afro-American Experience*, vol. 2, ed. Nathan I. Huggins, Martin Kilson, and Daniel M. Fox. New York: Harcourt Brace Jovanovich, 1971.

Kitwana, Bakari. *The Hip-Hop Generation: Young Blacks and the Crisis in African-American Culture.* New York: Basic Civitas Books, 2002.

Kovner, Josh. "State Voter Registration Dips." *New Haven Register* (November 2, 1989): 6.

Kretschsmer, Kelsy and David S. Meyer. "Platform Leadership: Cultivating Support for a Public Profile." *American Behavioral Scientist* 50, no. 10 (June 2007): 1395–1412.

Krinsky, John and Ellen Reese. "Forging and Sustaining Labor-Community Coalitions: Workfare Justice in Three Cities." *Sociological Forum* 21, no. 4 (December 2006): 623–658.

Kromm, Chris. "Black Belt Power: African Americans Come Back South, Change Political Landscape." *Race, Poverty & the Environment* 18, no. 2 (2011): 17.

Landry, Bart. *The New Black Middle Class.* Berkeley: University of California Press, 1987.

Lang, Clarence. *Grassroots at the Gateway: Class Politics and the Black Freedom Struggle in St. Louis, 1936–75*. Ann Arbor: University of Michigan Press, 2009.

———. "Political/Economic Restructuring and the Tasks of Radical Black Youth." *Black Scholar* 28, nos. 3–4 (Fall–Winter 1998): 30–38.

Lauter, Paul and Dan Perlstein. "Introduction." *Radical Teacher*, no. 40 (Fall 1991 [1964]): 2–5.

Lee, Chana Kai. *For Freedom's Sake: The Life of Fannie Lou Hamer*. Urbana: University of Illinois Press, 1999.

Lenin, V. I. *What Is to Be Done? Burning Questions of Our Movement*. New York: International, 1969.

Linsin, Christopher E. "Something More Than a Creed: Mary McLeod Bethune's Aim of Integrated Autonomy as Director of Negro Affairs." *Florida Historical Quarterly* 72, no. 1 (Summer 1997): 20–41.

Lipset, Seymour. *Rebellion in the University*. Boston: Little, Brown, 1971.

LISTEN, Inc. "An Emerging Model for Working with Youth." New York: Funders' Collaborative on Youth Organizing Occasional Paper Series on Youth Organizing No. 1, 2003.

Lofland, John. *Social Movement Organizations: Guide to Research on Insurgent Realities*. New York: Aldine, 1996.

Lovell, John Jr. "Youth Programs of Negro Improvement." *Journal of Negro Education* 9, no. 3 (July 1940): 379–387.

Lusane, Clarence. "Congratulations, It's a Crime Bill." *CovertAction*, no. 50 (Fall 1994): 14–21.

Males, Mike and Dan Macallair. *The Color of Justice: An Analysis of Juvenile Adult Court Transfers in California*. Washington, D.C.: Coalition for Juvenile Justice, January 2000.

Mannheim, Karl. *Ideology & Utopia: An Introduction to the Sociology of Knowledge*. San Diego, CA: Harcourt Brace, 1985 [1936].

———. "The Sociological Problem of Generations." Pp. 352–369 in *Studies in Social Movements: A Social Psychological Perspective*, ed. Barry McLaughlin. New York: Free Press, 1969 [1951].

Marable, Manning. *Race, Reform, and Rebellion: The Second Reconstruction in Black America, 1945–1990*. Rev. 2nd ed. Jackson: University Press of Mississippi, 1991.

———. "Toward a Renaissance of Progressive Black Politics." Pp. 73–82 in *Speaking Truth to Power: Essays on Race, Resistance, and Radicalism*, ed. Manning Marable. Boulder, CO: Westview, 1992.

Marx, Gary T. "External Efforts to Damage or Facilitate Social Movements: Some Patrons, Explanations, Outcomes, and Complications." Pp. 94–125 in *The Dynamics of Social Movements: Resource Mobilization, Social Control, and Tactics*, ed. Mayer N. Zald and John D. McCarthy. Cambridge, MA: Winthrop, 1979.

Maryland General Assembly. House Bill No. 979. http://mgaleg.maryland.gov/webmga/frmMain.aspx?tab=subject3&ys=2005rs/billfile/hb0979.htm (accessed May 19, 2011).

———. House Bill 1303. Department of Legislative Services, February 11, 2005.

————. Senate Bill 616. Department of Legislative Services, February 4, 2005.

————. Senate Finance Committee Hearings on SB 773 [Audio]. Department of Legislative Services, March 17, 2005.

Masci, David. "$30 Billion Anti-crime Bill Heads to Clinton's Desk." *Congressional Quarterly Weekly Report* 52, no. 34 (August 27, 1994): 2488–2493.

Matthews, Tracye. "'No One Ever Asks What a Man's Role in the Revolution Is': Gender and the Politics of the Black Panther Party, 1966–1971." Pp. 281–293 in *The Black Panther Party [Reconsidered]*, ed. Charles E. Jones. Baltimore, MD: Black Classic Press, 1998.

Mattson, Kevin. "The Academic Labor Movement: Understanding Its Origins and Current Challenges." *Social Policy* 30, no. 4 (Summer 2000): 4–10.

Maxton, Ashindi. "Prisoners Raise Money for Black Student Leadership Network." *Miscellany News* (April 28, 1995): 6.

McAdam, Doug. *Freedom Summer*. New York: Oxford University Press, 1988.

————. *Political Process and the Development of Black Insurgency, 1930–1970*. Chicago: University of Chicago Press, 1985.

————. "Tactical Innovation and the Pace of Insurgency." *American Sociological Review* 48 (December 1983): 735–754.

McAdam, Doug, Sidney Tarrow, and Charles Tilly. *Dynamics of Contention*. New York: Cambridge University Press, 2001.

McBroome, Delores Nason. *African Americans in California's East Bay 1850–1963*. New York: Garland, 1993.

McCarthy, John D., Clark McPhail, and John Crist. "The Emergence and Diffusion of Public Order Management Systems: Protest Cycles and Police Response." Pp. 49–69 in *Globalization and Social Movements*, ed. Pierre Hamel et al. New York: Palgrave, 2001.

McCarthy, John D. and Mayer N. Zald. "Resource Mobilization and Social Movements: A Partial Theory." Pp. 15–42 in *Social Movements in an Organizational Society*, ed. Mayer N. Zald and John D. McCarthy. New Brunswick, NJ: Transaction, 1987.

McCormick, Joseph, II and Sekou M. Franklin. "Expressions of Racial Consciousness in the African American Community: Data from the Million Man March." Pp. 315–336 in *Blacks and Multiracial Politics in America*, ed. Yvette M. Alex-Assenoh and Lawrence J. Hanks. New York: New York University Press, 2000.

McDermott, Kathryn A. *Controlling Public Education: Localism versus Equity*. Lawrence: University Press of Kansas, 1999.

McDowell, Valerie. "Justice for Youth Coalition: No More Youth Jails Campaign." Pp. 58–59 in *No Turning Back: Promising Approaches to Reducing Racial and Ethnic Disparities Affecting Youth of Color in the Justice System*. Washington, D.C.: Building Blocks for Youth, October 2005.

McNeil, Genna Rae. "Youth Initiative in the African American Struggle for Racial Justice and Constitutional Rights: The City-Wide Young People's Forum of Baltimore, 1931–1941." Pp. 56–80 in *African Americans and the Living Constitution*, ed. John Hope Franklin and Genna Rae McNeil. Washington, D.C.: Smithsonian Institution Press, 1995.

Mendel, Richard A. *Less Hype, More Help: Reducing Juvenile Crime, What Works—and What Doesn't*. Washington, D.C.: American Youth Policy Forum, 2000.

Merrifield, Andy. "The Urbanization of Labor: Living-Wage Activism in the American City." *Social Text* 18, no. 1 (Spring 2000): 31–54.

Meyer, David S. and Sidney Tarrow. "A Movement Society: Contentious Politics for a New Century." Pp. 1–29 in *The Social Movement Society*, ed. David S. Meyer and Sidney Tarrow. Lanham, MD: Rowman & Littlefield, 1998.

Meyer, John W. and Brian Rowan. "Institutionalized Organizations: Formal Structure as Myth and Ceremony." *American Sociological Review* 83, no. 2 (1977): 340–363.

Meyerson, Harold. "Organize or Die." *American Prospect* 14, no. 8 (September 1, 2003): 39–42.

Milton, Catherine. "National Service: Secret Weapon in the Fight Against Crime." *Public Management* 76, no. 7 (July 1994): 6–10.

Minkoff, Debra C. "From Service Provision to Institutional Advocacy: The Shifting Legitimacy of Organizational Forms." *Social Forces* 72, no. 4 (June 1994): 943–969.

———. *Organizing for Equality: The Evolution of Women's and Racial-Ethnic Organizations in America, 1955–1985*. New Brunswick, NJ: Rutgers University Press, 1995.

Montejo, Victor. *Voices from Exile: Violence and Survival in Modern Maya History*. Lawton: University of Oklahoma Press, 1999.

Moriarty, Brooks. "NAACP Mourns Slayed Youths." *Yale Daily News* (February 2, 1989): 3.

Morris, Aldon D. "Birmingham Confrontation Reconsidered: An Analysis of the Dynamics and Tactics of Mobilization." *American Sociological Review* 58 (October 1993): 621–636.

———. "Black Southern Student Sit-In Movement: An Analysis of Internal Organization." *American Sociological Review* 46, no. 6 (1981): 744–767.

———. *The Origins of the Civil Rights Movement: Black Communities Organizing for Change*. New York: Free Press, 1984.

Morris, Aldon D. and Suzanne Staggenborg. "Leadership in Social Movements." In *The Blackwell Companion to Social Movements*, ed. David A. Snow, Sarah A. Soule, and Hanspeter Kriesi. Oxford: Blackwell, 2003. http://www.blackwellreference.com/subscriber/tocnode?id=g9780631226697_chunk_g97806312266979 (accessed June 28, 2012).

Morrison, Minion K. C. *Black Political Mobilization: Leadership, Power, and Mass Behavior*. Albany: State University of New York Press, 1987.

Morrison, Toni, ed. *To Die for the People: The Writings of Huey P. Newton*. New York: Writers and Readers, 1995 [1972].

Moses, Robert P. and Charlie Cobb, Jr. "Organizing Algebra: The Need to Voice a Demand." *Social Policy* 31, no. 4 (Summer 2001): 4–12.

Mueller, Carol. "Ella Baker and the Origins of 'Participatory Democracy.'" Pp. 51–70 in *Women in the Civil Rights Movement: Trailblazers and Torchbearers, 1941–1965*, ed. Vicki L. Crawford, Jacqueline Anne Rouse, and Barbara Woods. Brooklyn, NY: Carlson, 1990.

Musser, Denise Casamento. "Public Access to Juvenile Records in Kansas." *Corrections Today* 63, no. 3 (June 2001): 112–113.

Myrdal, Gunnar. *The American Dilemma*. New York: Harper & Row, 1944 [1962].

"NAACP Reports Takes Aim at Black Crime." *Detroit News* (July 15, 1992): 1.

NAACP Youth Council News. "We Build Together a World of Justice, Freedom, Equality." *Crisis* 44, no. 7 (July 1937): 217.

Naison, Mark. *Communists in Harlem during the Depression*. Urbana: University of Illinois Press, 1973.

Nathan, Richard P., Fred C. Doolittle, and Associates. *The Consequences of Cuts: The Effects of the Reagan Domestic Program on State and Local Governments*. Princeton, NJ: Princeton Urban and Regional Research Center, 1983.

Neufeld, Matt. "Students Take Time to Paint, Canvass Artful Volunteers Aid Communities." *Washington Times* (September 21, 1992): B3.

Nieves, Evelyn. "California Voters in Conservative Initiatives." *New York Times* (March 12, 2000): 2.

Noel, Peter. "Soul on Ice." *Village Voice* (November 24, 1998): 66.

Nolte, Carl. "Bay Area Voters Are State's Contrarians." *San Francisco Chronicle* (March 10, 2000): A17.

Nwafor, Azinna. "The Revolutionary as Historian: Padmore and Pan-Africanism. A Critical Introduction to George Padmore: Pan-Africanism or Communism." Pp. xxvi–xxvii in *Pan-Africanism or Communism*, by George Padmore. Garden City, NY: Doubleday, 1971.

O'Donoghue, Jennifer L., Benjamin Kirshner, and Milbrey W. McLaughlin. "Introduction: Moving Youth Participation Forward." *New Directions for Youth Development: Theory, Practice Research, and Youth Participation* 96 (February 2003): 15–26.

Ogbar, Jeffrey O. G. *Hip-Hop Revolution: The Culture and Politics of Rap*. Lawrence: University of Kansas Press, 2007.

Oliver, Melvin L. and Thomas M. Shapiro. *Black Wealth/White Wealth: A New Perspective on Racial Inequality*. New York: Routledge, 1995.

Olson, Mancur. *Logic of Collective Action*. Cambridge, MA: Harvard University Press, 1965.

"O'Neil Rejects Using Troops in Drug Fight." *New York Times* (May 6, 1989): 30.

Orgeman, Teague. "Principles and Power: The AFL-CIO under John Sweeney." Unpublished manuscript, Williams College, Williamstown, MA, August 2002.

Orr, Marion. "Congress, Race, and Anticrime Policy." Pp. 225–256 in *Black and Multiracial Politics in America*, ed. Yvette M. Alex-Assensoh and Lawrence J. Hanks. New York: New York University Press, 2000.

Ortiz, Paul. *Emancipation Betrayed: The Hidden History of Black Organizing and White Violence in Florida from Reconstruction to the Bloody Election of 1920*. Berkeley: University of California Press, 2005.

Outlaw, Marpessa Dawn and Matthew Countryman. "The Autobiography of Deidre Bailey: Thoughts on Malcolm X and Black Youth." Pp. 233–237 in *Malcolm X in Our Own Image*, ed. Joe Woods. New York: St. Martin's, 1992.

Pappas, Takis S. "Political Leadership and the Emergence of Radical Mass Movements in Democracy." *Comparative Political Studies* 41, no. 8 (August 2008): 1117–1140.

Parsons, Kezia. "Trial Size." *City Limits* 23, no. 7 (September/October 1998): 5.

Payne, Andrea Maneulita. "One Step Forward." *City Limits* 21, no. 4 (April 1996): 8–9.

Payne, Charles M. "Ella Baker and Models of Social Change." *Journal of Women in Culture and Society* 14, no. 4 (1989): 885–899.

———. *I've Got the Light of Freedom: The Organizing Tradition and the Mississippi Freedom Struggle.* Berkeley: University of California Press, 1995.

Payne, Charles M. and Carol Sills Strickland, eds. *Teach Freedom: Education for Liberation in the African-American Tradition.* New York: Teachers College Press, 2008.

Peyser, Marc and Thomas Rosentiel. "She's Taking Her Stand." *Newsweek* 127, no. 24 (June 10, 1996): 32.

Piven, Frances Fox and Richard A. Cloward. *The New Class War: Reagan's Attack on the Welfare State and Its Consequences.* New York: Pantheon, 1982.

———. *Poor People's Movements: Why They Succeed, How They Fail.* New York: Vintage, 1979 [1977].

Plotke, David. "What's So New about New Social Movements." Pp. 113–136 in *Social Movements: Critiques, Concepts, Case-Studies*, ed. Stanford Lyman. New York: New York University Press, 1995.

Poe, Eileen and Michael A. Jones. *And Justice for Some: Differential Treatment of Minority Youth in the Justice System.* Washington, D.C.: Youth Law Center's Building Blocks for Youth Initiative, April 2000.

Polletta, Francesca. "Free Spaces in Collective Action." *Theory and Society* 28 (1999): 1–38.

———. "The Structural Context of Novel Rights Claims: Southern Civil Rights Organizing, 1961–1966." *Law & Society Review* 34, no. 2 (2000): 367–406.

Prothrow-Stith, Deborah with Michael Weismann. *Deadly Consequences.* New York: HarperCollins, 1991.

Purdum, Todd S. "Dinkins Calls for Healing in Brooklyn." *New York Times* (August 26, 1991): B1.

Puritz, Patricia and Mary Ann Scali. "Beyond the Walls: Improving Conditions of Confinement for Youth in Custody." Washington, D.C.: American Bar Association/ Juvenile Justice Center, January 1998.

———. "Civil Rights of Institutionalized Persons: CRIPA Can Be Used to Eliminate Unlawful Conditions of Confinement in Juvenile Facilities." *Corrections Today* 60, no. 5 (August 1998): 80.

Quiroz-Martinez, Julie, Diana Pei Wu, and Kristen Zimmerman. *ReGeneration: Young People Shaping Environmental Justice.* Oakland, CA: Movement Strategy Center, 2005.

Rae, Douglas W. *City: Urbanism and Its End.* New Haven, CT: Yale University Press, 2004.

———. "Making Life Work in Crowded Places." *Urban Affairs Review* 41, no. 3 (January 2006): 271–291.

Ransby, Barbara. *Ella Baker and the Black Freedom Movement: A Radical Democratic Vision*. Chapel Hill: University of North Carolina Press, 2003.

Reckdahl, Katy. "Interrupted." *Gambit Weekly* 24, no. 81 (July 13, 2004): 22.

Record, Wilson. *The Negro and the Communist Party*. New York: Atheneum, 1971 [1951].

———. *Race and Radicalism: The NAACP and the Communist Party*. Ithaca, NY: Cornell University Press, 1964.

Reed, Adolph, Jr. "Demobilization in the New Black Political Regime: Ideological Capitulation and Radical Failure in the Postsegregation Era." Pp. 182–208 in *The Bubbling Cauldron: Race, Ethnicity, and the Urban Crisis*, ed. Michael Peter Smith and Joe R. Feagin. Minneapolis: University of Minnesota Press, 1995.

———, ed. *Without Justice for All: The New Liberalism and Our Retreat from Racial Equality*. Boulder, CO: Westview, 2001.

Reger, Jo. "Organizational Dynamics and Construction of Multiple Feminist Identities in the National Organization for Women." *Gender and Society* 16, no. 5 (October 2002): 710–727.

Richards, Johnetta. "The Southern Negro Youth Congress: A History." Doctoral dissertation, University of Cincinnati, 1987.

Robnett, Belinda. "African-American Women in the Civil Rights Movement, 1954–1965: Gender, Leadership, and Micromobilization." *American Journal of Sociology* 101, no. 6 (May 1996): 1661–1693.

———. *How Long? How Long? African American Women in the Struggle for Civil Rights*. New York: Oxford University Press, 1997.

Rooks, Daisy. "The Cowboy Mentality: Organizers and Occupational Commitment in the New Labor Movement." *Labor Studies Journal* 28, no. 3 (Fall 2003): 33–62.

Rose, Fred. *Coalitions across the Class Divide: Lessons from the Labor, Peace, and Environmental Movements*. Ithaca, NY: Cornell University Press, 2000.

Rose, Tricia. *Black Noise: Rap Music and Black Culture in Contemporary America*. Wesleyan, CT: University Press of New England, 1994.

Ross, B. Joyce. "Mary McLeod Bethune and the National Youth Administration: A Case Study of Power Relationships in the Black Cabinet of Franklin D. Roosevelt." *Journal of Negro History* 60, no. 1 (January 1975): 1–28.

Rucht, Dieter. "Movement Allies, Adversaries, and Third Parties." In *The Blackwell Companion to Social Movements*, ed. David A. Snow and Sarah A. Soule. Oxford: Blackwell, 2003. http://www.blackwellreference.com/subscriber/tocnode?id=g9780631226697_chunk_g97806312266979 (accessed June 28, 2012).

Russ, Hilary. "Making Change: Two Turntables and a Megaphone." *City Limits* 27, no. 10 (December 2002): 32–33.

Santoro, Wayne A. and Gail M. McGuire. "Social Movement Insiders: The Impact of Institutional Activists on Affirmative Action and Comparable Worth Policies." *Social Problems* 44, no. 4 (November 1997): 503–517.

Sanyal, Bishwapriya. "NGOs' Self-Defeating Quest for Autonomy." *Annals of the American Academy of Political and Social Science* 554 (November 1997): 21–32.

Scales, Ann. "Clinton to Sign Welfare Bill into Law." *Boston Globe* (August 22, 1996): A23.

Schiraldi, Vincent and Mark Soler. "The Will of the People? The Public's Opinion of the Violent and Repeat Juvenile Offender Act of 1997." *Crime and Delinquency* 44, no. 4 (October 1998): 590–601.

Schneider, Beth E. "Political Generations and the Contemporary Women's Movement." *Sociological Inquiry* 58 (Winter 1988): 4–21.

Schock, Kurt. *Unarmed Insurrections: People Power Movements in Nondemocracies.* Minneapolis: University of Minnesota Press, 2004.

Schumer, Ellen and Susan O'Donnell. "Turning Parents into Strong Community Leaders." *Shelterforce Online* (November/December 2000): 4. http://www.shelterforce. com/online/issues/114/schumerodonnell.html (accessed November 24, 2013).

Scott, James C. *Domination and the Arts of Resistance.* New Haven, CT: Yale University Press, 1990.

———. "Patron-Client Relations and Political Change in Southeast Asia." *American Political Science Review* 66, no. 1 (1972): 91–113.

Seawright, Jason and John Gerring. "Case Selection Techniques in Case Study Research: A Menu of Qualitative and Quantitative Options." *Political Research Quarterly* 61, no. 2 (June 2008): 294–308.

Sen, Rinku. "Race and Occupy Wall Street." *Nation* (October 26, 2011). http://www.the-nation.com/article/164212/race-and-occupy-wall-street# (accessed August 22, 2012).

Shaw, Todd C. *Now Is the Time! Detroit Black Politics and Grassroots Activism.* Durham, NC: Duke University Press, 2009.

Shepard, Karen B. "Understanding Disproportionate Minority Confinement." *Corrections Today* 57, no. 3 (June 1995): 114.

Sherman, Daniel J. "Disruption or Convention? A Process-Based Explanation of Divergent Repertoires of Contention among Opponents to Low-Level Radioactive Waste Disposal Sites." *Social Movement Studies* 7, no. 3 (December 2000): 265–280.

Sherwood, Kay E. and Julie Dressner. *Youth Organizing: A New Generation of Social Activism.* Philadelphia: Public/Private Ventures, 2004.

Simon, Stephanie. "Yale Pledges $1.5M to City, Easing Town-Gown Relations." *Boston Globe* (April 8, 1990): 74.

Simpson, Andrea Y. *The Tie That Binds: Identity and Political Attitudes in the Post–Civil Rights Generation.* New York: New York University Press, 1998.

Singh, Robert. *The Congressional Black Caucus: Racial Politics in the U.S. Congress.* Thousand Oaks, CA: Sage, 1998.

Sitkoff, Harvard. *A New Deal for Blacks: The Emergence of Civil Rights as a National Issue. Volume 1: The Depression Decade.* New York: Oxford University Press, 1978.

Smith, Robert C. "Black Power and the Transformation from Protest to Politics." *Political Science Quarterly* 96, no. 3 (Autumn 1981): 431–443.

———. "Politics Is Not Enough: The Institutionalization of the African American Freedom Movement." Pp. 97–126 in *From Exclusion to Inclusion: The Long Struggle for African American Political Power*, ed. Linda Williams and Ralph Gomes. Westport, CT: Praeger, 1992.

————. *We Have No Leaders: African American Leadership in the Post–Civil Rights Era.* Albany: State University of New York Press, 1996.

Snow, David A. and Robert D. Benford. "Ideology, Frame Resonance, and Participant Mobilization." Pp. 197–218 in *International Social Movement Research: From Structure to Action*, ed. Bert Klandermans, Hanspeter Kreisi, and Sidney Tarrow. Greenwich, CT: JAI, 1988.

————. "Master Frames and Cycles of Protest." Pp. 133–155 in *Frontiers in Social Movement Theory*, ed. Aldon Morris and C. McClurg Mueller. New Haven, CT: Yale University Press, 1992.

Snyder, Howard N. "Juvenile Arrests 2001." *Juvenile Justice Bulletin*. Washington, D.C.: Office of Juvenile Justice and Delinquency Prevention, December 2003.

Snyder, Howard N. and Melissa Sickmund. "Juvenile Justice System Structure and Process." Pp. 4–12 in *Essential Readings in Juvenile Justice*, ed. David L. Parry. Upper Saddle River, NJ: Pearson, 2005.

SOBU News Service. "The Elections." *African World* 1, no. 3 (November 21, 1970): 3.

————. "N.C. YOBU Shows Growth." *African World* 2, no. 15 (May 9, 1972): 5.

————. "North Carolina Youth Organization for Black Unity Purpose and Program." *African World* 11, no. 3 (November 13, 1971): 4X.

————. "SOBU Explains National Program." *African World* 1, no. 1 (October 17, 1970).

Soler, Mark. *Public Opinion on Youth, Crime and Race: A Guide for Advocates.* Washington, D.C.: Youth Law Center's Building Blocks for Youth Initiative, October 2001.

Soule, Sarah A. "The Student Divestment Movement in the United States and Tactical Diffusion: The Shantytown Protest." *Social Forces* 75, no. 3 (March 1997): 855–883.

Sparks, Holloway. "Dissident Citizenship: Democratic Theory, Political Courage, and Activist Women." *Hypatia* 12, no. 4 (Fall 1997): 74–110.

Spence, Lester. *Stare in the Darkness: The Limits of Hip-Hop and Black Politics.* Minneapolis: University of Minnesota Press, 2011.

Spillane, Margaret. "Newhallville Turns It Around; A Tale of Two Schools—II." *Nation* 255, no. 8 (September 21, 1992): 290–291.

Spitzer, Alan B. "The Historical Problem of Generations." *American Historical Review* 78, no. 5 (December 1973): 1353–1385.

Stafford, Walter W. "The National Urban League Survey: Black America's Under-35 Generation." Pp. 19–64 in *The State of Black America*, ed. Lee A. Daniels. Washington, D.C.: National Urban League, 2001.

Staggenborg, Suzanne. "The Consequences of Professionalization and Formalization in the Pro-Choice Movement." *American Sociological Review* 53 (August 1988): 585–606.

————. "Social Movement Communities and Cycles of Protest: The Emergence and Maintenance of a Local Women's Movement." *Social Problems* 45, no. 2 (May 1998): 108–204.

Staples, Robert. "The Post Racial Presidency: The Myths of a Nation and Its People." *Journal of African American Studies* 14, no. 1 (March 2010): 128–144.

Stolle-McAllister, John. "Local Social Movements and Mesoamerican Cultural Resistance and Adaptation." *Social Movement Studies* 6, no. 2 (September 2007): 161–175.

Strolovitch, Dara Z. *Affirmative Advocacy: Race, Class, and Gender in Interest Group Politics*. Chicago: University of Chicago Press, 2007.

[Strong] Jackson, Augusta V. "Southern Youth Marches Forward." *Crisis* 45, no. 6 (June 1938): 47.

———. "Southern Youth's Proud Heritage, No. 1, 1964." Pp. 16–20 in *Freedomways Reader: Prophets in Their Own Country*, ed. Esther Cooper Jackson and Constance Pohl. Boulder, CO: Westview, 2000.

Sullivan, John. "African Americans Moving South—and to the Suburbs." *Race, Poverty & the Environment* 18, no. 2 (2011): 16–19.

Sullivan, Lisa Y. "Beyond Nostalgia: Notes on Black Student Activism." *Socialist Review* 20, no. 4 (October–December 1990): 21–28.

———. "Hip-Hop Nation: The Undeveloped Social Capital of Black Urban America." *National Civic Review* 86, no. 3 (Fall 1997): 235–243.

Summers, Mary E. and Phillip Klinker. "The Daniels Election in New Haven and the Failure of the Deracialization Hypothesis." *Urban Affairs Quarterly* 27, no. 2 (December 1991): 202–215.

———. "The Election of John Daniels as Mayor of New Haven." *PS: Political Science & Politics* (June 1990): 142–145.

Tanehaus, David S. *Juvenile Justice in the Making*. Oxford: Oxford University Press, 2004.

Tannock, Stuart and Sara Flocks. "'I Know What It's Like to Struggle': The Working Lives of Young Students in an Urban Community College." *Labor Studies Journal* 28, no. 1 (Spring 2003): 1–30.

Tarrow, Sidney. *Power in Movement: Social Movements, Collective Action and Politics*. New York: Cambridge University Press, 1994.

Taylor, Judith. "Organizational Elaboration as Social Movement Tactic: A Case Study of Strategic Leadership in the First US School-Sponsored Program for Gay and Lesbian Youth." *Social Movement Studies* 6, no. 3 (December 2007): 311–326.

Taylor, Verta. "Gender and Social Movements: Gender Processes in Women's Self-Help Movements." *Gender & Society* 13 (1999): 8–33.

Taylor, Verta and Nancy E. Whittier. "Collective Identity in Social Movement Communities: Lesbian Feminist Mobilization." Pp. 104–129 in *Frontiers in Social Movement Theory*, ed. Aldon D. Morris and Carol McClurg Mueller. New Haven, CT: Yale University Press, 1992.

Thomson, Robert. "Howard Board Sets Emergency Meeting on Student Unrest." *Washington Post* (March 15, 1989): C1.

Tilton, Jennifer. *Dangerous or Endangered? Race and the Politics of Youth in Urban America*. New York: New York University Press, 2010.

Tough, Paul. *Whatever It Takes: Geoffrey Canada's Quest to Change Harlem and America*. Orlando, FL: Houghton Mifflin Harcourt, 2009.

Tracy, Paul E. *Decision-Making and Juvenile Justice: An Analysis of Bias in Case Proceedings*. Westport, CT: Praeger, 2005.

Tripp, Luke. "The Political Views of Black Students during the Reagan Era." *Black Scholar* 22, no. 3 (Summer 1992): 45–51.

Ture, Kwame. "Kwame Ture Address, University of Massachusetts, April 14, 1997." Reprinted in *Black Scholar* 27, nos. 3–4 (Fall–Winter 1997): 2–31.

U.S. Department of Justice. "Investing in Girls: A Twenty-First Century Strategy." *Journal of the Office of Juvenile Justice and Delinquency Prevention* 6, no. 1 (October 1999): 3–13.

Violence Policy Center. *Firearms Production in America: 1975–1997—A State-by-State Breakdown*. Washington, D.C.: Violence Policy Center, 2000.

Von Drehle, David. "Eager Advocates of Change Are Told to Await New Clinton Team's Results." *Washington Post* (December 14, 1992): A4.

Walters, Ronald W. *Pan-Africanism in the African Diaspora: An Analysis of Modern Afrocentric Political Movements*. Detroit, MI: Wayne State University, 1993.

Walters, Ronald W. and Robert C. Smith. *African American Leadership*. Albany: State University of New York Press, 1999.

Walton, Hanes. *When the Marching Stopped: The Politics of Civil Rights Regulatory Agencies*. Albany: State University of New York Press, 1988.

Warren, Dorian. "A New Labor Movement for a New Century? The Incorporation of Marginalized Workers in U.S. Unions." Doctoral dissertation, Yale University, New Haven, CT, December 2005.

Washington Post Editorial Board. "Trouble for Troubled Youth." *Washington Post* (April 9, 2005): A22.

Watkins, Celeste M. "A Tale of Two Classes: The Socio-economic Divide among Black Americans Under 35." Pp. 67–85 in *The State of Black America*, ed. Lee A. Daniels. Washington, D.C.: National Urban League, 2001.

Watkins, S. Craig. *Hip Hop Matters: Politics, Pop Culture, and the Struggle for the Soul of a Movement*. Boston: Beacon, 2006.

Watson, Bruce. *Freedom Summer: The Savage Season That Made Mississippi Burn and Made America a Democracy*. New York: Viking, 2010.

We Interrupt This Message. *Soundbites and Cellblocks: An Analysis of the Juvenile Justice Media Debate & a Case Study of California's Proposition 21*. San Francisco: We Interrupt This Message, 2001.

White, Aaronette M. "All the Men Are Fighting for Freedom, All the Women Are Morning Their Men, but Some of Us Carried Guns: A Race-Gendered Analysis of Fanon's Psychological Perspectives on War." *Signs: Journal of Women in Culture and Society* 32, no. 4 (2007): 857–884.

White, Walter. "The Youth Council of the N.A.A.C.P." *Crisis* 44, no. 7 (July 1937): 215.

Whittier, Nancy. "Political Generations, Micro-cohorts, and the Transformation of Social Movements." *American Sociological Review* 62, no. 5 (October 1997): 760–778.

Wilkins, Fanon Che. "In the Belly of the Beast: Black Power, Anti-Imperialism, and the African Liberation Solidarity Movement, 1968–1975." Doctoral dissertation, New York University, 2001.

Williams, Jane. "Restructuring Labor's Identity: The Justice for Janitors Campaign in Washington, D.C." Pp. 203–217 in *The Transformation of U.S. Unions: Voices, Visions, and Strategies from the Grassroots*, ed. Ray M. Tillman and Michael S. Cummings. Boulder, CO: Lynne Rienner, 1999.

Williams, Juan. *Enough: The Phony Leaders, Dead-End Movements, and Culture of Failure That Are Undermining Black America—and What We Can Do about It.* New York: Crown, 2006.

Williams, Terry and William Kornblum. *The Uptown Kids: Struggle and Hope in the Projects.* New York: Putnam, 1994.

Williams, Yohuru. "No Haven: Civil Rights, Black Power, and Black Panthers in New Haven, Connecticut, 1956–1971." Doctoral dissertation, Howard University, Washington, D.C., 1998.

Wilson, William Julius. "The Economic Plight of Inner-City Black Males." Pp. 55–70 in *Against the Wall: Poor, Young, Black, and Male*, ed. Elijah Anderson. Philadelphia: University of Pennsylvania Press, 2008.

———. *When Work Disappears: The New World of the Urban Poor.* New York: Knopf, 1996.

Wittner, Lawrence S. "The National Negro Congress: A Reassessment." *American Quarterly* 22, no. 4 (1970): 883–901.

Wolman, Leo. "The Turning Point in American Labor Policy." *Political Science Quarterly* 55, no. 2 (June 1940): 161–175.

Wolters, Raymond. *Negroes and the Great Depression: The Problem of Economic Recovery.* Westport, CT: Greenwood, 1970.

———. *The New Negro on Campus: Black College Rebellions of the 1920s.* Princeton, NJ: Princeton University Press, 1975.

Woodard, C. Vann. *The Strange Career of Jim Crow.* 3rd rev. ed. New York: Oxford University Press, 1974 [1955].

Wright, Marian Thompson. "Negro Youth and the Federal Emergency Programs: CCC and NYA." *Journal of Negro Education* 9, no. 3 (1940): 397–407.

Wyn, Johanna and Rob White. *Rethinking Youth.* London: Sage, 1997.

YOBU News Service. "Building the Black Assembly." *African World* 2, no. 30 (September 30, 1972): 3.

———. "Carmichael Announces New Political Party." *African World* (November 11, 1972): 15.

———. "YOBU Unites Students and Community." *African World* 3, no. 10 (March 3, 1973): 12.

Young Wisdom Project of the Movement Strategy Center. *Making Space, Making Change: Profiles of Youth-Led and Youth-Driven Organizations.* Oakland, CA: Movement Strategy Center, 2004.

Youth Force. *In Between the Lines: How the New York Times Frames Youth.* New York: We Interrupt This Message, 2001.

Youth Force Coalition. *Schools Not Jails: A Report on the Northern California Youth Movement Against Proposition 21*. San Francisco, April 2000.

Youth Media Council. *Speaking for Ourselves: A Youth Assessment of Local News Coverage*. San Francisco: We Interrupt This Message, 2002.

Zald, Mayer N. and John D. McCarthy. "Social Movement Industries: Competition and Conflict." Pp. 161–180 in *Social Movements in an Organizational Society*, ed. Mayer N. Zald and John D. McCarthy. New Brunswick, NJ: Transactions, 1987.

Ziedenberg, Jason. *Models for Change: Building Momentum for Juvenile Justice Reform*. Washington, D.C.: Justice Policy Institute, December 2006.

Zinn, Howard. *SNCC: The New Abolitionists*. Boston: Beacon, 1965.

ARCHIVES AND ORAL HISTORY DOCUMENTATION

Black Student Leadership Network/Black Community Crusade for Children Collection File. Archives and documentation collected by Sekou M. Franklin.

Civil Rights Documentation Project Vertical File Collection. Moorland-Spingarn Library, Manuscripts Division, Howard University, Washington, D.C.

Ed Strong Papers. Moorland-Spingarn Research Center, Howard University, Washington, D.C.

Federal Bureau of Investigation Files. U.S. Department of Justice, Washington, D.C.

George Meany Memorial Archives. National Labor College, Silver Spring, MD. (The Union Summer files are not processed. Access to these documents requires special permission from the Secretary-Treasurer's office.)

Juvenile Justice Reform Movement Collection File. Archives and documentation collected by Sekou M. Franklin.

Papers of the National Negro Congress. Library of Congress, Manuscript Division, Washington, D.C.

Records of the National Urban League. Library of Congress, Manuscript Division, Washington, D.C.

Student Nonviolent Coordinating Committee Papers. Founders Library, Howard University, Washington, D.C.

Student Organization for Black Unity Newspaper, *African World*. Moorland-Spingarn Research Center, Howard University, Washington, D.C.

INTERVIEWS

Baker, Ella. Interview by John Britton, June 19, 1968, 1–98. Ralph J. Bunche Oral History Collection, Civil Rights Documentation Project, Moorland-Spingarn Research Center, Howard University, Washington, D.C.

Drake, St. Claire. Interview by Robert E. Martin, July 28, 1969, 1–210. Ralph J. Bunche Oral History Collection, Civil Rights Documentation Project, Moorland-Spingarn Research Center, Howard University, Washington, D.C.

Richardson, Gloria. Interview by John Britton, October 11, 1967, 32. Ralph J. Bunche Oral History Collection, Civil Rights Documentation Project, Moorland-Spingarn Research Center, Howard University, Washington, D.C.

INTERVIEWS BY SEKOU M. FRANKLIN

Abramson, Lauren. June 2, 2005.

Aird, Enola. January 25, 2002.

Allen, Phillip. August 23, 2003.

Armstrong, Kimberly. June 2, 2005.

Barron, Cameron. June 27, 2003.

Bervera, Xochitl. July 14, 2004.

Black, Tim. March 13, 1999.

Blackwell, Angela Glover. August 13, 1999.

Brown, Drema. April 19, 2000.

Brown, Sylvia. May 28, 2003.

Burrowes, Nicole. May 2, 2000.

Canada, Geoffrey. January 4, 2001.

Chatmon, Kia. August 17, 2000.

Choice, Crandall. June 30, 2003.

Coleman, Milton. August 3, 2000.

Conyers, Angela. July 14, 2004.

Countryman, Matthew. September 13, 2000.

Coursey, Tanza. May 28, 2003.

David, Marian. May 1, 2000.

Davis, Kim. April 24, 2000.

Esdaile, Scot X. February 27, 2003.

Farrow, Kenyon. July 14, 2004.

Faruqee, Mishi. July 22, 2004.

Fisher, Helene. August 16, 1999.

Fletcher, Bill. July 10, 2003.

Foggy, Andrea. January 31, 2000.

Ford, Patricia. August 20, 2003.

Franklin, Kamua "Karl." May 23, 2000.

Gavins, Raymond. April 18, 2000.

Graham, Rikkia. May 28, 2003.

Gray, Richard. March 15, 2000.

Greene, Sean. April 11, 2000.

Griffith, Mark Winston. April 5, 2000.

Hallmon, Maceo. July 21, 2004.

Hardin, Chino. July 22, 2004.

Hawkins, Channing. June 26, 2003.

Hodge, Gregory. August, 27, 1999.

Holder, Andre. July 22, 2004.

Hoy, Darriel. September 9, 2000.

Jackson, Esther Cooper. May 16, 2000.

Jackson, James. May 16, 2000.

James, Taj. August 15, 1999.

Jennings, Keith. August 30, 1999.

Joe, Sean. February 8, 2000.

Johnson, Nelson. August, 6, 2000.

Johnson, Nicole. April 12, 1999.

Jones, Kasey. June 17, 2000.

Kelly, Malikah J. July 22, 2004.

Lydia, Malkia. November 2, 1999.

Mahr, Corlita. July 15, 2004.

Marthol, Marie Monique. May 22, 2000.

McDavid, Lolita. December 12, 2001.

McKenzie, Sarah. September 4, 2003.

Middleton, Tamika. July 15, 2004.

Miles, Cameron. July 27, 2004.

Mims, Thomas. July 22, 2004.

Minter, Steve. January 18, 2002.

Nembhard, Jessica Gordon. January 30, 2002.

Patterson, Anita. March 6, 2002.

Perkins, Greg. July 20, 2004.

Peterkin, Robert. December 12, 2001.

Petgrave, Sheldon. July 23, 2004.

Porchia, Felicia. June 2, 2003.

Prothrow-Stith, Deborah. January 23, 2002.

Rhee, Kate. August 5, 2004.

Sabol, Barbara. January 29, 2002.

Sawyer, Melissa. July 14, 2004.

Scott, Patrick. June 19, 2003.

Simms, Lisa. May 8, 2000.

Smith, Stacy. June 4, 2005.

Sullivan, Lisa Y. May 3, 2000.

Taaffe, Claudine "Candy." April 24, 1999.

Tuckson, Reed. February 11, 2002.

Utter, David. July 14, 2004.

Walker, Jason. March 16, 2000.

Walton, Audrey. July 22, 2003.

White, Steven. March 3, 2000.

Wilkens, Desiree. July 14, 2003.

Wilson, Danté. July 21, 2004.

Womack, Gina. August 25, 2004.

Young, James. April 7, 2000.

A. Philip Randolph Institute (APRI), 246,
252
Abolish the Poll Tax Week, 59
Abramson, Lauren, 228
activism and activists, black youth: as
bridge-builders, 6, 48, 96–97, 258;
BSLN's work with, 129, 130, 142–143;
case studies of, 5–8; challenges to, 99;
collective, 115–116, 184; conceptualizing,
28–45, 111; creative organizing by, 37–42,
69, 97, 98; difficulties faced by, 2, 93–94;
direct action, 212; framing strategies
used by, 43–44; fund-raising for, 170;
low-income, 32, 34–35, 133; militancy
among, 35–36, 75, 79; multiple identities
of, 5–6, 21–23; networks of, 29, 117, 253,
255–256, 258; organizations encompass-
ing, 1–5; political involvement, 3–4, 31,
38, 69, 97–98, 125–126, 165–166, 180;
post-World War II, 72; progressive, 78,
96; resource dilemma, 257–259; transformational, 93, 95, 256; workers' rights,
35, 236, 246, 251. See also juvenile justice
reform movement (JJRM); mobilization: youth-based; movements: intergenerational; post-civil rights era generation; students, black; youth, black
adult organizations and adults, 94, 102–
103, 116, 175, 229; activist, 18, 21, 24–26,
62, 71, 73, 212, 261; in advisory roles,
54, 64, 68, 74, 129–130, 138; control
over youth movements, 20, 201; generational cleavages, 25, 184, 188, 258;
lobbying groups, 92, 124; relationship
with youth activists, 26, 177, 255–256,
258, 261; as youth group allies, 29–30,
44, 53, 57, 125, 256–257. See also bridge-
builders, movement; generations;
young adults
Advanced Service and Advocacy Workshops (ASAW), 129, 174, 178, 196
Adventures in Excellence, 174
advocacy, 35, 36, 259; direct-action, 132–
133, 150–151, 153, 161, 175; freedom school
curriculum directed toward, 149–150,
151, 152, 168; HIV/AIDS response, 31–32;
service, 152–153; single-issue, 33, 34;
training for, 132, 175, 186; typologies of,
5–6. See also adult organizations and
adults: as youth group allies
Advocates for Children and Youth in Bal-
timore, 224
Africa, 83, 85, 88, 250. See also Free South
Africa movement (FSAM)
African Americans. See blacks
African-American Women's Agenda, 107
African-American Young Adult Leader-
ship (AAYAL) meeting, 138–139, 140, 141
African-American Youth Congress (aka
Black Youth Political Coalition), 97,
99–109
African Descendants Awareness Move-
ment, 166
African Liberation Day, 83
African Liberation Support Committee
(ALSC), 83, 87, 88
African Project, SNCC, 90
African Students Association, 83

African World (newspaper), 83, 84, 87

Agricultural Workers Organizing Committee (AWOC), 38

Aird, Enola, 122, 161

Akron, Ohio, Union Summer organizing in, 244

Alabama, SYNC youth legislature in, 60

Alex Haley Farm, 3, 186, 303n7

Alfred D. Noyes Children's Center, 224

Alianza Dominicana of Washington Heights, Brooklyn, 167, 194

All African People's Revolutionary Party (AAPRP), 87, 88, 314n23

Alliance of African Men, 97

All-Southern Negro Youth Conference, 53–54, 67

Alston, C. Columbus, 48, 61

Amenia Conference, NAACP, 56, 139

American Committee on Africa, 92

American Council on Education, 23

American Dilemma, The (Myrdal), 66

American Federation of Labor (AFL), 50–51

American Federation of Labor-Congress of Industrial Organizations (AFL-CIO), 235, 238, 242–257. *See also* Agricultural Workers Organizing Committee; Congress of Industrial Organizations; Organizing Institute; Union Summer campaign

American Federation of State, County and Municipal Employees (AFSCME), 242, 244, 245, 249

American Negro Labor Congress (ANLC), 51

Americans Coming Together, 95

American Student Union (ASU), 54

American Youth Commission, studies by, 55

American Youth Congress (AYC), 54

AmeriCorps, 153–155

Amos, Kent, 148–149, 202

Annie E. Casey Foundation, 213

anti-affirmative action bill. *See* Proposition 209 (California)

Anti-Apartheid Act of 1986, 73

anti-apartheid movement, 24, 72, 88–93, 94, 125, 211

anti-lynching legislation, campaigns for, 56, 59

anti-violence campaigns, 227, 255; BCCC/BSLN, 157–163, 180–181, 205; direct action, 161; New Haven, 97, 98–102, 108, 111

Anti-Violence Network, 159

Anti-Violence Task Force (AVTF), 159–160, 162

antiwar movement, civil rights movement synthesized with, 41. *See also* Vietnam War, protesting

Apollon, Dominique, 4, 21–22, 34

APPLES program, 134

Applied Research Center, 5

appropriation, strategy of, 40–41, 44, 72–73, 217, 228, 233

Arbuthnot, Grover, 209–210, 212, 222

Armstrong, Kimberly, 228

Atlanta, Georgia: SCAR chapter, 90

Atlanta Project, SNCC, 75

at-risk youth: assistance to, 222, 226, 227, 254–255; criminal justice system treatment of, 210, 215, 216; in freedom schools, 150, 164; programs for, 119, 127, 135, 164

Atwater, Lee, 294n36; Howard University board appointment, 93, 126, 150

autonomy, 107, 259. *See also* Black Student Leadership Network: autonomy concerns; movements: autonomy concerns

Azabache coalition, 166–167, 179

Azania, as term for South Africa, 89

Bailey, Deirdre, 104, 106, 107, 109, 112

Baker, Ella, 71, 93, 109; as bridge-builder, 190; community organizing philosophy of, 132–133, 134, 136, 250, 252; and

SNCC formation, 24–25, 50, 73, 74, 77, 120. *See also* Ella Baker Child Policy Training Institute (EBCPTI)

Baltimore: Advocates for Children and Youth, 224; Buy Where You Can Work campaign, 50; Community Conferencing Center, 228; Gay Detention Center, 227; juvenile justice system in, 224–227, 256

Baltimore City Juvenile Justice Center, 224

Bandele, Lumumba, 166–167

Baraka, Ras, 150

Barnes, Claude W., Jr., 81

Barron, Cameron, 241, 250

Bates, Evelyn, 239

Battles, Wendy, 128

Bay Area Youth Caucus meeting, 179

Bedolla, Lisa García, 22

Bellagio retreat (Italy), 120–123, 124, 125

Bennettsville, South Carolina, community center, 174–175

Bervera, Xochitl, 221

Bethune, Mary McLeod, 54–55; letter to Franklin Roosevelt, 1, 3–4, 5

Bey, Kimoko Ferut, 85

Biondi, Martha, 80

Black Belt Thesis (aka Black Republic Thesis), 53

Black Community Crusade for Children (BCCC), 116, 117–126, 258, 262; anti-gun violence campaign, 157–163, 180–181, 205; CDF as coordinator of, 121–122, 124, 125–126, 259; Childhood Hunger Campaign, 172; Clinton administration connections, 145, 147, 153–154; founding of, 121–123; grassroots initiatives, 122, 141, 142–143, 187; intergenerational linkages built by, 122, 124–125; Juvenile and Family Court Judges Leadership Council, 159; objectives of, 122, 138–139; organizational challenges, 137–138; regional offices,

123–124, 293n28; Rheedlen Centers affiliation with, 169; Steering Committee, 137, 138; Steven White's tensions with, 184, 185, 188, 190; and Summer Freedom School Program, 144–155; tensions with BSLN, 170, 173, 184–185, 198–203; Working Committee, 123, 138, 201. *See also* Black Student Leadership Network: BCCC linkages with

Black Family Institute's Hawk Foundation, 177

Black Liberators, SNCC's alliance with, 44, 79, 80

Black Nia Force, 150

Black Panther Party (BPP): and freedom schools, 3, 167; SNCC's alliance with, 44, 79–80; women activists in, 191–192

Black Peoples' Union Party of North Carolina, 82

blacks, 124, 154, 177, 237; conscription of, 64, 68; HIV/AIDS response, 31–32; low-income, 34–35, 67, 68–69, 103, 255; middle-class, 36, 56, 69, 86, 119, 133, 152, 240; mobilization of, 48, 49, 125, 149, 259; poor, 82, 96, 97, 101, 108, 151–152, 261–262; in Union Summer campaign, 249–250, 251. *See also* children, black; marginalization: of black youth; students, black; youth, black

Black Student Leadership Network (BSLN), 3, 112, 115–141, 211; alternative conference, 197, 199, 200; anti-gun violence campaign, 157–163, 180–181, 205; ASAW training programs, 129, 174, 178, 196; autonomy concerns, 185, 193, 200–201, 202; BCCC linkages with, 125–126, 128, 142–144, 178, 180, 183, 187–189, 193, 259; Black Youth Vote project, 95, 162, 197, 198; CDF linkages with, 116, 126–128, 142–144, 180, 183, 187, 189–190, 193, 258–259; Citizenship 2000 campaign, 168, 197, 198, 199, 200, 201, 202, 203;

Black Student Leadership Network
(*continued*):
Clinton administration connections,
153–154; community organizing by, 140,
153, 178, 181; constitution and bylaws,
130–131, 178, 187, 191; creative organizing
strategies used by, 182, 203; demobilization of, 170, 179, 181, 183–205, 253;
diversity in, 136, 199–200; formation
of, 117, 125, 126–131; framing strategies
used by, 152–153; grassroots organizing
efforts, 15, 116, 132, 141, 142–143, 180–181,
195; indigenous groups linking with,
116, 143, 163, 180; intraorganizational
tensions in, 167, 168–169, 172, 180–181,
184, 185–193, 195; Issue Clusters created
by, 190–191; leadership cadre, 129, 136,
140–141, 148–149, 185, 193, 196, 201–202,
248, 255; Marlboro County, South
Carolina, campaign, 173–174; New York
Metro chapter, 15, 165–170, 178, 181, 194,
196; in North Carolina, 133–135, 140,
148, 170–173, 181; One Thousand by Two
Thousand project, 195, 198, 199, 203;
organizational structure, 7, 130, 203,
258; organizing activities, 163–180, 199,
297n6; People's Community Feeding
Program, 15, 166, 181; political context,
140, 198; positional strategies used by,
44; recruitment efforts, 143, 155, 156, 179,
195–196, 197, 202, 203; reorganization of,
193–198, 203, 235, 304n32; resources of,
137, 163; sexism in, 191–192; Sista II Sista
program, 170, 181; social change agenda,
138–139; Southern Region, 170–175;
Steering Committee, 130–131; Sullivan
as acting director of, 189, 190–191, 195–
196; Summer Freedom School Program,
3, 144–155, 163, 184, 185–186, 189, 203;
tensions with BCCC and CDF, 170, 173,
184–185, 198–203; voter mobilization activities, 161–162, 168, 196–197, 200, 201;
Voter Registration and Education in the

Black Community workshop, 197; West
Coast regional offices, 175–180, 181, 196;
Working Committee, 126–127; youth
participation in, 129, 130, 142–143. *See
also* mobilization: BSLN's efforts; Na-
tional Coordinating Committee, BSLN
Black Students United for Liberation, 81
Black Student Union of Hunter College,
166
Blackwell, Angela Glover, 123, 137, 146,
147–148, 176, 201–202
Black Youth Political Coalition. *See* African-American Youth Congress
Black Youth Vote project, 95, 162, 197, 198
Blue Dog Coalition, 238
Board of Young Adult Police Commissioners, New Haven, Connecticut, 110
Boggs, Carl, 238
Bond, Horace Mann, 54
Bond, Julian, 77
bridge-builders, movement: coordinating
movement infrastructures, 255–256,
261; creative strategies used by, 2–3,
38–39, 41, 42–43, 48; generation of, 26,
190; institutional leveraging used by,
82–83; in JJRM, 211–212; labor movement, 236; leadership styles of, 45, 46,
184; in New Haven campaigns, 98, 108;
organizational elaboration strategy
of, 79; positionality strategies used by,
44, 212; Sullivan as, 190–191, 253–254;
youth activists as, 6, 48, 96–97, 258. *See
also* adult organizations and adults;
civil rights movement; post-civil rights
era generation
Bridges Juvenile Center. *See* Spofford
Juvenile Center
British American Tobacco Company, 48,
58–59
Brock, Avis, 219
Brooklyn, New York: BSLN chapter,
165–170, 178, 181; Sisterhood of Black
Single Mothers, 192

Brown, Charlotte Hawkins, 54
Brown, H. Rap, 80
Brown, Sylvia, 249
Brue, Brenda, 210
Building Blocks for Youth initiative, 212–213
Building Local Organizing Communities (BLOC), 205
Bunche, Ralph, 51, 66
Bunnage, Leslie Allison, 248–249
Burnham, Louis, 48, 53, 54, 61, 65
Burrowes, Nicole, 134–135, 167, 169, 191
Bush administrations, 118, 119, 237; devolution policies of, 27, 92–93, 110, 158
Bynoe, Yvonne, 26

Cabral, Amilcar, 85
Calogero, Paul, 221
Canada, Geoffrey, 123, 162, 164, 201, 311n86
Carmichael, Stokely, 31, 77, 84–85, 87, 240
Carolina Alliance for Fair Employment, 243–244
Carson, Clayborne, 80, 178
Cease Fire (Rand and Sugarmann), 158
Central Brooklyn Partnership (CBP), 15, 165
Chambers, Jordan, 50
Charles Drew Development Corporation, 178
Charles H. Hickey, Jr., School, Maryland, 223, 310n60; closing of, 224, 225, 233
Charleston, South Carolina, Union Summer organizing in, 243–244
Chavannes, Dorothy, 165–166
Cheltenham youth detention center, Maryland, 223–224; closing of, 231, 233
Chicago Area Project, 229
Child Development Group of Mississippi (CDGM), 78
Childhood Hunger Campaign, 172
children, black: advocating for, 119, 125–126, 199; education of, 102–103,

144, 165; feeding, 108–109. See also Black Community Crusade for Children; Child Development Group of Mississippi; Children's Defense Fund; freedom schools; youth, black
children, Latino, 102–103, 108–109
Children Action Teams, 199
Children in Confinement in Louisiana (Human Rights Watch), 210
Children's Defense Fund (CDF): Alex Haley Farm, 3, 186, 303n7; as BCCC coordinator, 121–122, 124, 125–126, 259; Clinton administration connections, 145, 147–148, 200; founding of, 118–119; grassroots organizing by, 15, 124, 150, 187; gun violence reduction strategy, 158–159; Marlboro County, South Carolina, office, 155, 173–174; National Observance of Children's Sabbaths, 172, 173; Stand for Children campaign, 169, 170, 173, 185, 198–199, 200, 202, 203; Sullivan as field director of, 186–192; tensions with BSLN, 173, 180, 184–185, 198–203. See also Black Student Leadership Network: CDF's linkages with
Chong, Dennis, 20
Citizenship 2000 campaign, BSLN, 168, 197, 198, 199, 200, 201, 202, 203
City-Wide Young People's Forum (CWYPF), 50
civil rights movement: class divisions in, 151–152; demobilization of, 2, 72; generational debates in, 24–25; HIV/AIDS response by, 31–32; institutional leveraging during, 35, 36, 37, 40; militant phase of, 32, 215; in Mississippi, 30, 39, 76–77; motivations for, 192; movements intersecting with, 29, 41; northern strategy, 79; organizing efforts within, 93–94; SNCC's role in, 1, 30; television as tool of, 196; training activists for, 303n7; women activists in, 20

Civil Rights of Institutionalized Persons
Act (CRIPA) of 1980, 216, 223
Clark, Septima, 109
Clark, Tom, 68
class: growing divide in black community, 101, 132, 149; hierarchies of, 4, 21,
36, 61, 214; marginalization of, 249, 251;
in post-civil rights era, 236, 237–241; in
Union Summer movement, 247–251
Clemente, Rosa, 26
Clinton, Hilary Rodham, 118, 147; as CDF
staff attorney, 145, 200
Clinton administration: BCCC's connection to, 145, 147, 153–154; and child
poverty reduction, 145, 146–147; Edel-
man's ties to, 145, 200; *Putting People
First,* 146; Summer of Service program,
153–155; and welfare reform bill, 204
Coalition of Black Trade Unionists
(CBTU), 238, 252
coalitions, 106, 179; community-labor,
236, 241; cross-class, 96, 97, 100–101;
cross-racial, 61, 92; of indigenous
groups, 7; intergenerational, 92, 182;
multiethnic, 124. *See also* linkages
Cobb, Charlie, Jr., 39, 145, 297n8
Coca-Cola Company boycott, 90
Cohen, Cathy J., 4, 220, 239, 261
Cohen, Robert, 59, 61
Coleman, Milton, 84, 87
Coleman for Children & Youth's Youth
Making Change initiative, 179
collective security issue, World War II, 52,
53, 63–64
college campuses: and civil rights protests, 40, 47, 88; mobilization activities
on, 87, 90, 95, 117, 127, 241; movements
transcending, 81–83, 103, 129, 195, 196,
261–262; organizing students on, 47,
87, 90, 95; protesting reorganization
of colleges, 84–85; racial attacks on,
92–93; registering voters on, 97; youth-
based activism transcending, 7, 19. *See*

also New Haven youth movement; students, college; *and individual colleges*
Columbus, Ohio: Stop the Violence conference, 162; Union Summer campaign
in, 247
Combs, Sean "Puffy," 27
Comer, James, 121, 149
Commission on National and Community Service, 149
Communist Party (CP): in movement
infrastructure, 49; NNC's relationship
with, 52, 53, 62–63, 63–64; recruitment
of blacks by, 283n22; SNYC's relationship with, 62–63, 65–67, 69, 259; World
War II policy, 68. *See also* Young Communist League
Community Conferencing Center, Baltimore, 228
Community Justice Center, New York
City, 229
community organizing: Baker's philosophy of, 132–133, 134, 136, 250, 252;
BSLN's initiatives, 140, 153, 178, 181;
freedom school curriculum directed
toward, 149–150, 151, 152, 155; intergenerational tensions, 124; JJRM's,
233; labor movement's, 236; radical
ideological approach to, 167–168, 227;
SNCC campaigns, 1, 73–74; training in,
3, 132, 186; transformational, 233. *See
also* organizing activities
Community Organizing and Family Issues (COFI), 220
community service movement, 152,
153–155
Communiversity program, North Carolina, 134
Comprehensive Anti-Apartheid Act of
1986, 91
Concerned Citizens of Tillery, North
Carolina (CCT), 134, 135
conflict mediation activities (aka community conferences), 150, 226, 228

Congregations Offering Preventative Education, 172

Congressional Black Caucus, 145

Congress of Industrial Organizations (CIO), 49, 59, 62–63, 66. *See also* American Federation of Labor-Congress of Industrial Organizations

Congress of Racial Equality (CORE), 6, 25, 30, 73

Connor, "Bull," 67

Consequences for Juvenile Offenders Act of 1999, 214

conservatives and conservatism: generational associations with, 20–21; get-tough measures endorsed by, 214–215; rise of, 2, 33, 36, 86, 92–93, 205, 237; southern strategy, 215, 294n36. *See also* Bush administrations; Reagan administration; right, the, shift toward

contained movements, 17–18, 255

Conway, Norman H., 225

Conyers, Angela, 222

Cosby, Bill, 220, 221

Cotton, Dorothy, 178

Council of Federated Organizations (COFO), 30–31

Countryman, Matthew, 154, 175, 292n46; and BSLN, 112, 125–126, 127, 133, 136, 137, 189–190; on child poverty, 146–147; as director of EBCPTI, 150, 186, 191, 259; and divestment movement, 89, 90–91; and freedom schools, 149–150, 151

Coursey, Tanza, 247

Covington, Olive, 124

Crane, George T., 2

creative organizing strategies, 37–45; of black students and youth, 69; bridge-builders' use of, 2–3, 38–39, 41, 42–43, 46, 48; BSLN's use of, 182, 184, 203; case studies, 6–7; consequences and outcomes, 42–45, 43; labor movement's use of, 246, 251; in New Haven youth movement, 97, 98

crime: draconian policies on, 157, 161, 217; prevention/reduction programs, 97, 98–102, 157–163, 180, 205, 226–229; punitive measures for, 214–215. *See also* anti-violence campaigns; gun violence; Omnibus Crime Bill of 1994

Criminal Violence and Justice Working Group, 160

Crist, John, 214

Critical Resistance South, 277n37

Crown Heights neighborhood, Brooklyn, violence in, 165, 167

Curtis, Russell L., 29

Daniels, John, 97, 100, 105, 106–109, 110–111, 188, 290n8

David, Marian, 173

Davis, John P., 51–52, 62, 64

Davis, Kim, 157, 200

Davis, Ray, 89

Dawson, Michael C., 239

Day, Noel, 297n8

deindustrialization, 36, 99, 104, 111, 157–158, 227, 237. *See also* underemployment and unemployment

Democracy Multiplied Zone (DMZ), 230

Democratic Party: Jesse Jackson's struggles within, 92–93, 104; moderates and conservatives in, 146, 237–238; Progressive, 60

Democratic Party, Mississippi, segregation in, 30, 35, 74, 76–77. *See also* Mississippi Freedom Democratic Party (MFDP)

Democratic Socialists of America, Youth Section, 90–91

Dennis, David, 178

Denver, Union Summer organizing in, 244–245

detention centers, juvenile, abuses in, 209–210, 216–217, 223–224, 256. *See also* incarceration; juvenile justice system; prisons, youth; *and individual detention centers*

Detroit, Union Summer organizing in, 244

DiLieto, Biagio, 103, 106

Dillahunt, Dara, 171

Dilulio, John J., Jr., 159

divestment movement, 7, 73, 88–93

Dodd, Christopher, 160

Domhoff, G. William, 34

Donahue, Thomas, 236

Doss, Kelli, 162, 297n6

Double V (Double Victory) campaign, 65

Dow, John, 97, 102, 103, 106

Dressner, Julie, 29

Dubois, W. E. B., 54, 56

Dudley High School, Greensboro, North Carolina, 81

Durham Congregations in Action, 172

Each One, Teach One Leadership Program, 232–233

Eaton, Susan, *Union Leadership Development in the 1990s and Beyond,* 242–243

Edelman, Jonah, 199

Edelman, Marion Wright, 117–120; and BCCC, 119–124, 137, 139; birthplace of, 173; and BSLN, 117, 127, 128; and CDF, 118–119, 187, 201; Clinton administration ties, 145, 200; and freedom schools, 147, 148, 149, 156; and Haley Farm, 303n7; protesting child poverty, 203–204; and Stand for Children campaign, 198–199, 202

Edelman, Peter, 23, 204

education, 102–103, 144, 164–165, 168, 181. *See also* freedom schools; schools

Education, Not Incarceration initiative, 230

Educational Enrichment and Leadership Development project, 174

Effective Coalition for Juvenile Justice, Louisiana, 222

Ehrlich, Bob, 225, 226

elaboration, strategy of, 7

electioneering and elections: blacks' involvement in, 82; BSLN and, 168; corporate interests in, 256; mobilizing students for, 74, 97, 200–201, 202; municipal, 83; New Haven youth movement and, 103–111; presidential, 7, 92–93, 94, 95, 104, 145–146, 197. *See also* Voter Registration and Education in the Black Community, BSLN

elite groups: financial, 152; industrial, 48; mobilization of, 34, 259–260; political, 40, 79, 97, 152, 176

Ella Baker Child Policy Training Institute (EBCPTI), 132–137; Countryman as director of, 150, 186, 191, 259; graduates from, 137–138; leadership philosophy of, 139, 140; Sullivan's involvement with, 187, 190–191; training for freedom school staff, 116, 148, 150, 174, 184, 186. *See also* Baker, Ella

Ellington, Marty, 89

Elm City Nation, 102

El Puente, 167, 194

Epstein, Laura, 249

Esdaile, Scot X, 97, 99–100, 102, 104, 108

families, black, 82, 119, 122, 148, 221, 256, 261. *See also* Black Community Crusade for Children; Community Organizing and Family Issues

Families and Friends of Louisiana's Incarcerated Children (FFLIC), 219, 221–222

Family Preservation and Support Services Act of 1993, 164

Fanon, Franz, 80

Farmer, James, 76

farm workers movements, 38. *See also* United Farm Workers

Farrow, Kenyon, 217

Faruqee, Mishi, 231, 232

February 1st Movement, 85

Federal Bureau of Investigation (FBI), infiltration of black organizations, 67, 68, 82

Federal Housing Act of 1949, 104
Feld, Barry C., 215
Fellowship for Racial Reconciliation, 25
50 Cent, 27
Fisher, Helene, 150–151, 187
Fletcher, Bill, 240–241, 250, 262
Fletcher, Marguerite, 89
Flocks, Sara, 241
Food Action Research Council, 172
Fordice, United States v., 172–173
Forman, James, 80, 240
Forster, Nancy S., 225
Foundation for Community Development, 81
framing, strategy of, 39–40, 233, 255;
    bridge-builders' use of, 48; BSLN's
    use of, 152–153; labor movement's use
    of, 48, 236, 246; New Haven youth
    movement's use of, 98, 103, 108, 109;
    SNYC's use of, 43–44; SOBU's use of,
    72–73, 85
Franklin, John Hope, 121, 145, 146
Franklin, Kamau (aka Karl Franklin), 166,
    167, 170
Frederick Douglass Society, City College
    of New York, 54
freedom schools, 60, 191, 297n8; chal-
    lenges to, 155–157, 180, 181; costs of,
    299n42; curriculum for, 149–150, 151,
    155, 173, 186; in Mississippi, 144–145,
    235; in New York City, 164; sexism in,
    191; Sullivan's involvement with, 149–
    150, 151, 156, 187; training staff for, 116,
    148, 150, 174, 184, 186. *See also* Summer
    Freedom School Program, BSLN
Freedom Summer campaign of 1964, 75,
    144, 246
Freedom Vote campaign, 60, 74
Freeman, Jo, 19
Freeman, Kim, 128
Free My People Youth Organization, 127
Free South Africa Movement (FSAM), 3,
    73, 88–93, 255

Frosh, Brian E., 225
Fuller, Howard. *See* Sadauki, Owusu
Fund for Southern Communities, 133

Gantt, Harvey, 121
Ganz, Marshall, 38
Garden-Vazquez, Adrianne, 154
Gavins, Raymond, 172, 183, 185, 195
Gay Detention Center, Baltimore, 227
Gay Youth Project, Urban Justice Center,
    216
gender equality issues, 26, 39, 60–61, 131,
    191–192, 242, 247–251
generations: divide between, 24–25, 38,
    101, 184, 188, 254; hip-hop, 26–27; resis-
    tance in, 20. *See also* bridge-builders,
    movement; movements: intergenera-
    tional; post-civil rights era generation
Generation S program, SEIU, 251, 254
Georgia Progressive Black Student Alli-
    ance (GPBSA), 90
Ginwright, Shawn A., 227
Giuliani, Rudy, 168, 218, 230, 232
Gordon, Edmund, 149, 151
Government Employees United Against
    Racial Discrimination, 85
Graham, Rikkia, 247
Grant, Gary, 135
Gray, Richard, 127, 128, 189–190, 205
Great Depression, 44, 45, 69; deprivation
    of black youth during, 48, 50, 51, 54,
    55, 69
Greater New Haven NAACP Youth
    Council, 97. *See also* National Associa-
    tion for the Advancement of Colored
    People: Youth Council
Green, Celena, 168
Greene, Sean, 135, 177
Greensboro Association of Poor People
    (GAPP), 81, 83
Griffith, Mark Winston, 165, 189
Griffith, Michael, 92
Guevara, Che, 80

gun violence: BCCC/BSLN campaign to reduce, 157–163, 180-181, 205; New Haven reduction campaign, 97, 98–102, 108, 111; 1980s explosion of, 118; welfare cutbacks as cause of, 157–158, 160. *See also* anti-violence campaigns; crime

Haines, Herbert, 32
Hallmon, Maceo, 211, 227
Hamer, Fannie Lou, 76–77, 109
Harambe Organization, 85
Hardin, Pamanicka "Chino," 231–232
Harlem: black political activity in, 56; freedom schools in, 164, 191
Harlem Brotherhood, 167
Harlem's Children's Zone, 164, 311n86
Harm Free Zone (HFZ), 230
Harrington, Picket, 174
Harrison, Cedric, 174
Harvard University, Black Student Collective, 85
Hayden, Tom, 15, 36
"A Healthy Start, a Safe Start, a Fair Start, and a Head Start" campaign, 122–123
Height, Dorothy, 121, 145–146, 147
hierarchies, 32, 34–35, 215; class, 4, 21, 36, 61, 192, 214; in movement infrastructures, 40, 183–184; racial, 4, 31, 36, 51, 96, 213, 214, 215–216. *See also* inequalities
Higginbotham, Leon, 147
Highlander Folk School, Tennessee, 31, 144, 303n7
Highsmith, Gary, 97, 100
Hill, Norman, 246
Hillard, Easter, 134–135
Hinds, Laura, 226
hip-hop culture, 21, 26–27, 95
Hip Hop Summit Action Network, 27
Hitler, Adolf, SNYC's campaign against, 65
Hobgood, North Carolina, Citizen's Group, 134, 135

Hodge, Gregory, 176, 180
Holder, Andre, 230
homophobia, 32
Honey, Michael, 238–239
Hood Work, 26. *See also* hip-hop culture
Hooks, Benjamin, 96
Horton, Myles, 109, 303n7
HoSang, Daniel, 29
Hotel and Restaurant Employees (HERE), 236, 244
hotel workers, South Carolina, unionizing, 243–244
house party model of mobilization, 129
Houston, Kevin D., 97, 100–101
Howard University: Atwater's appointment to board of, 93, 126, 150; Black Nia Force, 117
Hoy, Darriel, 136, 170–173, 175, 183, 185, 195, 200
Human Rights Watch: *Children in Confinement in Louisiana*, 210
Hunter, Tera, 38
Hutchings, Phil, 80

identities: activist, 21–23, 24, 27–28, 184; grievances based on, 249; masculine, 32
immigrants, 22, 179, 236. *See also* Latinos; youth, Asian; youth, Latino
incarceration: aftercare programs lacking, 209, 211, 219, 222; black youth disproportionately targeted for, 40, 160, 162, 205, 213, 218, 234. *See also* crime; detention centers, juvenile, abuses in; juvenile justice system; prisons, youth; Proposition 21 (California), mobilization against; *and individual facilities*
indigenous groups: activating, 41, 261; BSLN's linkages with, 116, 143, 163, 180; collaborating with, 7, 150, 255; in Los Angeles, 177–178; transforming, 44
inequalities, 115, 132, 227; in juvenile justice system, 233–234; racial, 6, 21, 152;

socioeconomic, 101, 255, 261; structural, 6, 101, 118, 220; systemic, 4, 5, 154, 225, 256. *See also* hierarchies

infrastructures, movement: adult-led, 24; advantaged/disadvantaged subgroups, 31, 43; BCCC/BSLN/CDF linkages, 125, 144, 203; black-led, 48–49, 82, 255; black youth's influence in, 71–72; bridging, 41, 261; complex, 6, 21; diverse, 69, 183–184; of grassroots organizations, 260; hierarchies within, 31–32, 40; institutional leveraging in, 18, 33–37, 45–46; institutional niches in, 33, 34, 35, 45; intergenerational, 115–116, 184, 255; of JJRM, 211–212; parent-youth formations, 258–259; progressive, 240; racial tensions in, 92; sexism in, 35, 192; SNCC's, 78; SNYC's, 61; sustainability of, 2, 184; youths' role in, 28–37, 38, 45, 62, 71–72, 94, 140

institutionalism, parallel, 60, 74

institutional leveraging, 18, 33–37, 45–46; bridge-builders' use of, 82–83, 96; in CDF/BCCC/BSLN infrastructure, 144, 152, 185, 203; challenges associated with, 2, 3, 256; labor movement's use of, 236, 246; New Haven youth movement's use of, 98, 110, 111; poverty reduction through, 146; among prominent black groups, 73, 259–260; shift toward, 86–87; SNCC's use of, 72, 76, 78–79

institutional niches, 33, 34, 35, 45, 152, 200

interest convergence, 40–41

International Negro Youth Movement, 54

International Union of Operating Engineers (IUOE), 244

Ivey, Ron, 84

Jackson, Esther Cooper, 47, 48, 60–61, 65

Jackson, James, 54, 58–59, 61, 62, 66, 239; "The World Beyond the Campus" speech, 47–48, 254

Jackson, Jesse: anti-gun violence campaign, 160–161; and New Haven youth movement, 7, 94, 96; presidential campaigns, 7, 92–93, 94, 95, 104

Jackson, Juanita, 50

James, Errol, 126, 160, 179

James, Taj, 176, 178–179, 181, 204, 205

Janey, Kim, 134

janitors, Union Summer organizing of, 247, 250–251

Jefferson, Michael, 97, 100, 101

Jeffries, Hasan Kwame, 35

Jennings, Keith, 88, 89, 90, 138, 139

Jessamy, Patricia, 225

Jim Crow segregation: combating, 31, 48, 65, 71; in juvenile justice system, 23, 218–219, 224; as obstacle to organizing black workers, 61–62

jobs, loss of. *See* deindustrialization; underemployment and unemployment

Jobs with Justice, Student Labor Action Coalition, 236

Joe, Sean, 165, 196, 262

Johnson, Charles S., 54

Johnson, Glenda Hatchett, 159, 202

Johnson, Jawana, 134

Johnson, Nelson, 81–82, 82–83, 86, 87, 94

Johnson, Nicole, 153

Johnson, Otis, 138, 202

Jones, Bill, 105, 106, 107

Jones, Kasey, 126, 128, 150

Just 4 Me Mentoring, 228

justice. *See* racial justice; social justice

Justice 4 Youth Coalition, 231, 232

Juvenile and Family Court Judges Leadership Council, BCCC, 159

Juvenile Detention Alternatives Initiative (JDAI), 217–218

Juvenile Justice Delinquency and Prevention Act of 1988, 216

Juvenile Justice Project of Louisiana (JJPL), 210, 218, 220, 221

Juvenile Justice Reform Act of 2003, Louisiana, 221, 233

juvenile justice reform movement (JJRM), 209–234; ameliorative policies, 158–159; appropriation strategies used by, 217, 228, 233; black-led, 3, 6, 7–8; bridge-builders in, 211–212, 255; institutional leveraging used by, 259–260; in Louisiana, 218–223, 254–255; in Maryland, 223–228; mobilization campaigns for, 22–23, 205; in New York City, 23, 212, 229–233; positionality strategies used by, 44, 217, 233; in San Francisco Bay Area, 212

juvenile justice system: aftercare programs lacking in, 209, 211, 218, 222, 225, 226–227; black and Latino youth overrepresented in, 162, 215, 228, 307n10; entrenched problems in, 209–210, 212, 213–218, 221; in Maryland, 211, 216; in New York City, 231; POMS, 214, 215, 217, 218, 225; racial disparities/hierarchies in, 4, 31, 36, 51, 96, 162, 210–211, 213–216, 223–224; systemic changes in, 225, 228, 233; trying youth as adults, 16, 214, 215, 308n31. *See also* detention centers, juvenile, abuses in; incarceration; juvenile justice reform movement (JJRM); prisons, youth

Kelley, Christine, 24
Kelly, Robin, 67, 173
Kendig, Rebecca, 222
Kiddie Korner. *See* New Haven youth movement
Kid's First ballot initiative (Oakland), 179
Killian, Wendy, 151
King, Martin Luther, Jr.: and NAACP, 277n35; nonviolence direct action campaigns, 40, 161; Poor People's Campaign, 118, 198; at SNCC founding conference, 26, 76, 276n35. *See also* Southern Christian Leadership Conference (SCLC)

King, Rodney, rioting over verdict, 298n31
Kirkland, Lane, 236, 242
Kirshner, Benjamin, 20
Koen, Charles, 80

labor movement, 235–252; black youth participation in, 234, 243, 251, 255; and civil rights movement, 29; community tradition of, 109; organizing strategies, 48, 58, 236, 246, 251; progressives in, 235, 242; training activists for, 303n7
labor schools, 59, 144
labor unions: black leaders of, 58, 238; exclusionary practices in, 47, 48, 50–51, 243; militancy of, 24; racism in, 69, 243. *See also* American Federation of Labor-Congress of Industrial Organizations
Latinos, 124, 154, 177, 179, 236, 251. *See also* children, Latino; youth, Latino
Lawson, Ifetayo, 176
Lawson, James, 276n35
League of Women Voters, 95
League of Young Southerners, 66–67
Lee, Chana Kai, 60, 108–109
Lee, Richard, 103–104
lesbian, gay, bisexual and transgendered (LGBT) youth, 216–217
Levin, Andy, 243, 247
Lillard, Toya, 154
linkages: cross-movement, 44, 72, 79, 83, 217; cross-racial, 89, 179; intergenerational, 122, 124–125, 220; multiethnic, 179. *See also* coalitions
Locke, Alaine, 54
Los Angeles: BSLN regional offices in, 175, 177–178; Rodney King verdict rioting, 298n31; Union Summer organizing in, 244

Louis, Errol T., 165

Louisiana: Ad Hoc Juvenile Advisory Board, 221; JJRM campaign in, 22–23, 218–223, 229, 232, 233, 254–255; Juvenile Justice Commission, 221; treatment of black youth in juvenile justice system, 210–211. *See also* Tallulah Correctional Center for Youth, Louisiana

Louisiana Appleseed (lobbying group), 222

Lovell, John, Jr., 49

Lowndes County Freedom Party, Alabama (LCFP), 35

Loyal Democrats of Mississippi, 77. *See also* Democratic Party, Mississippi, segregation in

Lubow, Bart, 217, 232

Lydia, Malkia, 161

Lynch, William, Jr., 121

Lyn-Cook, Richard, 151

Mahr, Colita, 222–223

Malcolm X, 80

Malcolm X Grassroots Movement, 167

Malcolm X Liberation University, 81

Mamiya, Lawrence, 164

Manley, Renaye, 235, 236

Mannheim, Karl, 20

Marable, Manning, 115, 116

March on Washington: in 1941, 64, 65; in 1983, 88

marginalization: of black youth, 39–40, 44, 100, 213, 251, 261; class, 249, 251; combating, 93; degrees of, 31; economic, 177; gender, 242; of poor blacks, 151–152; racial, 242, 251; secondary, 220, 261; of working class blacks, 220, 238–239, 239–240

Marlboro County, South Carolina, activism in, 155, 173–174

Marshall, Joe, 162

Marthol, Marie Monique, 166, 167

Marxism, among SNYC activists, 61, 69, 87

Maryland: JJRM campaign in, 211, 216, 223–228, 229, 232

Maryland Juvenile Justice Coalition, 211, 224–228, 310n61

Massengale, Tony, 142, 178, 202, 296n1

McAdam, Doug, 32, 38, 40

McCarthy, John D., 214

McDavid, Lolita, 123

McFate, Katherine, 157

McGillicuddy, Kim, 229

McGuire, Gail M., 102

McKaine, Osceola, 60

McLaughlin, Milbrey W., 20

McPhail, Clark, 214

Meany, George, 236

media coverage, of black and Latino youth, 5, 16, 39–40, 215–216, 229

Mendel, Richard A., 216

Mentoring Male Teens in the Hood, 227

Miami, Union Summer organizing in, 244

Miami Shipbuilding Company, 59

Middleton, Tamika, 230, 277n37

Midwest Academy/United States Student Association Grassroots Organizing Weekends, 133

Miles, Cameron, 225, 227, 228

Miller, Thomas V. "Mike," 225

Mims, Thomas, 233

Minkoff, Debra C., 33, 152, 260

Minter, Steve, 122

Mississippi: civil rights movement in, 30, 39, 76–77; freedom schools in, 144–145, 235

Mississippi Action Plan, 78

Mississippi Freedom Democratic Party (MFDP), 30–31, 60, 74, 76–77

Mitchell, Clarence, 50

mobilization: black-led, 48, 49, 125, 149, 259; BSLN's efforts, 128–130, 136–141, 176, 181, 183, 196–197, 199, 202, 262; changing contexts for, 260–261; on college campuses, 87, 90, 95, 117, 127, 241; contained, 17–18; direct action, 36, 77, 161; of elite groups, 34, 259–260; house party model, 129; for juvenile justice reform movement, 22–23, 205; of post-civil rights era generation, 2, 9, 18, 28–46; transformational, 17, 18, 71, 73, 82, 93; youth-based, 9, 30, 32, 33, 96, 140. *See also* activism and activists, black youth; youth, black: mobilization of

Moody, Leslie, 244

Moore, Greg, 90

moral pragmatism, 108–109

Morris, Aldon D., 40, 115, 184

Moses, Robert P., 39, 109

Mothers Alone Working, 192

Mount Vernon/New Rochelle Group (aka Pat Robinson Group), 192

movements: appropriation strategies in, 44, 217; autonomy concerns, 25, 60, 62, 63, 65, 74, 79, 91–92; building, 5, 24, 34, 170; cross-class, 151–152; disputes in, 183–184; extra-systemic pressures on, 11, 17, 24, 41; federated, 143–144; intergenerational, 7, 18–19, 30, 48, 205, 212, 236, 254; national governing bodies *vs.* local affiliates, 143–144, 168–169, 172, 180–181; political contexts, 69, 139, 180; post-civil rights era generation, 15–46; remedying inequalities, 233–234; single-issue, 34, 41, 91; student, 77, 89, 91–92, 92–93, 197–198, 202; youth-based, 19–45, 97, 116, 197–198, 258, 259. *See also* infrastructures, movement; *and specific movements*

Movement Strategy Center, San Francisco, 181

Muhammad, Rahman, 251

music. *See* hip-hop culture; rap music

Nashville, Tennessee, Union Summer organizing in, 244, 248

National African Youth Student Alliance, 90

National and Community Service Act of 1993, 153

National Association for the Advancement of Colored People (NAACP): activism through, 6, 30, 48; competition with SCLC, 277n35; middle-class culture of, 56; and New Haven Youth movement, 100–109, 127; voter registration drives, 83; Youth Council, 50, 56–58, 69, 95, 97, 99, 100–101

National Black Political Assembly (NBPA), 82

National Black Political Convention (NBPC), 82

National Coalition of Advocates for Students, 127

National Conference of Negro Youth, 54–55

National Conference on Problems of the Negro and Negro Youth, 4, 54

National Congress of Puerto Ricans, 194

National Coordinating Committee, BSLN (NCC): membership of, 131, 160, 175, 195–196; restructuring by, 185, 193–194; Stand for Children campaign, 200; tensions in, 202

National Day of Action Against Violence (NDAAV), 161–162, 172; cities holding protests, 300n63, 300n70

National Hip-Hop Political Convention, 26

National Labor Relations Act of 1935 (Wagner Act), 58

National Negro Congress (NNC): CIO members joining, 62–63, 63–64; CP activists in, 62, 63–64; movement infrastructure, 48; SNYC's relationship with, 54, 62, 64, 67; Youth Council/

Youth Continuations Committee, 50, 51–52, 52–53, 68–69
National Observance of Children's Sabbaths, 172, 173
National Save and Change Black Schools Project, 85
National Student Association, 25
National Student Christian Federation, 25
National Student League (NSL), 54
National Youth Administration (NYA), 23
National Youth Center Network, 196
National Youth Organization, 88
Nazi-Soviet Pact, World War II, 63
Neely, Sandra, 84
Negron, Louis, 194
Negro Sanhedrin movement, 283n13
Nembhard, Jessica Gordon, 201
neoliberalism and neoliberals, 4, 26, 27, 251
network-affiliated groups, 5–6, 19, 30, 255, 261
Network of Underground Artists, 166
networks, 40, 110, 218; youth-oriented, 29, 117, 253, 255–256, 258
Newark, New Jersey, Union Summer organizing in, 250–251
New Haven youth movement, 3, 95–112, 255; antiviolence/community intervention campaigns, 97, 98–102, 108, 111; appropriation strategies used in, 44; and BSLN formation, 7, 117; framing strategies used in, 98, 103, 108, 109; as grassroots organization, 97, 110, 111–112; high school students in, 96, 107; institutional leveraging used in, 110, 111; and Jesse Jackson campaign, 7, 94, 96; police-community relations, 260–261; school funding campaign, 102–103; voter registration efforts, 97, 104, 106, 108–109, 127, 292n46. See also Daniels, John
New Orleans, JJRM campaign in, 222, 256
Newton, Huey, 240–241

New York City: BSLN chapter in, 15, 165–170, 178, 181, 194, 196; Community Justice Center, 229; freedom schools in, 164; JJRM activists in, 23, 212, 216–217, 229–233; Rheedlen Centers, 164, 169; United Youth Committee, 50
New York Metro chapter, BLSN, 15, 165–170, 178, 181, 194, 196
New York/Northeast Region, 163–170
Nia NuArts Liberation School, 165–166, 167, 170
Nia Youth Collective, 166, 167
Nixon, E. D., 54
Nixon administration, 93, 98
Nkrumah, Kwame, 314n23
No More Youth Jails, 231
North Carolina: APPLES program, 134; Black Peoples' Union Party; BSLN's organizing work in, 133–135, 140, 148, 170–173, 181; Communiversity program, 134; Greensboro Association of Poor People, 81, 83; Hobgood Citizen's Group, 134; Raleigh freedom school, 156, 171
North Carolina A&T University, 81, 85
North Carolina Black Assembly (NCBA), 82
North Carolina Hunger Network, 172
North Carolina Student Rural Health Coalition, 171
North Carolinians Against Racial and Religious Violence, 134
Nwafor, Azinna, 283n22

Oakland, California: BSLN regional office in, 3, 176, 179; Kid's First ballot initiative, 179
Obama, Barack, 4
Occupy Harlem, 5
Occupy the Hood, 5
Occupy Wall Street movement, 4–5, 21–22
O'Donoghue, Jennifer L., 20
Olson, Mancur, 20

Omega Boys Club, San Francisco, 162, 177
Omnibus Crime Bill of 1994, 159–160, 161, 181, 214, 216, 308n31
One Thousand by Two Thousand project, BSLN, 195, 198, 199, 203
Open Society Institute, 213
Operation Big Vote, New Haven, 108
organizational elaboration, strategy of, 79
organizing activities: for black unity, 80–88; BSLN's, 199, 297n6; difficulty sustaining, 69, 93–94; direct action, 3, 10, 150–151, 153, 177, 197, 212; federated, 143–144; intergenerational, 188; local-level, 163–180; models of, 29, 40, 255; moral pragmatic approach to, 108–109; political, 140, 152; progressive, 54, 125–126; race-based, 61; women's, 106. See also creative organizing strategies
Organizing Institute (OI), 236, 242, 243, 245, 247, 249, 254
Ounce of Prevention Fund, 160

Pan-African Students Association, 83
Pan-African Students' Organization, 83
Pastore, Nicholas, 109–110, 111
Pat Robinson Group. See Mount Vernon/ New Rochelle Group
patron-client relationships, 24, 34–35, 106, 111, 257–258, 259
Patterson, Frederick, 54
Payne, Charles, 19, 77
People's College of Tennessee, 85
People's Community Feeding Program, BSLN, 15, 166, 181
Perkins, Gregory, 224
Personal Responsibility and Work Opportunity Reconciliation Act of 1996 (aka Welfare Reform Bill), 169, 198, 204
Peterkin, Robert, 204
Petgrave, Sheldon, 232–233
Plotke, David, 21

police: brutality of, 59, 99, 105, 109–110, 111, 160, 169; community relations, 260–261; stop-and-frisk tactics, 127
Polletta, Francesca, 143
Poor People's Campaign, 118, 198
Porchia, Felicia, 247
positionality, strategy of, 41–42, 44–45, 48, 212, 217, 233, 261–262
post-civil rights era generation: activists of, 17, 28, 96, 255; challenges to, 2, 4; class divisions in, 240; identities of, 27–28, 96; institutional leveraging by, 34, 45–46, 259; labor and, 237; mobilization of, 9, 18, 28–45, 45–46; movement activism of, 15–46; political orientations of, 16, 21, 95, 251; radicalism of, 20–21; social media as tool of, 196; youth as social and political variable, 19–28, 116
postracialism, 4–5
Poughkeepsie, New York, BSLN chapter in, 163–164
Price, Hugh, 120–121, 147, 148
Primary Enrichment Program, Marlboro County, South Carolina, 174
Prison Moratorium Project (PMP), 230–231
prisons, youth: abuses in, 209–210, 212, 216, 223–224, 310n61; expansion of, 99, 160, 174–175, 211, 214; in Maryland, 223–224; racism as factor in sentences, 159, 179, 211, 214–215. See also detention centers, juvenile, abuses in; incarceration; juvenile justice system
Proctor, Deidre, 297n6
Progressive Black Student Alliance (PBSA), 88
Progressive Democratic Party, 60. See also Democratic Party
progressive movements and progressives: antidemocratic tendencies in, 191; black, 48–49, 139, 146; coalitions of, 106; generational associations with,

20–21; institutional leveraging in, 33, 36; labor movement, 235, 240, 242; political activity, 104; resources for, 126; social movement, 17; white, 25, 61–62; youth-based, 78, 96, 110

Progressive Student Network, 90

Proposition 21 (California), mobilization against, 16, 30, 41–42, 181, 277n38

Proposition 184 (California), 180

Proposition 187 (California), 22, 179, 180

Proposition 209 (California), 179–180

Prothrow-Stith, Deborah, 161

public health crises, black community, 162, 256, 260; as causes of crime and violence, 98, 101–102, 111, 116, 118, 121, 124, 222

public order management system (POMS), 214, 215, 217, 218, 225. *See also* juvenile justice system

Putting People First (Bill Clinton campaign treatise), 146

Quick, Paulette, 134

race: AFL's position on, 50–51; Clinton administration dialogue on, 146; disparities in juvenile justice system, 162, 213, 215–216, 223–224; hierarchies of, 4, 31, 36, 51, 96, 213, 214, 215; marginalization of, 242, 251; politics of, 6; in post-civil rights era, 236, 237–241; in Union Summer movement, 247–251

racial justice: fighting for, 5, 22, 45, 65, 93, 152; heightening consciousness around, 73, 93; SNYC's commitment to, 64, 68, 69; SOBU's mobilization around, 72

Racial Justice Day (RJD), 169

racial profiling, 16, 40, 260–261

racism: combating, 79, 87, 89, 91–92, 127, 132, 134–135, 169; in juvenile justice system, 162, 210–211, 213, 215–216, 223–224; in labor unions, 69, 243; systemic, 93, 152; in U.S. Army, 64, 65. *See*

also inequalities: racial; postracialism; segregation, racial

radicalism and radicals: antidemocratic tendencies among, 191; black power movement, 74, 80–81, 83, 86; of black youth, 48–49; hip-hop, 26–27; in NAACP, 56; positional strategies used by, 45; in post-civil rights era generation, 20–21; self-limiting, 34; white, 62, 63

Rainbow Coalition, anti-gun violence campaign, 160–161

Raleigh, North Carolina, freedom school, 156, 171

Rand, Kristen, X., *Cease Fire,* 158

Randolph, A. Philip, 51–52, 62, 63, 72; March on Washington (1941), 64, 65. *See also* A. Philip Randolph Institute

Ransby, Barbara, 25

rap music, 27. *See also* hip-hop culture

Reagan administration, 118, 119, 237; devolution policies of, 27, 36, 92–93, 98, 110, 158

Reclaiming Our Children and Community Projects, Inc., 226

Reed, Adolph, Jr., 36

Reger, Jo, 143–144

Reid-Green, Carolyn, 123–124

religion and religious groups, 62, 172, 178

Republican Party, 19, 237, 238

resources, 115, 125–126, 152, 170; indigenous, 40, 72, 162–163, 260–261; shortages of, 115, 137, 255, 257–259

restructuring, global, 26, 251

Rhee, Kate, 230, 231

Rheedlen Centers for Children and Families, New York, 164, 169

Richards, Dona, 90

Richardson, Gloria, 74

Richardson, Judy, 178

right, the, shift toward, 117, 119, 146, 237. *See also* conservatives and conservatism: rise of

Right to Vote Campaign, BSLN, 59
Riley, Boots, 26, 277n38
rites-of-passage programs, 100, 174, 176–177, 178, 227
Robinson, Jeff, 126–127
Robnett, Belinda, 38–39, 131–132
Rock the Vote, 95
Rodgers, Martin, 126, 127, 133, 145
Rooks, Daisy, 250
Roosevelt, Franklin, 23, 65; Bethune's letter to, 1, 3–4, 5
Rucht, Dieter, 29
Rustin, Bayard, 72, 76

Sabol, Barbara, 121, 122
Sadauki, Owusu (aka Howard Fuller), 83
Safe Start Cease the Fire! initiative, 161
safety net programs, elimination of, 237, 238
San Francisco: Omega Boys Club, 162, 177
San Francisco Bay Area: BSLN regional offices in, 175–180; JJRM activists in, 212; Movement Strategy Center, 181; Youth Media Council, 16, 39–40
sanitation workers, Memphis, strike of 1968, 29, 238–239
Sankofa Community Outreach and Restoration Center, 220
Santoro, Wayne A., 102
Sawyer, Melissa, 222
schools: African-centered, 176, 177; dropout rates, 222; equitable funding for, 102–103; labor, 59; public, 97. See also education; freedom schools
Schuyler, George, 50
Scott, Patrick, 239, 246
Scottsboro case, 49, 71
Scot X. See Esdaile, Scot X
segregation, racial: combating, 16, 35, 49, 50, 64, 66, 69, 73, 132; in Democratic Party, 30, 74; industrial, 64, 69. See also Jim Crow segregation; racism
Sen, Rinku, 5

Service Employment International Union (SEIU), 236, 247, 250–251; Generation S program, 251, 254; and Union Summer, 247
sexism, 35, 60, 61, 132, 191–192, 243
Shabazz, YaSin, 128
Shalala, Donna, 118, 145
Sharecropper's Union, 67
Shaw, Clifford, 229
Shaw, Todd C., 37–38
Sherwood, Kay E., 29
Shock, Kurt, 28
Shriver, R. Sargent, 78
Simba, Inc., 177
Simkins, Modjeska, 60
Simmons, Russell, 27
Simms, Lisa, 199, 205
Simon, Paul, 160
Simpson, Andrea Y., 16
Sista II Sista program, BSLN, 170, 181
Sisterhood of Black Single Mothers (Brooklyn), 192
Socialist Party (SP), 52
social justice: campaigns for, 48, 94, 211; hierarchies of, 32; movement activism for, 18, 33, 45, 152; narratives, 28; radical healing approach, 222; SNYC, 68. See also juvenile justice reform movement
social movements: black participation in, 48; engaging youth in, 116; fundraising for, 170; incubator programs for, 181; infrastructure support for, 125; institutional leverage in, 98; internal discriminatory patterns in, 192; mass-based, 183; militant, 215; trajectory of, 255; typologies of, 5–6
South, the: black resettlement in, 237; conservatives' southern strategy, 215, 294n36; mobilization of blacks in, 64, 87, 109, 246, 259; religion in, 62; sit-in movements, 25, 72, 73; SNCC's concentration on, 74, 79. See also Jim Crow

segregation; *and individual southern states and cities*

South African Pan-African Congress, 89

South African Students' Organization, 88

South Carolina, activism in, 60, 181, 243–244

Southern Christian Leadership Conference (SCLC), 25, 30, 41, 144. *See also* King, Martin Luther, Jr.

Southern Connecticut State University, 96

Southern Negro Youth Congress (SNYC): All-Southern Negro Youth Conference, 67; autonomy of, 65–66; CP's relationship with, 62–63, 65–67, 69, 259; demobilization of, 67–68, 86; establishment of, 48, 50, 53; FBI infiltration of, 67, 68; framing strategies used by, 43–44; geographic scope of, 7; justice efforts, 64; labor movement activism, 24, 59, 144, 251; leadership of, 248; Marxism among members, 61, 69, 87; maturation of, 56–57; movement activism and, 1, 47, 58–62, 71, 255, 262; NNC's relationship with, 54, 62, 67, 68–69; Right to Vote Campaign, 59; SNCC and, 74; women's role in, 60–61, 65; World War II policy, 64–65, 68, 258

Southwide Leadership Conference, 25, 73

Soviet Union. *See* Communist Party (CP); Nazi-Soviet Pact, World War II

Soweto Student Representative Council, 88

Sparks, Holloway, 17

Spelman College, SCAR chapter, 90

Spence, Lester, 4, 27

Spingarn, Joel, 56

Spofford Juvenile Center (aka Bridges Juvenile Center), 229, 231–232

St. Louis, Union Summer organizing in, 244

Staggenborg, Suzanne, 184

Stalder, Richard, 218–219

Stand Action Center, 199

Stand for Children campaign, 169–170, 173, 185, 198–199, 200, 202, 203

State University of New York (SUNY), in JJRM campaign, 230–231

Stop the Violence conference, Columbus, Ohio, 162

strikes, labor, black workers', 29, 58–59, 238–239

Strolovitch, Dara Z., 31

Strong, Ed, 48, 52–53, 54, 61, 62

Strong Jackson, Augusta V., 67

Student Coalition against Apartheid and Racism (SCAR), 90

Student Conference on Negro Student Problems, 54

Student Movement for African Unity, 83

Student Movement for Liberation of Southern Africa, 83

Student Nonviolent Coordinating Committee (SNCC): activists in, 6, 19–20, 67, 93, 261; African Project, 90; and anti-apartheid movement, 89–90; Atlanta Project, 75; Baker and, 120; Black Liberators' alliance with, 44, 79, 80; Black Panther Party's alliance with, 44, 79–80; civil rights movement and, 30, 41, 73–80; collapse of, 79, 86; feeding programs, 15; formation of, 1, 26, 50, 118, 276n35; and freedom schools, 3, 144; Freedom Vote, 60, 74; generational debates in, 23, 24–25; influences on, 31; institutional leveraging used by, 72, 76, 78–79; internal operations of, 74–75, 78; international outlook of, 75–76; leadership cadre, 286n3; organizing work of, 72, 94, 149, 255; Union Summer campaign modeled after, 7, 235, 248; White Folks Project, 75; women activists in, 191–192

Student Organization for Black Unity (SOBU): *African World* newspaper, 83, 84, 87; collapse of, 86–87; framing strategies used by, 43–44, 72, 84; geographic scope of, 7; mobilization efforts, 81–82, 262; movement activism of, 1, 88, 93, 240, 255, 261; support for black political party, 82–83; YOBU merger with, 84–87

Student Power Network, 167

students, black: electioneering, 103–111; mobilizing, 90, 176, 202, 203, 241; movement activism among, 47–58, 68–69, 140; New Haven youth movement and, 103–111; recruitment of, 245–247; training for activism, 140; twentieth-century movements of, 49–58, 72, 78; unity organizations, 80–88

students, college: in BSLN, 130–131, 145, 149, 156, 160, 170, 172, 174, 193–194, 196, 205; in JJRM campaign, 230–231; in New Haven youth campaign, 10, 109; protests by, 102–103; recruitment of, 235–252, 254; in SNCC, 79, 90; in social change activities, 81, 83, 140; in Union Summer campaign, 239–241, 247–249; and voter registration campaigns, 109. *See also* college campuses; National Association for the Advancement of Colored People: Youth Council

students, high school, in New Haven youth movement, 96, 107

Students for a Democratic Society, 25

Sugarmann, Josh, *Cease Fire,* 158

Sullivan, Lisa Y.: and BCCC, 124–125; and BSLN, 112, 127, 130, 133, 205; as BSLN acting director, 189, 190–191, 194, 195–196; as CDF field director, 186–192; and community service movement, 154; death of, 253; Edelman's meeting with, 117, 120; and freedom schools, 149–150, 151, 156, 187; and New Haven youth movement, 97, 100–101, 107–108; "On

Leadership," 253–254; Steven White's dissension with, 184, 187–190

Summer Food Service Program, USDA (SFSP), 147–148, 150, 157, 166, 172

Summer Freedom School Program, BSLN, 3, 144–155, 163, 184, 185–186, 189, 203. *See also* freedom schools

Summer of Service program, Clinton administration, 153–155

super-predators image, 159–160

Surdna Foundation, 213

Swanson Correctional Center for Youth. *See* Tallulah Correctional Center for Youth, Louisiana

Sweeney, John, 235, 243; New Voices campaign, 242, 257

Taaffe, Claudine "Candy," 194, 196, 205

Tallulah Correctional Center for Youth, Louisiana, 209–210, 218, 223; closing of, 221, 222, 231, 233

Tannock, Stuart, 241

Tarrow, Sidney, 40

Taylor, Judith, 79

Teenage Leadership Core, 174, 175

Teen Summit (television show), 175

Tennessee: Alex Haley Farm, 3, 186, 303n7; Highlander Folk School, 31; Memphis sanitation workers' strike of 1968, 29, 238–239; Nashville Union Summer organizing in, 244

Thompson, Marcia, 134

Three Strikes crime bill. *See* Proposition 184 (California)

Till, Emmit, murder of, 49, 71

Tilly, Charles, 40

Tilton, Jennifer, 4, 30

Tobacco Stemmers and Laborers Industrial Union, 58–59

trade unions. *See* labor unions

Training Institute. *See* Ella Baker Child Policy Training Institute (EBCPTI)

TransAfrica Forum, 92, 250

transformational movements, 2, 46, 82, 86, 170, 250, 254; importance of, 240, 246; institutional leveraging in, 34, 35, 37, 260; mobilization, 17, 18, 71, 73, 82, 93; youth-oriented, 33, 49, 133, 255–256, 261. *See also* appropriation, strategy of

Tuckson, Reed, 121, 177

Ture, Kwame. *See* Carmichael, Stokely

Turner, John B., 121

21st Century Leadership, 127

Twenty-Sixth Amendment, U.S. Constitution, 35–36

Tyson, Althea, 97, 105–106, 108

underemployment and unemployment: in black communities, 173, 251; Carolina Alliance for Fair Employment, 243–244; criminal behavior related to, 99, 216; gun violence related to, 157–158; youth, 42, 50, 98, 241. *See also* deindustrialization

Union Leadership Development in the 1990s and Beyond (Eaton), 242–243

Union of Needle Trades, Industrial, and Textile Employees (UNITE), 236

Union Summer campaign, 242–251; blacks' participation in, 237, *245*, 247, 249–250; blitz campaigns, 250, 252; bridge-builders' role in, 255, 261; countering strategies, 238; creative organizing strategies of, 3, 6, 44; funding for, 314n32; recruiting for, 254, 257; SNCC compared to, 7, 235–236

United Brotherhood of Carpenters, 242, 244

United Farm Workers (UFW), 38, 244, 246–247

United Food and Commercial Workers (UFCW), 242, 244

United States Student Association (USSA), 90

United States v. Fordice, 172–173

United Students Against Sweatshops, 236

United Youth Committee, 50

universities. *See* college campuses; students, college

Urban Justice Center (Gay Youth Project, New York City), 216

Urban Strategies Council (Oakland, California), 3, 176, 178

US Action, 95

Utter, David, 210, 218–219

Vann, Roger, 97, 100

Vassar Gathering, 205

Vassar Green Haven Prison Program, 164

Vietnam War, protesting, 35, 75, 80

View, Jenice, 168, 197

violence, 59, 179, 227, 255; Crown Heights, Brooklyn, 165, 167; Rodney King verdict riots, 298n31. *See also* antiviolence campaigns; gun violence

Violence Policy Center, 158

Violent Crime Control and Law Enforcement Act of 1994. *See* Omnibus Crime Bill of 1994

Violent Youth Predator Act of 1996, 214

voter education/mobilization/registration: BSLN initiatives for, 161–162, 168, 196–197, 200, 201; campaigns for, 6, 57, 59, 95, 292n46; NAACP drives, 83; New Haven youth movement, 97, 104, 106, 108–109, 127, 292n46

Voter Education Project (VEP), 77

Voter Registration and Education in the Black Community, BSLN, 197

Voting Rights Act of 1965, 23, 94

Wagner Act. *See* National Labor Relations Act of 1935

Walker, Naomi, 162, 183, 185, 195, 297n6

Wallace, Henry, 68

Walters, Ronald W., 86

Walton, Audrey, 247, 248

Warren, Dorian, 249

Washington Heights neighborhood, Brooklyn, violence in, 167, 194

Watson-Davis, Leslie, 127, 197

Waxler School for Girls, 224

We Interrupt This Message, 16, 215–216, 229

Welfare Reform Bill. *See* Personal Responsibility and Work Opportunity Reconciliation Act of 1996

Wellstone, Paul, 210

Wessels and Pautch law firm, 238

West, Cornel, 121

White, Aaronette M., 32

White, Rob, 22

White, Steven, 95; BCCC tensions with, 184, 185, 188, 190; as BSLN director, 112, 127–128, 137, 141; and Daniels' mayoral campaign, 106, 107, 127; and freedom schools, 149, 151, 156; resignation from BSLN, 184, 185–186, 190, 193; Sullivan's dissension with, 184, 187–190

White, Walter, 56, 57

White Folks Project, 75

whites, 61, 75, 88, 89, 124, 167, 176, 213

Whittier, Nancy, 23

Wilkens, Desiree, 249

Wilkins, Amy, 126

Wilkins, Che, 85

Wilkins, Roger, 121, 146, 147

Wilkins, Roy, 31, 76–77, 83

Williams, Juan, 220

Williamson, Leah, 127

Wilson, Danté, 226, 228

Womack, Gina, 219, 220

women, black: excluded from leadership positions, 32, 131–132, 133; as heads of families, 221; incarceration rates of, 216; organizations of, 3–4, 106; in SNCC, 191–192; in SNYC, 60–61, 65; in tobacco industry workforce, 59, 239

World War II: black radicals influenced by, 49, 69; collective security issue, 52, 53, 63–64; Double V campaign, 65; Nazi-Soviet Pact, 63; SNYC's policy on, 64–65

Wyn, Johanna, 22

Yale University, 91, 96, 99

Yergan, Max, 62

Young, James, 174–175

young adults: as advisors, 127–128, 188–190, 193, 205; in AFL-CIO, 242; in BPP, 79; inner-city, 9, 98, 99; mobilizing, 17–18, 168; noncollege, 257, 261; as organizers, 28, 139, 250; in SCAR, 90; in SNYC, 48, 67; in SOBU, 84; in social movements, 5–6, 11, 45, 49, 56, 69, 129. *See also* students, college

Young Communist League, 23, 66–67. *See also* Communist Party (CP)

Young Lords, 194

Young Negro Cooperative League, New York City, 50

Young Turks, 56

youth: concept of, 22, 23–24; as vanguard of social change, 19–28, 68–69, 81, 93–94, 96, 116

youth, Asian, 194, 243, 245

youth, black: civil unrest concerns, 166–167; competing identities among, 27–28; crises affecting, 42, 152, 256; Depression-era deprivation of, 48, 50, 51, 54, 55, 69; disproportionately targeted by juvenile justice system, 127, 162, 205, 211, 213, 228; gun-related deaths among, 157, 163; labor movement's recruitment of, 66, 235–252; low-income, 85, 205, 241, 261; marginalization of, 39–40, 41, 44, 100, 251, 261; media coverage of, 16, 40, 215–216, 229; militancy among, 36, 259; mobilization of, 1–5, 9, 41, 115–117, 128–130, 136, 140, 176, 181, 183, 199–200, 241, 262; movement activism among, 6,

20–21, 69, 71–73, 86, 194, 204, 205; New Haven youth movement and, 103–111; political status of, 3–4, 6, 21, 23, 38; sociopolitical activity of, 38, 48, 54; super-predators image applied to, 159–160; unequal school funding for, 102–103; unfairly impacted by crime legislation, 160, 161; Union Summer recruitment of, 243, 249–250; urban, 26, 102; working-class, 18, 44. *See also* activism and activists, black youth; students, black

youth, Latino: in BSLN, 199–200; civil unrest concerns, 166–167; competing identities among, 27–28; disproportionately targeted by police, 162, 205, 213; media coverage of, 5, 16, 40, 215–216, 229; protesting Proposition 187, 22; stop-and-frisk tactics targeting, 127; strengthening ties with black youth, 194; super-predators image applied to, 159–160; unequal school funding for, 102–103; Union Summer recruitment of, 243, 245

youth, white, 167, 213

Youth Action, 292n46

Youth and Student Network Initiative, 250

youth-based movements, 28–45; creative organizing strategies used by, 2–3, 37–45; federated, 7–8; infrastructures, 28–38; institutional leveraging in, 2, 33–37; shared identities of, 23; shortcomings of, 20

Youth Empowerment Project (YEP), 222

Youth Enhanced Services (YES) for Mental Health, 223

Youth Force, 16, 39–40, 229–230, 232

Youth for the Unity of a Black Society, 81

Youth Law Centers, Building Blocks for Youth initiative, 212–213

Youth Media Council, San Francisco, 16, 39–40

Youth Organization for Black Unity (YOBU), 84–87

YouWho Coalition, 222

Zepeda, Tony, 178

zero-tolerance policies: disproportionate impact on youth of color, 160, 216, 234; mobilization against, 8, 16, 144, 159; in New York City, 214, 217, 230

Zinn, Howard, 178

Zirkin, Bobby, 226

Zulu Nation, 170

Zurcher, Louis A., 29

Sekou M. Franklin is an Associate Professor in the Department of Political Science at Middle Tennessee State University (MTSU) and is the Coordinator of the Urban Studies Minor Program at MTSU. He has published works on urban politics, social movements, juvenile justice, the anti–death penalty movement, youth activism, Venezuelan politics, African American politics, and state and local politics. He has also been active with numerous social justice organizations and performs expert preparation analyses for voting rights and redistricting cases.

SEP 2 6 2014